MW01598342

Fair as the
Moon

Fair as the Moon

Discovering the New Moon
within Yahweh's Love Story

W. J. Ragan

Fair As The Moon
Copyright © 2017 by W.J. Ragan

No part of this publication may be reproduced, distributed, or
transmitted in any form or by any means, including photocopying,
recording, or other electronic or mechanical methods, without the
prior written permission of the author, except in the case of brief
quotations embodied in critical reviews and certain other non-
commercial uses permitted by copyright law.

Tellwell Talent
www.tellwell.ca

ISBN

978-1-77302-181-2 (Hardcover)
978-1-77302-182-9 (Paperback)
978-1-77302-180-5 (eBook)

Yours, Yahweh, is the greatness,
the power, the glory, the victory, and the majesty!
For all that is in the heavens and in the earth is Yours.
Yours is the kingdom, Yahweh, and
You are exalted as head above all.

1 CHRON.29:11

Dedication

This book is dedicated first to my Heavenly Father,
who with love, patience and faithfulness has covered
and cared for me every step of the way.

To my wonderful husband and family and
all I learned sharing life with them.

Special thanks to my earthly Father who
taught me to see the world with eyes of wonder
and introduced me to the Creator of it all.

Words on a page could never thank each of you
enough for the treasures that I hold in my
heart because of you.

Table of Contents

PROTECTION

PREPARATION

PRACTICE

POSTLUDE

Preface

THERE ARE MANY MYSTERIES WITHIN THE WAYS AND WORDS OF YAHWEH; so many that a person could spend their entire life searching them out and still only scratch the surface of His Wonder and Majesty! Each time we encounter even a glimpse of who our God truly is it spurs us on to seek more of Him. Then, from each glorious glimpse to the next, we continue to seek after Him until the day He gathers us home, and we see Him face to face.

Can you fathom the mystery of God? Or can you probe the limits of the Almighty? Job 11:7

From a Biblical perspective, things are concealed or hidden for a time or season, and then at the appointed time, they are revealed. In English, the word mystery holds the same understanding and is described as hidden truth. When we seek the hidden truths or mysteries of Yahweh with humble hearts, He allows us to see and understand things that were hidden to us before.

..the mystery which has been hidden for ages and generations. But now it has been revealed to his saints, to whom God was pleased to make known what are the riches of the glory of this

mystery among the Gentiles, which is Christ in you, the hope of glory. Col.1:26,27

The above verse is telling us that there was a mystery or hidden truth for generations and the mystery was Yahshua. All of the Torah, Prophets, and Writings or what is commonly called the Old Testament, held the mystery of the Messiah until the appointed time that Yahshua came to us as a baby. His life on Earth revealed Yahweh's hidden truths to us in all that He did and said. When He had fulfilled His Father's plans, He then suffered and died to save us and restore righteousness! At that miraculous time, many more mysteries of Yahweh's Word were unveiled ... at least to those who had the eyes to see and the ears to hear.

But their minds were hardened, for until this very day at the reading of the old covenant the same veil remains because in Christ it passes away. But to this day, when Moses is read, a veil lies on their heart. But whenever one turns to the Lord, the veil is taken away. 2 Cor. 3:15,16

Without controversy, the mystery of godliness is great: God was revealed in the flesh, justified in the spirit, seen by angels, preached among the nations, believed on in the world, and received up in glory. 1Tim.3:16

In these last days, Yahweh is unveiling, even more understanding to His people. Many things that were once a mystery or hidden to us, are being revealed by the leading of Yahweh's Spirit and the revelation of Yahshua.

He said to them, "To you is given the mystery of God's Kingdom, but to those who are outside, all things are done in parables, that 'seeing they may see, and not perceive, and hearing they may hear, and not understand; lest perhaps they should turn again, and their sins should be forgiven them. Mark 4:11,12

The New Moon is one of these mysteries and has been shrouded in man's tradition and misunderstanding. For many people, including myself, it was a source of frustration and confusion. Mainstream churches don't speak of it, and the world twists it for their pagan agendas. Still, as people see the importance of keeping Yahweh's feast days and desire to keep pace with the Good Shepherd, it becomes apparent that the New Moon is a part of Yahweh's wonderful design.

Yahweh's appointed days are designed to renew us and prepare us for what lies ahead, and we must allow His Spirit to guide us into all truth. His Spirit will help us establish the principles by which we are called to stand and unite us as one. Those who are in the world are watching, and we need to give them sound answers for our actions and the assurance that the choices we are making are pleasing to Yahweh, more than man.

> *For you were once darkness, but are now light in the Lord. Walk as children of light, for the fruit of the Spirit is in all goodness and righteousness and truth, proving what is well-pleasing to the Lord. Eph.5:8-10*

Yahweh reveals hidden truths to guide and keep us in one accord during the difficult years that lie ahead, especially as the day of Yahshua's return draws near. Religious systems continue to disappoint believers. Sometimes the fault lies with individual people who have a selfish agenda, but not always. Most often it is simply the influence of cultures saturated in Hellenistic and Western mindsets. We are all products of systems because we are raised in them, whether religious, cultural or educational… but our Shepherd is calling us out of them. His desire is for us to repent of our ways and the ways that have been passed down to us, generation to generation, from our fathers.

> *Repent therefore, and turn again, that your sins may be blotted out, so that there may come times of refreshing from the presence of the Lord, and that he may send Christ Jesus, who was ordained for you before, whom heaven must receive until the times of restoration of all things, which God spoke long ago by the mouth of his holy prophets. Acts 3:19-21*

When we are restored and refreshed in His presence, our hearts and eyes will be opened to see the entire Word of Yahweh in its fullness, from Genesis to Revelation.

> *I have yet many things to tell you, but you can't bear them now. However when he, the Spirit of truth, has come, he will guide you into all truth, for he will not speak from himself; but whatever he hears, he will speak. He will declare to you things that are coming. He will glorify me, for he will take from what is mine, and will declare it to you. John 16:12-14*

The search for truth is not an easy one though. It is humbling and often lonely for the way is narrow. We are in need of the Spirit of Yahweh and His Word, which is ultimately revealed to us in Yahshua, to be our final authority on all that we seek. Then we will find truth and unity. Our caution is to discern men's words over Yahweh's Word. Man's words fill the airways and resound in our gatherings. We must pray for discernment and look for the fruit in the lives of those who speak so that we are not led astray by wolves in sheep's clothing.

> *I have other sheep, which are not of this fold. I must bring them also, and they will hear my voice. They will become one flock with one shepherd. John 10:16*

> *Beware of false prophets, who come to you in sheep's clothing, but inwardly are ravening wolves. By their fruits you will know them. Do you gather grapes from thorns, or figs from thistles? Matt.7:15,16*

Scientists have discovered how animate and inanimate things in Yahweh's Creation naturally synchronize together. For example, if you put metronomes, or pendulums in a room together they will eventually unite and move to the same beat. You also see this natural phenomenon in flocks of birds and schools of fish. As sojourners on Earth, our ultimate goal is the same, to be led by the same Shepherd, down the same path, to the same end, which of course is it to be home with Yahshua for all eternity. One day there will be a remnant of Yahweh's people united in one accord. It is not my desire to persuade you to change your mind or your ways. That is in Yahweh's hands alone, and each of us must choose our walk with Him. Still, we *are* called to exhort, encourage and edify one another in love.

Therefore exhort one another, and build each other up, even as you also do. 1 Thess.5:11

The heart of this book is to share with you what Yahweh revealed to me in my search for answers about the New Moon. It has been a very humbling and amazing experience. I honestly never expected to find such awe and beauty in the way of the New Moon. I hope and pray that the things I share with you will touch your life as they have mine. Please take what I have prepared, test it and prayerfully seek Yahweh for the truth of our Beloved's heart.

Yahweh looked down from heaven on the children of men, to see if there were any who did understand, who did seek after God. Ps.14:2

Wendy Joy Ragan

ALL SCRIPTURE IS QUOTED FROM THE WORD ENGLISH
BIBLE UNLESS OTHERWISE MARKED.

PRELUDE

Principles

MUCH OF OUR LIVES ARE GOVERNED BY PERSONAL CHOICE. IN MANY CASES, decisions for family, religion, and education are being based on social acceptance and pleasure. The world is changing, and sound principles established on foundational truth are no longer the basis of right and wrong choices. The reality of long-term consequences for the choices we are making is being undermined with apathy and tolerance. We may not fully see the effect of this on our lives today, but it will dramatically affect the lives of our children and their children. If we do not return to the sound principles of Yahweh's heart found in His Word and His Creation we will be unable to navigate the lies and deception safely. Noah Webster's 1828 Dictionary describes principle as:

In a general sense, the cause, source or origin of any thing; that from which a thing proceeds; as the principle of motion; the principles of action.

-Ground; foundation; that which supports an assertion, an action, or a series of actions or reasoning. On what principle can this be affirmed or denied? He justifies his proceedings on the principle of expedience or necessity. He reasons on sound principles.

Are we living in a time where we are losing sound principles? The culture we are raised in dramatically affects our lives and produces reference points for our actions, choices, and understanding. In a world that is uniting through networking and online community, many cultures are converging to become a melting pot of principles that people live by. Each person or community is taking on ideals within the smorgasbord of thought and values as it suits their lifestyle and desires. This is not the way of truth. We need Yahweh's principles! The principles of life found in Yahweh's Word. His principles of life, motion, and reason are lovingly designed to guide us and help us determine right and wrong. With fear and trembling, we must return to Yahweh's principles, for we are in danger of being led off the path that Yahweh designed for us from the beginning. There is a fitting quote by Thomas Paine:

"Man cannot make or invent or contrive principles. He can only discover them and he ought to look through the discovery to the Author."

Yahweh is the Designer, Composer, Author, and Finisher of all we see and can ever hope to know or understand. The principles of our faith are based on evidence of Who He is; evidence that resounds all around us of an Author we cannot see. When you walk into a house wired with electricity, you cannot see it, but by faith, you flick a switch or plug in a toaster, and instantly there is proof of what is unseen. Likewise, if we live by faith in Yahweh from His Word and Creation we will discover His sound and unchanging principles. For what we observe around us in Creation is evidence or proof of the character and principles of the Creator and Author.

> Set your mind on the things that are above, not on the things that are on the earth. Col.3:2

> Beware lest anyone cheat you through philosophy and empty deceit, according to the tradition of men, according to the basic principles of the world, and not according to Christ. For in Him dwells all the fullness of the Godhead bodily; and you are complete in Him, who is the head of all principality and power. Col.2:8-10

Yahweh is calling to all who have the ears to hear, to come to the Him and be saved. He desires that none should perish, but we must be willing to know Him and follow Him. The true path of righteousness is a path that few want to travel, for it is not the easy or popular way. Yahshua calls it narrow and restricted.

> Enter in by the narrow gate; for wide is the gate and broad is the way that leads to destruction, and many are those who enter in by it. How narrow is the gate, and restricted is the way that leads to life! Few are those who find it. Matt.7:13,14

Even so, what could be more wonderful than finding the gate that leads to everlasting life, no matter how arduous the journey? We all have hopes and dreams of living a long and prosperous life here on Earth, but we must not forget that when the end comes and Yahshua returns, we will all be judged for the way we live our lives, and our eternal destiny will be sealed. All that we embrace in this life can be an opportunity to love, overcome and touch the lives of those around us or serve ourselves. Whatever trials or challenges we face in our search for the truth that leads to life, will seem like nothing compared to the glorious future that we may have with the Messiah … if we find the narrow gate.

> For our light affliction, which is for the moment, works for us more and more exceedingly an eternal weight of glory; while we don't look at the things which are seen, but at the things which are not seen. For the things which are seen are temporal, but the things which are not seen are eternal.2 Cor. 4:17,18

As the seed of Abraham and sojourners on our way home, we need to understand Yahweh's principles, patterns and promises to help us navigate through the deception. These treasures will be found in the quiet places where there is no other distraction. Then as we let go of our worldly identity and humble ourselves before the King of the Universe, he will give us understanding.

> Give me understanding, and I will keep your law. Yes, I will obey it with my whole heart. Ps. 119:34

Understanding comes when we see the Author and Creator of the Universe for who He is and then apply His principles to all that He made. If you have ever studied art, you will know that there are principles of design. These principles are used throughout a design to give it balance and consistency. The artist who designed the artwork is easily identified when you can see the principles of their design repeated in each of their works of art. When we see Yahweh as the magnificent Artist of all that He Created from this perspective, we will be able to discern truth more accurately by His repeated principles of design. Each principle and pattern that He placed within His Masterpiece is evidence of His loving character and awesome design. When we learn to see His principles and apply them to our lives, they will give us the foundational truth we need to persevere until the end.

The Masterpiece

SOME MAY SEE SCRIPTURE AS A COLLECTION OF MANY STORIES, BUT FROM Yahweh's perspective, there is only one magnificent story, His Love Story. Scene after glorious scene plays out through each generation and in each one of our lives; day after day, month after month, year after year, down through the centuries from the beginning of time. The principles and patterns within His story are real, alive and faithful, like His signature on His artwork. They stand true and unchanged, just as He is unchanged.

"For I, Yahweh, don't change;" Mal.3:6a

When we accept the redemption price of Yahshua, Yahweh's only Son, which is His shed blood for us, we are choosing to become an intimate part of His heartfelt story. As His betrothed, we are to learn the ways of His heart and willingly submit to the beauty of each part of His design. We must lay down our plans and the agenda of man's systems for His design alone and seek to find the ways of His heart at all costs...even when the majority is going a different way. If we take the way of the majority, it often leads to compromise and the putting aside of our differences for the sake of unity. This may sound peaceful and good at first; even wise in small matters, but in the end, it usually leads to indifference and complacency. Too often, it is the most popular ways that take the lead, and our differences on important matters are subdued for common ground.

When we live life in a compromised way we miss out on the promise of abundant life that Yahshua paid for us to have.

Yahweh is the Master of immaculate precision, balance, rhythm, and song. His story is unfolding, in His timing, according to His will, on His calendar no matter what we may think about it. His plan is for us to become one with Him, and abide by His principles, for they were established with wisdom before the foundations of this world were spoke into existence. His story is the original, epic love story of all time and all others since the beginning of Creation are mere shadows and reflections of His. When we see Creation and Yahweh's Word from this perspective, we can then understand that everything is one, as opposed to a myriad of isolated points. It helps us to see the details of His Word, history and our present life as pieces of one magnificent story. He is the Master, and everything is a piece in His Masterpiece!

No matter who you are, where you live, or what you believe, you are playing a part within Yahweh's story. Even satan has a part to play. His role as Yahweh's adversary is to distort the Masterpiece and deceive Yahweh's people with the doctrine of men and the distractions of life. Satan's goal is to confuse us and entice us away from Yahweh with counterfeits and distortions of the truth, including at times blatant lies. He woos people with pride and self-gratification. Our part is to be aware of his schemes and not lose our zeal for Yahweh, fighting the good fight for His Name sake. It is important that we exhort one another to follow the Way, the Truth and the Life as never before ... always being circumspect and watching.

Be sober and self-controlled. Be watchful. Your adversary, the devil, walks around like a roaring lion, seeking whom he may devour. 1Pet. 5:8

Though this may seem difficult at times in a world that is so far removed from the ways of the Creator, the voice of Yahweh's Spirit still calls to us. His call to us is to come out of the world and hear the song of Yahweh's love story. This is why we must be separate and seek Him with all our heart away from man's influence.

…who saved us and called us with a holy calling, not according to our works, but according to his own purpose and grace, which was given to us in Christ Jesus before times eternal, 2 Tim.1:9

I heard another voice from heaven, saying, "Come out of her, my people, that you have no participation in her sins, and that you don't receive of her plagues, Rev.18:4

With our hearts established and secured in Yahweh's purpose for our life we will be able to see as He sees. We will then know Him as He truly is and our hearts will join in harmony with His beautiful plans for us. Through each step of the journey that He takes us on, whether through meadows, upon mountaintops, down in valleys or through desolate desert places, we must always remember that it is our hearts that Yahweh is concerned with first and foremost.

But Yahweh said to Samuel, "Don't look on his face, or on the height of his stature, because I have rejected him; for I don't see as man sees. For man looks at the outward appearance, but Yahweh looks at the heart." 1 Sam.16:7

Each place Yahweh chooses for us to travel is designed to challenge us and prepare our hearts to receive and keep His Word, just as He did when He took His people out of Egypt to His mountain in the wilderness. Now instead of stone tablets, He has chosen to write His Covenant on our hearts and to dwell within us by His Spirit.

I will also give you a new heart, and I will put a new spirit within you; and I will take away the stony heart out of your flesh, and I will give you a heart of flesh. Ez. 36:26

But you are not in the flesh but in the Spirit, if it is so that the Spirit of God dwells in you. But if any man doesn't have the Spirit of Christ, he is not his. If Christ is in you, the body is dead because of sin, but the spirit is alive because of righteousness. But if the Spirit of him who raised up Jesus from the dead dwells in you, he who raised up Christ Jesus from the dead will also give life to your mortal bodies through his Spirit who dwells in you. Rom.8:9-11

This is something He will not force upon us; it is our choice. We have the choice to answer the call of the Father, submitting our hearts to His glorious story or staying within the world. Once we accept Yahweh and His ways, we need to guard our hearts, for they are passionate, sensitive and fickle and can quickly deceive us.

The heart is deceitful above all things, and it is exceedingly corrupt: who can know it? Jer.17:9

Because, knowing God, they didn't glorify him as God, neither gave thanks, but became vain in their reasoning, and their senseless heart was darkened. Rom.1:21

Keep your heart with all diligence, for out of it is the wellspring of life. Prov.4:23

The Hebrew word for keep in Proverbs 4, is Strong's #H5341 נצר natsar, which means; to watch, guard from danger, keep secret, blockade, watchman and is usually translated as keep, preserve and watchman. Natsar is also used in other verses about keeping the testimony and words of Yahweh.

Blessed are those who keep his statutes, who
seek him with their whole heart. Ps.119:2

As we allow Yahweh to write on our hearts all that is precious to His heart, our hearts naturally become one with His! Our new life with Him holds the responsibility to preserve and watch over what is precious to His heart so that the world will know the reality of Who Yahweh is. As His treasured people and watchmen, our first duty is to be sure that our hearts do not hold on to things from our past life, especially things that do not align with Yahweh's Masterpiece. If we do, our pride, heartaches, and fears will dictate what we are able to understand. We must allow Yahweh's Spirit to have full reign in our hearts and lives, and be willing to leave our old baggage behind. Only then will we be able to take an honest and clear look at the truth, not compromising it to protect our pride or comforts. Yahweh's Masterpiece will then unfold before us without our preconceived scenarios, established habits, ideals or allegiance to another man.

Ironically when we make our personal fears and ideals greater than our fear of Yahweh, it keeps us away from Him and the safety of His care. We are all living lives that allow us to choose easier or more convenient ways. In the increasingly tolerant culture we live in, where we do most of our communication through a device, it is also becoming increasingly easier to avoid overcoming our fears, habits, and mindsets. Avoiding the truth may seem peaceful for a time, but the only truly safe and peaceful place on Earth is found when we overcome our fears, submit to Yahweh's plans and dwell in His presence. The realities of Yahweh's Kingdom are all that will save us and keep us. Our only hope of knowing them is to hear His voice and follow the leading of His Spirit.

> *For if you live after the flesh, you must die; but if by the Spirit you put to death the deeds of the body, you will live. For as many as are led by the Spirit of God, these are children of God. For you didn't receive the spirit of bondage again to fear, but you received the Spirit of adoption, by whom we cry, "Abba! Father!" Rom. 8: 13-15*

May it become our delight to seek Yahweh with all our heart, allowing Him to reveal His truth to us, and learning to trust Him completely.

> *Blessed is the man who trusts in Yahweh, and whose trust Yahweh is. For he shall be as a tree planted by the waters, who spreads out its roots by the river, and shall not fear when heat comes, but its leaf shall be green; and shall not be careful in the year of drought, neither shall cease from yielding fruit. Jer. 17:7,8*

> *He gave some to be apostles; and some, prophets; and some, evangelists; and some, shepherds and teachers; for the perfecting of the saints, to the work of serving, to the building up of the body of Christ; until we all attain to the unity of the*

faith, and of the knowledge of the Son of God, to a full grown man, to the measure of the stature of the fullness of Christ; that we may no longer be children, tossed back and forth and carried about with every wind of doctrine, by the trickery of men, in craftiness, after the wiles of error; but speaking truth in love, we may grow up in all things into him, who is the head, Christ; from whom all the body, being fitted and knit together through that which every joint supplies, according to the working in measure of each individual part, makes the body increase to the building up of itself in love. Eph. 4:11-16

It is time to walk together as one in truth and love to become Yahshua's spotless bride; a bride that seeks to know her Bridegroom for who He truly is, rather than letting religious systems dictate who He is. Only then can we become a bride willing to lay down all selfish endeavors to seek our Beloved with all our heart.

Test all things, and hold firmly that which is good. 1Thess. 5:21

But from there you shall seek Yahweh your God, and you shall find him, when you search after him with all your heart and with all your soul. When you are in oppression, and all these things have come on you, in the latter days you shall return to Yahweh your God, and listen to his voice. Deut 4:29,30

Now is the time to hear and see with fresh eyes and an open heart, the wonder, and beauty of Yahweh's Masterpiece. Then we can rightfully test and prove all things, comprehending the glory that the heavens are declaring. As we see the fullness of His Story and Masterpiece it will give us the firm foundation we need to stand on, and help us to align our words and actions with His. Yahweh's Word is first revealed to us in all that He Created. Each amazing and breathtaking piece compliments and confirms all that He wrote in His Word. Together they are witnesses of His character and establish His truth. In the next chapters, we are going on an amazing journey of seeking Yahweh and building our foundation of faith by discovering Yahweh's masterful patterns and pictures.

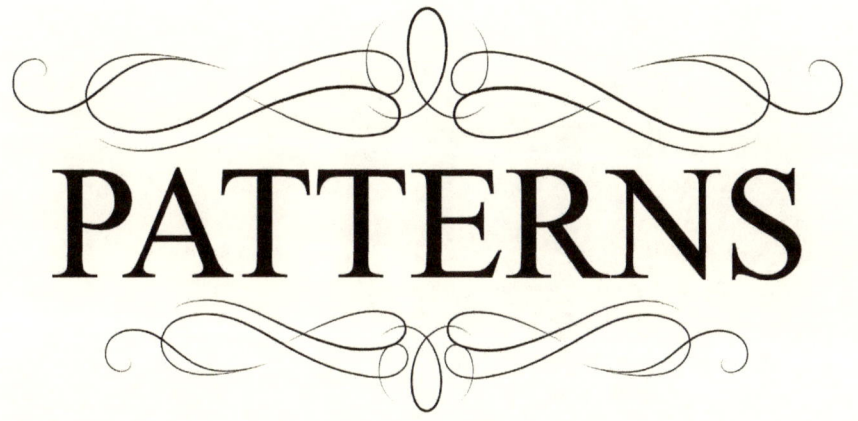

PATTERNS

The Foundation Pattern

Of old You laid the foundation of the earth.
The heavens are the work of Your hands.
Ps. 102:25

PATTERNS ARE EXTREMELY IMPORTANT. THEY ESTABLISH THE TRUTH and purpose of a person, system or thing. The word pattern in the Merriam-Webster dictionary is described as; an artistic, musical, literary, or mechanical design or form, a reliable sample of traits, acts, tendencies or other observable characteristics of a person, group or institution; an original design or model considered deserving of imitation or being copied. Likewise, the consistent traits and acts of someone make up their character. The patterns of a person's character traits prove who they are and the motivation of their heart. For example, when someone is selfish or offensive most of the time but then acts kind when they want to impress someone the pattern reveals their true character. They are not truly kind but motivated by selfish gain. The same is true for the opposite. If someone is kind and considerate most of the time and then suddenly strikes out in an unkind way, breaking their good character pattern, it usually reveals that there is hurt or something wrong in their life that needs to be resolved. The secret to really knowing someone is of course, to spend time with them and to get to know their heart through their characteristics. With time and care, you will see whether their words match their actions and consequently understand the true motivation of their heart. If we don't take set apart time to get to know someone we will then have trouble understanding him or her, especially if his or her actions are inconsistent. Often this brings assumptions and misunderstandings to our relationships ... including our relationship with our Heavenly Father.

Yahweh has expressed His characteristics to us in countless ways, but if we do not take time to see Yahweh's heart and the patterns that He created from the very beginning, we run the risk of misunderstanding His Word and being led astray by false doctrine. Consequently division and confusion get a grip on us. Yahshua rebuked people for their inconsistency and hypocrisy because their ways and their misinterpretation of Yahweh caused others to become disheartened and confused. The same is true today. Many people claim with their words that they follow a certain standard, whether a religious code of moral conduct, or some other code of living, but often their actions do not match their spoken convictions. Over the centuries many have claimed to keep the Word of Yahweh, but because they misrepresent who Yahweh is in their actions and in the words they speak, it causes misunderstanding and hurt. It is for this reason that many who do not yet to know Yahshua as their Savior, avoid the truth and are led astray by false, religious systems.

If we want to truly know Yahweh, we must be willing, first and foremost, to spend intimate time with Him ... listening to His voice and discovering His patterns. Knowing His patterns will give us a foundation to test our search for truth on and to build our faith on. Yahweh's Word reveals many patterns to us, but there is one key pattern that envelops them all, and will play a crucial part in discerning false teachers and doctrine. This is the pattern of being hidden or concealed in darkness first, until the revealing of life or light. We will focus on this pattern throughout the following chapters of this book. Before we begin though, let's look at the word pattern from Yahweh's perspective.

The Hebrew word for pattern brings insight into the source of Yahweh's pattern. It is Strong's #8403 תבנית tabaniyth (tabaneet), which is described as; structure, model, form, likeness, and pattern. The first thing to notice about this word תבנית tabaniyth, is that it begins and ends with the same

Hebrew letter; the tav ת. The letter tav is the 22nd and last letter in the Hebrew aleph-bet and means; a seal, a sign, a mark or covenant. When we take this letter back to its original picture or paleo form, it looks like a cross ✗. The fact that the tav means sign or mark is very intriguing because within Yahweh's design we find that the number seven is very important as the number of completion. The number three is also a number that holds the meaning of fullness and completion. We could then see the Hebrew aleph-bet as three sets of seven for a total of 21 letters with the tav standing alone at the end, as a sign or signature from Yahweh's hand. The Hebrew word for pattern, as we have seen, has a tav at the beginning and the end. In other words, the Hebrew word tabanith for pattern is encompassed on both ends with the sign of the covenant. Amazingly this reveals that a pattern, from Yahweh's perspective holds the meaning or likeness of a seal, sign or covenant. Also, in the Noah Webster's 1828 Dictionary we find the English word pattern described as;

An original or model proposed for imitation; the archetype; an exemplar; that which is to be copies or imitated, either in things or in actions; as the *pattern* of a machine; a *pattern* of patience. Christ was the most perfect *pattern* of rectitude, patience and submission ever exhibited on earth.

If Christ or the Messiah is the most perfect pattern, then of course His pattern is of great importance to us. Could Yahshua be the source or key to all of Yahweh's patterns? Let's go deeper to see if there is more confirmation to this. The Noah Webster' 1828 dictionary describes a sign as;

A token; something by which another thing is shown or represented; any visible thing, any motion, appearance or event which indicates the existence or approach of something else.

A wonder; a miracle; a prodigy; a remarkable transaction, event or phenomenon. Through mighty signs and wonders.

Some visible transaction, event or appearance intended as proof or evidence of something else; hence; proof; evidence by sight.

Michelle
Gumaga + Nana
John!

A memorial or monument; something to preserve the memory of a thing.

To mark with characters or one's name. To *sign* a paper, note, deed, etc. is to write one's name at the foot, or underneath the declaration, promise, covenant, grant, etc., by which the person makes it his own act, subscription of one's name; signature

Each of these powerful meanings confirm the importance of a sign or covenant seen in the tav, and leads us to an even more compelling part of the Hebrew word תבנית tabaniyth for pattern. Between the two covenant letter tavs א ת, there is another three letter Hebrew word בני baniy; which means to build and restore. We can then say that a pattern holds the message of building and restoring the Covenant. The tav is also a sign, memorial, wonder or token of what will be rebuilt and restored in the future. This is fascinating! Now, if we take our search one step further, we will find that within the Hebrew word baniy for restore and rebuild, is the two letter root word בנ ben, which means 'son!' ... There it is! Complete confirmation that Yahweh's pattern of life is ultimately found in His Son, Yahshua! How fitting that the word for pattern itself would begin and end with the letter tav which is the sign of the Covenant and the essence of the pattern itself. Yahweh's pattern of darkness first and then life or light is a memorial sign or signature of life, hope and repentance because it reveals His Son Yahshua, as our Savior! Here we find the very heart behind all of Yahweh's patterns and all that Yahshua did while He walked on Earth. Each pattern or sign from Yahweh testifies of the One who created them! Yahshua came to us to reveal the true character qualities of His Father and to be the foundation pattern for us to follow.

Wow.

> *According to the grace of God which was given to me, as a wise master builder I laid a foundation, and another builds on it. But let each man be careful how he builds on it. For no one can lay any other foundation than that which has been laid, which is Jesus Christ. 1 Cor. 3:10,11*

Then through the pattern of His death and resurrection, Yahshua made a way for us to be restored back to His Father. The Hebrew word, tabaniyth for pattern is a phenomenal sign of love to us. Starting from the center of the word we have; Yahshua (Yahweh's son, בנ ben) who came to renew, rebuild and restore (בני baniy), Yahweh's Covenant (revealed in the two ת's placed at the beginning and end of the word). The renewed Covenant was established through Yahshua's death on the cross giving us the pattern(תבנית tabaniyth) of life. Yahshua confirmed this pattern when He referred to Jonah as His sign.

> *But he answered them, "An evil and adulterous generation seeks after a sign, but no sign will be given it but the sign of Jonah the prophet. For as Jonah was three days and three nights in the belly of the whale, so will the Son of Man be three days and three nights in the heart of the earth. The men of Nineveh will stand up in the judgment with this generation, and will condemn it, for they repented at the preaching of Jonah; and behold, someone greater than Jonah is here." Matt.12:39-41*

Jonah was hidden in the depths of the sea for three days and three nights, just as Yahshua was hidden in the earth for three days and three nights. Here is Yahweh's pattern of life; first concealing something or someone until the appointed time for it or them to be revealed. The Son came in the likeness of His Father to reveal the pattern of His Father's heart and to build, restore and establish the pattern found in the heavens.

The Hebrew word tabaniyth is the word used to describe what Yahweh revealed to Moses in the Wilderness. The pattern or tabaniyth of the Tabernacle that Moses received on Mt. Sinai revealed the Heavenly pattern of Yahweh's dwelling. Yahweh's dwelling place, in turn, revealed His Son, who would come to establish and rebuild His Father's kingdom on Earth. Yahshua's desire and mission was to reveal the character of His Father, Yahweh.

> *"If you had known Me, you would have known My Father also. From now on you know Him and have seen Him." John 14:7*

Yahweh's patterns, especially His pattern of life, are woven into all that He has made. They are imbedded in His Word and in all Creation as fingerprints and signatures from His hand. When He spoke into the darkness at the beginning, His patterns became the fabric and design within all He called into existence. Yes, there will always be counterfeits, but if you truly know the pattern of the original, you will not be fooled by a fake. That is the message that Yahshua came to tell us. Only when man interferes with Yahweh's Masterful design that His wonderful patterns are distorted and lost. To properly seek the truth we must first know Yahweh's heart through His patterns, which, as we have seen, hold the revelation of His Son.

> *For by him all things were created, in the heavens and on the earth, things visible and things invisible, whether thrones or dominions or principalities or powers; all things have been created through him, and for him. He is before all things, and in him all things are held together. He is the head of the body, the assembly, who is the beginning, the firstborn from the dead; that in all things he might have the preeminence. For all the fullness was pleased to dwell in him; and through him to reconcile all things to himself, by him, whether things on the earth, or things in the heavens, having made peace through the blood of his cross. Col. 1:16-20*

The truth of Yahshua being at the center of all Yahweh has done is also found hidden in a mysterious two letter Hebrew word found throughout the Hebrew text of the Old Testament or Tanak. This small little word is a sign of the Messiah and yet many people do not even know that it exists. Those who do know that it exists do not always see it as a sign of the Messiah. Yahshua revealed the mystery of these two letters in Revelation when He said,

> *"I am the Alpha and the Omega, the First and the Last, the Beginning and the End".*

When we read His statement as an English translation of a Greek text, we miss something important, for Yahshua was actually revealing the mystery of this small two-letter word. Again, the mystery cannot be understood in English or Greek; we must see it through Yahweh's Hebrew aleph-bet.

If you have ever looked at the Old Testament in its original Hebrew text, you will find this two-letter word את placed throughout. Amazingly, this word is not translatable! It simply stands as a sign or mark strategically placed throughout Yahweh's Word. We have seen that the letter tav ת is the sign of the covenant and that in its original picture or paleo form looks like a cross ✕. Now let's look at the aleph א.

The aleph א in its original picture or paleo form, looks like the head of an ox Ɀ, and holds the meaning; strong, mighty or leader. When we put these two meanings together, we find; "the strength of the covenant" or "the leader of the cross!" There is only one who can claim this title, and that is our Mighty Redeemer, Yahshua! What was hidden or concealed in the Old Testament? The revelation of the One who would come forth at the appointed time is to be a pattern for us. He is the Aleph and the Tav, the beginning and the end and that is why He proclaimed,

> *For if you believed Moses, you would believe me; for he wrote about me. John 5:46*

Yahweh's pattern of life, revealed in Yahshua's life, is woven throughout all of Scripture and is the pattern that we must lay our foundation for truth upon. As we search for answers about the New Moon, or any other matter of Scripture, we must see that all things align with Yahweh's original pattern, for He does not change even if all else passes away.

> *"They will perish, but You will endure.*
> *Yes, they will wear out like a garment.*
> *You will change them like a cloak, and they will be changed.*
> *But You are the same,*
> *And Your years will have no end.*
> *The children of Your servants will continue.*
> *Their descendants will be established before You."*
> *Ps. 102:26-28*

The mighty voice of Yahweh is what spoke the Heavens and Earth into existence. The planets orbit, creatures migrate, winds rush in their courses, tides swell and withdraw, and the seasons turn as all of Yahweh's Creation twirls, flows and dances day after day, month after month, and year after year, by the power of His voice. When we take the time to be still, watch and listen, we will see and hear that Yahweh's cycles and rhythmic movements are at the heartbeat of all He created and that they are all a part of His masterful composition that brings forth and sustains all life!

If the foundations are destroyed,
what can the righteous do? Ps.11:3

We have the privilege to seek and search for the truth, not so that we can have more knowledge or become puffed up, but on the contrary, to humbly search for our Heavenly Father and find our way home to Him. With Yahshua as our foundation for all truth, we will be able to build our faith and discern truth. This is how we will discover the beauty of the New Moon. Though it may seem to be one of the smaller pieces within Yahweh's Masterpiece, it holds important patterns and pictures for Yahshua's bride. Our motivation for searching out truth, in the New Moon or any other part of life within Yahweh's kingdom, is to seek Yahweh's heart and be prepared for the time of His coming. Let's now look at the patterns of Yahweh as signs that give us confirmation and guidance in seeking the New Moon and its part in Yahweh's amazing Love Story and Song.

The Creation Pattern

I have made the earth, and created man on it.
I, even my hands, have stretched out the heavens,
and all their host I have commanded. Is.45:12(KJV)

THOSE WHO SPEND TIME IN RESEARCH REALIZE THAT THE BEGINNING IS where we find the source and pattern for how things function and have life. The background, beginning or source of someone or something establishes their motives and character history. This method is used to find answers all the time; for example, if you want to find out about a person you go back to their beginnings and look at their childhood. If you want to know about an organization you ask about the values or mission statements to why they began, etc. The same is true with Yahweh; we must go to Genesis and see how He designed all that He created to understand the rest of His Word. Genesis gives us a phenomenal narrative of Creation from the perspective of the Physicist, Designer, Author, Composer, and Architect who made it. What He chose to make and how He set it all into motion speaks volumes of who He is.

The opening words of Scripture tell us that Yahweh spoke into existence the heavens and Earth within a six-day pattern and rested on the seventh day. From that time on He has astounded generation after generation of scientists, astronomers, and physicists with His infinite and yet intricate designs. Every element obeys Him and moves to His command and rhythm. Richard Swenson, M.D. describes the Creator in his book, "More than Meets the Eye" like this:

"Nothingness obeys his voice. He controls time space matter and light. He monitors the position of every elementary particle. He is sufficient unto Himself. He does not need anybody or anything to accomplish his purposes. He answers to no one. He obeys his own counsel. He works on thousands of levels all at the same time. His scientific sophistication is unfathomable. He created the laws of physics and appears to be a pure mathematician. His intelligence is so superior according to Einstein, that in comparison "of all the systematic thinking and acting of human beings is an utterly insignificant reflection."

The magnitude of Yahweh's power and precision is far beyond our comprehension! When we see Him as the Creator of ALL, we cannot help but fear Him. He truly is the King of the Universe, and there is none to compare with Him. In awe and wonder, we as His children have the privilege of seeking His heart in all that He has made. We can come to Him with our questions and trust that as a loving Father, He will give us good answers and help us understand how we should respond to His leading. Then we can apply the truth of His Word to our lives and grow into mature, strong servants in His Kingdom.

In our search we will focus mainly on Yahweh's pattern of life. His pattern will give us the framework of how His design functions. The second verse of Genesis is where Yahweh begins His description of how the Universe began:

The earth was formless and empty. Darkness was on the surface of the deep and God's Spirit was hovering over the surface of the waters.Gen.1:2

With these powerful opening words of Creation's history, Yahweh reveals to us the pattern of life and revelation. First, there was darkness and a covering and then the manifestation of what was covered or hidden in the darkness. The pattern revealed in this verse foreshadows the way Yahweh would work with His people including the way of salvation. The ultimate plan is found in His only Son who was hidden within the patterns of Creation and the lives of the patriarchs for thousands of years ... until the appointed time. When the appointed time came to fruition, Yahshua was manifested or revealed to the world. Yahweh's pattern will be the same at the end. Genesis gives us the pattern of life that carries the full revelation of the Author and Finisher found in Revelation. That is what the word Revelation is telling us. Below is Noah Webster's 1828 dictionary description of revelation.

Revelation: The act of disclosing or discovering to others what was before unknown to them; appropriately, the disclosure or communication of truth to men by God himself, or by his authorized agents, the prophets and apostles.

I believe the pattern of life that Yahweh wants us to see is that in His timing He will reveal what was hidden. The Hebrew word for Revelation is Hitgalut and is described as: to expose or unveil something that was hidden or concealed. We know that Yahshua is the Messiah because His life was the revelation and fulfillment of the Words in the Torah, Prophets and Writings. His life followed the pattern of Yahweh.

..who was foreknown indeed before the foundation of the world, but was revealed at the end of times for your sake, who through him are believers in God, who raised him from the dead, and gave him glory; so that your faith and hope might be in God. 1Peter 1:20,21

For nothing is hidden that will not be revealed; nor anything secret that will not be known and come to light. Luke 8:17

The word 'revealed' in the above Scripture is also translated as manifest in some versions. In other words, this verse may be interpreted as; all that couldn't be seen or was hidden from our sight will be made manifest and come into the light at its appointed time. All of Yahweh's Creation functions by things being hidden until the time comes for them to be manifested or revealed to our sight.

For the creation waits with eager expectation for the children of God to be revealed. Rom. 8:19

Yahweh desires that our lives match the pattern of life and the revealing of what was or is hidden. We are to be the ones that manifest our belief in what cannot be seen. When our actions match our belief, we prove to the world Who Yahweh is and what He cares about. As we submit ourselves to Yahweh's statutes and press on daily toward a time that is hidden from us, we are proving that we are betrothed and waiting to go to a place that is being prepared for us. That is what our faith is all about! How we live and show Yahweh our love for Him is the manifestation or revealing of what is true, even though for a time it is unseen or hidden. Of course this is not new but bears repeating because it is so important in the overall picture. Yahshua wants our belief in Him to be rooted in our trust in Him, not simply in physical evidence. Yahshua admonished Thomas for needing to see.

> *Jesus said to him, "Because you have seen me, you have believed. Blessed are those who have not seen, and have believed." John 2:29*

> *Now faith is assurance of things hoped for, proof of things not seen. Hebrews 11:1*

We must believe in the Creator for who He is and His faithfulness to His Word, not for what we see with our eyes of flesh. Remember that it was because Abraham believed that Yahweh called him righteous.

> *He believed in Yahweh, who credited it to him for righteousness. Gen.15:6*

Now let's return to the second verse of Genesis and look at the account of the Spirit of Yahweh hovering over the waters.

> *The earth was formless and empty. Darkness was on the surface of the deep and God's Spirit was hovering over the surface of the waters. Gen.1:2*

Notice that darkness covered the deep as the Spirit of Yahweh hovered over the waters to bring forth life. There within the darkness of His covering Yahweh was breathing life into the elements; just as a mother bird hovers over her young vibrating her wings to give life and oxygen to her young ones. These opening moments of Creation are the foundational picture of how Yahweh brings life to us. Genesis continues to tell us that an evening or darkness followed by morning or light gives us Yahweh's pattern for a day, which also follows His pattern for life. First, darkness covers, then His Words call forth to the light, and the revelation of what was hidden in the dark is made manifest.

Seeing Yahweh's pattern is imperative to how we understand Yahweh's heart. In our search through Scripture, we will find that this pattern of darkness first and then life or light is repeated throughout. Over and over darkness envelops something and then at the appointed time, what was covered in darkness is exposed to light. Within this pattern you will also discover how when something is covered or hidden, revelation and life are brought forth in the hidden place. In our convenient world of electricity and enterprise, the awesome beauty of Yahweh's design is being lost.

On our journey to find the truth, we must always look at Yahweh's full picture displayed in all that He has made. When we see Creation from the perspective of the Creator and don't try to fit His things into our preconceived paradigms, our minds are opened and refreshed with His ways and life. Could this also be true with the word darkness? Often we are told to associate darkness with satan or evil. Though it is true that satan is filled with darkness, his darkness is the opposite of what is related to Yahweh. The darkness of satan is absent of true light and harbors death. Satan's darkness is corrupt, filled with deception and destruction. There is by Yahweh's design another kind of darkness or covering. Just as there is more than one kind of light there is also more than one kind of darkness. Satan's tactics always include a counterfeit or a lie to try and deceive us. We, on the other hand must be alert and watching. I am not at all suggesting that anything of satan's darkness is good. This would be deceptive and evil to Yahweh;

Woe to those who call evil good, and good evil;

who put darkness for light,
and light for darkness;
who put bitter for sweet,
and sweet for bitter! Is.5:20

Yahshua declared that He is the Light and the revelation of what is unseen. He came to make a clear separation between His true light and satan's false light, and His protective darkness from satan's evil darkness.

Jesus cried out and said, "Whoever believes in me, believes not in me, but in him who sent me. He who sees me sees him who sent me. I have come as a light into the world, that whoever believes in me may not remain in the darkness. John 12:44-46

There is a positive and negative side to all things and we MUST discern carefully what we are seeing. In the material world, we call these counterfeits or imitations. You can buy the real thing or a copy of the real thing. Usually, the copy is cheaper and poorly made. In the spiritual realm, it is critical to not succumb to the copy of the original because the copy or counterfeit will lead to death. The choice is for everyone to make. We can choose what is real and true or settle for a cheap, deceptive counterfeit. One of the main reason's people choose the copy or the counterfeit is that it is less expensive. Most people can't afford the price of the genuine product, so they settle for a cheaper copy. When it comes to our Messiah though, we cannot afford to settle for anything or anyone else but Him. The reality is that, just as it is in the material world, true and genuine things come at a price. Our redemption came at a high price, and likewise there is a price for following the true Redeemer and King. There is the living Messiah leading to everlasting life, and there is the counterfeit antiMessiah leading to destruction and death. Both have light!

For such men are false apostles, deceitful workers, masquerading as Christ's apostles. And no wonder, for even Satan masquerades as an angel of light. 2 Cor.11:13,14

We are in need of Yahweh's pattern to discern which light is the true light. If we simply say that Yahweh is only found in the light and never seek the source or pattern of Yahweh's light we run the risk of being deceived. Yahweh's light is found within the pattern of life, which is revealed after darkness. Look at Solomon's words.

> *It came to pass, when the priests had come out of the holy place, that the cloud filled Yahweh's house, so that the priests could not stand to minister by reason of the cloud; for Yahweh's glory filled Yahweh's house. Then Solomon said, "Yahweh has said that he would dwell in the thick darkness. 1Kings 8:10-12*

Notice that Yahweh's presence is described as a cloud. Clouds are a wonderful picture of Yahweh's covering, which will talk more of later. As you search the Scriptures, you will see Yahweh's pattern comes alive in everything He made and that He comes to us in darkness first and then reveals His Light. How do we discern the difference between true light and false light or one darkness and another? For most people there is an obvious answer; one is *with* the presence of Yahweh, and one is *without* the presence of Yahweh. One is the place of evil and will lead to death and punishment, and one is the place of life and growth leading to blessing and promise. Just as it is important to be aware that there is a light that is deceptive and filled with lies and man's ways, so it is with the darkness. Here again we see that one revelation of darkness is void of His presence leading to death and the other is a place of covering and protection leading to life.

> *But if your eye is evil, your whole body will be full of darkness. If therefore the light that is in you is darkness, how great is the darkness! Matt. 6:23*

> *Therefore see whether the light that is in you isn't darkness. Luke 11:35*

These compelling Scriptures show us that we have the potential to harbor a deceptive light that isn't light at all, but darkness. This is so very important to understand! If there is a light in us that is in reality darkness, how will we recognize it? There is a wonderful answer! His Name is above all Names!

The people who walked in darkness have seen a great light.
Those who lived in the land of the shadow of
death, on them the light has shined.
For to us a child is born. To us a son is given; and the
government will be on his shoulders. His name will
be called Wonderful, Counselor, Mighty God,
Everlasting Father, Prince of Peace. Is.9:2,6

Again, therefore, Jesus spoke to them, saying, "I am the light of
the world. He who follows me will not walk in the darkness, but
will have the light of life. John 8:12

The One and only true light is Yahshua, the Light of the world. He is
our standard for how to determine light. He said that through Him we
have the light of life. We must study His Word and follow His way by
aligning our hearts with His, for we are not of this world and we are not
to pattern ourselves after the subtle, false light of the enemy. We are
children of the One and only Light and called to dwell in His Light
alone.

Let no one deceive you with empty words. For because of
these things, the wrath of God comes on the children of
disobedience. Therefore don't be partakers with them. For you
were once darkness, but are now light in the Lord. Walk as
children of light, for the fruit of the Spirit is in all goodness
and righteousness and truth, proving what is well pleasing
to the Lord. Have no fellowship with the unfruitful deeds of
darkness, but rather even reprove them. For the things which
are done by them in secret, it is a shame even to speak of. But
all things, when they are reproved, are revealed by the light, for
everything that reveals is light. Therefore he says, "Awake, you
who sleep, and arise from the dead, and Christ will shine on
you." Eph.5:6-14

Paul's letter to the Ephesians is warning us again to not be deceived by
false light. The light of the Messiah is to be our One true light. His
light will reprove and expose what is false and reveal righteousness and
truth. The pattern of life is seen in how Yahweh chooses to conceal His

Light in darkness for a time and then reveal what was hidden at His appointed time. As He takes us to Himself and walks us through His pattern, we will see His glorious light, just as He did at the beginning of all that He Created.

The Garden Pattern

My beloved has gone to his garden, to the beds of spices,
To feed in the gardens, and to gather lilies. Song of S. 6:2

IF YOU ARE SOMEONE WHO LOVES SPENDING TIME IN THE GARDEN, YOU
know that it is filled with many life lessons. Unlike the man-made world
of the city, the garden, the vast open country, and rugged wilderness are
the places where we find things alive and growing. Everywhere you look
in nature there are insights to the character of our Creator, but it is most
compelling in the garden where we become caretakers of what is growing.
As we work with the soil, planting, watering and pulling weeds, many
Scriptures come alive right before our eyes. As we care for and protect our
gardens, Yahweh reveals His idea of how relationships and bearing fruit
work in His kingdom.

The Genesis account of Yahweh's relationship with Adam in the garden
gives us understanding of His original desire for a relationship with Him.
Yahweh desired to be personally and physically involved in the creation
of man. He personally gathered the dirt up in His own hands when He
formed Adam.

Yahweh God formed man from the dust of the ground, and breathed into his nostrils the breath of life; and man became a living soul. Gen.2:7

Then Yahweh personally planted the Garden of Eden as a place to commune with Adam.

Yahweh God planted a garden eastward, in Eden, and there he put the man whom he had formed. Gen. 2:8

Yahweh's garden was designed for fellowship with Adam. They walked and talked together in its beauty, and Yahweh lovingly gave Adam a part in His creative work by asking Adam to name all the animals. Then in Yahweh's timing and in His order, He creates a helpmate for Adam.

Yahweh God said, "It is not good that the man should be alone; I will make him a helper suitable for him." Gen.2:18

Only this time Yahweh did something extraordinary! Adam's helpmate did not come from the dirt as he did; she was hidden at his side in keeping with Yahweh's pattern.

Yahweh God caused a deep sleep to fall on the man, and he slept; and he took one of his ribs, and closed up the flesh in its place. He made the rib, which Yahweh God had taken from the man, into a woman, and brought her to the man. Gen.2:21,22

The way Eve came to Adam foreshadowed the way that the bride of the Messiah would also come forth. The bride for the first Adam was hidden within his own body until the appointed time. Likewise Yahshua Who is referred to as the second Adam, will one day have His bride brought forth from His side where she is now hidden.

So also it is written, "The first man, Adam, became a living soul." The last Adam became a life-giving spirit. However that which is spiritual isn't first, but that which is natural, then that which is spiritual. The first man is of the earth, made of dust. The second man is the Lord from heaven. 1Cor.15:45-47

These records of Yahweh's first relationship with man and His desire to fellowship with us and be involved in our lives are breathtaking! They show us Yahweh's heart for the future when all things are restored. One day we will return to a time when everything will be made new, a time of renewed intimate fellowship with our Beloved King in His garden. The garden shows us pictures of Yahweh's heart and how important the garden is to Him and that He desired it first. Thousands of years later when Yahweh's Son, Yahshua came to us, He used many terms and parables that referenced gardening and other agricultural matters, to teach us how to care for the things of His Father's heart. That is why it is crucial to understand the principles found in the garden and then apply them to the many times Yahweh speaks of them in Scripture. Yahshua confirmed Yahweh's heart for the garden when He told us that the parable of the seed was the most important parable and the key to understanding all His parables.

He said to them, "Don't you understand this parable? How will you understand all of the parables? Mark 4:13

To understand the parable of the seed, we must understand the garden pattern, found in the life of a seed and then see how it applies to our lives. A tiny seed has three parts that together make up all the potential of the full grown plant; whatever that plant may be, from a delicate flower to a mighty cedar. Those three parts are the embryo, the endosperm and the seed covering, sometimes called a seed coat. When given the right conditions these three will play their part in becoming a mature plant, which will produce its own fruit, which in turn will hold many more seeds.

At the appointed time or season, when the conditions for growth are right, a place is made for a seed in good soil. The seed is then carefully set into the ground and covered with enough soil to protect it. While safely hidden in the earth, the seed's hard outer covering or seed coat softens and breaks open. With the hard coating broken, the embryo and endosperm release new life. The conditions of covering and safety give the seed what it needs to grow strong. If that same seed had been left out on the top of the soil or was not completely covered, it would have been exposed to the weather or even worse, devoured by predators. On the other hand, when it is safely tucked away in the ground, the elements of nature are not life threatening but life giving. While the seed is covered, the warmth of the Sun and the nourishing rain cause the seed to vibrate with life. Soon roots and shoots are sent forth. Then as the roots reach down into the soil, the shoots push up and break through the darkness to reach for the light. With these familiar pictures in mind let's read the parable of the seed.

> *The farmer sows the word. The ones by the road are the ones where the word is sown; and when they have heard, immediately Satan comes, and takes away the word which has been sown in them. These in the same way are those who are sown on the rocky places, who, when they have heard the word, immediately receive it with joy. They have no root in themselves, but are short-lived. When oppression or persecution arises because of the word, immediately they stumble. Others are those who are sown among the thorns. These are those who have heard the word, and the cares of this age, and the deceitfulness of riches, and the lusts of other things entering in choke the word, and it becomes unfruitful. Those which were sown on the good ground are those who hear the word, and accept it, and bear fruit, some thirty times, some sixty times, and some one hundred times. Mark 4:14-20*

The Seed in Yahshua's parable is the Word of Yahweh, which we also know is Yahshua.

> *The Word became flesh, and lived among us. We saw his glory, such glory as of the one and only Son of the Father, full of grace and truth. John 1:14*

The most precious Seed is our Redeemer and our only hope. It's important to note that the seed in Yahshua's parable, which we are freely given, has varying chances of life. Those different chances are based on our individual lives and determine whether the Seed of Yahweh will bring forth fruit or die.

There is another intriguing picture of seed we find in relation to Abraham's offspring, which are also referred to as seed.

Now to Abraham and his Seed were the promises made. He does not say, "And to seeds," as of many, but as of one, "And to your Seed," who is Christ. Gal.3:16(NKJ)

When we accept Yahshua as our Savior and turn from the ways of the world, we are accepting the power of His Holy Spirit into our life and allowing our fleshly life to die. Yahweh then puts His seed within us, by way of the Holy Spirit and we become born again seeds of Abraham, and heirs to the Covenant. We are now one of the many children that Abraham was promised when he gazed into the night sky and the vast array of stars.

And if you are Christ's, then you are Abraham's seed, and heirs according to the promise. Gal.3:29(NKJ)

That is, those who are the children of the flesh, these are not the children of God; but the children of the promise are counted as the seed. Rom. 9:8(NKJ)

Another reference to seed that goes beyond our individual identity as seed is when the Kingdom of Heaven is likened to a seed.

He set another parable before them, saying: "The Kingdom of Heaven is like a grain of mustard seed, which a man took and sowed in his field. Matt. 13:31

Again we see the pattern of Yahweh established. The seed needs to be sown in the ground or covered in darkness for it to have life and bear fruit. As partakers of the Kingdom of Heaven and the seed of Abraham, we will naturally experience the different life applications of a seed. One of the more difficult things about the life of a seed is the waiting. For a time the life of a seed is covered and hidden from all eyes, but just as the gardener must patiently wait for the revealing of the seed's life, so we must patiently wait for Yahweh to reveal the things of His Kingdom and the fullness of our life with Him.

Be patient therefore, brothers, until the coming of the Lord. Behold, the farmer waits for the precious fruit of the earth, being patient over it, until it receives the early and late rain. James 5:7

We must keep in mind that our heavenly Father is the gardener. In His patience and timing, He waits for us to become fruit bearing. He is ultimately the one who will give us the best conditions for life. Yahshua also refers to His Father as the vinedresser revealing to us that Yahweh's goal is and always has been for us to bear much fruit.

In this is My Father glorified, that you bear much fruit; and so you will be My disciples. John 15:8

The life of a seed in the garden also teaches us principles about the pattern of bearing fruit. Fruit bearing does not happen based on our own ideals. Man's ways cannot bear good fruit. Good fruit must come by the design of the Gardener and His Seed.

By their fruits you will know them. Do you gather grapes from thorns, or figs from thistles? Even so, every good tree produces good fruit; but the corrupt tree produces evil fruit. A good tree can't produce evil fruit, neither can a corrupt tree produce good fruit. Every tree that doesn't grow good fruit is cut down, and thrown into the fire. Therefore by their fruits you will know them. Matt. 7:16-20

This simple yet amazing process comes through the pattern of life. A seed is sown in the ground and with care will produce fruit that holds much more seed after its own kind. We know this well in the physical, but could it be that we take it for granted in the spiritual; especially in a world that causes us to be dependent on world's systems to meet our needs more than our own efforts to grow seeds? When we remove ourselves from the natural and physical realities of a seed it becomes more difficult to understand what it means to us spiritually. We must see and understand the patterns of the Creator, especially the pattern of life. This pattern helps us to know Him intimately so that we can walk through our lives with the purpose of growing and bearing fruit.

The beginning of our journey with Yahweh, just as with the life of a seed starts in darkness or death. Our human nature does not initially respond well to this because like a seed's hard outer coat, we too have a worldly veneer that needs to soften and break. We cry out to the Father for new life, and we are met with death. Yet this is the most crucial step that leads us to life. A seed kept in the gardener's hand, pocket or storehouse will not have life in itself. Of course, it is good to store seed for future planting, as Joseph did when he prepared for famine, but a seed's main purpose is to die and be buried to bring forth new life. As Yahshua said:

Most certainly I tell you, unless a grain of wheat falls into the earth and dies, it remains by itself alone. But if it dies, it bears much fruit. John 12:24

You foolish one, that which you yourself sow is not made alive unless it dies. 1 Cor.15:36

The physical or natural way of a seed's life reveals to us that spiritual seeds are also destined to die in order to have everlasting life.

However that which is spiritual isn't first, but that which is natural, then that which is spiritual. 1Cor. 15:46

As the natural seed must die to give life to the plant inside, so our natural, carnal self must die to give way for the Seed of Yahshua to have life within us. The death of a seed from Yahweh's perspective is a sign of true love. If we try to keep or preserve ourselves and do not willingly die to our selfish nature, we will not have life or produce fruit.

Whoever seeks to save his life loses it, but whoever loses his life preserves it. Luke 17:33

Whoever is born of God doesn't commit sin, because his seed remains in him; and he can't sin, because he is born of God. 1John 3:9

Good fruit comes from identifying with the Seed of the Word, which is Yahshua and His death and burial. Good fruit is also manifest by the attributes of the Seed of Yahshua within it; which is predominately revealed in love. If spiritual fruit does not come forth in love, it is not of Yahshua our Messiah.

We know that we have passed out of death into life, because we love the brothers. He who doesn't love his brother remains in death. 1John 3:14

John is telling us that if we do not love we remain in death, do not grow and consequently will not bear good fruit. We must allow the death to ourselves to have its full work for the Seed of Yahshua to have life. Abundant life can only happen through the pattern of life! As we die to our selfish nature in the hidden place of our heart and allow the Seed of Messiah to take root, His love will grow in our lives.

Greater love has no one than this, that someone lay down his life for his friends. You are my friends, if you do whatever I command you. John 15:13,14

By this we know love, because he laid down his life for us. And we ought to lay down our lives for the brothers. 1 John 3:16

Once our selfish love dies it makes way for abundant new life; now our life is not our own but hidden in the Messiah and His life. When we humbly accept the Seed that was planted in our heart and guard it against the ways of the world, it will take root and be demonstrated in our words and actions. Our works of love will be evidence of who Yahweh is in our lives.

In days to come, Jacob will take root.
Israel will blossom and bud.
They will fill the surface of the world with fruit. Is.27:6

Even so, let your light shine before men; that they may see your good works, and glorify your Father who is in heaven. Matt.5:16

Yahweh desires us to walk through a physical application of what is happening spiritually within us. This is seen in the process of baptism. As we identify with Yahshua's death and are submerged under water, our old self is washed away, and we are raised up to new life. His Spirit then fills us with a love for Him and His Covenant that we could never achieve in our flesh and all is made new. Our expression of faith in Yahshua is displayed to all who witness us being buried under water as a testimony of the Seed we have accepted into our heart. All of this is simply the physical action of what is miraculously happening within us.

I have been crucified with Christ, and it is no longer I that live, but Christ living in me. That life which I now live in the flesh, I live by faith in the Son of God, who loved me, and gave himself up for me. Gal.2:20

Or don't you know that all we who were baptized into Christ Jesus were baptized into his death? We were buried therefore with him through baptism to death, that just as Christ was raised from the dead through the glory of the Father, so we also might walk in newness of life. Romans 6:3,4

The parable of the seed tells us that the sower generously spread the seed on all types of ground, but the seed only finds life in soft, rich soil. The parable goes on to describe what happens to the seed in the different types of soil, and the consequences of it. The life of the seed and the fruit that comes from it will ultimately depend on the soil and the soil in Scripture is then likened to our hearts. If our hearts are filled with the things of the world and our selfish motives, they will be hard to the things of Yahweh, but if our hearts are soft or humble the Seed or Word of Yahweh will be able to enter our hearts and have life. As mentioned before, this comes from guarding our heart just as a gardener protects his field so that the seed will prosper and bear much fruit.

The heart is deceitful above all things, and it is exceedingly corrupt: who can know it? I, Yahweh, search the mind, I try the heart, even to give every man according to his ways, according to the fruit of his doings. Jer. 17:9,10

These verses in Jeremiah reveal that the condition of our hearts and the fruit we bear will have consequences. The need for our Heavenly Father to have full reign in our heart and to make it a Holy Place for Him to dwell is vital. We are often deceived by our feelings and the fleshly desires that the world seduces us with, but He is our Master and Judge and will test all that we harbor in our heart.

Of course, dying to self is an extremely difficult process, yet as we die to ourselves, we learn to fully entrust our life into our Master's hands. If we humbly submit our hearts to Yahweh and then keep them safe from the world, we will find that eventually ... His desires become our desires. Then our hearts become worthy of having His Covenant commands written upon them and His Holy Spirit living within.

Seeing our heart as the soil for the seed of Yahweh and the Holy place of His dwelling should make us more aware of our heart's condition. A good farmer is very concerned for the condition of the soil. He prepares the soil by restoring to it what is lacking and pulling out weeds to make a safe place for the seed. The way soil is cared for is true for our hearts as well. Have you ever felt that your heart was being torn apart or tested? Yahweh is always checking the condition of our hearts. As the gardener of our heart's soil, He too is restoring to us what is lacking in our heart and weeding out what doesn't belong.

Many people are taking renewed interest in growing their own food, which includes finding the best ways of preparing soil for planting. One of the ways that is being rediscovered aligns with Yahweh's pattern of life. In a DVD called "Back to Eden," Paul Gautschi shares how God has taught him the benefits of covering the soil. He explains how covering the soil makes it soft, fertile and protected from harsh weather. Paul's garden and his method of covering the soil is becoming renowned for its ease of care and the bounty it produces. He makes this intriguing statement; **"when the soil is uncovered, it becomes vulnerable and lost."**

If this is true in the natural, it must then be true in the spiritual. When we look at our hearts as the soil we can also see that having Yahweh's covering over our heart will make it soft, humble and ready to receive His seed or Word. Once we have His seed covered within us, the covering will keep it safe from the world's harshness and allow it to fully mature and bear much fruit. Can you see how covering or concealing is important and vital for life? Without Yahweh's covering, we are exposed to the world, and our hearts become hard and unable to receive His seed. We become prideful, stiff-necked and separated from Yahweh. Consequently, His Word or Seed is not able to reach its fullness of life in us; our fruit bearing is then hindered and the Seed at risk of being lost.

This I say therefore, and testify in the Lord, that you no longer walk as the rest of the Gentiles also walk, in the futility of their mind, being darkened in their understanding, alienated from the life of God, because of the ignorance that is in them, because of the hardening of their hearts; who having become callous gave themselves up to lust, to work all uncleanness with greediness. Eph.4:17-19

Understanding that Yahweh's pattern of life begins with darkness first is so important. In the quiet, hidden place of Yahweh's covering, we become humble, soft and broken; ready to receive His Word, hear His voice and develop a deep root. Yahweh's pattern gives us insight to the root of the plant as well, for the root is what remains covered and hidden in the soil. There in the dark, it reaches deep into the soil for nourishment and life; for without the root the plant would die. The hidden and protected root teaches us about the kingdom of Yahweh because what is unseen is the very thing that sustains the whole plant. The deeper the roots go, the more stable and strong the plant. It should also be noted that a plant with a deep root will survive a drought, whereas a shallow root will quickly wither. The same is true in our walk with Yahshua. Scripture tells us that as we seek to know Yahweh in a deeper way and trust Him, the more secure our root. On the other hand, if we have a hardened heart the root will not be able to sink deep into the soil, our growth will be stunted, and when drought comes, we will not survive.

Blessed is the man who trusts in Yahweh, and whose trust Yahweh is. For he shall be as a tree planted by the waters, who spreads out its roots by the river, and shall not fear when heat comes, but its leaf shall be green; and shall not be careful in the year of drought, neither shall cease from yielding fruit. Jer. 17:7,8

If we do not submit fully to Yahweh, choosing our own way or the ways of man, we expose ourselves to the plight of the world. Our choices will bring consequences that are very difficult and in the end could even be fatal.

Yahweh says: Cursed is the man who trusts in man, and makes flesh his arm, and whose heart departs from Yahweh. For he shall be like the heath in the desert, and shall not see when good comes, but shall inhabit the parched places in the wilderness, a salt land and not inhabited. Jer. 17:5,6

When the sun had risen, it (the plant) was scorched; and because it had no root, it withered away. Mark 4:6 (parenthesis mine)

Notice that Jeremiah is comparing our trust in Yahweh with two different types of plants and the soil that they are in. Those who trust Yahweh are like a tall tree planted by waters where the soil is soft and rich, and they are unscathed when drought comes. Those who trust in man are like the heath. Heath is an uncultivated wasteland land with poor coarse soil and bad drainage that only allows for small shrubs to grow. This is where we get the word heathen from, referring to a people that desire to live out in the wasteland away from Yahweh's abundant goodness and grace.

There are also those who may look fine on the surface and do well during good times, but only have a shallow root. When difficult times come their shallow root will not sustain them. All that needed to develop in the secret or hidden place, where a good root is developed, did not take place and so when trial comes, they are exposed and unprotected.

These in the same way are those who are sown on the rocky places, who, when they have heard the word, immediately receive it with joy. They have no root in themselves, but are short-lived. When oppression or persecution arises because of the word, immediately they stumble. Mark 4:16,17

To gain a deeper understanding of this (pun intended) there is a picture found in four Hebrew words used to describe how to study the Scriptures. These four words are Parshat, Remez, Darash and Sud. The Hebrew word PARDES is an acronym of the first letters of these four words. As you can see when you take the P-R-D-S from the beginning of each word and add vowels, you get the word PARDES. Amazingly, the Hebrew word PARDES means "garden" or "orchard" and is sometimes even referred to as Paradise... which takes us back to the beginning of Yahweh's story and His heart, which is revealed in the Garden of Eden. Each of these four words takes us on a journey of understanding Yahweh's Word more intimately. Each word reveals a layer that is deeper and more intense than the last. Just as Yahweh has desired from the beginning for us to seek Him in the garden, these words paint a beautiful picture of how Yahweh desires for us to seek Him now. As we saw earlier it was Yahweh that planted the Garden of Eden. He wants us as His children to delight in seeking Him in the wonder and beauty of all He created. Let's look at each of these four Hebrew words to help us seek Him and deepen our roots.

The first level of seeking is seen in the word parshat, which portrays the surface or literal understanding of something. The pashat level is simply what you see and feel the first time you walked through a garden, like a child sees, full of excitement at seeing everything for the first time. This is when you try to take in and experience everything around you. Usually you will remember only a few things that stood out to you personally, but return with joy to seek for more.

The next word is remez, which portrays the wonder or allegorical meaning hidden beyond what is easily seen. The remez level of searching is when you realize that there is purpose and meaning hidden within all that you see and hear. Also, the remez level opens our eyes and makes us think. Yahshua used this level when He spoke in parables. Remez searching usually fills you with a sense of curiosity that leaves you pondering thoughts that fill you with questions.

The third word in our journey is d'rash. The d'rash level of searching is when you want your questions answered and so you dig for truth. D'rash searching cannot be compared to the things we typically look for on a daily basis, like looking for your keys or the missing match to your sock. This search, is driven by love and compared to the desperate search for a lost child or spouse. The d'rash level understands that there is priceless value in what you are searching for. We see the d'rash level throughout Scripture, in the many ways Yahweh portrays His love for us, and Yahshua revealed it when He said:

> *Which of you men, if you had one hundred sheep, and lost one*
> *of them, wouldn't leave the ninety-nine in the wilderness, and*
> *go after the one that was lost, until he found it? Luke 15:4*

In the Song of Solomon we also see this level used as the writer portrays pictures of Yahweh's love story and His bride seeking for Him.

> *I sought him whom my soul loves.*
> *I sought him, but I didn't find him.*
> *I will get up now, and go about the city;*
> *in the streets and in the squares I will*
> *seek him whom my soul loves.*
> *I sought him, but I didn't find him.*
> *The watchmen who go about the city found me;*
> *"Have you seen him whom my soul loves?"*
> *I had scarcely passed from them,*
> *when I found him whom my soul loves.*
> *I held him, and would not let him go ...*

We now come to the fourth and final word in our journey of searching which is sud or sometimes called sode. We get our English word sod meaning, a piece of grassy earth with roots, from this word. At this final level of seeking we reach the deepest place. Sode is the level that reveals to us the root or source of life. The sode part of our journey is where we find the reward for all the other seeking we have done, for it takes us to the source of all we had hoped to find. Here is the revelation of what is hidden or unseen; the destination of our heart's fulfillment. The fullness of the Hebrew word sode will ultimately be revealed at Yahshua's return, for

He is our source of life and the prize we seek. From the garden perspective, the sode level is the evidence of what is beneath the soil or unseen by man's eye. When we find the intimate place of the sode level understanding, we will have complete peace because what we could not understand on the surface now makes perfect sense. In the sod or root level, we find the hidden place where Yahweh entrusts us with the intimate things of His heart. In the verse below the word translated as secret is Strong's #H5475 סוד sode.

For the perverse person is an abomination to the Lord,
But His secret counsel is with the upright. Prov.3:32 (NKJ)

Notice that it is with the upright that Yahweh gives His secret or sode level of counsel. Again this truth was revealed to the disciples when Yahshua explained to them the parable of the seed.

The disciples came, and said to him, "Why do you speak to them in parables?"

He answered them, "To you it is given to know the mysteries of the Kingdom of Heaven, but it is not given to them. For whoever has, to him will be given, and he will have abundance, but whoever doesn't have, from him will be taken away even that which he has. Therefore I speak to them in parables, because seeing they don't see, and hearing, they don't hear, neither do they understand. Matt. 13:10-13

The disciples had died to their old life and gave their life to following Yahshua. Their commitment to Him and their daily walk with Him, brought them to a different understanding than those outside.

But blessed are your eyes, for they see; and your ears, for they hear. For most certainly I tell you that many prophets and righteous men desired to see the things which you see, and didn't see them; and to hear the things which you hear, and didn't hear them. Matt.13:16,17

The sode or root is the part of the plant that seeks or thirsts for the deep waters of righteousness. When we hunger and thirst for righteousness, we too will go deeper with Yahweh seeking the Living Water found in the secret place of intimacy with Him.

> *God, you are my God. I will earnestly seek you. My soul thirsts for you. My flesh longs for you, in a dry and weary land, where there is no water. Ps.62:1*

> *As therefore you received Christ Jesus, the Lord, walk in him, rooted and built up in him, and established in the faith, even as you were taught, abounding in it in thanksgiving. Col. 2:6,7*

> *He who sits on the throne said, "Behold, I am making all things new." He said, "Write, for these words of God are faithful and true." He said to me, "It is done! I am the Alpha and the Omega, the Beginning and the End. I will give freely to him who is thirsty from the spring of the water of life. Rev.21:5,6*

The hidden place is where the Living Water satisfies our thirst! The depth of the roots or what is unseen will then establish our strength and stability as fruit-bearing trees. The evidence of what is established in secret will then be made manifest in our words and deeds.

> *Watch over your heart with all diligence, For from it flow the springs of life. Prov. 4:23*

> *Blessed is the man who doesn't walk in the counsel of the wicked, nor stand in the way of sinners, nor sit in the seat of scoffers; but his delight is in Yahweh's law. On his law he meditates day and night. He will be like a tree planted by the streams of water, that brings forth its fruit in its season, whose leaf also does not wither. Whatever he does shall prosper. Ps.1:1-3*

In the dark, concealed place, away from harsh elements and exposure to the world, new life and strength is developed. However, without Yahweh's covering we become like exposed soil; vulnerable, lost and effected by man's ways. We apply this truth in our lives when a part of our body is wounded. Carefully the wound is cleansed and then covered to protect it and allow it to heal properly. With proper covering, our skin stays soft and safe, so that the wound can be fully restored with very little to no scarring. If we then take this natural truth to the body of the Messiah, it becomes clear that our wounds and heartaches also need to be covered in the secret place where we are healed and restored to whole. When we are washed in the Living Water and covered in the secret place we will see that Yahshua bore our wounds so that we could be healed.

For to this you were called, because Christ also suffered for us, leaving you an example, that you should follow his steps, who did not sin, "neither was deceit found in his mouth." Who, when he was cursed, didn't curse back. When he suffered, didn't threaten, but committed himself to him who judges righteously; who his own self bore our sins in his body on the tree, that we, having died to sins, might live to righteousness; by whose stripes you were healed. 1 Pet. 2:21-24

Bless the LORD, O my soul,
and all that is within me,
bless his holy name!
Bless the LORD, O my soul,
and forget not all his benefits,
who forgives all your iniquity,
who heals all your diseases, Ps.103:1-3

Of course, the most beautiful display of Yahweh's pattern of life is seen in the awe of childbirth, for it is in the secret place of a woman's womb that a seed is planted. When the conditions are right, a new life begins to develop away from the eyes of world.

If I say, "Surely the darkness will overwhelm me;
the light around me will be night";
even the darkness doesn't hide from you,
but the night shines as the day.
The darkness is like light to you.
For you formed my inmost being.
You knit me together in my mother's womb.

I will give thanks to you,
for I am fearfully and wonderfully made.
Your works are wonderful.
My soul knows that very well.
My frame wasn't hidden from you,
when I was made in secret,
woven together in the depths of the earth. Ps. 139:11-15

The most profound reality of the secret place is revealed in this hidden place of covering that brought each of us into life. There hidden in a mother's womb new life develops and grows until the appointed time of our arrival into the light and life of the world. Here again we see that the natural way of life and birth also gives us insight to the spiritual.

Yahshua told us that we needed to be born again to have new life. This can only be possible by a miraculous encounter with Yahweh. When Nicodemus questioned returning to our mother's womb to be born again, Yahweh's told him that we must be born of the Spirit.

Jesus answered him, "Most certainly, I tell you, unless one is born anew, he can't see the Kingdom of God." John 3:3

We see this truth pictured in the life of a butterfly. A butterfly begins life as a mere caterpillar bound to the earth. The lowly caterpillar spends his days crawling around gardens devouring and destroying plants. Then at an appointed time, the caterpillar conceals himself in a covering and is hidden away in the secret place of its newly made chrysalis. There in secret something mysterious and amazing happens away from the eyes of the world; something that changes the caterpillar forever. At another appointed time the covering or chrysalis begins to break open. Slowly, what used to crawl upon the Earth on its belly, emerges from within the secret place as a butterfly with wings of beauty. The once caterpillar is no longer bound to Earth and devouring plants. No! It is now a new creature that has flight and participates in bringing forth life and fruit in the garden by pollinating it. This is Yahweh's desire for our life.

Don't be afraid, you worm Jacob, and you men of Israel. I will help you," says Yahweh, "and your Redeemer is the Holy One of Israel. Is.41:14

The Hebrew word translated as worm in the above verse is Strong's #H8438 tola'ath which means maggot, and comes from the Hebrew word yala, meaning to utter inconsiderately or devour. Tola'ath or maggot pictures the life we have when we don't have Yahshua as our Savior. Thankfully, in our helpless state Yahshua comes to us in the secret place of our heart to transform us into new creatures! There He reveals to us the secrets of His Covenant, and we emerge not bound to this world any longer. We are now new creatures that are in the likeness of Yahshua ready to do His will and bring forth fruit.

> *I will give you the treasures of darkness*
> *And hidden riches of secret places,*
> *That you may know that I, the Lord,*
> *Who call you by your name,*
> *Am the God of Israel. Is.45:3*

But alas, we are not like the caterpillar because we have been given the gift of free will. The new life we are given requires daily personal choice, for we are creatures of habit and selfish patterns. The negative habits and patterns that are intergraded into our lives are the hardest to let go of because we are so used to them and often don't even recognize that we have them. As born again children of Yahweh we must choose to listen to His voice and respond to the new life He has so graciously given us. Often we let our emotions and past experiences affect our future, but this is not the way of the butterfly. As a new creature, the old ways are gone and our new life is all that is important.

Therefore if anyone is in Christ, he is a new creation. The old things have passed away. Behold, all things have become new. 2 Cor. 5:17

We therefore were buried with Him through baptism into death, in order that, just as Christ was raised from the dead through the glory of the Father, we too may walk in newness of life. Rom. 6:4

As new citizens of a heavenly kingdom, we are called to express who we have become to the world. Often we take our miraculous transformation lightly, forgetting that our thoughts and words have life. We must have the courage and faith to overcome the negative. Below is quote from Michael S. Tyrrell who has discovered the power of positive frequencies in our life through music and sound.

Now here's a secret, when a thought becomes a belief, it translates as a pure signal or frequency and it has the power to alter matter. And nothing will be impossible to him that…believes. Another word for unwavering belief is faith. And faith is what pleases God…why? Faith allows the object of God's affection, you and I, to live a supernatural life instead of a merely mundane, faithless existence. And that's why it is impossible to please God without faith, think of it as the difference between living as a caterpillar or a butterfly. Faith is transformational!

We must not allow our thoughts and words to rob us of the abundant life Yahshua paid for us to have.

> *..for the weapons of our warfare are not of the flesh, but mighty before God to the throwing down of strongholds, throwing down imaginations and every high thing that is exalted against the knowledge of God, and bringing every thought into captivity to the obedience of Christ; 2 Cor.10:4,5*

Yahweh has designed a place of covering for us. A place where the Seed of His Word can grow, flourish and bear fruit. There under His loving care, we can heal from our past wounds and be restored to a new life. Each day we are given is an opportunity to walk in victory with our King or fall into the old habits and patterns we developed in the world, leaving us exposed and vulnerable. Our choices in word and deed affect our hearts and consequently our testimony. May our hearts become soft and humble under Yahweh's covering and display to the world who Yahweh truly is in all that we do and say.

Who can understand his errors?
Cleanse me from secret faults.
Keep back Your servant also from presumptuous sins;
Let them not have dominion over me.
Then I shall be blameless,
And I shall be innocent of great transgression.
Let the words of my mouth and the meditation of my heart
Be acceptable in Your sight,
O Lord, my strength and my Redeemer. Ps. 19:12-14

The Covenant Pattern

He remembers His covenant forever,
the word He commanded for a thousand generations. Ps.105:8

YAHWEH ALWAYS STANDS BY IS WORD WITH INTEGRITY AND HONOR, AND when He makes a Covenant, it is forever! He never forsakes it. His Word is faithful and true, His heart is steadfast, and He willingly takes the responsibility of His Covenant conditions upon His shoulders. The Covenant that Yahweh made thousands of years ago with our forefathers; Abraham, Isaac, and Jacob is being fulfilled by Him throughout each generation. This is very real, reaching to our generation and beyond! Our modern generation has lost the understanding of how serious a vow or covenant is. In today's western culture, breaking a promise or a contract is common and acceptable, especially if a person is no longer happy or satisfied. From Yahweh's perspective though, a covenant is everlasting and His Covenant is at the heart of all that is unfolding over time.

The gravity of Yahweh's promises and the depth of His love are far beyond the world's comprehension. Yahweh has chosen to share His holy Covenant moments and times of intimacy with His people in private and away from the eyes and criticism of the world. Some may find this difficult to comprehend in a world that accepts it as normal to announce every thought and activity online, but it was common practice in times past to treat intimacy with *extreme privacy*. Yahweh desires a set apart time with His beloved people; a time away from the crowds and often hidden in darkness.

We must consider how important this is to our relationship with Him. An honorable covenant relationship will not want to share private time with a group of people. On the contrary, they will look for time away from the crowds to be alone together. This has been Yahweh's heart from the very beginning of time. When He desires heartfelt communion with His people, Yahweh creates a covering that protects them and sets them apart. These are precious times that Yahweh desires to spend with His beloved and express to her the desires of His heart. It was true in the beginning, and it will stand true at the end of days. Let's look at the scene when Yahweh made a Covenant with His trusted friend Abraham.

> *When the sun was going down, a deep sleep fell on Abram. Now terror and great darkness fell on him. Gen.15:12*

> *It came to pass that, when the sun went down, and it was dark, behold, a smoking furnace, and a flaming torch passed between these pieces. Gen.15:17*

We see here that Abram (who is not yet called Abraham) is covered in a great horror of darkness as well as the dark of the night. Yahweh designed a set apart place right where they were. Abram was then covered in darkness and sleep to remove from him the consequences of breaking the Covenant conditions, for the Covenant would encompass all the generations who would come after him. Yahweh's promises to Abram and the magnitude of the responsibilities that it held would rest upon Yahweh's shoulders alone for all generations. Does this mean that the Covenant doesn't apply to us? No! On the contrary! The Covenant conditions apply to all who come to Yahweh and the consequences of breaking the Covenant are death.

> *Abram fell on his face. God talked with him, saying, "As for me, behold, my covenant is with you. You will be the father of a multitude of nations. Your name will no more be called Abram,*

but your name will be Abraham; for I have made you the father of a multitude of nations. I will make you exceedingly fruitful, and I will make nations of you. Kings will come out of you. I will establish my covenant between me and you and your offspring after you throughout their generations for an everlasting covenant, to be a God to you and to your offspring after you. I will give to you, and to your offspring after you, the land where you are traveling, all the land of Canaan, for an everlasting possession. I will be their God. Gen.17:3-8

These powerful words of Yahweh's Covenant with Abram apply to you and me and every generation to come until He returns. When we become a part of the family of Yahweh, we also become Abraham's seed and heirs to the Covenant conditions. How does this happen? In harmony with the way of Yahweh's pattern, we find the pattern of darkness and then light comes alive again in the pattern of a Covenant. The darkness fell upon Abram and Yahweh came to him as a flaming torch. Then Yahweh personally passed between the sacrifices; taking full responsibility of the promises made. As the centuries have rolled by, Yahweh's people have turned away from Him and played the harlot by indulging in the ways of the world and its gods. Yahweh's Covenant was forgotten, and those who claimed to be His became adulterous and worthy of death according to the Covenant conditions.

"When a man takes a wife and marries her, then it shall be, if she finds no favor in his eyes, because he has found some unseemly thing in her, that he shall write her a bill of divorce, and put it in her hand, and send her out of his house. When she has departed out of his house, she may go and be another man's wife. If the latter husband hates her, and write her a bill of divorce, and puts it in her hand, and sends her out of his house; or if the latter husband die, who took her to be his wife; her former husband, who sent her away, may not take her again to be his wife, after that she is defiled; for that is abomination before Yahweh. You shall not cause the land to sin, which Yahweh your God gives you for an inheritance. Deut.24:1-4

Once Yahweh's people (His betrothed) had forsaken His Covenant and played the harlot, He could not receive them back according to His Word, and so Yahweh took the penalty we deserved for breaking His Covenant with Abram upon Himself. In His holiness He could never break His Word, nor could He marry a harlot. Yahweh had to divorce His people because they had forsaken Him for other gods.

> *I saw when, for this very cause, that backsliding Israel had committed adultery, I had put her away and given her a bill of divorce, yet treacherous Judah, her sister, had no fear; but she also went and played the prostitute. Jer. 3:8*

Over time Yahweh's people have strayed from His Covenant and disregarded the things of His heart. We all have sinned and fallen short of His Covenant requirements and are deserving of death. According to Yahweh's Word, He had to divorce us from Himself and His Kingdom. A righteous, holy King could not accept a harlot as His betrothed. We were lost and without hope, but Yahweh knew from the beginning that we would fall short. That is why He relieved Abram from taking the full responsibility of the Covenant. In His great love and mercy, He took on the restoration of the Covenant and made way for us to return to Him. Yahweh's relationship with Abram, who Yahweh later called Abraham, foreshadowed His plan of redemption.

Remember that Abraham and Sarah waited until they were beyond child-bearing for a son and heir. Isaac was miraculously born to them in their old age; their only son, the son of promise. When Isaac became a young man, Yahweh asked Abraham to give up the son they had waited for so long as a sacrifice to Him. In faithfulness to Yahweh, Abraham takes his son Isaac to the mountain as Yahweh asked him to. This display of love that Abraham, our father showed Yahweh foreshadowed the day Yahweh would reciprocate His love for Abraham and all his descendants. For at the appointed time Yahweh gave His only Son as an act of love in return. Yahshua's sacrifice was a sign of Yahweh's love for Abraham and His faithfulness to the conditions of the Covenant.

Sending Yahshua to die for us made way for two amazing things to happen. One; Yahshuah took our punishment and paid the penalty of death for our sin, establishing the way for us to return to the Covenant with His Father. And two; Yahshuah was buried and then rose from the dead as a new man, victorious over the grave. Yahshua resurrected as a new man restoring the Covenant, and we now have the awesome privilege of also becoming new, counted as Abraham's seed and accepted back into Yahweh's Covenant relationship.

..how much more will the blood of Christ, who through the eternal Spirit offered himself without blemish to God, cleanse your conscience from dead works to serve the living God?

For this reason he is the mediator of a new covenant, since a death has occurred for the redemption of the transgressions that were under the first covenant, that those who have been called may receive the promise of the eternal inheritance. Heb.9:14,15

The term New Testament does not do justice to this amazing truth. The Hebrew translation, Brit Chadashah or Renewed Covenant more accurately describes all that Yahshua accomplished for us, for now, all the conditions of the Covenant Yahweh made with Abraham are restored to us.

For you are all children of God, through faith in Christ Jesus. For as many of you as were baptized into Christ have put on Christ. There is neither Jew nor Greek, there is neither slave nor free man, there is neither male nor female; for you are all one in Christ Jesus. If you are Christ's, then you are Abraham's offspring and heirs according to promise. Gal. 3:26-29

There are no words to truly express the mercy and loving-kindness is of a Father who would go to such amazing lengths for those He loves. As we accept the sacrifice that Yahshua made and the conditions of the Covenant, we become heirs to the promise that Yahweh made with Abraham. Yahweh's promise was and is that He would take us under the safety of the Covenant conditions and the blood covering of the Messiah. Now as the seed of Abraham, Yahweh will protect and fight for us because we are His.

After these things Yahweh's word came to Abram in a vision, saying, "Don't be afraid, Abram. I am your shield, your exceedingly great reward." Gen.15:1

For those who follow Yahweh, it is an honor and a pleasure to keep the terms of the Covenant; for the terms of the Covenant show our love to Yahweh and keep us from being separated from Him. As we guard and treasure Yahweh's precious Covenant, we learn more each day about how it was designed and orchestrated as a pattern to identify and glorify His Holy character. The below verses are a statement from Yahweh telling us how He feels about His everlasting Covenant, which was established with Abraham, Isaac, and Jacob and confirmed in David.

"My covenant I will not break,
Nor alter the word that has gone out of My lips.
Once I have sworn by My holiness;
I will not lie to David:
His seed shall endure forever,
And his throne as the sun before Me;
It shall be established forever like the moon,
Even like the faithful witness in the sky." Ps.89:34-37

It should then come as no surprise that Yahshua's death followed the Covenant pattern. At the time of Yahshua's death, Yahweh covered the world in darkness. This darkness was not a natural eclipse of the Sun, for it lasted hours. The day was covered in darkness by the hand of Yahweh creating Covenant conditions as He always has and always will. Yahshua, His only Son, was then hidden in a tomb for three days until the revealing of His glorious life and light.

Now from the sixth hour there was darkness over all the land until the ninth hour. Matt.27:45

It was now about the sixth hour, and darkness came over the whole land until the ninth hour. The sun was darkened, and the veil of the temple was torn in two. Jesus, crying with a loud voice, said, "Father, into your hands I commit my spirit!" Having said this, he breathed his last. Luke 23:44-46

Abraham's love for Yahweh brought him to a place of obedience, even to the death of his only son. He did not have to sacrifice his only son that day though because Yahweh provided the ram in the thicket. Thousands of years later Yahweh proved His love and commitment to Abraham by sacrificing His only Son on what many believe to be the same mountain. Yahshua was sacrificed to fulfill Yahweh's Covenant promise to Abraham and renew the Covenant. We will see as we continue our search, that the Sun and Moon are witnesses to this Covenant and that the darkness of the Moon's conjunction plays an important part in Yahweh's overall story.

There is another parallel for this Covenant pattern that played out during the Exodus when Yahweh rescues His people from Egypt. Let's take a moment to refresh our memory with this pivotal time in history. Yahweh commissions Moses to confront Pharaoh saying, "Give Me My (Israel) firstborn or I am going to kill your firstborn."

You shall tell Pharaoh, 'Yahweh says, Israel is my son, my firstborn, and I have said to you, "Let my son go, that he may serve me"; and you have refused to let him go. Behold, I will kill your son, your firstborn.'" Ex.4:22,23

As you know, Pharaoh did not meet the conditions Yahweh had set before him and Egypt was plagued with nine judgments because of Pharaoh's hardened heart. The ninth judgment began with the Covenant pattern, as thick darkness fell over the land for three days. This was a prelude to Yahweh's Covenant conditions.

Yahweh said to Moses, "Stretch out your hand toward the sky, that there may be darkness over the land of Egypt, even darkness which may be felt." Moses stretched out his hand toward the sky, and there was a thick darkness in all the land of Egypt for three days. Ex. 10:21,22

Then Yahweh issued the tenth and final judgment; the death of the first-born that Yahweh had warned Pharaoh of at the very beginning! Pharaoh repeatedly refused to let Yahweh's firstborn go free and now all the first-borns in Egypt would pay for His refusal to listen.

In Yahweh's mercy and grace, He gives Moses instructions for *the only way* of safety from this judgment. Each household who chose to believe the words of Yahweh and protect their firstborn would take a spotless lamb in its first year, kill it and place its blood on the doorposts and lintel of their homes. Their act of faith and obedience showed Yahweh that they believed Him and accepted His Covenant terms. This foreshadowed the blood covering that Yahweh's only Son (the only way of redemption) would provide for us.

Those who chose the way of faith and obedience to the Mighty God of Israel were hidden safely in their homes that dreadful night, as the shadow of death swept through Egypt. The firstborns within the homes that had the blood covering on their doorway were safe under the shadow of His protection. Those who refused the Covenant conditions were NOT protected! It's that simple! When the darkness lifted and the first light of dawn appeared, the revealing of the firstborns of the Covenant also appeared. Again we see Yahweh's awesome life changing pattern of darkness first and then the revelation of new life.

The story continues as Moses leads the newly revealed Children of Israel to the mountain of His choosing in the desert. There in the wilderness away from all the world's eyes, Moses tells the Children of Israel to cleanse themselves for three days to prepare to stand in the presence of Yahweh. Can you imagine the great anticipation to meet the One who had just displayed His Mighty hand of power over all of Egypt?

> *Yahweh said to Moses, "Behold, I come to you in a thick cloud, that the people may hear when I speak with you, and may also believe you forever." Moses told the words of the people to Yahweh. Yahweh said to Moses, "Go to the people, and sanctify them today and tomorrow, and let them wash their garments, and be ready against the third day; for on the third day Yahweh will come down in the sight of all the people on Mount Sinai. Ex.19:9-11*

At the end of the three days, there was a great, long blast of a shofar, thunderings, lightening and a thick, dark cloud that came down upon the mountain! In awe the people witnessed the presence of Yahweh descend upon the mountain. The mountain was shrouded in what appeared to be a fierce storm, causing the mountain and the people to tremble.

> *On the third day, when it was morning, there were thunders and lightnings, and a thick cloud on the mountain, and the sound of an exceedingly loud trumpet; and all the people who were in the camp trembled. Moses led the people out of the camp to meet God; and they stood at the lower part of the mountain. All of Mount Sinai smoked, because Yahweh descended on it in fire; and its smoke ascended like the smoke of a furnace, and the whole mountain quaked greatly. When the sound of the trumpet grew louder and louder, Moses spoke, and God answered him by a voice. Yahweh came down on Mount Sinai, to the top of the mountain. Yahweh called Moses to the top of the mountain, and Moses went up. Ex.19:16-20*

Yahweh's account of one of the most breathtaking moments in Scripture reveals Moses' heart compared to the hearts of the rest of the people. Moses knew Yahweh like no one else! When he heard Yahweh call to him, he responded without fear and did not hesitate to climb into the dark and intense storm conditions to be with Him. To those who did not know Yahweh, this intense setting was reason enough to keep their distance. From Yahweh's perspective, this was a set-apart time of intimacy that He had waited for. Moses willingly climbed the mountain and was hidden with the Most High for forty days. He was covered in darkness and safe in the presence of Yahweh; receiving the terms of the Covenant in a similar setting to that of Abraham, only this time Moses was fully awake.

These are astounding pictures of how incredibly fearful it is to be in Yahweh's Presence. Most people let their fear overtake them and choose to keep their distance as the Children of Israel did. Only the few who truly know Yahweh willingly answer His call and walk into His awesome presence, allowing His glory to envelope them in the secret place. These Scriptures reveal and confirm this amazing reality:

Yahweh has said that he would dwell in
the thick darkness. 2Chron.6:1b

He made darkness his hiding place, his pavilion around him,
darkness of waters, thick clouds of the skies. Ps.18:11

Clouds and darkness are around him.
Righteousness and justice are the
foundation of his throne. Ps. 97:2

Within Yahweh's Love Story, this is an integral piece of His over all Masterpiece and as the Artist, is one of His principles of design and a repeated pattern. Our part in His Covenant is to align ourselves with His pattern as we walk with Him month by month. The Covenant pattern teaches us that if we dwell with Him in the secret place and abide in Him and Him in us, we will be hidden and protected in times of trouble and judgment. The enemy has tried to distort this truth in so many ways, but he cannot touch the wonder and beauty of the heavens and all that they are declaring ... if we have the eyes to see.

But as it is written, "Things which an eye didn't see, and an ear
didn't hear, which didn't enter into the heart of man, these God
has prepared for those who love him." 1 Cor.2:9

The Heavenly Pattern

He alone spreads out the heavens,
And treads on the waves of the sea. Job 9:8

WE HAVE ALL BEEN BLESSED AND AWED BY THE BEAUTY AND THE MAJESTY
of the heavens. Yahweh has spread them out as a glorious canvas or scroll
to tell His magnificent story on and to display His heart to His people.
This is the hand of our loving Father, and His overwhelming desire is
for us to know Him. One day when His story's closing scenes come to
completion Scripture tells us that Yahweh will roll up the heavens again
like a scroll. When this happens, we will want to be close by His side and
protected under His covering.

The sky was removed like a scroll when it is rolled up.
Every mountain and island were moved
out of their places. Rev.6:14

All of the army of the sky will be dissolved.
The sky will be rolled up like a scroll, Is.34:4a

Yahweh placed the Sun, Moon, planets and stars across the heavens in His
divine order. Each one is placed in such a precise manner that Earth and
all who dwell there are the sole audience to their fullness and wonder. A

quote from Guillermo Gonzalez and Jay W. Richards book, Privileged Planet reads:

Simply stated, the conditions allowing for intelligent life on Earth also make our planet strangely well suited for viewing and analyzing the universe. The fact that our atmosphere is clear; that our moon is just the right size and distance from Earth, and that its gravity stabilizes Earth's rotation; that our position in our galaxy is just so; that our sun is its precise mass and composition — all of these facts and many more not only are necessary for Earth's habitability but also have been surprisingly crucial to the discovery and measurement of the universe by scientists. Mankind is unusually well positioned to decipher the cosmos.

By Yahweh's Masterful design, we have been given front row seating for the glory of the heavens, and all of its astonishing story telling movement! Any other position or variation in the Earth's location would not allow for us to view Yahweh's wonderful story playing out or have sustainable life on our small, yet vibrant planet. This is the heart of our Creator and our loving Father choosing to display His story in a sparkling night sky for all to see. What other response could we have but to look up?!

My voice You shall hear in the morning, O Lord;
In the morning I will direct it to You, And
I will look up. Ps. 5:3(NKJ)

But when these things begin to happen, look up, and lift up your heads, because your redemption is near. Luke 21:28

Many great men in history that loved Yahweh did just that ... they looked up ... searching the heavens in their efforts to know Him. Many believe that when Yahweh told Abraham to look up and count the stars that He was actually telling him to make a record of the constellations and the story that He had written in the heavens.

"Yahweh brought him outside, and said, "Look now toward the sky, and count the stars, if you are able to count them." He said to Abram, "So will your offspring be." Gen. 15:5

The Hebrew word translated as count, in the above verse, is Strong's #H5608 ספר saphar; which means; to record, tell or recount a story. Saphar confirms that Yahweh was literally asking Abraham to make a record of the story that He had written in the heavens. Abraham then passed down his insight throughout his generations. We see later that Daniel too was skilled in seeing and understanding the signs and story of the heavens. Daniel then passed on his knowledge and understanding of the heavens to the Magi who also looked up. What the Magi understood of the heavens gave them the discernment for determining the birth of the Messiah.

As Yahweh's children and Abraham's seed, we too should look up for we are living in a time when Yahweh's story draws very near to His final chapters. If we listen with our hearts, we will hear His symphony crescendo as the grand finale of His story unfolds. It is important though, that we see the story from the Creator's perspective; the way that He established things in His Word and not according to the distorted ways of man. I cannot emphasize this enough, for the ways of man and the perverted ways of the world will lead to distraction and eventually destruction.

> *There is a way which seems right to a man,*
> *but in the end it leads to death. Prov. 14:12*

But Peter and the apostles answered, "We must obey God rather than men." Acts 5:29

As we saw earlier, we must go to the beginning to establish Yahweh's heart on a matter. This is especially true for the heavenly pattern.

God said, "Let there be lights in the expanse of sky to divide the day from the night; and let them be for signs to mark seasons, days, and years; and let them be for lights in the expanse of sky to give light on the earth"; and it was so. God made the two great lights: the greater light to rule the day, and the lesser light to rule the night. He also made the stars. God set them in the expanse of sky to give light to the earth, and to rule over the day and over the night, and to divide the light from the darkness. God saw that it was good. There was evening and there was morning, a fourth day. Gen.1:14-19

The way that Yahweh designed and established darkness and light gives us His pattern for a day, which follows His pattern for life. As one day closes and another day begins, we enter into a period of darkness that was designed for rest and restoration. Once restored in the darkness of night, we rise to life in the light of the day. In a world that has moved away from the natural patterns of Creation with artificial light and technology, people are suffering. Science has proven that because we don't have complete darkness when we sleep, we are not receiving the rest and restoration that the night was meant to bring us. We are missing out on Yahweh's pattern for life.

The pattern of a day also reveals Yahweh's plan for oneness; the darkness and the light compliment each other to make one whole day. There are some that contend that because Yahweh separated the darkness from the light that they cannot be seen together as one day. The thought is that darkness represents evil and thus it was separated out of the light. This concept does not follow Yahweh's pattern. Yahweh revealed the picture of oneness when He separated woman from the side of man. Though a man and a woman are different in their role and purpose in life (opposites in many ways) they are meant to be one and compliment each other in their differences bringing fullness to life. Darkness first and then light also brings the fullness of life to a day.

In a similar way, the Sun and the Moon work together in the heavens to bring the fullness of one day. The Sun is the greater light given to rule over the day, and the Moon is the lesser light given to rule over the night; each fulfills a different role but work together to bring the fullness of one day. Later as we look at the deeper meaning for the Sun and Moon, we will understand how important and beautiful this picture is. If we choose to see the night and the day as separate, great confusion is stirred up and we loose sight of how time is to be kept. If we put the day before the night or change the day to begin at midnight, we are allowing man to manipulate what was clearly stated in Genesis as Yahweh's pattern of life.

Genesis also states that the lights in the heavens are to be signs for us. The word sign in Hebrew is Strong's# H226 אות oth which means: sign, remembrance or miracle. Notice that this word is similar to the two-letter, Aleph Tav we looked at earlier, except for the Hebrew letter vav ו in the middle of the word. The letter vav in the original Hebrew pictograph or paleo form is a nail, which means: to add or secure something. If we agree that Yahshua is the Aleph and the Tav, who took the nail in His hands and feet to renew the Covenant and confirm the pattern of life by being buried and then rising from the dead, then we can also agree that a sign from Yahweh will secure and confirm this.

There are many amazing stories of signs in the heavens recorded throughout Scripture, especially during the time of Yahshua's birth and death. There are also many heavenly signs recorded throughout history. How people discern or respond to these signs ranges from, those who feel that these signs affect nothing here on Earth, to those who feel that what is happening in the heavens affects their life daily through false claims in astrology. These worldly extremes cannot dictate our response to Yahweh's signs. The ways of Yahweh are balanced, orderly and intricately designed, not random. We may not always understand them, but that is because we are not always seeing Yahweh's design from His overall Masterpiece and so our discernment is skewed.

As Yahshua's triumphant return draws near Yahweh is opening our eyes and hearts to see and understand how the signs of the heavens affect us in these latter days. It is of great importance to align ourselves with the timing of our Father and not our own timing. Looking to the signs of heaven for discernment and understanding is how we will learn to keep pace with Him and bring unity to the body of the Messiah. Some say it doesn't matter what day we keep Yahweh's feast days just as long as we keep them. Others say that the signs in the heavens and the way they affect the calendar are a stumbling block to our walk. Still, others say that going with the majority and keeping the unity of the brethren is more important than our differences. In our search for Yahweh's heart in these matters, we should not become discouraged or give up. On the contrary, let us seek Him all the more as we see the Day of His return approaching, trusting that He will work all things together for His purposes.

From a secular perspective, we all have appointments that we must keep. If we overlook our prescheduled dates with dentists, doctors, etc., we often suffer the consequences, such as cancellation fees or simply a bad reputation. Likewise, if you are called for a job interview and don't show up at the right time, will it matter? If you were invited to perform before dignitaries at a gala event, would it matter what time you performed? The proper attitude when invited to participate in a grand event is that of honor and privilege. An invitation to perform or be a part of an event on any level puts you in a position of accountability to the coordinator and the other participants. In spite of how minor your part may seem in a grand event, your concerns for being completely in sync with those who planned it should only be heightened … not diminished. The honor of being asked to attend an event should cause you to do your best to impress the producers and coordinators and play your part with excellence. This shows your care and concern for the outcome of the event and for those who planned it.

Our journey in this life is played out in a similar way. When we see Yahweh's grand and spectacular appointments as His set apart days for us to meet with Him alone, then we must treat them with the same or more respect as any worldly event may receive. Each of us has a vital role to play and should be concerned for each other's part in His Love Story so that the outcome He desires is achieved.

The best example of being at the right place at the right time is seen through the eyes of a relationship between a man and a woman. In their time of building a relationship, each outing or meal together is important because it helps them get to know each other. If one of them has no regard for their time together and does not show up to a prescheduled date, like a dinner, a party or worse still, their own wedding rehearsal … what then?

What if the man in the relationship was the one who had given his time and heart into organizing an event for his betrothed? Would he care if she made an effort to be on time? What if he had specifically told her a time and place to be and instead she chose to go to a friend's event? To take this picture a step further, what if she asks her betrothed to forfeit the plans he had made and join her at the other gathering? Of course, this sounds silly and ludicrous because it would obviously matter a great deal to any man or woman how their fiancé responded to them because it is a reflection of their love for them.

As blatant and obvious as this may seem in the world, it is often the way we treat our Beloved Yahweh. Our frustration with the many voices and choices that fill the airways on how to meet with Him is causing us to give up on seeking Him with all our heart. He is NOT the author of confusion but the Master of order and precision. Understanding Yahweh's design and His signs, especially the New Moon is so important. They are specifically designed by Yahweh to keep us, warn us and bring us to His important preplanned rehearsals and appointments. Our natural response as His betrothed is to know His appointed times and then seek to be with Him on those days to the best of our ability. So in honor of our Beloved and as His betrothed let us take up the privilege of pursuing His heart and His times.

We will first look for the wonder of His Love Story through the main players in the heavens, the Sun and the Moon.

He appointed the moon for seasons.
The sun knows when to set.
Ps.104:19

The Hebrew word for seasons in this verse is Strong's #H4150 מוֹעֵד moed which means; "appointed time, festival or rehearsal." Yahweh fashioned the Moon to help us keep pace with Him and to reveal His appointed times and His special days. Our heavenly Father is calling us to come out of the worldly systems, which embrace every cultural celebration and pagan tradition passed down through centuries, and join Him in His celebrations and rehearsals.

You shall not walk in the customs of the nation, which I am casting out before you: for they did all these things, and therefore I abhorred them. Lev.20:23

Sadly, the world's ways have permeated everything that we know, even our places of worship. Yahweh's desire is to take us away from the traditions of man, no matter how familiar and endearing they have been in the past and teach us His ways. When we learn the ways of Yahweh and meet Him on His appointed days we learn what matters to His heart and eventually our hearts will become like His.

> *Don't be conformed to this world, but be transformed by the renewing of your mind, so that you may prove what is the good, well-pleasing, and perfect will of God. Rom.12:2*

As Yahshua's bride, we are to joyfully anticipate time with our beloved King on His appointed days. His bride's efforts to seek Him and find His way reveal her love for Him, for it is her honor and privilege to be with Him and serve Him alone. Yahshua's bride will watch and listen for His leading as she walks with Him through each day. She will learn the signs in the heavens that are given to her by her Beloved; allowing His Word and the guidance of His Holy Spirit to help her find her way home.

I know that for many, the idea of watching and discerning the heavens seems daunting and even impossible, especially if you live where there are many days of cloud cover. Nevertheless His Word says;

> *The heavens declare the glory of God;*
> *And the expanse shows His handiwork.*
> *Day after day they pour out speech,*
> *And night after night they display knowledge.*
> *There is no speech nor language*
> *Where their voice is not heard.*
> *Ps.19:1-3*

Our question must be, no matter what our circumstances; "What is the glory of Yahweh that the heavens are declaring?" Is it such a great mystery that the average person cannot comprehend it? Remember that a mystery is placed before us to cause us to seek it out with wonder and awe. Now let's put the four different levels of seeking, Parshat, Remez, Darash and Sud, that we saw in the Creation chapter, to work. We must seek Yahweh with all heart, digging deeper than what is comfortable or common. Simply looking at the beauty of the heavens from time to time will not bring us understanding. We must be careful and discerning for some want to distort Yahweh's heavenly message for their pagan beliefs.

Thankfully we have been given Yahweh's truth and His Spirit to guide us on our journey of discovery. The only way to truly understand the heavens is to understand their Maker. Again, this can only come from developing an intimate relationship with Him, for though the heavens are astonishingly beautiful there is a deeper glory within their design. The heavens are declaring the love story of the King; the awesome King of glory.

> *Who is this King of glory?*
> *Yahweh of Armies is the King of glory!*
> *Ps.24:10*

I believe that we can know the glory that the heavens are declaring if we know *who* the King of glory is. He promised that we would find Him if we seek Him with all of our heart. Always remember that our heavenly Father is the great Author and Composer and His grand symphony is playing all around us. As a loving Father, Yahweh has placed picture after picture before us to tell us of His heart. Each picture is a part of His overall Masterpiece. So now…let us take up the privilege of kings and seek the glory of our beloved King displayed for us in the heavens.

PICTURES

Yahweh's Story

FROM THE TIME WE WERE BORN, EACH AND EVERY PERSON LONGS TO BE loved in some way. Love or the lack of it affects our lives very deeply. This is because we are wired for love as a part of Yahweh's wonderful story. Yahweh has created all things from the perspective of His awesome and relentless love.

For God so loved the world, that he gave his one and only Son, that whoever believes in him should not perish, but have eternal life. John 3:16

Beloved, let us love one another, for love is of God; and everyone who loves is born of God, and knows God. He who doesn't love doesn't know God, for God is love. 1 John 4:7,8

.. that Christ may dwell in your hearts through faith; to the end that you, being rooted and grounded in love, may be strengthened to comprehend with all the saints what is the width and length and height and depth, and to know Christ's love which surpasses knowledge, that you may be filled with all the fullness of God. Eph.3:14-19

Yahweh's love is unfathomable and encompasses all that He created. How many of us would give up our only son or daughter to die and make a way for those who are lost to return home? Such a great love should never be taken for granted, for the One who has such an amazing capacity to love, also has a great desire to be loved.

> *Jesus said to him, "'You shall love the Lord your God with all your heart, with all your soul, and with all your mind.' This is the first and great commandment. Matt.22:37,38*

We have seen that the Earth has front row seating to the glory of the heavens, and it's astonishing story telling movement! May we never forget that each meticulously planned and precious piece of Yahweh's Word is a part of a magnificent love story that spans all time. Yahweh's story is so amazing and full of wonder that we could never see its fullness from our finite perspective. That is why our heavenly Father has chosen to show us His heart through pictures and stories and patterns. Imagine now that you are seated in the grandest theater in the entire Universe. The theater is called the Milky Way, and there is an epic love story playing. As the story unfolds, it captures your heart and pulls you to the edge of your seat as the ending draws near. The last battle between the Bridegroom and His enemy for the bride intensifies as the climax mounts. You sit up and hold your breath as the music crescendos and the final scenes grip your heart! Yahweh's final chapters are the breathtaking time that we live in and you are a part of this awesome story!! All that is playing out around us is a part of Yahweh's design and composition. It is our privilege to earn His trust as we love, follow and trust Yahweh. He will then give us of the "ever after" that awaits us beyond all that we could imagine. These glimpses of His glory will touch a place in our hearts that longs for Him and compels us to press on to the goal of spending eternity with Him as His bride.

The Garden of Eden was so pure and pristine that some scientists believe you could have heard the stars resonate in song. Yahweh's first chapters in the Garden was a time of pure oneness with Yahweh in every aspect. That glorious time is what Yahweh desires for us to return to. Only this time it will be even more glorious than at the beginning. Though we have been scattered and lost for centuries, Yahweh longs for the time when He will gather us home to be one with Him and all will be restored to a splendor that surpasses even the Garden of Eden.

> *For behold, I create new heavens and a new earth:*
> *and the former shall not be remembered,*
> *nor come into mind. Is.65:17*

> *I saw a new heaven and a new earth; for the first heaven and*
> *the first earth have passed away and the sea is no more.*
> *He who sits on the throne said, "Behold, I am*
> *making all things new. Rev.21: 1,5*

Our wayward hearts and cultural influences have taken us far from His original design. It is only by Yahshua's shed blood that we can come back to the Father. Yahweh's mercy has made a way for us to be one or echad with Yahshua as He is one with His Father. Yahshua spoke of this often and made it clear that He was not on a mission of His own but a mission of His Father's heart to bring home those who are lost.

> *"I do not pray for these alone, but also for those who will believe*
> *in Me through their word; that they all may be one, as You,*
> *Father, are in Me, and I in You; that they also may be one in*
> *Us, that the world may believe that You sent Me. And the glory*
> *which You gave Me I have given them, that they may be one*
> *just as We are one: I in them, and You in Me; that they may*
> *be made perfect in one, and that the world may know that You*
> *have sent Me, and have loved them as You have loved Me."*
> *John 17:20-23*

Yahshua is expressing His love for His disciples and for all who would follow after them. His love is a love that our western culture has lost. In the western world, love is commonly expressed for anything in life. We express the same for love food, entertainment and material things as we do people. Yahweh's love is profoundly different. He incessantly desires to draw those who have been lost and scattered to come back to Himself so that they will be together as a family. Just as the father in the story of the prodigal son waited patiently for his son to return, so Yahweh patiently waits and calls to His bride to come home.

We know and have believed the love which God has for us. God is love, and he who remains in love remains in God, and God remains in him. 1 John 4:16

The fact that everything that was created resonates with the love song that Yahweh designed may sound fanciful to some, but quantum physicists have discovered that it is not simply a romantic ideal. Research reveals that the Universe was brought into existence by an energized vibration of sound. Yahweh's opening scenes did not happen by a random sound or even a big bang. Though science will not admit it, there is only ONE sound that has the power to create and that is the mighty voice of Yahweh! His voice is often described as a thunder that causes mountains to tremble. The most amazing two words in all Scripture is "Yahweh said!" For thousands of years, men have been researching, exploring and discovering the results of all that He spoke into existence. Yet with all of our advanced technology, we are unable to comprehend its magnitude. The more we search, the more we realize how infinitely amazing and divinely unique our world is.

By faith, we understand that the universe has been framed by the word of God, so that what is seen has not been made out of things which are visible. Heb.11:3

By Yahweh's word, the heavens were made;
all their army by the breath of his mouth.
He gathers the waters of the sea together as a heap.
He lays up the deeps in storehouses.
Let all the earth fear Yahweh.
Let all the inhabitants of the world stand in awe of him.
For he spoke, and it was done.
He commanded, and it stood firm.
Ps.33:6-9

Let them praise Yahweh's name,
For he commanded, and they were created. Ps.148:5

Our heavenly Father designed, composed and set in motion a symphonic story that we have the privilege of being a part of every day. In spite of the wars and the encroaching evil, the small blue planet we live on is vibrant, beautiful and filled with wonder. We must not become so caught up in the world that we forget to notice the moments and places that take our breath away and fill us with awe. The enemy may attempt to drown out Yahweh's song with his distorted and perverted sounds, but Yahweh's melody is eternal and continues to resonate all around us. You have heard it in a newborn's cry, in the resonance of a bird's song, in the clicking and buzzing of insects, in the whirling, whispering winds, the rolling thunder, the crack of lightening, in the rush and babbling of waters through its courses and the countless myriad of other wondrous sounds that are playing out daily. Each solitary element of Creation has its specific part to play, and together they obey the Master composer and conductor of the Masterpiece ... all that is ... except man.

We are set-apart created beings that Yahweh has given a choice. We can choose to walk in Covenant with Him and play our part in His song; aligning ourselves with His voice and learning be in one accord with His Symphony ...or not. Whatever we choose though and how we respond will come with consequences. For every action, spoken word and choice has a reaction and an eternal consequence because, as we have seen, our words and actions also have a frequency that affects something or someone else around us. As insignificant as our daily words and actions may seem, they determine our future.

> *I tell you that every idle word that men speak, they will give account of it in the day of judgment. For by your words you will be justified, and by your words you will be condemned. Matt.12:36,37*

> *For we must all be revealed before the judgment seat of Christ; that each one may receive the things in the body, according to what he has done, whether good or bad. 2 Cor. 5:10*

Within Yahweh's Creation, words and music profoundly affect us and our surroundings. Some words and music calm us, and others make us excited and happy; sometimes even frightened or sad. The entertainment world, advertising industry and many types of therapy understand this very well and use words and music to affect our emotions. You may have heard of the studies done in Japan where scientists tested the effects of words and sound on water. The test exposed one portion of water to positive sound and another portion to negative sound. The positive sound was simply kind words, such as 'thank-you' and the negative sound was unkind words such as 'you fool.' Surprisingly the positive words caused the water molecules to form into a clear, symmetrical water crystal similar to a snowflake and the negative words caused the water to be distorted and without form.

The same scientists did a similar study exposing one portion of water to classical symphony music and another to hard rock music. The results were remarkably similar to the positive and negative spoken words. The water exposed to the sound of a symphony formed a symmetrical shape and the one exposed to the hard rock music became dark and deformed. This amazing truth affects us daily. Our bodies are made up of mostly water. Consequently the positive and negative things that we hear influence us greatly. We cannot change the words that others may say to us, but we can choose to speak life to those around us to edify one another and build one another up. So often simple, accusing or derogatory words are casually used and deeply hurt the hearer. Therefore, we must guard our heart against the negative. The enemy is the 'accuser of the brethren,' and we should never take sides with him, for we are children of light called to bring forth life. Scripture warns us of the power of our words and their consequences.

Death and life are in the power of the tongue;
those who love it will eat its fruit. Prov.18:21

Let no corrupt speech proceed out of your mouth, but only what is good for building others up as the need may be, that it may give grace to those who hear. Eph.4:29

Don't be drunken with wine, in which is dissipation, but be filled with the Spirit, speaking to one another in psalms, hymns, and spiritual songs; singing, and making melody in your heart to the Lord; giving thanks always concerning all things in the name of our Lord Jesus Christ, to God, even the Father; subjecting yourselves to one another in the fear of Christ. Eph.5: 18-21

When we speak, we are exercising the power to bring forth life or death to the one we are speaking to. One day we will give an account for every word we chose to speak and even those we chose not speak. Our words need to be in one accord with Yahweh not in discord. For if we speak without His love we are the horrible sound of a clanging brass within His symphony.

If I speak with the languages of men and of angels, but don't have love, I have become sounding brass, or a clanging cymbal. 1 Cor. 13:1

You offspring of vipers, how can you, being evil, speak good things? For out of the abundance of the heart, the mouth speaks. The good man out of his good treasure brings out good things, and the evil man out of his evil treasure brings out evil things. I tell you that every idle word that men speak, they will give account of it in the day of judgment. For by your words you will be justified, and by your words you will be condemned." Matt. 12:34-37

Though physicists are only now seeing the power of sound and its affect on Creation and us, the truth remains that Yahweh's voice is the single most powerful sound in all the Universe and every particle responds to it.

Yahweh's voice is on the waters.
The God of glory thunders,
even Yahweh on many waters.
Yahweh's voice is powerful.
Yahweh's voice is full of majesty.
Yahweh's voice breaks the cedars.
Yes, Yahweh breaks in pieces the cedars of Lebanon.
He makes them also to skip like a calf;
Lebanon and Sirion like a young, wild ox.
Yahweh's voice strikes with flashes of lightning.

Yahweh's voice shakes the wilderness.
Yahweh shakes the wilderness of Kadesh.
Yahweh's voice makes the deer calve,
and strips the forests bare.
In his temple everything says, "Glory!"
Psalm 29:3-9

Our sojourn here on Earth is a mere vapor in comparison to Yahweh's astonishing overall story and our response to Him will affect our eternal life. Yahweh's Word clearly reveals to us that His story was designed before He made the heavens and the Earth and what has happened over the span of the last six thousand years is the manifestation of it. We can think what we like, believe what we like, and do what we like ... but you cannot stop His story from playing out exactly the way He designed it to. Every 'jot and tittle' will be fulfilled and His finale will consume the entire Universe. He is calling us to come into harmony with Him and all that He has created, but we must make our own decision. In truth, each of us only has two choices in this life; one brings us into oneness with the Father leading to everlasting life, and the other brings us into discord leading to death.

I call heaven and earth to witness against you today, that I have set before you life and death, the blessing and the curse. Therefore choose life, that you may live, you and your descendants; to love Yahweh your God, to obey his voice, and to cling to him; for he is your life, and the length of your days; that you may dwell in the land which Yahweh swore to your fathers, to Abraham, to Isaac, and to Jacob, to give them. Deut. 30:19,20

A choral symphony is a large musical composition that includes multiple parts including an orchestra, a choir, and soloist. A symphony like this wonderfully describes the way Yahweh has composed the Universe. There are many parts that come together to make His symphony complete. Each part of His creation has been given a part in His choral symphony, and each is moving and vibrating to His orchestrated Word. Physicists are now discovering this truth in that, all matter, time and space are vibrating like countless stringed instruments playing a symphony of one story or song. As never before in history, technology allows our vision to stretch further than we ever could have imagined. Scientists now have astonishing insights both in the macro things of the billions of galaxies in our Universe that go far beyond our eyesight, to the micro things of the atomic world within our world, too small for our eyes to see. What an amazing time to be alive! We are seeing more of the beauty and wonder of Creation than ever before, even if science doesn't believe in the Creator or shall I say, Composer of the song that they are beginning to hear. Below is a quote by physicist, Michio Kaku:

So all the subatomic particles that make up our body are nothing but different notes on many, many, many tiny little violin strings, little rubber bands, and that physics is nothing but the laws of harmony of these vibrating strings. Chemistry is nothing but the melodies you can play on these vibrating strings. The universe is a symphony of strings, and the mind of God that Einstein wrote eloquently about the last 30 years of his life, is cosmic music resonating through 11-dimensional hyperspace.

Doesn't this take your breath away?! All Creation is singing in harmony, and there is only one song that is being sung … the love song of Yahweh! His song is the story of a Bridegroom and His bride, and it is at the center of all we know. This includes the rise and fall of kingdoms and the many wars that rage across the nations because the adversary hates Yahweh's story. Satan's goal is to distort and destroy Yahweh's song in whatever way he can, for as long as he can. Yahweh's magnificent and symphonic love story is the overwhelming reality He has woven into all we can see and even beyond what we see.

When you search the word Universe online or in an average dictionary, you will find many technical descriptions of its origin, including the probable Latin word that gives the etymological meaning behind it.

The Latin word derives from the poetic contraction Unvorsum — connects un, uni (the combining form of unus, or "one") with vorsum, versum (a noun made from the perfect passive participle of vertere, meaning "something rotated, rolled.

An alternative interpretation of unvorsum is "everything rotated as one" or "everything rotated by one."Wikipedia

The above description of the Universe agrees with Yahweh's cyclical design and that He rolled everything out as though upon a scroll. Yes, the great Composer and Creator of the Universe rolled out His song and story across the entire heavens like an epic musical score. From a simple child-like perspective though, the word Universe is a compound word made up of two parts. The first part is "uni" which means one and is the root for all words that express oneness like uniform, union, and unison. The second part is "verse" which means, a part of a song or poem. These two parts together reveal the true meaning of Universe … "one song!" To add to the wonder of this, it has been discovered that every Hebrew letter has a corresponding musical note. A Hebrew teacher named Uri Harel put together a project that takes the Hebrew Scripture into the world of music.

Today, new evidence confirms the idea that the original text of the Hebrew Bible is multi-layered and goes much deeper than the surface story. Mysterious codes embedded in the text contain information that could have not been written or obtained by human beings. "Why," Uri has asked himself, "would one of the layers of this complex text not be music?" And if there is music in the text, how would one find it? The answer Uri came up with was probably the simplest one: assign a musical note to each Hebrew letter and let the Bible "play itself..." hebrewworld.com

These studies bring confirmation to the understanding that as a Master Composer and Musician, Yahweh sang all things into existence. Now it is our turn to respond and seek our part in His song. Below is a piece from an article called, God's Symphony of Praise by Patricia L. Williams.

One of the marks of greatness of a classical composer is his ability to manipulate melodic fragments into various constructs and then reorganize them into even more meaningful patterns. Full enjoyment of a symphony on this second, deeper level depends upon our ability to remember the melodies heard previously, and when, after a some-times prolonged interlude, they reappear in all their majesty, it is like reuniting with an old friend. The more familiar we become with the

composition, the more we anticipate the arrival of that recognizable melody. The same is applicable to the Bible's major themes. Just as a symphony, with its different movements, is united by its thematic material, so is the Bible. The themes are manipulated, maneuvered, transformed, and sometimes disguised, but study and meditation can often reveal them. A musician who has studied the composition will understand it in greater depth and see the marvelous intricacies better than someone hearing it for the first time. However, the conductor, or in our analogy, the Holy Spirit can guide us into a more complete understanding.

Let us digress at this point as we ponder the role of the conductor. He (or she) <u>never</u> adds to, subtracts, or in any way changes the score that the composer has written. The job of the conductor is to interpret the information on the page and to lead, guide and direct the musicians in the performance. As pertains to the matter of interpretation, there are certain notations that may not be changed; for example, the notes themselves may not be altered unless there is an obvious misprint. The work must be performed in the same key that was chosen by the composer because a certain mood or impression can be generated through this choice of key. However, when the composer writes, "allegro" on the score, to define the speed at which the music is to be performed, just how fast is "allegro"? If he writes, "pianissimo" on a section, just how soft is that? The conductor determines these criteria within certain universal parameters and thus puts his signature on the performance.

I urge you to take time to think of Yahweh in this light, for you will never hear of anything more awesome and beautiful than that of the King or Conductor of the Universe singing His heart's Love Story into existence. His love is so great it encompasses all He made ... this is the world you and I have the privilege of living in! May we ever thank Him and praise Him for the wonder of this life, for even though we have fallen away and there is so much discord, there remains so much beauty that man can never destroy.

As we open our eyes and ears to the realty of Yahweh's heart and how it is displayed through music, it should then be of no surprise that many words used for celebrating and dance in Scripture are related to whirling or moving in a circle. Dance is the basis of how most of Creation moves; planets, moons, atoms, and much more all move cyclically, responding in praise to the one true Creator and Conductor of the Song of the Universe. All around us we see that the migration of birds, animals and fish, the design of flowers, spider webs and so much more also express Yahweh's cyclical design. Everything has been given a design and purpose that declares the character of the Creator and takes part in praising Him and His glorious Name.

Praise the Lord!Praise Yah!
Praise Yahweh from the heavens!
Praise him in the heights!
Praise him, all his angels!
Praise him, all his army!
Praise him, sun and moon!
Praise him, all you shining stars!
Praise him, you heavens of heavens,
You waters that are above the heavens.
Let them praise Yahweh's name,
For he commanded, and they were created.
He has also established them forever and ever.
He has made a decree which will not pass away.
Praise Yahweh from the earth,
you great sea creatures, and all depths!
Lightning and hail, snow and clouds;
stormy wind, fulfilling his word;
mountains and all hills;
fruit trees and all cedars;
wild animals and all livestock;
small creatures and flying birds;
kings of the earth and all peoples;
princes and all judges of the earth;
both young men and maidens;
old men and children:
let them praise Yahweh's name,
for his name alone is exalted.

His glory is above the earth and the heavens.
He has lifted up the horn of his people,
the praise of all his saints;
even of the children of Israel, a people near to him.
Praise Yah! Ps. 148

The thrilling and wondrous reality of the Universe is that every one of its innumerable galaxies, especially our Milky Way and every living thing on our privileged planet are dancing and praising Yahweh in harmony with His song. He is calling you to join in harmony with Him. The choice is yours. Look at the words of Zephaniah.

The Lord thy God in the midst of thee is mighty; he will save, he will rejoice over thee with joy; he will rest in his love, he will joy over thee with singing. Zeph.3:17 (KJV)

Can you imagine the Creator and King of all the Universe rejoicing over His bride with singing? How marvelous for such a precious and glorious moment to be true, yet this is Yahweh's heart. I encourage you to look up the words in this verse and ponder them in your heart. The first word translated as joy is simchah, which may be familiar to you; it is the basis of the expression "Simchat Torah" and simply means to be glad or joyful. The second word translated as joy, is the Hebrew word "giyl" which gives us a different picture of joy than simchah. It's the kind of joy that cannot be contained within words alone. Giyl means to spin around for joy. Could this be what 'jumping for joy' would look like? Yahweh "giyl" over you or we could say, He leaps and dances for joy over you.

Now I ask you ... have you ever felt so overwhelmed with joy for your Maker and King that you wanted to leap, dance and sing? King David did. When the Ark of the Covenant was safely returned, King David was so overwhelmed with joy that he humbly removed his royal garment and danced (giyl) with joy.

David danced before Yahweh with all his might; and David was clothed in a linen ephod. 2 Sam. 6:14

As Yahweh's betrothed, we too should be like David who was called a man after Yahweh's own heart and dance before our King. Even though David was the king of all Israel, he submitted in love to the King of the Universe continually bringing songs of worship before Him.

A gentleman who is well trained in dance will take his lady partner in his arms and lead her across the dance floor (often in circles) in harmony with the music. If the lady is a good partner, she will submit to his leading and the music's rhythm. She is not concerned with the direction they are moving across the dance floor for her gaze is fixed upon her partner alone, and she fully trusts him to lead. Beloved of the Most High, this is Yahweh's extended hand to you; to come and join in dance with Him. If you listen for His song, take hold of His hand and submit to His leading, you will experience the most wonderful dance that you could ever imagine.

Therefore, if the heart of our Beloved Bridegroom desires to express joy for His bride through dance and song, then what should the response of His bride be? Naturally, her loving response should be joyful praise and the willingness to take His hand and follow Him with all her heart ... but if she resists Him and remains silent, it will be just as Yahshua said when He spoke to His disciples.

> *... He answered and said to them, "I tell you that if these should keep silent, the stones would immediately cry out." Luke 19:40*

Yahweh's Word tells us in Luke 6, that out of the abundance of treasure in a man's heart the mouth speaks. From all that we have seen, we can then say that out of the abundance of Yahweh's heart, the Universe and all we see, hear, smell, taste and touch, was spoken into being. How wonderful it is to see Yahweh's Universe this way. The 'One Song' that Yahweh composed is His magnificent symphony and the outpouring of His heart, which has been faithfully playing since his opening scene in Genesis and will continue until the final scene closes and His bride is home with Him.

So again I ask you, what is your part in His song? Everyone is given the chance to be in relationship with Yahweh through Yahshua and His shed blood for our sin. If you choose to follow His leading and love Him, He will show you by His Word the way to be in harmony with Him. Then just as a child learning to play an instrument, the Spirit will guide you through His song. Each year as you practice and rehearse, His verses and chorus found in His cycles of righteousness will become more familiar. Most people who have mastered an instrument will tell you that the discipline of setting apart time to practice is not easy. You must be diligent, patient and faithful. This too is the way of learning Yahweh's heart. The longer you endure with practicing and rehearsing the more familiar you become with the song of His heart. Then like a wonderful melody that you know by heart, you will find His song or Word will flow with ease through your life, and you will be in harmony with Him.

"Behold, God is my salvation. I will trust, and will not be afraid; for Yah, Yahweh, is my strength and song; and he has become my salvation."Is.12:2

"Make a joyful shout to God, all the earth!
Sing out the honor of His name;
Make a joyful shout to God, all the earth!
Sing to the glory of his name!
Offer glory and praise!
Tell God, "How awesome are your deeds!
Through the greatness of your power,
your enemies submit themselves to you.
All the earth will worship you,
and will sing to you;
they will sing to your name."
Ps.66:1-4

There is one important caution though. New Age and Kabbalah take the wonder of Yahweh's design and twist it to suit their own way and you do not want to be lead astray by their mysticism. Remember that Yahweh's truth will always draw you closer to His Word and to His heart ... not away from it. The truth will lead you to the narrow path of righteousness, the path leading to everlasting life. Our heavenly Father is the *Master*. His patterns give us a foundation to unlock the mysteries of His Word and help us know Him above all counterfeits.

So now, with the pattern of life and Yahweh's love story laid out as a backdrop, we will look to the heavens, which are untouched by man. His heavenly pictures will confirm His love story and help us unlock Yahweh's mystery behind the New Moon and His plan for the bride of the Messiah.

Please let me emphasize that as we look to the heavens I am in *no way* suggesting that any created thing is a replacement for who Yahweh is. We look to the heavens to discover the Designer and His design alone. The Sun is NOT Yahweh! Nor is it in any way a god to be glorified, it is a heavenly player designed to play a part in revealing Yahweh's power and His purposes. The same is true for the Moon and any other created thing. Nothing created is ever to replace the Creator. The second command of the Ten Commandments declares; "You shall have no other gods before Me." Yahweh is the One who created all we see and know, and it is an insult to give anything He made precedence over Him. Yahweh was so angered at the golden calf that Aaron made because it was used as a replacement for Him. All things in heaven and Earth are subject to the mighty voice of Yahweh and were designed to speak of Him and to draw our attention to His greatness and glory.

For great is Yahweh, and greatly to be praised!
He is to be feared above all gods.
For all the gods of the peoples are idols,
but Yahweh made the heavens.
Honor and majesty are before him.
Strength and beauty are in his sanctuary.
Ps.96:4,5,6

Praise Yah!
Praise Yahweh from the heavens!
Praise him in the heights!
Praise him, all his angels!
Praise him, all his army!
Praise him, sun and moon!
Praise him, all you shining stars!
Ps.148: 1-3

Let's submit to the leading of the Master and join in His glorious love story that is ringing out in the heavens. I invite you now to join me in a discovery of the amazing players in Yahweh's great Love Story and Song; players created by His voice and set in the heavens to declare His glory.

There is one glory of the sun, another glory of
the moon, and another glory of the stars;
for one star differs from another star in glory. 1Cor. 15:41

The Sun

THE SUN IS THE MOST DYNAMIC AND POWERFUL PLAYER IN OUR SOLAR
system. Its presence on the evening and morning horizon is a beautiful
sight that we all have enjoyed countless times. We love the Sun's warmth,
brightness, and beauty. Yet I wonder if we take for granted how vitally
important it is to our life. Below are two descriptions of how amazing the
Sun is.

**"The Sun is the brightest object in our Universe. It gives us light, heat
and energy. It may seem that energy comes from other sources such as
gasoline and electricity but the ultimate source of energy for the Earth
is nothing else but the sun. Without the sun life on Earth would not
exist. It would be so cold that no living thing would be able to survive
and our planet would be completely frozen." Nasa**

**"It holds the solar system together; pours life-giving light, heat, and
energy on Earth; and generates space weather." National Geographic**

The Sun is so massive that scientists estimate one million, three hundred
thousand Earths would fit inside of it. Its temperature averages an overwhelming ten thousand degrees Fahrenheit. The extraordinary heat and
power of the Sun is matched only by the absolute precision of where it
is in relationship to us on Earth. If the Earth were even 5% closer to the

Sun, all the water on Earth would boil. If the Earth were a mere 15% further from the Sun all the water on earth would freeze. These remarkable statistics remind us that our beautiful, blue planet is dependent on the Sun for life.

In the context of Scripture, what do these statistics reveal about the glory of the heavens? I would like to humbly consider the following Scriptures that compare Yahweh's attributes to that of the Sun.

> *For Yahweh God is a sun and a shield.*
> *Yahweh will give grace and glory.*
> *He withholds no good thing from those who walk blamelessly.*
> *Ps.84:11*

He had seven stars in his right hand. Out of his mouth proceeded a sharp two-edged sword. His face was like the sun shining at its brightest. When I saw him, I fell at his feet like a dead man. Rev.1:16,17

For the Lord your God is a consuming fire, a jealous God. Deut. 4:24(NKJ)

Therefore, receiving a Kingdom that can't be shaken, let us have grace, through which we serve God acceptably, with reverence and awe, for our God is a consuming fire. Heb. 12:28,29

There are many other places in Scripture that tell us that Yahweh revealed Himself within fire or by fire. He appeared to Moses as a burning bush and His presence with Israel in the wilderness was as a pillar of fire. He also was the fourth person in the blazing furnace with Shadrach, Meshach, and Abednego.

Then these men were bound in their pants, their tunics, and their mantles, and their other clothes, and were cast into the middle of the burning fiery furnace. Therefore because the king's commandment was urgent, and the furnace exceeding hot, the flame of the fire killed those men who took up Shadrach, Meshach, and Abednego. Dan.3: 21,22

Consider also that Yahweh appeared as a blazing furnace or smoking oven when He met with Abraham to make a Covenant with him.

> *And it came to pass, when the sun went down and it was dark, that behold, there appeared a smoking oven and a burning torch that passed between those pieces. Gen.15:17*

We need to take heed to what Yahweh is revealing to us. He is the source of all power and light, and His presence would kill us if we drew near to Him uncovered. In a similar manner, we have all been warned of the danger of looking at the Sun without eye protection or spending too long in the Sun for fear of being burned, even though the Sun is 150 million kilometers away! Yahweh expressed this compelling truth when Moses asked to see His glory.

> *He said, "You cannot see my face, for man may not see me and live."Ex.33:20*

These are stunning parallels of Yahweh's attributes and the Sun; both have a heat and a light that can blind, burn or kill; yet both are our *only* source of light and life. James tried to put this into perspective when he compared us to a vapor.

> *Whereas you don't know what your life will be like tomorrow. For what is your life? For you are a vapor, that appears for a little time, and then vanishes away. James 4:14*

May we never forget this unnerving reality! It is not cliché or poetic. Man is seventy-five percent water and Yahweh is a consuming fire. Imagine what would happen if a vapor of water came near to a blazing inferno. This is the awesome power of *WHO* we serve. He is the Almighty King of the Universe, and there is none like Him. If these realities don't make you tremble in humility and fear, it should at the very least renew your awe of Yahshua our Messiah. Who being one with His Father was clothed in flesh and came to us. How incredible it is that we did not die in the presence of one so powerful. Yet Yahweh clothed His only Son in flesh so that He could dwell with us and then die in our place. Truly this is too wonderful for words and the most powerful act of love ever.

> *Have this in your mind, which was also in Christ Jesus, who, existing in the form of God, didn't consider equality with God a thing to be grasped, but emptied himself, taking the form of a servant, being made in the likeness of men. And being found in human form, he humbled himself, becoming obedient to death, yes, the death of the cross. Therefore God also highly exalted him, and gave to him the name which is above every name; that at the name of Jesus every knee should bow, of those in heaven, those on earth, and those under the earth, and that every tongue should confess that Jesus Christ is Lord, to the glory of God the Father. Phil. 2:5-11*

I have seen in myself and with others that as time passes, we have a tendency to become familiar with Yahweh and comfortable with our faith. Yet Scripture compels us to always keep our minds on the incredible work that Yahshua did for us. He is so unfathomable in power that He is described as having the attributes of the Sun, as His Father does, and their power demands our attention, fear, and respect ... always and forever.

Again…please allow me to assure you that I am not suggesting that the Sun is in any way a substitute for Yahshua or Yahweh, or that it should be worshiped or revered. There has been much concern about Sun worship and the many pagan practices that it entails, yet the Sun was made by Yahweh, and its light is a mere reflection of the One who created it. It was strategically set in the Universe to display the truth of its Creator. As powerful as it is, compared to Yahweh it is a mere instrument of His making. If we see even hint of Yahweh's power through this picture, it will help us revere our Master and King. He is so deserving of our adoration for Him, for He willingly laid down His majesty and awesome power to come as a servant to us all.

> *Oh the depth of the riches both of the wisdom and the knowledge of God! How unsearchable are his judgments, and his ways past tracing out! Rom.11:33*

The Hebrew word for Sun is Strong's #H8121 שמש, shamash. If you have ever celebrated Chanukah, also known as the Feast of Dedication or the Festival of Light, this word will be familiar to you. Each night of Chanukah's eight nights, candles are lit upon a nine-branched menorah. The center candle on the menorah is known as the shamash. It is spelled the same as the Hebrew word for Sun, but it means, "to serve," and so it is called the servant candle. Each night the shamash candle is lit first and then gives its light to each of the other candles. In other words the shamash or servant is the only true source of light in the celebration and is the one that serves all the other candles by giving them its light. This beautiful family tradition reflects the magnificent reality of Yahshua as the Light of the world. Just as the shamash candle is the source of light for all other candles, the Sun or shamash is the only source of light for the Moon, which we will look at deeper in the chapters to come.

Another note of interest is that the root word for shamash comes from the Hebrew word, Strong's # H8034 shem שם, which means name. In Hebrew thought a name is far more than the title you were given at birth. The word shem or name, means honor, authority and character. The word shamash for the Sun is telling us something of the awesome character of Yahshua who's character was the true revelation of His Father. I have chosen to spell His name as Yah - shua for this reason; Yah being the common name for the Father and the Son. Yahshua came to bring Yahweh's salvation to the world and honor and authority to His Father's name ... not His own.

Sing to God! Sing praises to his name!
Extol him who rides on the clouds: to Yah, his name!
Rejoice before him! Ps.68:4

Blessed is the man whom you discipline, Yah,
and teach out of your law; Ps.94:12

Let us now allow Scripture to reveal to us pictures of Yahshuah, as the shamash, שמש through Yahweh's design in the heavens.

But to you who fear My name
The Sun (H8121) of Righteousness shall arise

With healing in His wings;
And you shall go out
And grow fat like stall-fed calves. Malachi 4:2(NKJ)

For Yahweh God is a sun (H8121) and a shield.
Yahweh will give grace and glory.
He withholds no good thing from those
who walk blamelessly. Ps. 84:11

Clearly, Yahweh is drawing our attention to a picture here. The attributes of the Sun that He placed in the heavens is revealing a shadow picture of the greatness of who He is; for He is our light and our salvation, without Him we are lost and have no hope of life.

There was a set apart moment for a few of Yahshua's close friend's during Tabernacles when Yahshua took them up a mountain and allowed them to see His true identity:

He was transfigured before them. His face shone like the sun, and his garments became as white as the light. Matt.17:2

Also, the disciple who is known as the closest to Yahshua describes Him like this;

In the beginning was the Word, and the Word was with God, and the Word was God. He was in the beginning with God. All things were made through Him, and without Him nothing was made that was made. In Him was life, and the life was the light of men. And the light shines in the darkness, and the darkness did not comprehend it. John 1:1-5 (NKJ)

May we never forget that Yahshua is the only light we will ever need. He is our source for all our needs; light, bread, living water, breath, revelation, inspiration, healing and so much more.

That was the true Light, which gives light to every man coming into the world. John 1:9(NKJ)

At the end of time as we know it, the truth of our King will become overwhelmingly real, for we will behold the fullness of His light. The Sun will no longer be needed, for it was only meant to be a physical picture of the glory of who Yahweh is. One glorious day we will finally be together with Him in the New Jerusalem, and Yahshua will be the only light we need.

For who in the skies can be compared to Yahweh?
Who among the sons of the heavenly beings is like Yahweh,
a very awesome God in the council of the holy ones,
to be feared above all those who are around him? Ps. 89:6,7

The sun will be no more your light by day;
nor will the brightness of the moon give light to you,
but Yahweh will be your everlasting light,
and your God will be your glory. Is.60:19

The city has no need for the sun, neither of the moon, to shine, for the very glory of God illuminated it, and its lamp is the Lamb. Rev.21:23

In the light of this amazing truth let's continue to look at Yahweh's glorious story and the Sun's faithful companion in the heavens.

The Moon

THE NEXT PLAYER IN YAHWEH'S LOVE STORY IS THE MOST OBSERVED AND misunderstood. Man has always been enamored with the Moon and its presence in our night sky because it is the one object in the heavens that we can easily gaze upon. Faithfully the Moon dances around the Earth every 29.5 days reflecting eight different phases to us every month in beautiful symmetry. Seven of the phases are visible to us, and one is not. The dark or invisible phase of the Moon is where it transitions from one cycle to the next, commonly known as the conjunction or New Moon. Conjunction is the time between the visible phases where the Moon is renewed or as some say, 'born again.'

These eight phases of the Moon are for man to watch and keep track of the month that is passing, not for counting. Once we establish the first day of the New Moon, we then count days, not phases. The phases, on the other hand, play out a picture of Yahweh's pattern of life in the heavens. The fact that there are eight phases is very intriguing because the number eight in Hebrew understanding is the number for 'new beginning.' We see this at the time of Noah where there were eight who were saved and started a new beginning after the flood. Seven, as we have seen in the Menorah is the number Yahweh has designed for completion and fullness. The number eight represents the abundant overflow that comes after the completion or fullness of something and the beginning of what is next or new. We see this in the way of our Moon, which displays seven visible phases and then a dark phase, which is a new beginning. Below is a quote by E. W. Bullinger, from his book 'Number in Scripture,' describing the meaning and symbolism of the number eight.

"In Hebrew the number eight is Sh'moneh, from the root Shah'meyn, 'to make fat,' 'cover with fat,' 'to super-abound.' As a participle it means 'one who abounds in strength,' etc. As a noun it is 'super-abundant fertility,' 'oil,' etc. So that as a numeral it is the super-abundant number. As seven was so called because the seventh day was the day of completion and rest, so eight, as the eighth day, was over and above this perfect completion, and was indeed the FIRST of a new series, as well as being the eighth. Thus it already represents two numbers in one, the first and eighth."

We find a special picture of the number eight as a new beginning at the end of Tabernacles. First, we have seven days of celebrating in a tent or sukkah, followed by the set apart eighth day.

> *Seven days you shall offer an offering made by fire to Yahweh. On the eighth day shall be a holy convocation to you; and you shall offer an offering made by fire to Yahweh. It is a solemn assembly; you shall do no regular work. Lev.23:36*

The eighth day after Tabernacles has been given two traditional names; Shemini Atzeret which means, Eighth Assembly, and Simchat Torah which, as mentioned earlier means the Joy of Torah. Both names reflect the abundant joy and new life this day brings. The eighth day holds the beauty of completion, for it comes at the end of all Yahweh's seven appointed days and the seven days in the sukkah. With great joy and satisfaction, we take this appointed time to linger in the presence of our King; reflecting back on all we have enjoyed walking the path of righteousness behind us and looking forward to the path that lies ahead. For those who follow the readings of the Torah, it is also the day when you return to Genesis and begin reading anew. When Yahshua returns to fulfill these fall feast days, the time of Tabernacles will be the awesome millennial reign of the

Messiah. This will be a time like none other in history, when we dwell or tabernacle in the presence of our King and worship with joy before Him. The day that follows will be the precious day when Yahshua's bride lingers in the presence of her Beloved and Yahweh makes all things new. Then the final chorus of Yahweh's great symphony will have been sung, and an eternal future in the New Jerusalem will come to those who have become His bride and royal priesthood.

> *"For, behold, I create new heavens and a new earth;*
> *and the former things will not be remembered,*
> *nor come into mind. Is.65:17*

> *I saw a new heaven and a new earth: for the first heaven and the*
> *first earth have passed away, and the sea is no more. Rev.21:1*

Seeing Yahweh's design from the perspective of renewal and rebirth gives us a better understanding of all His patterns and pictures, especially the New Moon. Yahweh's endings are also His beginnings, for the end or death of a cycle, season or person is the point of new life and new beginning. You can see this best when you think of walking on a circular path or the way the planets orbit for the place of beginning and ending is the same, just as we read in E.W. Bullinger's explanation for the number eight. The Moon's eight phases are a faithful witness to the wonder of this truth each month.

> *It will be established forever like the moon,*
> *the faithful witness in the sky. Ps.89:37*

The Moon's relationship with the Sun in the heavens is displaying something very beautiful to us. We have seen that the Sun is Yahweh's heavenly picture of the Bridegroom; a picture of Yahshua. Now we are going to focus on how the Moon carries the attributes of the bride of Yahshua who is called to become a royal priesthood. Remember that the Tabernacle in the Wilderness revealed the pattern of Yahweh's heavenly Tabernacle. The Levites were set apart as the only ones to serve Yahweh within the Holy Place and then reflect His heart's desire to the twelve tribes around Him. The Moon in a similar way is the heavenly player called to reflect the Sun in the midst of the twelve constellations. These both are pictures of the bride of Messiah who is called to be Yahweh's set apart royal priesthood preparing for a future with her Beloved.

> *But you are a chosen race, a royal priesthood, a holy nation, a people for God's own possession, that you may proclaim the excellence of him who called you out of darkness into his marvelous light: who in time past were no people, but now are God's people, who had not obtained mercy, but now have obtained mercy. 1 Pet. 2:9,10*

The ultimate goal for those who choose to be Yahshua's bride is to serve Him within Yahweh's Kingdom and to follow the ways of their King. They desire to become like their Bridegroom and reflect His glorious light to all those around them. As we come together in true unity, worshipping Yahweh in spirit and truth, we will experience the fullness of life Yahweh's desires for us to have. We see this pictured in the middle of the Moon's cycle when it is full and bright in the night sky. Just as the bride of Messiah sets her face toward her Beloved to reflect His light to a dark world, so the Moon sets its face toward the Sun and reflects its light in the night sky. When the Moon is full, it rises in the East and crosses the night sky just as the Sun does in the day.

> *"So let all your enemies perish, Yahweh,*
> *but let those who love him be as the sun when*
> *it rises in its strength." Judges 5:31*

After the Moon is full, it rises later and later in the night sky as it wanes or decreases, until it becomes a faint sliver in the morning's twilight on the eastern horizon. Then, at last, it slips away from our sight into the glorious light of the Sun. At this time the Moon is hidden or concealed from the eyes of all the world. As we have seen through Yahweh's pattern of life, this is an important picture of His design. If we look at Yahweh's patterns through the lens of His story and remove man's traditions, the wonder of Yahweh's heart comes alive before us. As we continue our search for Yahweh's heart in the New Moon we will see that it is a picture of Yahshua's priestly bride dwelling in the secret place of the Most High. During the time of the full Moon, the Moon is alone in the dark night sky. This is a picture of Yahshua's bride strong and obedient to reflect the light of her Beloved. Then in humility and faithfulness, she returns to her only source of light and life to be refreshed and renewed in His presence. This is the pageantry the Moon is faithfully revealing to us. When we see the New Moon through Yahweh's Masterpiece, it will teach us much about our role as His bride and *our* place within His great Love Story.

The Moon's role in the heavens as a picture of Yahshua's bride and royal priesthood helps us understand how the glory of the heavens relates to us. In the next chapters, we are going to search each word used for Moon in Scripture to uncover the deeper meaning of the Moon's purpose and the pictures it portrays. We will look at the three Hebrew words that are translated into English as moon or New Moon. The first word is לבנה levana, the second is ירח yerach, and the third or last, חדש codesh. Each of these words will give us insight into the attributes of Yahshua's bride. My prayer is that as we look to each of these words, that they will bring life and joy to our call to celebrate the New Moon.

Ultimately, the purpose behind our search through Yahweh's Word is to wash us with His truth so that we will become renewed and able to understand His heart. No matter how man distorts the pictures Yahweh has created ... the truth *will* forever stand and unfold, as it is ordained to do. It stands to reason then, that as the last days unfold Yahweh's enemy, satan wants to bring division and distortion to our understanding of Who Yahweh is; in hopes of turning us away from Yahweh to believe a lie. Yet if we see everything as echad or one, we will also see that that all Yahweh created joins as one in praise to His Name to tell of His glorious love story ... all of it!

Praise Yah!
I will give thanks to Yahweh with my whole heart,
in the council of the upright, and in the congregation.
Yahweh's works are great,
pondered by all those who delight in them.
His work is honor and majesty.
His righteousness endures forever. Ps.111:1-3

Levana

OUR FIRST HEBREW WORD FOR MOON IS STRONG'S #H3842 LEVANA, לבנה
which means white or brick. At first glance, we might simply make the
connection between the Moon and levana through the white color of
the clay used for brick and the white color of the Moon. Yet if we look
deeper I believe there is much more that levana for Moon is meant to
show us. Bricks are usually associated with the kind of work related to
slavery or with the building of an empire. Levana is first found in Genesis
and translated as bricks at the time when all the people of Earth gathered
together in one accord to build a tower.

> *They said to one another, "Come, let's make bricks, (levana)
> and burn them thoroughly." They had brick for stone, and they
> used tar for mortar. They said, "Come, let's build ourselves a
> city, and a tower whose top reaches to the sky, and let's make a
> name for ourselves, lest we be scattered abroad on the surface of
> the whole earth."Gen.11:3,4*

What needs to be noticed here is that the people chose to build their
tower out of bricks instead of stones. Those who desired to build empires
that would stand against the ways of Yahweh typically made them with
bricks. We see it with the Tower of Babel, which was made with pride by

a united people, to prove that they could build something to reach into the heavens. Their tower was meant as a sign of power to boast of their strength and abilities and make a great name for themselves.

Later in Exodus, the Children of Israel are forced to make bricks for Pharaoh. Pharaoh too was a man of power and pride. His goal was to build a great empire and name for himself. Though Yahweh's people were captive, lost and in need of a Savior, their life of slavery had become all the Children of Israel knew. Even in their harsh environment, they learned to overcome and thrive.

> *Now there arose a new king over Egypt, who didn't know Joseph. He said to his people, "Behold, the people of the children of Israel are more and mightier than we. Come, let us deal wisely with them, lest they multiply, and it happen that when any war breaks out, they also join themselves to our enemies, and fight against us, and escape out of the land." Therefore they set taskmasters over them to afflict them with their burdens. They built storage cities for Pharaoh: Pithom and Raamses. But the more they afflicted them, the more they multiplied and the more they spread out. They were grieved because of the children of Israel. The Egyptians ruthlessly made the children of Israel serve, and they made their lives bitter with hard service, in mortar and in brick, and in all kinds of service in the field, all their service, in which they ruthlessly made them serve. Ex.1:8-14*

> *The midwives said to Pharaoh, "Because the Hebrew women aren't like the Egyptian women; for they are vigorous, and give birth before the midwife comes to them." Ex.1:19*

In the midst of their trials the Children of Israel stayed strong, worked hard and their families grew. I cannot help but wonder if they, as we often do, looked for ways to make the best of a bad situation? Could this be revealing to us that Yahweh's people were conforming to the ways of the Egyptian system as a way of surviving? It appears that they had become like the bricks they were being forced to make. They, like bricks, were being shaped by the system and hardened in their hearts; serving man rather than the truth of Yahweh. At first, this may sound like a harsh judgment on the Children of Israel for Pharaoh did try to control them with heavy work. It is later when Yahweh rescues His people, and they are away from Egypt, that this truth is revealed. For once they were away from Egypt, and in the Wilderness, they longed to go back.

> *The whole congregation of the children of Israel murmured against Moses and against Aaron in the wilderness; and the children of Israel said to them, "We wish that we had died by Yahweh's hand in the land of Egypt, when we sat by the meat pots, when we ate our fill of bread, for you have brought us out into this wilderness, to kill this whole assembly with hunger." Ex.16:2,3*

> *The mixed multitude that was among them lusted exceedingly: and the children of Israel also wept again, and said, "Who will give us flesh to eat? We remember the fish, which we ate in Egypt for nothing; the cucumbers, and the melons, and the leeks, and the onions, and the garlic; but now we have lost our appetite. There is nothing at all except this manna to look at." Num.11:4-6*

This picture is also true for us today. We are slaves to the world's system and all that it brings upon us. Our thoughts are formed by the world and the culture we live in; shaped into the likeness of our culture by the media, social structure, personal acceptance and religious viewpoint. Like bricks, we are used for building worldly empires of all shapes and sizes, by many different Pharaoh figures. Like the Children of Israel in Egypt, we too usually make the best of bad situations in order to survive. Sadly this conforms us to the world, as we look for success and purpose within it. The deliverance that Yahshua paid for His us to have is often compromised by our attachment to the world. Below is a verse from Sara Groves' song, Painting Pictures of Egypt that sums up our struggle.

The past is so tangible
I know it by heart

Familiar things are never easy
To discard
I was dying for some freedom
But now I hesitate to go
I am caught between the Promise
And the things I know

The familiar things, no matter how difficult they are, shape us. We find this in the picture within the Hebrew word levana for Moon. Just as Moses was sent by Yahweh to save the Children of Israel and take them out of Egypt, so Yahshua was sent by Yahweh to save us and take us out of the world and its systems. We are not to become like a brick that is shaped by the world and used to build worldly empires. We are sons and daughters of the King and called to live in Yahweh's kingdom according to His Word. To be in the world and not of the world takes great discernment and caution for we are so easily conformed to the lifestyle around us and the world's subtle influence.

I pray not that you would take them from the world, but that you would keep them from the evil one. They are not of the world even as I am not of the world. John 17:15,16

Don't be conformed to this world, but be transformed by the renewing of your mind, so that you may prove what is the good, well-pleasing, and perfect will of God. Romans 12:2

Revelation warns us that being 'of the world' will give us a false sense of security and dupe us into thinking we can make it by our strength.

Because you say, 'I am rich, and have gotten riches, and have need of nothing;' and don't know that you are the wretched one, miserable, poor, blind, and naked; Rev. 3:17

The New Testament also warns us that we have a new life in Messiah and to not be entangled or involved in the ways of the world any longer.

You were made alive when you were dead in transgressions and sins, in which you once walked according to the course of this world, according to the prince of the power of the air, the spirit who now works in the children of disobedience; among whom we also all once lived in the lust of our flesh, doing the desires of the flesh and of the mind, and were by nature children of wrath, even as the rest. Eph. 2:1-3

Don't love the world or the things that are in the world. If anyone loves the world, the Father's love isn't in him. For all that is in the world, the lust of the flesh, the lust of the eyes, and the pride of life, isn't the Father's, but is the world's. The world is passing away with its lusts, but he who does God's will remains forever. 1 John 2:15-17

Yahweh's call to come out of the ways of the world is more urgent than ever before. Many have heard His call and have responded. Each of us having a unique story of how we were born again, and our lives were changed; how we came away from the ways of the world and into His Kingdom. This is where the deeper meaning for levana is seen most beautifully. When Yahweh calls us to Himself, and we accept the power of Yahshua's shed blood for us something awesome happens. He takes each worldly brick through a process of renewal and being born again. This refining process reshapes us to become His living stones. As we conform to His likeness, He takes His living stones and builds His Temple or Assembly.

So then you are no longer strangers and foreigners, but you are fellow citizens with the saints, and of the household of God, being built on the foundation of the apostles and prophets, Christ Jesus himself being the chief cornerstone; in whom the whole building, fitted together, grows into a holy temple in the Lord; in whom you also are built together for a habitation of God in the Spirit. Eph. 2:19-22

Putting away therefore all wickedness, all deceit, hypocrisies, envies, and all evil speaking, as newborn babies, long for the pure milk of the Word, that with it you may grow, if indeed you have tasted that the Lord is gracious: coming to him, a living stone, rejected indeed by men, but chosen by God, precious. You also, as living stones, are built up as a spiritual house, to be a holy priesthood, to offer up spiritual sacrifices, acceptable to God through Jesus Christ. 1Peter 2:1-5

Yahweh is challenging us to leave behind all that previously shaped us and follow Him at all costs. Still, stones shaped in the hands of our Creator, even living stones have no light of their own. Just like the Moon Yahweh's living stones are called to reflect their only source of light ... Yahshua. Studying the Moon through this Hebrew word levana meaning brick or white, shows us that the Moon is a constant reminder of how we are being transformed from a worldly brick into a white living stone to be used in the building of Yahweh's Temple. Just as the Moon travels through its cycle, we too walk day by day, through Yahweh's cycles being renewed into the likeness of our Master and reflecting His light.

But we all, with unveiled face seeing the glory of the Lord as in a mirror, are transformed into the same image from glory to glory, even as from the Lord, the Spirit. 2 Cor. 3:18

With unspeakable joy, we are called to obey the Words of our Savior, Shepherd, and King willing to be built into a spiritual house that reflects the light of our Beloved. We like the Moon are a dull stone with no light but called to be a luminary that reflects the light of our Savior.

Now I would like to show you another amazing picture related to levana, which comes from a Hebrew word that has the same spelling as levana. It is a word you are familiar with in English; Strong's #H3828 levana לבנה, translated as frankincense. Frankincense is a very compelling word for it also means white, just as it did when translated as brick. Strong's Concordance describes levana for frankincense this way; the whiteness of the smoke that rises when it is burned as incense. The incense or smoke of the frankincense represents our prayers that are to rise before Yahweh's throne as a sweet smelling aroma.

Let my prayer be set before you like incense;

the lifting up of my hands like the evening sacrifice. Ps. 141:2

The pattern of the Tabernacle, the Temple, and all their elements apply to our lives in a real and intimate way; for our service to Yahweh happens first and foremost within us as we become His Temple. All the elements that we read about in the Torah are teaching us how to serve Yahweh in ways that are acceptable to Him. This is not found in the ways of the world.

> *Therefore, I urge you, brothers and sisters, in view of God's mercy, to offer your bodies as a living sacrifice, holy and pleasing to God—this is your true and proper worship. Do not conform to the pattern of this world, but be transformed by the renewing of your mind. Then you will be able to test and approve what God's will is—his good, pleasing and perfect will. Rom.12:1,2 (NIV)*

I used the New International Version here because the translators chose to use the word pattern, which portrays that it is the pattern of Yahweh that we seek, not the world's. As Yahweh's children, we are to seek the pattern of life which is revealed in, darkness or concealing first and then life. This is what the heavens are declaring! Yahshua admonished us to pray for the ways of heaven to be established here on Earth in His model prayer, "On earth as it is in heaven." The pattern of the heavenly Tabernacle is to be our pattern of living as we sojourn here on Earth. Revealing the elements of the Tabernacle is the way we prove to the world what is acceptable to our heavenly Father.

> *For you were once darkness, but are now light in the Lord. Walk as children of light, for the fruit of the Spirit is in all goodness and righteousness and truth, proving what is well pleasing to the Lord. Eph.5:8-10*

As Yahshua's bride and royal priesthood, the service of the Tabernacle will become a delight to us because it is what our Beloved deems as acceptable. As Yahweh's children adopted into His family, we are learning the ways of His household for we have become the dwelling for His Spirit until He return's to take us home.

Or don't you know that your body is a temple of the Holy Spirit which is in you, which you have from God? You are not your own, for you were bought with a price. 1 Cor. 6:19

Frankincense or levana was one of the required elements in the Tabernacle or Temple. It was used in the making of the holy anointing oil and in the mixture of spices that burned on the altar of incense. Frankincense was also placed on the showbread every Shabbat and was used with the grain and meat offerings. Still, when you hear the word frankincense it usually brings to mind the time of Yahshua's first coming when the Magi brought Him gifts of gold, frankincense, and myrrh.

We know that each of each of these gifts held great value, but I would like to focus on the frankincense. The world today is recognizing more and more that frankincense has powerful healing properties and is becoming renowned in the battle of cancer. From Yahweh's perspective, frankincense played a significant part in the Tabernacle. Its qualities and fragrance are important to Him and I believe we will understand even more about it when we see Him face to face.

Yahshua called the Temple His Father's 'house of prayer' and frankincense played an integral part in the picture of prayer, for it was burned before the Holy of Holies as a sweet smelling aroma. The word levana for Moon reminds us that as Yahweh's living stones we are in a process of becoming a sweet smelling aroma to Him through our prayer and worship.

Has this house, which is called by my name, become a den of robbers in your eyes? Behold, I, even I, have seen it," says Yahweh. Jer. 7:11

He said to them, "It is written, 'My house shall be called a house of prayer,' but you have made it a den of robbers!" Matt. 21:13

Just as the altar of incense was to constantly burn before the Holy of Holies, our prayers also are to be constantly brought before Yahweh.

Let my prayer be set before you like incense;
the lifting up of my hands like the evening sacrifice. Ps.141:2

But we will continue steadfastly in prayer and in the ministry
of the word. Acts 6:4

Another angel came and stood over the altar, having a golden
censer. Much incense was given to him, that he should add it
to the prayers of all the saints on the golden altar which was
before the throne. Rev.8:3

We are now Yahweh's house of prayer, and all we bring before Him must be as pleasing to Him as the sweet fragrance from the altar of incense that rose before His throne. Remember that levana also pictures us as worldly bricks that need to be transformed into His white, fragrant living stones. Yahweh does not tolerate the ways of the world or man's perversion of His ways. These are a foul smell to Him.

I hate, I despise your feast days, and I will
not smell in your solemn assemblies.
Amos 5:21 (KJV)

As His living stones we must follow Yahweh with all our heart and seek His ways for He is our only Light and Salvation.

Yahweh is my light and my salvation.
Whom shall I fear? Ps.27:1a

Frankincense teaches us about the refining process that Yahweh takes us through when we commit to following Him. The refining is designed to remove the patterns of the world that have shaped us like a brick and then teach us Yahweh's patterns which will make us a living stone; fit for His presence. Our best human efforts are not pleasing before Yahweh. They are a stench before His Throne. When we worship and pray by His Spirit and His Truth, we become pleasing to His heart. On the contrary, if we bring our Sabbaths, New Moons or any gathering of *man's* design before Him they are a burden to Him, for they are not designed by Him or acceptable before His throne.

"When you come to appear before Me,
Who has required this from your hand,
To trample My courts?
Bring no more futile sacrifices;
Incense is an abomination to Me.
When you come to appear before me,
who has required this at your hand, to trample my courts?
Bring no more vain offerings.
Incense is an abomination to me;
new moons, Sabbaths, and convocations:
I can't bear with evil assemblies.
My soul hates your New Moons and your appointed feasts.
They are a burden to me.
I am weary of bearing them. Is.1:12-15

Many believe that this Scripture is telling us that Yahweh doesn't want us to keep His Sabbath, New Moon or festivals. Nothing could be further from the truth! Instead, Yahweh is referring to His people's disregard of His things. He speaks of His courts being trampled and bringing before Him *our* New Moons, Sabbaths, and festivals ... NOT HIS! Our stuff is worldly, filled with prideful ambition and used to serve other gods. To become a sweet smelling aroma, we must come to Him on His terms. He is the Way, the Truth and the Light and He desires to see His people return to His ways. When we hear His voice and leave behind the world to follow Him, we show Him how much we love Him.

> *This is how we know that we know him: if we keep his commandments. One who says, "I know him," and doesn't keep his commandments, is a liar, and the truth isn't in him. But whoever keeps his word, God's love has most certainly been perfected in him. This is how we know that we are in him: he who says he remains in him ought himself also to walk just like he walked. 1John 2:3-6*

As we daily walk with Him and learn of His heart, we become a pleasing aroma to Him, like the frankincense within the Holy place. Yahshua's bride will willingly do all she can to please her Bridegroom; for there is no love in bringing the things of the world before the Throne of Grace. The things of our past life that Yahshua freed us from are not going to please our Beloved. Our whole life is to be transformed so that we may become like Him and take His fragrance and light to a lost world.

> *Now thanks be to God, who always leads us in triumph in Christ, and reveals through us the sweet aroma of his knowledge in every place. For we are a sweet aroma of Christ to God, in those who are saved, and in those who perish; to the one a stench from death to death; to the other a sweet aroma from life to life. Who is sufficient for these things? 2 Cor. 2:14-16*

Here the meaning for levana as frankincense comes alive. The fragrance within the Tabernacle was upon the sacrifices and in the incense that rose before Yahweh. We now are the living sacrifices that die to ourselves and then bring worship and prayer as incense before our King in intercession. No longer are we bricks shaped by the world and our selfishness. Now we have the freedom to choose to be living stones that align with Yahshua, the Chief Cornerstone, ready to reflect the light of our Beloved.

> *As you come to Him, the living stone, rejected by men, but chosen and precious in God's sight, you also, like living stones, are being built into a spiritual house to be a holy priesthood, offering spiritual sacrifices acceptable to God through Jesus Christ. For it stands in Scripture:*
>
> *"See, I lay in Zion a stone,*
> *a chosen and precious cornerstone;*
> *and the one who believes in Him*
> *will never be put to shame." 1 Pet.2:4-6*

Later we will look more deeply at frankincense as we study the character of Yahshua's bride and the importance of submitting to the leading of His Spirit. Levana teaches us that we are to come before our King with prayerful humility; always quick to lay down our ways for the ways of our Master Yahshua.

> *"Heaven is my throne, and the earth is my footstool.*

What kind of house will you build to me?
Where will I rest?
For my hand has made all these things,
and so all these things came to be," says Yahweh:
"but to this man will I look,
even to he who is poor and of a contrite spirit,
and who trembles at my word. Is.66:1,2

As Yahshua's bride let's now look at the next Hebrew word for Moon to help us understand the importance of fearing Yahweh and trembling at His Word.

Yerach

THE SECOND HEBREW WORD USED FOR MOON IN SCRIPTURE IS STRONG'S #H3394 yerach ירח. At first, you will see that yerach is simply described as the moon in most concordances, but as we look a little deeper, we find something more. The Etymological Dictionary of Biblical Hebrew states that yerach means "impact" as in the impact the Moon has on vegetation. Keep in mind that we are searching out how Yahweh's heavenly players are revealing truth to us. What is the Moon showing us through these different names? Science and Yahweh's Word are not separate, nor do they oppose one another. On the contrary, one works hand in hand with the other to bring life and understanding. The key is that we must use concrete scientific fact found in Creation and Yahweh's Word alone, not man's opinion, theory or bias to come to our conclusions.

The Moon, as you know, has a great impact on our watery blue planet. Our beautiful home in the Universe is seventy per cent water, making most of our Earth's surface subject to the rhythm of the Moon's gravitational pull. When we stand on the beach and enjoy the rhythmic waves, we don't always think of the Moon's part in its motion, yet it is the amazing pattern of the heavens that is touching our lives all the time.

Our Moon's impact on Earth stabilizes its rotation, which in turn effects our seasons and consequently the harvests; both vital to us for life and for playing our part in Yahweh's celebrations. For centuries people involved in agriculture have looked to the different phases of the Moon and how the moisture in the ground is affected by each phase.

The lunar phase controls the amount of moisture in the soil. This moisture is at its peak at the time of the new and the full moon. The sun and moon are lined up with earth. Just as the moon pulls the tides in the oceans, it also pulls upon the subtle bodies of water, causing moisture to rise in the earth, which encourages germination and growth. Tests have proven that seeds will absorb the most water at the time of the full moon. (gardeningbythemoon.com)

In many cases, new age, folklore, and superstition have grabbed ahold of this truth and distorted it, but it cannot be denied that what happens in Creation is the result of Yahweh's design and physical reality. Below is a Scripture that references the Moon "bringing forth" or impacting the precious things of the Earth.

And for the precious fruits brought forth by the sun, and for the precious things put forth by the moon, Deut.33:14

The rhythm of our tides helps remove pollutants from our shoreline and circulates nutrients to ocean plants and animals that they need to survive. Without the regular washing of the tides, the complex and abundant ocean life would die, and food resources would diminish. Soon our water would become contaminated, and we too would die. Often we hear of the hope of life on other planets when scientists find a hint of moisture on a barren rocky planet. In a way the comparison is laughable. We are alive here on this Earth because of unfathomable intricate details that are in motion every moment of every day. How can we compare our abundantly rich, watery Earth to any other planet?

For most of us though, when we think of our Moon and its impact on our lives, it can be narrowed down to the spectacular way it travels through our night sky, designing our months and lighting up the darkness. As amazing as this is, it seems that its wonder is being compromised through technology. The ease of communication and research that is at our fingertips obviously has a multitude of pros and cons. One of the pros is that we have made the world a smaller place and can connect with people worldwide giving us a global awareness. Another pro is the ease of finding information. I am old enough to remember the days when the very thought of searching for the truth about a topic was a daunting task that could mean hours, days and maybe even weeks of hunting. Now we can search almost anything, anytime and nearly anywhere. And so it is with knowing the phase of the Moon; no matter what the weather conditions, you can know the phase of the Moon with a glance at your phone.

The con side of the ease we have in research is that it is somewhat addicting. We are driven to know everything from how and what everyone is doing, to health, shopping, entertainment of every sort and every other detail of life. Our search for more information keeps us occupied in a cyber world on a daily basis. We spend many hours looking at a screen and not discerning the signs in the heavens. How many of us in this generation forget to look up at the Moon or ever consider how it impacts our lives? Nevertheless, from the beginning of time Yahweh placed it in the heavens to tell us so much!

It will be established forever like the moon (yarach),
the faithful witness in the sky.Ps. 89:37

He appointed the moon (yarach) for seasons.
The sun knows when to set. Ps. 104:19

These verses compel us to leave our devices, step away from our busy lives and go outside to look up at the witness Yahweh has placed in the night sky. For whether we are aware of it or not, the Moon remains faithful in the heavens above. It was designed to show us the seasons of Yahweh as He commanded it to and it will continue until the very end. In the verse of Psalm 104, the word seasons is Strong's #H4150 מועד moed, which as we saw earlier means; appointment, fixed time, specifically a festival. It is the same word used in Genesis for seasons.

God said, "Let there be lights in the expanse of sky to divide the
day from the night; and let them be for signs to mark seasons,
days, and years; Gen.1: 14

The word moed implies that there is an assembly or a place of meeting. Moed comes from the root word Strong's # H3259 יעד ya'ad, which means; to fix upon by agreement or appointment, to summon or engage in marriage. A season or moed is then of extreme importance from Yahweh's perspective because it is the set apart time of meeting or gathering together with Him at His appointed times. Notice that unity is implied in it's meaning; to fix upon by agreement or appointment. To fix upon by agreement is the very reason for the Moon's impact on Yahweh's people; to faithfully define the times of meeting with their Beloved. Though we are still discovering the details of what this looks like in practical terms, it is not something we should become frustrated with. We need to see the Moon as a counterpart to the Sun and what role it has in Yahweh's story so that we can come together with joy on Yahweh's appointed days.

The word yerach ירח for Moon is closely related to another important word; Strong's #H3384 ירה yarah, which means; to cast forth like rain or to shoot at a target. The first two Hebrew letters are the same as in yarach for Moon. The only difference is a small connecting space between the Hebrew letters chet ח in yarach and hey ה in yarah. When a two-letter root word is the same in Hebrew words they become a part of a cognate family of words giving deeper meaning and understanding to each other. This is true with yarach and yarah. The word yarach defined as Moon and yarah defined as casting forth rain or shooting at a target beautifully ties together the impact of the Moon and our walk with Yahshua.

The meaning behind yarah clearly comes to life in the garden and in the applications of traditional archery. We will look at both applications, but first, let's look at archery and the ways of shooting at a target. Traditional archery, as I have found out through my youngest son, has so many amazing life lessons. As he shared his experience in training, I realized that it is not as simple as picking up a bow and arrow and shooting. When you choose to learn the skill of archery, you must first learn to stand by planting your feet under your shoulders on solid ground (or may I suggest the Rock). Learning a solid stance is crucial in training your body to be a base or foundation for the bow. Scripture exhorts us to apply this principle to our lives. We are called to develop a firm stand and not waver or be tossed about by the world.

Watch! Stand firm in the faith! Be courageous! Be strong!
1 Cor.16:13

Therefore put on the whole armor of God, that you may be
able to withstand in the evil day, and, having done all, to
stand. Eph.6:13

When your body learns the proper stance, it will not easily return to
its original slack form. A serious archer will train his body to conform
to a pattern that will bring repeated accuracy at hitting the center of the
target.

But I discipline my body and bring it into subjection, lest, when
I have preached to others, I myself should become disqualified.
1 Cor. 9:27(NKJ)

Once an archer has mastered his stance, he then needs to become familiar
with his bow. Now with a firm foundation, an archer can practice holding
and drawing back his bow over and over until he can quickly and repeatedly bring his bow and arrow into place. As easy as this may sound it takes
time to develop form and habit. When stance and draw are mastered, the
archer finally begins to practice shooting at the target. Here is where the
steadiness of hand and eye come into play. The average person has great
difficulty keeping their hand steady enough to hit the center of the target.
There is a method though that archers use to train their eye and hand to
find the center. The archer takes his stance and draws his bow. While in
position he begins to eye the target by making an imaginary circle with the
tip of his arrow around the target's center. Gradually he tightens the circle,
making it smaller and smaller so that the tip of his arrow draws closer to
the center of the target. Once at center, the archer lets his arrow fly!

Archery's intriguing picture relates so beautifully to our cognate word
yarah, meaning to shoot at a target. Can you see how this process and
imagery parallels our walk with Yahshua? Both the archer and the arrow
hold life applications. On one side we are to learn to be like an archer that
trains to hit the center of the target. On the other side we are like arrows
in the hand of our Master Yahshua. Day after day, week after week, month
after month and year after year we go through the cycles (or circles) of

Torah drawing closer and closer to the center of our target. What is the center of our target? To be in the likeness of our Master Archer, Yahshua!

If a man doesn't relent, he will sharpen his sword;
he has bent and strung his bow.
He has also prepared for himself the instruments of death.
He makes ready his flaming arrows. Ps.7:12,13

For indeed I bend Judah as a bow for me.
I have filled the bow with Ephraim;
and I will stir up your sons, Zion,
against your sons, Greece,
and will make you like the sword of a mighty man.
Yahweh will be seen over them;
and his arrow will go flash like lightning;
and the Lord Yahweh will blow the trumpet,
and will go with whirlwinds of the south. Zech.9;13,14

As we follow Yahshua and allow the Holy Spirit to guide us, we will draw closer and closer to Him and His likeness. Each monthly cycle unfolds into years as we walk the path of righteousness laid out for us in Torah. Each time we walk the path of His cycle, our Master reveals to us a little more until we understand and grow closer to the center of our target.

As disciples of Yahshua, we are in training as an archer to fight the good fight and then train others to be His disciples and also hit the target.

Go, and make disciples of all nations, baptizing them in the name of the Father and of the Son and of the Holy Spirit, Matt. 28:19

This is pictured in the relationship between a Rabbi and his followers.

This man came to Jesus by night and said to Him, "Rabbi, we know that You are a teacher come from God; for no one can do these signs that You do unless God is with him." John 3:2

The followers of a Rabbi are called talmid or in plural, talmidim meaning "disciples." Talmidim leave everything behind to study and follow the ways of their Rabbi or teacher. The goal or target for a talmid is to perfectly reflect his master in speech, action, and mannerism. To reflect the mannerism of their Master was also the target for Yahshua's disciples and it remains the same today. We know it as the great commission that Yahshua called us to; helping others to become His talmidim or disciples. The royal priesthood or bride of the Messiah must learn to be His talmidim, reflecting all that their Master or Rabbi teaches them. Then our words and actions will not be our own or bring glory to ourselves in any way, but to the One who has trained us.

He who speaks from himself seeks his own glory, but he who seeks the glory of him who sent him is true, and no unrighteousness is in him. John 7:18

How does all of this relate to the Moon? The duty of the talmidim is to reflect everything the Rabbi does. In fact, you could know a talmid's Rabbi just by spending time with them. Yahshua came to show us this in the way He lived. Everything He did reflected the ways of His Father. He was totally submitted to the leading of Yahweh and came to glorify and reflect the light of the One who sent Him.

Jesus said to them, "My food is to do the will of him who sent me, and to accomplish his work. John 4:34

So Jesus replied, "Truly, truly, I tell you, the Son can do nothing by Himself, unless He sees the Father doing it. For whatever the Father does, the Son also does. John 5:19

For I have come down from heaven, not to do my own will, but the will of him who sent me. John 6:38

Now we are Yahshua's talmidim or disciples. We like the Moon have no light of our own and are called to come out the world's affairs to follow and reflect the One True Light ... Yahshua. Our goal is to be like Him to the extent that the Father in Heaven is glorified.

Even so, let your light shine before men; that they may see your good works, and glorify your Father who is in heaven. Matt.5:16

The more we become set-apart or holy, just as Yahshua is holy, the more of His light we reflect. When we submit to His teaching, we then become like sharpened arrows hidden in His quiver.

And He has made My mouth like a sharp sword;
In the shadow of His hand He has hidden Me,
And made Me a polished shaft;
In His quiver He has hidden Me." Is. 49:2

Here again we see Yahweh's pattern of life! In the covered or hidden place of Yahweh's hand we are prepared for battle becoming a polished instrument that can reflect His Light. He hides us within His quiver to keep us safe in His presence. When it is time He then releases us as we have seen in the pattern of the Moon!

There is one more very important analogy in archery that sums up the meaning of the word yarah and the picture of shooting at a target. In archery no matter how close an archer's arrow may get to the center of the target, any shot outside of the center is called 'sin.' Our walk with Yahweh is to be the same, for we called as followers of Yahshua to be holy.

Whoever commits sin also commits lawlessness, and sin is lawlessness. 1 John 3:4

The word yarach for Moon is revealing that for us to impact the world with the light of our Master we must be holy or sinless just as He was. The verse above reveals that sin is Torah-lessness. Often we are taught that the Torah is legalism without grace, but the Torah reveals Yahweh's righteousness, mercy, and grace. When we come into Covenant with Yahweh, we become partakers of the Covenant Torah. Yahweh's righteousness is found when we see His heart through His Torah which is His Word. We as His arrows must allow Him to shape us and aim us in order to achieve the target's center. We must humbly submit to His hand because we have been misshaped by the world and its crooked ways.

In our own strength, we could never hit the center of the target; which is holiness or being sinless. That is why we are in desperate need of Yahshua our Savior, and all that He did for us. When we accept Yahshua as our Savior and Rabbi we can become holy because His shed blood covers our sin. Now we can have a life that reflects the Light of Yahshua and points the way to the target. Yahshua kept the Torah and calls us to keep it by the leading of His Spirit so that we glorify the Father ... this is our target.

> *Like arrows in the hand of a warrior,*
> *So are the children of one's youth.*
> *Happy is the man who has his quiver full of them;*
> *They shall not be ashamed,*
> *But shall speak with their enemies in the gate. Ps.127:4,5*

For He made Him who knew no sin to be sin for us, that we might become the righteousness of God in Him. 2Cor. 5:21

Now by this we know that we know Him, if we keep His commandments. He who says, "I know Him," and does not keep His commandments, is a liar, and the truth is not in him. But whoever keeps His word, truly the love of God is perfected in him. By this we know that we are in Him. He who says he abides in Him ought himself also to walk just as He walked. 1 John 2:3-6

If we are to walk as Yahshua walked and hit the target, we must learn the ways of His Father and the Covenant that He came to restore. In our love for Him, we will keep His Covenant requirements found in Torah, and it will not be a burden to us. Just as a wife delights to take care of her husband and keep their home in order, so will we lovingly uphold all the things of Yahweh's household. Yahshua beckoned us to this when He said;

Come to Me, all you who labor and are heavy laden, and I will give you rest. Take My yoke upon you and learn from Me, for I am gentle and lowly in heart, and you will find rest for your souls. For My yoke is easy and My burden is light. Matt. 11:28-30

Now we come to the second meaning for yarah, which is; to cast forth like rain. This Hebrew word is also the root word for Torah. Yarah brings fullness to all that we saw in the garden pattern. Yahweh's Torah or instructions for righteousness are sent to us in the same way Yahweh casts the forth rain to the earth to sustain and awaken life. The pattern for life is revealed here again in the picture of how rain comes to us. Before the rain is cast forth, the earth is covered or concealed with cloud. The sky is darkened, as the clouds grow heavy with the rain. Then under the canopy of dark clouds, rain is poured out upon the Earth bringing life. When we see the rain likened to Torah, we can also see that the way of the rain follows Yahweh's pattern, for it is under a cloud covering that Yahweh pours forth His Word to bring life. Over and over we see that Yahweh chooses to come to us in a cloud covering. Clouds encompass Yahweh's presence, and of course where His presence is, so is His Word cast forth.

Yahweh said to Moses, "Behold, I come to you in a thick cloud, that the people may hear when I speak with you, and may also believe you forever." Ex.19:9

Yahweh spoke these words to all your assembly on the mountain out of the middle of the fire, of the cloud, and of the thick darkness, with a great voice. Deut. 5:22

While he was still speaking, behold, a bright cloud overshadowed them. Behold, a voice came out of the cloud, saying, "This is my beloved Son, in whom I am well pleased. Listen to him." Matt.17:5

Yahweh uses clouds to create a covering over us, and then the rain or Word of Yahweh comes forth nourishing the soil and bringing life to the ground. If the seed, which is Yahshua is covered in good ground (our heart), then the rain (Torah) will cause it to sprout, grow and bear fruit. In other words, if we have the seed of Yahshua in our heart and nourish it with the Torah; allowing it to have life in our words and actions, we will then bear fruit. These pictures of Yahweh's pattern of life are most beautifully seen in the spring after the land has laid cold and dormant through winter.

Winter covers the ground with fallen leaves, ice and snow, but when the warmth of the spring comes, and the clouds pour out the rain, the Earth is awakened to new life.

In the light of a king's face there is life, and his favor is like the clouds that bring the spring rain. Prov.16:15(ESV)

For as the rain comes down and the snow from the sky,
and doesn't return there, but waters the earth,
and makes it grow and bud,
and gives seed to the sower and bread to the eater;
so is my word that goes out of my mouth:
it will not return to me void,
but it will accomplish that which I please,
and it will prosper in the thing I sent it to do. Is.55:10,11

These verses wonderfully confirm all that yarah is revealing to us. In the presence of our King, there is light and favor. He brings us into His covering which is like a cloud that covers us, where we receive His Word which brings renewed life to us, just as the spring rain brings renewed life to the Earth. The phenomena of cloud cover is a breathtaking picture of Yahweh's pattern of life. Yahweh's presence within the Tabernacle revealed this truth as well.

Then the cloud covered the Tent of Meeting, and Yahweh's glory filled the tabernacle. Moses wasn't able to enter into the Tent of Meeting, because the cloud stayed on it, and Yahweh's glory filled the tabernacle. When the cloud was taken up from over the tabernacle, the children of Israel went onward, throughout all their journeys; but if the cloud wasn't taken up, then they didn't travel until the day that it was taken up. For the cloud of Yahweh was on the tabernacle by day, and there was fire in the cloud by night, in the sight of all the house of Israel, throughout all their journeys. Ex.40:34-38

Without the favor of Yahweh's presence, the Children of Israel were not to move. Only with His presence and His light were they to make their journey; just as the New Moon teaches us. Yahweh's presence, like a cloud, covers us and His Word pours out like rain on our heart. Then the seed of Yahshua, which dwells within us is refreshed and nourished, bringing new life.

> "Rain down, you heavens, from above,
> And let the skies pour down righteousness;
> Let the earth open, let them bring forth salvation,
> And let righteousness spring up together.
> I, the Lord, have created it. Is.45:8

> "Men listened to me, waited, and kept silence for my counsel.
> After my words they didn't speak
> again. My speech fell on them.
> They waited for me as for the rain. Their
> mouths drank as with the spring rain.
> Job 29:21-23

Remember though, that everything has a positive and negative effect depending on our choices. The Torah or rain is Yahweh's measure of righteousness. Our responsibility is to find favor with Him by receiving His instructions as spring rain on a humble and soft heart. If we do not have a humble heart, the rain will come, but it will not penetrate a hardened, prideful and stony heart. Our stubborn pride will bring down the rain as the judgment of His righteousness poured out on our lives. Just as the rain was used to judge and cleanse the Earth from unrighteousness at the time of Noah, so Yahweh's rain or Torah will judge us at the end. Noah was a humble and righteous man, and Yahweh hid him in the ark, while the rain lifted him above the storm to safety, but for those who were hardened in sin, the rain swallowed them in judgment.

The similarity in the cognate words, yarach, for Moon and the word yarah, for casting forth rain compels us to soften our hearts and receive the refreshing rain of Torah into our lives. When we are born again and begin to seek the heart of Yahweh, He opens our eyes to see that His Word (Torah), like the Moon and the rain has an impact on everything. Yahweh's Word pours out on all things, bringing forth life wherever there is good seed.

But I say to you, love your enemies, bless those who curse you, do good to those who hate you, and pray for those who spitefully use you and persecute you, that you may be sons of your Father in heaven; for He makes His sun rise on the evil and on the good, and sends rain on the just and on the unjust. Matt.5:44,45

Keep in mind that these pictures are faithfully playing out in the heavens to declare Yahweh's great Love Story. Just as the Moon impacts the Earth with its rhythm and the reflected light of the Sun, so the bride of the Messiah impacts the world around her with works of love that reflect Yahweh's truth and light. Without partiality, the rain brings life to the ground and water to the thirsty. Yahshua's bride without partiality brings the Living Water (Yahshua) to a lost world with the outpouring of Yahweh's Word (rain) and the good news of salvation in Yahshua. Psalm 72 reveals that the Moon has its time and purpose, just as Yahweh's rain has its time and purpose.

They shall fear You
As long as the sun and moon endure,
Throughout all generations.
He shall come down like rain upon the grass before mowing,
Like showers that water the earth.
In His days the righteous shall flourish,
And abundance of peace,
Until the moon is no more. Ps.72:5-7

For the past six thousand or so years, the Moon has been serving its purpose in Yahweh's heavenly story, but when Yahweh's story is complete, and all things have been fulfilled, the Moon will no longer be needed. Nor will the Sun; for then all things will be made new, and we will live by the light of Yahshua alone.

For now, the Moon is a faithful witness, and we can look to it as a symbol of our walk as the bride of Messiah. It is worth noting that two of Yahweh's appointed feast days are designed to come at the time of the full Moon when it is big and bright; one is at Passover or Pesach, and the other is Tabernacles or Sukkot. If the sky is clear on these appointed times,

Yahweh's people will be found celebrating together under the incandescent light of the Moon. These appointments with the King are His bride's 'time to shine' as she rehearses her Beloved's return with great joy and anticipation. Her fervent love for Him is a beacon in a dark world, as she glorifies Yahweh in her obedience and consistency in keeping what is dear to His heart. Her light is meant to bring joy, hope, and peace to those who are lost, alone, thirsty and hungry. For now this may not seem vital, but as the time of the end draws near Yahshua's bride will become a critical source of light to a world that is spiraling into satan's darkness. With confidence in her King, Yahshua's bride will then fulfill the prophecy written about her in Isaiah.

> *Arise, shine;*
> *For your light has come!*
> *And the glory of the Lord is risen upon you.*
> *For behold, the darkness shall cover the earth,*
> *And deep darkness the people;*
> *But the Lord will arise over you,*
> *And His glory will be seen upon you.*
> *The Gentiles shall come to your light,*
> *And kings to the brightness of your rising. Is. 60:1-3*

Let your light so shine before men, that they may see your good works and glorify your Father in heaven. Matt.5:16

Then the righteous will shine forth as the sun in the kingdom of their Father. He who has ears to hear, let him hear! Matt.13:43

For it is the God who commanded light to shine out of darkness, who has shone in our hearts to give the light of the knowledge of the glory of God in the face of Jesus Christ. 2 Cor. 4:6

Another intriguing word that comes from yarach ירח for Moon, is Strong's #H3405, Jericho ירחן. Jericho may help us put all the pieces together for the full picture of what yarach is revealing. As you know, Jericho was the mighty city that Joshua was called to conquer, sometimes referred to as the City of the Moon. Some say that Yahweh commissioned Joshua to overthrow Jericho to show that the Moon is not meant to have any part in our observance of time. While I agree that the story of Jericho holds a message about the Moon, I disagree that it is a message against the Moon. It is man's ways that Yahweh is against, not His own created signs. The Moon and the Sun were created to serve Yahweh as His signs and for His purposes from the very beginning. So let's look at the account of Joshua overtaking Jericho from the pattern perspective to see if there is more for us to discover.

> Now Jericho was tightly shut up because of the children of Israel. No one went out, and no one came in. Yahweh said to Joshua, "Behold, I have given Jericho into your hand, with its king and the mighty men of valor. All of your men of war shall march around the city, going around the city once. You shall do this six days. Seven priests shall bear seven trumpets of rams' horns before the ark. On the seventh day, you shall march around the city seven times, and the priests shall blow the trumpets. It shall be that when they make a long blast with the ram's horn, and when you hear the sound of the trumpet, all the people shall shout with a great shout; and the wall the city shall fall down flat, and the people shall go up, every man straight in front of him. Josh.6:1-5

Notice that Joshua does not formulate a strategy of his own. It is Yahweh's mission and His strategy. He tells Joshua from the start that He has given him the city and then lays out a cycle or pattern for him to follow. The priests and soldiers take their place, and Yahweh's Ark or Throne of authority is carried around Jericho, the City of the Moon, six times in silence. Joshua's battle was not a battle of man's power, but faith demonstrated through obedience and action. What was the final victory? The victory was over a stronghold that was impossible for them to conquer in their own strength. Jericho is a picture of the seemingly hopeless amount of worldly and pagan powers that try to rule us. Joshua had the faith and fear in Yahweh to overcome all that stood before him.

Jesus answered them, "Have faith in God. For most certainly I tell you, whoever may tell this mountain, 'Be taken up and cast into the sea,' and doesn't doubt in his heart, but believes that what he says is happening; he shall have whatever he says. Mark 11:22,23

The pattern of soldiers and priests walking around the city seven times is the same cycle we walk with Yahweh each year from the first month to the seventh month. By faith, we walk against the strongholds of this world and the schemes of the enemy through Yahweh's seven-day and seven-month cycle designed for His appointed days. As we walk in obedience with Yahshua, who's name is likened to Joshua and uphold His Covenant, seen in the Ark of the Covenant, Yahweh gives us the victory, and we learn to overcome! Our fear and faith in Yahweh gives us the courage and strength to walk out His Word and bring down the walls and principalities that want to keep us from all that Yahweh has promised us.

The account of Jericho holds a striking resemblance to the keeping of the New Moon. We begin in the spring with the first month and continue through six monthly cycles until the seventh month approaches. Then with the blowing of the trumpet and shouts of joy, the feast of Trumpets or Yom Teruah arrives. We will look deeper at Yom Teruah later, but it is the day of victory for Yahweh's people and the day of destruction for those who reject Him. Here is where we find the answer to why Yahweh would destroy Jericho or the City of the Moon. It is not because we are to disregard the Moon, but at the same time, we are not to worship it. As I emphasized at the beginning of this book, there is no way that I want to present the Sun or the Moon as something to be worshiped. They are mere signs, instruments, and players in a greater picture that shows us Yahweh's heart. No other god or image is ever to stand in His place. Yet this is not the way that many people choose. Over and over people choose an image as their point of worship. In the time of Joshua, it was the same as today. Archaeologists have uncovered many temples to the moon-god throughout the Middle East. There are many artifacts and wall paintings that have been found in ruined cities bearing the crescent moon symbol. From Turkey to the banks of the Nile, the most widespread religion of the ancient world was the worship of the moon-god. In many cultures worshipping the Moon is still in practice along with Sun worship. Symbols of the Moon and the Sun as gods in worldly worship are common. However, in the eyes of Yahweh's true bride, there will be no symbol or image to interfere with her fixed gaze upon her Beloved King.

"You shall have no other gods before Me.

"You shall not make for yourself a carved image—any likeness of anything that is in heaven above, or that is in the earth beneath, or that is in the water under the earth; you shall not bow down to them nor serve them. For I, the Lord your God, am a jealous God, visiting the iniquity of the fathers upon the children to the third and fourth generations of those who hate Me, but showing mercy to thousands, to those who love Me and keep My commandments. Ex. 20:3-6

The account of Joshua destroying a city that worshiped the Moon foreshadowed Yahshua's final victory over all false gods, including the antichrist. We as Yahshua's betrothed must diligently watch and follow Him alone. There is only one power to fear in all the Universe and that is Yahweh, and He does not compromise. We must have a sound real-ization of who Yahweh is and who we are in comparison to Him. King David understood the fear of Yahweh and wrote of it many times. The fear of Yahweh is not meant to drive us away from Him, on the contrary, it should cause us to run to Him because the One who loves us is the most the most powerful of all. As you read the Psalms below notice that there is a blessing that comes with fearing Yahweh.

Oh how great is your goodness,
which you have laid up for those who fear you,
which you have worked for those who take
refuge in you, before the sons of men!
In the shelter of your presence you will hide
them from the plotting of mans.
You will keep them secretly in a dwelling away
from the strife of tongues. Ps.31:19,20

Behold, Yahweh's eye is on those who fear him,
on those who hope in his loving kindness;
to deliver their soul from death,
to keep them alive in famine. Ps.33:18,19

For as the heavens are high above the earth,
so great is his loving kindness toward
those who fear him. Ps.103:11

Like a father has compassion on his children,
so Yahweh has compassion on those who fear him; Ps.103:13

As for man, his days are like grass.
As a flower of the field, so he flourishes.
For the wind passes over it, and it is gone.
Its place remembers it no more.
But Yahweh's loving kindness is from everlasting to everlasting
with those who fear him, his righteousness
to children's children;
to those who keep his covenant, to those who
remember to obey his precepts. Ps.103:15-18

Yahweh is near to all those who call on him,
to all who call on him in truth.
He will fulfill the desire of those who fear him.
He also will hear their cry, and will save them. Ps.145:19-20

Yahweh takes pleasure in those who fear him,
in those who hope in his loving kindness. Ps. 147:11

These verses are a staggering reminder that without the right perspective of fear we can jeopardize our relationship with Yahweh, becoming complacent, prideful and filled with many of our ideas. When this happens, we often find ourselves wrestling with a life that is based on what suits our flesh or culture. Handling life on our own may work for a time but it will not last and will have long-term consequences. If we loose sight of Who is in control and Who we will answer to at the final trumpet call, we also risk loosing our future with Him.

> For if we sin willfully after we have received the knowledge of the truth, there no longer remains a sacrifice for sins, but a certain fearful expectation of judgment, and fiery indignation which will devour the adversaries. Anyone who has rejected Moses' law dies without mercy on the testimony of two or three witnesses. Of how much worse punishment, do you suppose, will he be thought worthy who has trampled the Son of God underfoot, counted the blood of the covenant by which he was sanctified a common thing, and insulted the Spirit of grace? For we know Him who said, "Vengeance is Mine, I will repay," says the Lord. And again, "The Lord will judge His people." It is a fearful thing to fall into the hands of the living God. Heb. 10:26-31

The word yarah for Moon reminds us that we are frail humans at the mercy of the Almighty Creator and King. Fear keeps us in right standing with the One and Only Righteous Judge whom we will one day give an account. The above Scriptures should bring us to our knees or even better to our faces. Moses understood the fear of Yahweh and fell on his face often. Fear humbles us before Yahweh and brings His loving compassion, His protection and His attention to us. When we come to the place of seeing Yahweh in all His majesty and power, we as His children will find true shalom. The children of the mightiest King have nothing to fear of the outside world for they are always safe in His care. The world thinks that having no fear of anything brings them freedom. But true freedom comes when you know and fear the One who loves you. That is why Scripture tells us that love casts out fear.

> There is no fear in love; but perfect love casts out fear, because fear has punishment. He who fears is not made perfect in love. 1 John 4:18

When we come to know Yahweh and the power of His love, our fear of Him is put in its rightful place. Often, this is a fine line in our walk with

Him. Fear can cause us to run away or draw us close depending on our relationship with our Beloved. Scriptures tell us that Yahweh has compassion for those who fear Him because the ones who feared Him with love chose to press in closer and hear Him. The Greek word perfect in the above verse is Strong's #G5046, teleios which means: having reached its end, i.e., complete or perfect. Our fear of Yahweh and the wonder of His holiness and love should draw us closer and closer into an intimate relationship with Him. The deeper our relationship, the less we have to fear because our love for Him becomes complete as we follow in His ways. Many times Moses fell to his face in fear of Yahweh's righteous judgment, yet Yahweh said that Moses was the only one that He spoke to face to face ... the only one He trusted.

Yahweh spoke to Moses face to face, as a man speaks to his friend. Ex.33:11a

Those who simply fear Yahweh for His power alone and never draw close to His heart or follow in His ways do not find perfect or complete love. This will become very clear at the end when those who know Yahshua and the ways of His Father are gathered to Him and those who do not know Him are told to depart. May we never forget the greatness of our Almighty King and always worship before Him with fear and trembling, so that our love for Him may be complete in His eyes.

Chodesh

THE THIRD AND FINAL HEBREW WORD USED FOR MOON IN SCRIPTURE IS Strong's #H2320, chodesh חדש. You will find that chodesh is the word most often translated as New Moon and month when referencing Yahweh's appointed days. Chodesh comes from the word chadash, Strong's #H2318 חדש, which is spelled the same as chodesh and means; to renew, repair or restore. Chadash is also the root word for "chadasha" as in the Hebrew name for the New Testament, Brit Chadasha. Brit is the Hebrew word for Covenant, and so the New Testament could also be rightly called the Renewed Covenant. For Yahweh so loved the world and is so faithful to the Covenant that He made with Abraham, (who was willing to give his only son Isaac) that Yahweh sent His only Son Yahshua to die on our behalf, and then raise Him up from death as a new man so that the Covenant could be renewed! How amazing is our God and King!! He truly is a God of love and restoration, and the word chodesh for New Moon is a monthly reminder of the wonder and beauty of this truth. Chodesh is the phase of the Moon's cycle when the Moon is renewed or restored. Each chodesh, the Moon is hidden away at conjunction and passes through Yahweh's pattern of life. When the Moon's waxing sliver appears after conjunction, it is not a brand new Moon that we see in the sky, but the same Moon renewed and ready to begin its cycle once again. Women experience this monthly pattern as well. For in their childbearing years, in the secret place of their body, a time is set apart each month when the old is washed away, and a new beginning starts again. Often women find that their cycle is effected by the Moon's cycle because all is designed by the hand of Yahweh and bears His patterns. With these pictures in mind, it is not surprising that the Hebrew word 'molad' is used to describe the New Moon.

"Molad is a Hebrew word meaning "birth" that also generically refers to the time at which the New Moon is "born"." (Wikapedia)

You can see then, that each month the Moon is reminding us that we too must be born again and renewed to walk with Yahweh through His cycles.

> *Jesus answered him,"Most certainly, I tell you, unless one is born anew, he can't see God's Kingdom. John 3:3*

> *Therefore if anyone is in Christ, he is a new creation. The old things have passed away. Behold, all things have become new. 1 Cor. 5:17*

Some may wonder when the renewing actually happens. Is it before or after birth? Is it in public, for all eyes to see ... or in private? Our questions are easily answered through Yahweh's pattern of life. Over and over we see that His Creation reveals to us that renewing happens in private or in secret; hidden from the eyes of the world. In secret is where all new life and the renewing of life is formed. It happened in the natural when Yahweh knit us together in the secret place of our mother's womb, and it happens again in the spiritual when we find new life and transformation hidden away in the secret place of the Most High. Even now Yahshua beckons us to go into our closets and shut the door to spend time in prayer, for what happens in secret is what will be manifested as life to the world. This is the amazing picture that chodesh for New Moon is showing us.

> *But you, when you pray, enter into your inner room, and having shut your door, pray to your Father who is in secret, and your Father who sees in secret will reward you openly. Matt.6:6*

After the Moon is renewed at conjunction, the new sliver or crescent can be seen in the western sky. The Moon's journey then begins anew across the heavens. Faithfully it travels through each of its phases until at last, at the end of its cycle, it is once again hidden away from our sight for approximately three days. The same pattern was revealed through the Messiah when He died and was buried for three days and three nights in the tomb. During this breathless time in history, when Yahshua was hidden from our sight, He conquered death and made a way for renewed life and restoration! Halleluyah!

> *I therefore, the prisoner in the Lord, beg you to walk worthily of the calling with which you were called, with all lowliness and humility, with patience, bearing with one another in love; being eager to keep the unity of the Spirit in the bond of peace. There is one body, and one Spirit, even as you also were called in one hope of your calling; one Lord, one faith, one baptism, one God and Father of all, who is over all, and through all, and in us all. But to each one of us was the grace given according to the measure of the gift of Christ. Therefore he says, "When he ascended on high, he led captivity captive, and gave gifts to men." Now this, "He ascended", what is it but that he also first descended into the lower parts of the earth? He who descended is the one who also ascended far above all the heavens, that he might fill all things. Eph.4:1-10*

When Yahshua rose victorious, He rose as a new man for us. Again, this is the sign of Jonah and Yahweh's pattern of life!

> *But he answered them, "An evil and adulterous generation seeks after a sign, but no sign will be given it but the sign of Jonah the prophet. Matt.12:39*

By this awesome act of love, Yahshua made the way for us to be restored and reconciled back to His Father and become one with Him. As we follow Yahshua, Yahweh's mercy and grace renews, restores and repairs our wayward, broken hearts.

Not for these only do I pray, but for those also who believe in me through their word, that they may all be one; even as you, Father, are in me, and I in you, that they also may be one in us; that the world may believe that you sent me. The glory which you have given me, I have given to them; that they may be one, even as we are one; I in them, and you in me, that they may be perfected into one; that the world may know that you sent me, and loved them, even as you loved me. John 17:20-23

In the above prayer, Yahshua reveals the heart behind all that He did. His mission? … that we would know the love of His Father and be *one* with Him. Our journey here, as sojourners on Earth, is all about returning home to the Father. The Hebrew word used to show us the way back to the Father is Strong's #H7725 shuv, which means; to turn back, with the idea of returning to the starting point, to go home, restore, rescue, etc. Each Rosh Chodesh the Moon is our faithful witness in the heavens of this truth, as it returns or shuvs back to its source of light to be renewed and restored.

I will give them a heart to know me, that I am Yahweh: and they shall be my people, and I will be their God; for they shall return to me with their whole heart. Jer.24:7

Therefore tell them: Yahweh of Armies says: 'Return to me,' says Yahweh of Armies, 'and I will return to you,' says Yahweh of Armies. Zech.1:3

The wonder and revelation of this is found in what is known as the New Testament. Yahshua did not come to bring us a brand new Covenant. It was never Yahshua's desire to take us away from the heart of His Father. On the contrary, Yahshua came to restore the Covenant that Yahweh promised to Abraham, Isaac, and Jacob, and to Abraham's seed.

So often people forget that when they accept Yahshua as their Savior, they become a new person and enter into Covenant with the King! This magnificent reality is set before us in the heavens as a constant reminder of Yahweh's unfailing love! The Moon at Rosh Codesh or New Moon faithfully reminds us that it is not the old man that lives any longer, but a new man free to serve the King!

> But you did not learn Christ that way; if indeed you heard him, and were taught in him, even as truth is in Jesus: that you put away, as concerning your former way of life, the old man, that grows corrupt after the lusts of deceit; and that you be renewed in the spirit of your mind, and put on the new man, who in the likeness of God has been created in righteousness and holiness of truth. Eph.4:20-24

The New Moon is the landmark of restoration and renewal on our journey through each monthly cycle. It beckons us to stop and be refreshed in Yahweh's presence and calls us together as one. When we take a closer look at the word chodesh, we will see that the New Moon was meant for unity. Chodesh in its simplest form, originates from the two letter root word חד chad, which means; one, together or unity! Chad is the same root word that you will find for the word echad, Strong's #H259 אחד. This is the Hebrew word for one and has found its fame in the well known shema:

"Hear, O Israel: The Lord our God, the Lord is one!"

How ironic and compelling that the root for chodesh is unity (chad), when the New Moon is often the very reason for division. Yahweh is always concerned for the things that are lost or broken and desires to restore and renew them back to wholeness or oneness in His hand. We see this happen when He heals our bodies in the physical and it will happen in the end when he heals the body of Messiah in the spiritual.

> For as the body is one, and has many members, and all the members of the body, being many, are one body; so also is Christ. For in one Spirit we were all baptized into one body, whether Jews or Greeks, whether bond or free; and were all given to drink into one Spirit. 1 Cor.12:12,13

> For even as we have many members in one body, and all the members don't have the same function, so we, who are many,

are one body in Christ, and individually members one of another. Rom.12:4,5

The body of the Messiah is in need of much healing and restoration. In Yahweh's timing it will come, as the bride or body of the Messiah submits to her Beloved and allows Him to cover her and have His way in her life. Then with faith and fear, she will be restored as we saw in the words levana and yerach for Moon.

Wives, submit to your own husbands, as to the Lord. For the husband is head of the wife, as also Christ is head of the church; and He is the Savior of the body. Therefore, just as the church is subject to Christ, so let the wives be to their own husbands in everything.

Husbands, love your wives, just as Christ also loved the church and gave Himself for her, that He might sanctify and cleanse her with the washing of water by the word, that He might present her to Himself a glorious church, not having spot or wrinkle or any such thing, but that she should be holy and without blemish. Eph.5:22-27

When we submit to Yahweh's leading by the Holy Spirit, we will become one body; pure in love and bearing fruit for His Kingdom. Yahshua will then lead His bride on a journey to strengthen her and prepare her to endure until His return. All the parts of the body will work together as one to bring honor and glory to His Name in humility and loving service to others. Just as it is during winter, the bride will experience times when it feels dark, cold and lonely, but faithfully winter passes and all that was waiting beneath the soil will come to life.

Chodesh is teaching us about unity and oneness in the Messiah and the desire to become His spotless bride. When we accept Yahshua as our Savior, we are also accepting death to our old self. Again, this death and new life begin hidden from the eyes of the world... as it does with the Moon. At chodesh, the Moon is lost in the fullness of the Sun's bright glare and unseen by the world. When the Sun and Moon are together in the sky, it is the *only* time when the entire world sees the same thing ... a moonless sky. At this time, when the whole world is unified because no matter where you are on planet Earth, you will see the same thing at the same time ... amazing! This is Yahweh's picture of restoration and unity! This is the time when Yahshua's bride finds healing, restoration and safety.

Our differences in understanding the New Moon have sadly broken us apart on celebrating His Holy appointments. Often the best solution to this problem is to set aside our differences and find unity in the commonly accepted way. Unfortunately, if we disagree on the landmarks along the path, the journey can quickly become confusing and disheartening. Could this be the reasoning behind the Scripture in Amos?

Can two walk together, unless they are agreed?   Amos 3:3

As we saw in the chapter called Yahweh's Story, from Yahweh's perspective, there is only *one* breathtaking story that is playing out across the Universe and that is Yahweh's Masterpiece and Song. Yahweh is the Composer and Creator, and there is no other. Oh, there are many counterfeits, trying to distort and drowned out Yahweh's Masterpiece, but in the end, their attempts to copy or lie will be silenced, for Yahweh is not only the Composer of the symphony, He is also the Conductor. No matter how skilled a musician in an orchestra may be, it is the conductor who interprets the musical score and sets the tone. The conductor's direction and leading brings each individual musician together in one beautiful and harmonious sound. One glorious New Moon Yahshua will return, and the truth will prevail! The Hebrew word chodesh beckons us to play our part in Yahweh's great and masterful Love Story in harmony with His song. Our response is to be in one accord with the Composer and learn the music as a dedicated musician would. Then as we gather, we need to watch and listen for our Conductor to lead us in our part, allowing His Spirit to guide us into one accord with our Beloved.

Behold, God is my salvation,
I will trust and not be afraid;
'For Yah, the Lord, is my strength and song;
He also has become my salvation. Is.12:2

Yah is my strength and song.
He has become my salvation. Ps.118:14

Yah is my strength and song.
He has become my salvation.
This is my God, and I will praise him;
my father's God, and I will exalt him.Ex. 15:2

As we have seen, Yahweh's song and Masterpiece is nearing the closing scenes, and His intense grand finale is sweeping the world. His song is exalted above all the other noises of this crazy world and now is the time to join with the host of angels and all of Creation to be in harmony with Him. Noah Webster's 1828 Dictionary defines harmony as: the just adaptation of parts to each other, in any system or composition of things, intended to form a connected whole; as the harmony of the universe. Our call as one of Yahweh's family and especially Yahshua's bride is to be one with Yahweh and His ways. If we choose to be in harmony with the world or man's ways, we become in discord with Yahweh. Remember, it was when all was placed in His order, and the people were of one accord when His presence filled the Temple.

..when the trumpeters and singers were as one, to make one
sound to be heard in praising and thanking Yahweh; and when
they lifted up their voice with the trumpets and cymbals and
instruments of music, and praised Yahweh, saying,

"For he is good;
for his loving kindness endures forever!"

...then the house was filled with a cloud, even Yahweh's house,
so that the priests could not stand to minister by reason of the
cloud: for Yahweh's glory filled God's house. 2Chron.5:13,14

Yahshua promised to send His Holy Spirit to us. Our Beloved knew that we should not be left to our own ways and risk being lost or deceived. The Holy Spirit is our guide and comforter, to lead us into all truth and help us to always hear Yahweh's song through the chaos.

But the Counselor, the Holy Spirit, whom the Father will send in my name, he will teach you all things, and will remind you of all that I said to you. John 14:26

If we live by the Spirit, let's also walk by the Spirit. Let's not become conceited, provoking one another, and envying one another. Gal.5:25,26

When we walk by the leading of Yahweh's Spirit, we will have true harmony and be in one accord as the body of the Messiah. Those who are not following Yahweh can see that we are a divided people, who all claim to follow the same God. Obviously, this can be confusing, especially to those looking in from outside … yet the author of this awesome Masterpiece has nothing to do with confusion.

… for God is not a God of confusion, but of peace. As in all the assemblies of the saints. 1 Cor.14:33

Only when man's ways and the schemes of the enemy come into our gatherings are things distorted and the beauty of Yahweh's song lost. Often this brings confusion and separation within the body.

For where jealousy and selfish ambition are, there is confusion and every evil deed. But the wisdom that is from above is first pure, then peaceful, gentle, reasonable, full of mercy and good fruits, without partiality, and without hypocrisy. James 3:16,17

As the body of the Messiah, we must submit to our Beloved and be in harmony or one accord with His Word and His will for our lives. When we are in one accord with His Symphony, His presence will come.

Now when the day of Pentecost had come, they were all with one accord in one place. Suddenly there came from the sky a sound like the rushing of a mighty wind, and it filled all the house where they were sitting. Acts 2:1,2

Day by day, continuing steadfastly with one accord in the temple, and breaking bread at home, they took their food with gladness and singleness of heart, praising God, and having favor with all the people. The Lord added to the assembly day by day those who were being saved. Acts 2:46,47

There are various kinds of service, and the same Lord. There are various kinds of workings, but the same God, who works all things in all. But to each one is given the manifestation of the Spirit for the profit of all. For to one is given through the Spirit the word of wisdom, and to another the word of knowledge, according to the same Spirit; to another faith, by the same Spirit; and to another gifts of healings, by the same Spirit; and to another workings of miracles; and to another prophecy; and to another discerning of spirits; to another different kinds of languages; and to another the interpretation of languages. But the one and the same Spirit produces all of these, distributing to each one separately as he desires.

For as the body is one, and has many members, and all the members of the body, being many, are one body; so also is Christ. For in one Spirit we were all baptized into one body, whether Jews or Greeks, whether bond or free; and were all given to drink into one Spirit. 1 Cor. 12:4-13

The enemy is hard at work to destroy our attempts to be one with Yahweh and each other. His voice fills the airways with lies, mixed messages and worldly music that is becoming louder and more invasive than ever before. Our ears must become attuned to Yahweh's voice and His wonderful song so that it will play strong and steady in our hearts wherever we go. Then out of the abundance that His Words and melody bring us, we will love and edify one another, (not ourselves) in the gifts and calling that Yahweh has given each of us to live out. We will then have true unity and shalom as we become echad or one, just as Yahweh and Yahshua are one.

If there is therefore any exhortation in Christ, if any consolation of love, if any fellowship of the Spirit, if any tender mercies and compassion, make my joy full, by being like-minded, having the same love, being of one accord, of one mind; doing nothing through rivalry or through conceit, but in humility, each counting others better than himself; each of you not just looking to his own things, but each of you also to the things of others. Phil.2:1-4

Now the God of patience and of encouragement grant you to be of the same mind one with another according to Christ Jesus, that with one accord you may with one mouth glorify the God and Father of our Lord Jesus Christ. Rom.15:5,6

The time we spend in the presence of our Beloved prepares us to be in harmony with our brothers and sisters in Yahshua so that in one accord we will sing praises to Yahweh in all that we say and do. The Moon is our faithful witness to this goal. Each Rosh Chodesh, the Moon returns to the Sun and becomes echad or one within its glorious light and renewed in its presence. As Yahshua's bride it is our call to first be in harmony with the Composer and Conductor of the song of the Universe. Then we will see from His perspective that each of us has a part to play in His Majestic Symphony. As this becomes real in our lives, we will be like the Moon and bring Yahweh's light and life to those who are in darkness.

Holy Father, keep them through your name which you have given me, that they may be one, even as we are. John 17:11

Yahshua's Bride

"Come here. I will show you the wife, the
Lamb's bride." Rev.21:9

THE BRIDE OF THE MESSIAH OR THE LAMB'S WIFE AS REVELATION REFERS
to her, is like no other bride in all of history. Her purpose in life is
enveloped by her devotion to the King of the Universe. Yahshua's bride
understands that the things of this world are passing away and that she
is a sojourner on her way home. She only has eyes for her Beloved and is
anticipating the heavenly Jerusalem, which will be the dwelling place for
her Bridegroom when all is made new.

> *In my Father's house are many homes. If it weren't so, I would*
> *have told you. I am going to prepare a place for you. If I go*
> *and prepare a place for you, I will come again, and will receive*
> *you to myself; that where I am, you may be there also. Where I*
> *go, you know, and you know the way."John 14:2-4*

Yahshua's true bride will die to herself daily and hold no light of her own
or of the enemy. She will be ever transforming into the likeness and light
of her Beloved. Then like her Bridegroom, she will put others before
herself in love and humility. Her faith in her Beloved will be seen in her
works and in the end she will be clothed in radiant white linen revealing

her righteous acts. How remarkable that each attribute of the bride of the Messiah can also be seen in the attributes of the Moon found in Scripture and in the pictures Yahweh has placed in the heavens. Now we will use the three words for Moon and the patterns we have seen to take a deeper look at the Yahshua's bride and what her life looks like in this world.

A simple word search for Moon in the dictionary describes the Moon as Earth's natural satellite. For me, the word satellite quickly brought to mind images of man-made objects coursing the skies. A further look at the description for satellite brought an added surprise that I hadn't thought of, which is; a person who follows or serves another. Wow! This description matches the ways of the Moon as Earth's satellite so beautifully. It also confirms the description of the bride of Messiah as one who follows and serves her only source of light and life. Yahshua's bride will delight to faithfully follow and serve her Savior and King. She never forgets that she was bought with the lavish price of her Beloved's blood and that she is no longer her own or subject to the ways of man. Her body has become the temple of Yahweh, and her life is devoted to the one who freed her from the bondage of this world.

> *Or don't you know that your body is a temple of the Holy Spirit which is in you, which you have from God? You are not your own, for you were bought with a price. Therefore glorify God in your body and in your spirit, which are God's. 1 Cor. 6:19,20*

> *Only fear Yahweh, and serve him in truth with all your heart; for consider what great things he has done for you. 1Sam.12:24*

> *Then you shall return and discern between the righteous and the wicked, between him who serves God and him who doesn't serve him. Mal.3:18*

At the time of Yahshua's death, an interesting picture played out for us. Yahshua, the Son of Righteousness laid aside His heavenly glory to become like us and make a way for us to be with His Father. Everything He did was in full surrender and obedience to His Father. We too must become fully dependent on the Father for all our needs and should never shine or boast of our own efforts. When the time came for Yahshua to die, the soldiers put a scarlet robe upon Him. This robe represented the sin of us all and the price of redemption that He was taking upon Himself.

And they stripped Him and put a scarlet robe on Him. Matt.27:2

Yahshua's love and obedience to His Father fulfilled the very heart of Yahweh's great Love Story and made a way for Yahweh and His people to dwell together forever. As Yahshua's bride, we are to follow His example and submit fully to the ways of His Father and be willing to take up our cross daily.

Then He said to them all, "If anyone desires to come after Me, let him deny himself, and take up his cross daily, and follow Me. Luke 9:23

The every day trials set before us are designed to teach us to die to our selfish ways and worldly ideals, making us humble like our Beloved. The heavens will reveal this when the Moon or bride takes on a scarlet robe as her Beloved did for her.

The sun shall be turned into darkness,
And the moon into blood,
Before the coming of the great and awesome
day of the Lord. Acts 2:20

Just as our Beloved showed His great love for us by willingly taking upon Himself all that His idolatrous and sinful people deserved, so His bride will willingly suffer trial to show her love for Him. The disciples modeled this for us in the many trials they suffered for Yahshua's sake, as well as the uncountable others who have willingly suffered over the ages for the truth.

And when they had preached the gospel to that city and made many disciples, they returned to Lystra, Iconium, and Antioch, strengthening the souls of the disciples, exhorting them to continue in the faith, and saying, "We must through many tribulations enter the kingdom of God." Acts 14:21,22

When the Moon is turned to blood, it becomes a sign of our redemption from sin. The color scarlet is always looked upon as a reminder of Yahshua's redemptive blood and we must never loose sight of it, for it is the key that binds us to the Covenant. Without Yahshua's shed blood we have no way to the Father and consequently no eternal life. The scarlet cord was used as a sign of redemption on the azazel goat at Yom Kippur. A scarlet thread was woven into the curtains of the Tabernacle, and in the story of Rahab, a scarlet thread was bound to her window before the walls of Jericho came down, so that Rahab would be spared.

For Yahshua's bride, the redemptive covering of her Beloved's sacrifice is ever before her and is the motivation of her heart. There is a poignant picture of this in the Song of Songs that reflects the heart of Yahshua's bride. When He looks upon His beloved and sees that she is mindful of His redemptive work and their Covenant together, He sees her lips as a strand of scarlet.

> *Your lips are like scarlet thread.*
> *Your mouth is lovely. S. S. 4:3a*

What a beautiful picture of how all that we say and do, as the Lamb's wife should speak of Him crucified and His resurrection from death back to life. All our efforts to be righteous cannot be counted as worthy unless we are bound to His Covenant through the shed blood of our King. He is our all!

> *For I determined not to know anything among you, except Jesus Christ, and him crucified. 1 Cor.2:2*

The Lamb's wife will never forget all that her Beloved has done for her and that she has no righteousness of her own. Without Him, she would be forever lost and all her striving for righteousness worthless. Here we the revelation of levana as the Moon, faithfully declaring to the world that her light is His Light, and her righteousness is His righteousness. Even her best efforts to do what is right in her own eyes or serve Him in her own way are not pleasing in His sight as Isaiah reveals.

> *For we have all become like one who is unclean,*
> *and all our righteousness is like a polluted garment. Is.64:6*

Wash yourselves, make yourself clean.
Put away the evil of your doings from before my eyes.
Cease to do evil.
Learn to do well.
Seek justice.
Relieve the oppressed.
Judge the fatherless.
Plead for the widow."
"Come now, and let us reason together," says Yahweh:
"Though your sins be as scarlet, they shall be as white as snow.
Though they be red like crimson, they shall be as wool.
If you are willing and obedient,
you shall eat the good of the land;
but if you refuse and rebel, you shall
be devoured with the sword;
for the mouth of Yahweh has spoken it." Is.1:16-20

May Yahweh be praised for we are not bound to our sinful, hopeless state! We have redemption through His shed blood, which is our covering and the seal of the renewed Covenant. The most extraordinary reality seen in the picture of the blood Moon is that Yahshua's blood covering is the only way we can have righteousness at all. His redemptive blood gives us the right to become sons and daughters and the privilege to become like Him ... "white as snow"! This is so awesome!

His appearance was like lightning, and his clothing white as snow. Matt. 28:3

His head and his hair were white as white wool, like snow. His eyes were like a flame of fire. Rev.1:14

What an amazing transformation for us! When we are cleansed by the shed blood of our Messiah and King and then washed in His Word, we become white as snow and like our Beloved. As we saw earlier levana for Moon means white or brick revealing to us a picture of the bride who has walked away from the ways of the world that shaped her like a brick, to become washed in the blood of her Savior. King David, the man after Yahweh's heart, prayed for this.

> *Purify me with hyssop, and I will be clean.*
> *Wash me, and I will be whiter (levana*
> *H3835) than snow. Ps.51:7*

Remember that hyssop was used to put the blood of the spotless lamb upon the doorposts at the time of the first Passover. Then when the true Lamb of Yahweh came to us and hung on the cross to fulfill Passover, they used hyssop to apply bitter water to Yahshua's mouth.

> *Now a vessel full of vinegar was set there; so they put a*
> *sponge full of the vinegar on hyssop, and held it at his mouth.*
> *John 19:29*

The priests used hyssop to cleanse and purify, and so David references the hyssop when he asks Yahweh to cleanse him from his unrighteousness. Likewise, the suffering of Yahshua, the Lamb of Yahweh is connected to hyssop in that His suffering and death would cleanse and purify all those who would follow Him. When we allow ourselves to be purged and washed in His blood, taking up our cross and following Him we become white and prepared for our King. Daniel also prophesied of this.

> *Many shall purify themselves, and make themselves white*
> *(levana 3835) and be refined; but the wicked shall do wickedly;*
> *and none of the wicked shall understand; but those who are*
> *wise shall understand. Dan.12:10*

Here we see levana being used to describe the bride in the latter days! Notice that it is those who are wise who will understand what is required to become white. These amazing pictures and patterns are pieces to Yahweh's Masterpiece and reveal how the Moon represents the bride. Like the Moon, the bride is a living stone transformed into His image and shining as the Sun, just as the Song of Songs declares her to be!

> *Who is she who looks forth as the morning,*
> *Fair as the moon (levana H3842),*

Clear as the sun,
Awesome as an army with banners? S.S. 6:10

Yahshua's bride will be made up of those who reflect the light of their Beloved and go to into the world with the message of her Savior and nothing of herself. As the above Scripture declares, she will be as awesome as an army with banners because she is totally surrendered to her King and not ashamed to declare it to the world. She will then be as fair as the Moon and a pure reflection of His light alone!

Remember also that the other word that comes from levana is frankincense, and that frankincense is symbolic of our obedience in life and our prayers, that are to be a sweet smelling aroma before the throne of Yahweh. For us to see Yahshua's bride, 'fair as the Moon,' we need to tie the meanings for levana as white or brick and frankincense together. We find these two meanings in the intriguing life of a frankincense tree and the process of how frankincense comes to us.

Frankincense trees are remarkable because they grow in very harsh and unforgiving environments, such as drought and storm. The average frankincense tree survives and flourishes where other trees would quickly die. Some frankincense trees are so tenacious that they survive beyond the drought and storm conditions to even grow directly out of solid rock. Those few determined trees growing out of rock, obviously have no place to sink their roots like other frankincense trees. These trees are extremely vulnerable and exposed to all that the seasons may ravage upon them. One would naturally conclude that if a storm or any other harsh weather condition came upon these few obscure trees, they would soon wither or topple over because their roots are not anchored in the soil. Yet, these unique frankincense trees, or may I say levana trees, form a 'disc-like' growth at their base where their roots grip the rock. This growth secures them to the rock to ensure that they will not be torn away during harsh winds or violent storms.

Can you see the picture of Yahshua's remnant bride!? She is one of the few that has chosen to secure herself to the Rock, just as the Scripture tell us, "many are called, but few are chosen." These few endure the storms of life with no fear of the storms themselves! Why? ... because as we saw in the word yarach for Moon, she fears only one ... her Beloved! Scripture tells us many times that our Bridegroom is that Rock and those who have been redeemed and follow Yahshua are secured in Him.

He alone is my rock and my salvation, my fortress.
I will not be shaken.
With God is my salvation and my honor.
The rock of my strength, and my refuge, is in God.
Trust in him at all times, you people.
Pour out your heart before him.
God is a refuge for us. Ps.62:6-8

Don't fear,
neither be afraid.
Haven't I declared it to you long ago,
and shown it?
You are my witnesses.
Is there a God besides me?
Indeed, there is not.
I don't know any other Rock. Is. 44:8

For I will proclaim Yahweh's name.
Ascribe greatness to our God!
The Rock, his work is perfect,
for all his ways are just.
A God of faithfulness who does no wrong,
just and right is he. Deut.32:3,4

When Moses approached Yahweh for permission to behold His glory, he was put in the cleft of the Rock and covered as Yahweh passed by. How awesome this moment must have been! Do you ever long to be tucked away in the cleft of the Rock, safe from the world and covered by Yahweh's presence?

He said, "You cannot see my face, for man may not see me
and live." Yahweh also said, "Behold, there is a place by me,
and you shall stand on the rock. It will happen, while my glory

passes by, that I will put you in a cleft of the rock, and will cover you with my hand until I have passed by.. Ex.33:20-22

Being hidden in the cleft of the Rock is another awesome picture of all that the New Moon is revealing to us. Yahweh has promised to those who follow Him, that if we abide in Him, He will keep us safe from the world. He is our Rock and the source of all our needs. He is our hiding place, our refuge and strong foundation. As the storms of this world rage, the bride of the Messiah is secured in Him, safe under His hand and the shadow of His wing, overwhelmed by His glory and majesty.

> *My dove in the clefts of the rock,*
> *In the hiding places of the mountainside,*
> *Let me see your face.*
> *Let me hear your voice;*
> *for your voice is sweet, and your face is lovely.*
> *Song of Songs 2:14*

The frankincense or levana tree gives us a picture of how the bride is to cling to her Bridegroom and be nourished by Him for without Him she can do nothing, just as the branch cannot bear fruit without the vine. Notice in the above verse that the Beloved Bridegroom refers to His love as having a lovely face and a sweet voice. This is the result of having weathered the storms and being refined to reflect Him. Remember too that it was the Rock that followed the Children of Israel in the Wilderness and nourished them with water. Levana for Moon reminds us that as we go through trials to become white, we need to stay secured to the Rock, hidden in Him.

I am the vine. You are the branches. He who remains in me, and I in him, the same bears much fruit, for apart from me you can do nothing. If a man doesn't remain in me, he is thrown out as a branch, and is withered; and they gather them, throw them into the fire, and they are burned. John 15:5,6

Moreover, brethren, I do not want you to be unaware that all our fathers were under the cloud, all passed through the sea, all were baptized into Moses in the cloud and in the sea, all ate the same spiritual food, and all drank the same spiritual drink. For they drank of that spiritual Rock that followed them, and that Rock was Christ. 1Cor. 10:1-4

The frankincense trees that survive and overcome the harshest elements are ready for harvest at eight to ten years old. Each tree is then cut in a process called "striping" that allows the resin to bleed out of the tree. The resin that runs down the trunk of the tree is left to harden. These drops of resin that bleed out of the sides of the levana or frankincense trees are called "tears." Once they harden they are gathered like small stones varying in shades of amber, sepia, taupe and sometimes white. Later the hardened tears are broken into pieces and ground into powder for use. Below is a quote from an essential oil website:

Differences in soil and climate create even more diversity in the resin, even within the same species. In some places the desert environment is so harsh that the trees grow directly out of marble rock; the resin from these hardy survivors is considered superior.

To harvest frankincense, the outer bark of the tree is cut with a metal knife, causing the resin to bleed out. A few weeks later the harvesters return, gather the resin tears that have flowed from the tree, sort them into different grades, and store them in caves. The highest quality frankincense is in the tears which are almost pure white.

David Crow L.Ac

Notice in the quote that the frankincense trees that grow out of the rock have tears that are far more pure and superior to those that grow in soil or gravel. Amazingly, the tears from the few tenacious trees that grow out of rock are "white" ... which is the other meaning for levana! It is also worthy to note that the tears are hidden away in a cave away from the elements of the world. Here is another breathtaking picture of the bride being hidden away for safekeeping.

The most compelling parallel in the process of the frankincense tears is the suffering of the Messiah; for He was pierced or striped for us. His side was opened and poured forth blood and water so that His bride would have everlasting life and as His bride, we are to identify with His suffering.

For to this you were called, because Christ also suffered for us, leaving you an example, that you should follow his step.. 1 Pet.2: 21

These images may also bring to mind difficult things that you have suffered in your life, and the many tears of you have poured out before Yahweh. Have you ever felt that it was all you could do to cling to the Rock of Yahshua during a storm that ravaged your life? Sometimes the storms of life are so harsh that you feel you cannot hang on any longer and that you cannot cry anymore tears. Though these storms are very painful to go through at the time, there is a wonderful outcome for us when we cling to the Rock of our salvation.

Yahweh is near to those who have a broken heart,
and saves those who have a crushed spirit. Ps.34: 18

For thus says the high and lofty One who inhabits eternity,
whose name is Holy:
"I dwell in the high and holy place, with him also who is of a
contrite and humble spirit,to revive the spirit of the humble,
and to revive the heart of the contrite. Is.57:15

The word translated as contrite in the above verse is Strong's #H1793 dakka which means; crushed or broken to pieces (literally powder). Like the frankincense trees that grow out of the rock and produce the most precious frankincense tears, we too must accept that our heart's tears must be crushed to become useful within Yahweh's kingdom, especially in the service of the Tabernacle. If we are to be useful in our service to our King as His bride and priesthood, then this process is needed for us.

Blows that hurt cleanse away evil,
As do stripes the inner depths of the heart. Prov.20:30 (NKJ)

In the midst of heartbreak and pain have you ever wondered if the tears you have wept have any worth? Beloved of the Most High, your tears are cherished by Yahweh. He knows every single tear that you have shed and

He has heard every cry of your heart. All that we go through is a part of the needed refining to become pure and holy before Him. The trials we endure are designed to purge us of the world's selfish ways and prepare us for His purposes. As we humble ourselves before Him during these times, we learn more deeply to identify with all that Yahshua suffered for us. Each of these pictures are revealing that those who will be with Yahweh, in the end, are those who are humble and contrite in spirit. Scripture also tells us that every one of our tears are recorded in His book and gathered by Yahweh as a treasure.

You number my wanderings.
You put my tears into your bottle.
Aren't they in your book? Ps. 56:8

As Yahshua's bride we must walk as He walked, knowing without a shadow of doubt that the only way to become like our Savior is to die to ourselves and cling to Him alone. He is our Rock and our Refuge through even in the harshest of storms.

I love you, Yahweh, my strength.
Yahweh is my rock, my fortress, and my deliverer;
my God, my rock, in whom I take refuge;
my shield, and the horn of my salvation,
my high tower. Ps.18:1,

Be to me a rock of refuge to which I may always go.
Give the command to save me,
for you are my rock and my fortress. Ps.71:3

You will keep whoever's mind is steadfast in perfect peace,
because he trusts in you.
Trust in Yahweh forever;
for in Yah, Yahweh, is an everlasting Rock. Is.26: 3,4

Our response to the many trying things that we experience on the path of righteousness is what will determine our future. The above verse from Isaiah declares that Yahweh keeps those whose mind is steadfast in perfect peace. As we have seen in the attributes of the Moon, we must never take our eyes off of our One and only source of light and life. If we respond to trials with our trust in Yahweh and cling to Him for life and salvation, our lives will flourish, even through the raging storms. On the other hand, if we respond with our flesh and resist the Rock of our salvation instead of clinging to Him, we will suffer the consequences of having the world ravage and uproot us through the storms.

We, as Yahweh's royal priesthood and bride, must accept with joy, the training brought before us, learning to serve in the Tabernacle and dwell upon the Rock, as the following Psalm reveals.

> *One thing I have asked of Yahweh, that I will seek after,*
> *that I may dwell in Yahweh's house all the days of my life,*
> *to see Yahweh's beauty,*
> *and to inquire in his temple.*
> *For in the day of trouble he will keep*
> *me secretly in his pavilion.*
> *In the covert of his tabernacle he will hide me.*
> *He will lift me up on a rock.*
> *Now my head will be lifted up above my enemies around me.*
> *I will offer sacrifices of joy in his tent.*
> *I will sing, yes, I will sing praises to Yahweh. Ps.27; 4-6*

> *Hear my cry, God.*
> *Listen to my prayer.*
> *From the end of the earth, I will call to*
> *you, when my heart is overwhelmed.*
> *Lead me to the rock that is higher than I.*
> *For you have been a refuge for me,*
> *a strong tower from the enemy.*
> *I will dwell in your tent forever.*
> *I will take refuge in the shelter of your wings. Ps.61:1-4*

These Psalms confirm that Yahweh's desire is to hide us in the Holy of Holies or secret place and secure us there upon the Rock. As we abide in Him and choose to cling to the Rock of our salvation through the storms of life, our prayers and tears will become a sweet smelling aroma before His throne, like the frankincense. When we are born again and become a new man/woman or bride with eyes for our Husband alone, we will naturally attend to the desires of our Beloved's heart. The bride of the Messiah does not lean on her own understanding for answers to the difficult questions that life brings. She fully knows that her Beloved's ways are higher than her ways and she trusts Him to care for her and to protect her through every part of her journey home.

> *Trust in Yahweh with all your heart, and don't lean on your own understanding. In all your ways acknowledge him, and he will make your paths straight. Prov. 3:5-6*

> *"Therefore don't be anxious, saying, 'What will we eat?', 'What will we drink?' or, 'With what will we be clothed?' For the Gentiles seek after all these things; for your heavenly Father knows that you need all these things. But seek first God's Kingdom, and his righteousness; and all these things will be given to you as well. Matt.6: 31-33*

Isn't it extraordinary how these pictures tie together with the Moon? Truly the Moon is a faithful witness to us; revealing we should how we should walk as it travels through the heavens displaying the cycle of life we are to have with our Messiah.

> *His offspring will endure forever,*
> *his throne like the sun before me.*
> *It will be established forever like the moon,*
> *the faithful witness in the sky. Ps.89: 36,37*

Each monthly cycle impels us to seek our Beloved with all our heart and to dwell with Him in the secret place. Each New Moon we are given an opportunity to die to our own ambitions and seek the desires of Yahshua's heart alone, just as He seeks the will of His Father alone. The New Moon is a glorious time of renewal and intimacy with the One who paid the highest price possible for His beloved.

> *Jesus answered him, "Most certainly, I tell you, unless one is born anew, he can't see God's Kingdom." John 3:3*

We were buried therefore with him through baptism to death, that just as Christ was raised from the dead through the glory of the Father, so we also might walk in newness of life. Romans 6:4

Therefore if anyone is in Christ, he is a new creation. The old things have passed away. Behold, all things have become new. 2 Cor.5:17

In harmony with Yahweh's pattern of life, old things pass away each month, and all things are made new. This is true now and will be in the future when Yahshua returns! Each New Moon, the bride, takes her place alongside her Beloved where she is covered and concealed in His presence. After about three days she humbly appears in the West as a faithful witness to a lost world. She then travels eastward through the heavens moving closer and closer to her Beloved; each day waxing brighter until the middle of her journey when she shines in the night just as her Beloved shines in the day. At this time you will see the Moon rising in the East as the night closes in, just as her Beloved faithfully rises in the East at the break of day. The Moon's journey is a heavenly picture of how we are to learn to walk as our Beloved walks and to reflect His light into a dark world.

But the path of the righteous is like the dawning light, that shines more and more until the perfect day. Prov.4:18

After the bride's time of fullness, she humbly returns to her source of life and light, gradually waning smaller and smaller as she moves eastward toward her Beloved's glorious presence. Twice the Moon crosses the heavens in the same manner as the Sun; once when it is full and once when it is new. During the time when the Moon is full, it crosses the night sky alone mimicking the Sun and lighting the night to the point of casting shadows. The full Moon is a picture of Yahshua's bride strong and obedient bringing the light of her Beloved to a lost world. Her strength is found in Him and in humility she then returns to Him growing smaller each phase, until she is with her source of light and life.

He must increase, but I must decrease. John 3:30

The wonder and beauty that the New Moon is declaring is Yahshua's bride in full communion with her King before His throne. There in His presence, she is lost in His brightness as she takes her place by His side and they cross the heavens together. There is a description of this in Jay Ryan's book, Signs and Seasons:

During the time of the New Moon we cannot see the moon in the sky. The moon at this time is at a place in its orbit between the Earth and the Sun. In the sky, the moon is very close to the sun and is lost in the sun's bright glare. Also, when the moon is new its entire bright side is facing toward the sun, and the dark side is facing toward the earth. So even if the moon was not hidden by the sun's glare, it would not shine any light toward our world.

Like the sun, the moon has a day of its own. After rising, the moon climbs higher until reaching its own noon, where it crosses the Meridian. Then the Moon moves into the western sky, where it finally sets. But these risings and settings happen at different times of the day, depending on the phase. For most of the month the moon rises or sets during the daylight. When the moon is new, it rises close to the same time as the sun. The sun and the moon crossed the sky together, even though the moon is lost in the sun's bright glare. The moon crosses the Meridian with the sun close to high noon and sets invisibly sometime around the sunset.

The difference with the New Moon and the full Moon is that the Moon or bride is not alone in the sky at the New Moon. Just as a bride takes her place by the side of her bridegroom to waltz across a dance floor, so the Moon takes its place beside the Sun at the New Moon, in the Song of all Songs, to dance across the heavens enveloped in her Beloved's glorious light.

As our eyes and hearts are opened to see the heavens through the eyes of Yahweh, we will never look at them the same again! The wonder of Yahweh's great Love Story is ever before us. For those who are not taking the time to watch, these days will seem like any ordinary day, but for those who are watching, the New Moon is a precious time that foreshadows the day our Bridegroom will come to take us to His side and gather us home.

Notice that the Sun and Moon cross the Meridian together on this day, just as a groom takes his new bride across the threshold to their new home.

> *He has set a tabernacle for the sun,*
> *Which is like a bridegroom coming out of his chamber,*
> *And rejoices like a strong man to run its race.*
> *Its rising is from one end of heaven,*
> *And its circuit to the other end;*
> *And there is nothing hidden from its heat. Ps. 19:5,6(NKJ)*

The heavens declare as Psalm 19 is telling us that the place Yahweh made for the Sun is like a tent or tabernacle. The Hebrew word for tabernacle is Strong's #H168, ohel, which means; a tent, covering, home or tabernacle. Yahweh has set a tabernacle or dwelling for the Sun in the heavens as a picture of our future home. This is amazing because the word ohel comes from Strong's #H166, ahal, meaning to be clear or to shine. We see this in the Tabernacle in the Wilderness, for it displayed the wonder of all that Yahweh designed the heavens to declare. In the earlier chapter about the Sun, we looked at how the Menorah stands as the only light in the Tabernacle, just as the Sun is the only light in the tent that Yahweh placed in the heavens. In Psalm 19, the phrase "rejoices like a strongman" reveals a beautiful picture of this through the Hebrew word that is translated as 'rejoices.' This word is Strong's #H7797 שׂישׂ, siys meaning; to be bright or cheerful. When we look at this word's design you can see that its letters form the shape of a Menorah; one flame in the center and three flames on either side. As we have also seen, the Menorah and the Sun are symbols or pictures of the Messiah who is our *only* source of light. Psalm 19 is giving us wonderful insight into the heart of Yahshua, who loves His Father and loves to shine the light of His Father by doing His will. The joy He has in this is what He hopes for us to have. When you look upon the seven lights of the Menorah, think of Yahshua rejoicing to do the will of His Father, for this is the light that we too are meant to shine.

> *I am no more in the world, but these are in the world, and I am coming to you. Holy Father, keep them through your name which you have given me, that they may be one, even as we are. While I was with them in the world, I kept them in your name.*

Those whom you have given me I have kept. None of them is lost, except the son of destruction, that the Scripture might be fulfilled. But now I come to you, and I say these things in the world, that they may have my joy made full in themselves. John 17:11-13

Another intriguing Hebrew word in Psalm 19 is Strong's #H2646, chuppah which means; a canopy, covering, chamber, defense! In Psalm 19 this word is translated as the chamber where the Sun comes out to run its race. Traditionally a chuppah is used at weddings, especially Jewish weddings. This is a simple design of four poles covered in a cloth, tapestry or sometimes a prayer shawl, but its purpose is to reveal a greater biblical truth. Biblically the chuppah is a picture of Yahweh's secret place or dwelling; the place that Yahweh has designed for His bride to dwell with Him. Again, Yahweh's heart and ultimate plan has always been to cover His bride and take her to a place of intimacy and safety. When a bride and groom are wed, the chuppah pictures the dwelling place of the groom where the two of them will live and make their new life together.

So many of Yahweh's pictures lead us to the dwelling place of our King which is displayed in the Tabernacle. The Tabernacle in the heavens is the heart and blueprint of the Tabernacle in the Wilderness! The Tabernacle in the Wilderness was a foreshadow of the heavenly chamber or chuppah for the bride in the future when Yahshua comes to take her home.

The heavens declare the glory of God.
The expanse shows his handiwork. Ps.19:1

The heavens declare his righteousness.
All the peoples have seen his glory. Ps.97:6

Praise Yah! The heavens are shouting the awesome story of a Bridegroom and His beloved bride! They are declaring Yahweh's righteousness and the wonder of His heart. Imagine how amazing it would have been to walk with Abraham and hear all that Yahweh had revealed to him about the heavens. Or how awesome it would have been to climb the mountain with Moses and see or hear the patterns of Yahweh first hand. These breathtaking moments are recorded for us as memories of the past, but I believe that Yahweh wants to open our hearts and eyes to see them anew and apply them to our lives today. Yahweh is the same today as He has always been from before time began. The glory of the heavens and His patterns will remain until His story is complete and all things are made new.

> *Of old, you laid the foundation of the earth. The*
> *heavens are the work of your hands.*
> *They will perish, but you will endure. Yes, all*
> *of them will wear out like a garment.*
> *You will change them like a cloak, and they will be changed.*
> *But you are the same. Your years will have no end.*
> *The children of your servants will continue.*
> *Their seed will be established before you." Ps.102:25-28*

As we humble our hearts before Him, Yahweh's Spirit will reveal His ways to us. Now, especially as the last days unfold before us, we need to see what the heavens are declaring and singing out. As we look up, as our father Abraham did, Yahweh will reveal His glorious pattern of the twelve constellations, the Sun and Moon and stars dancing across the heavens.

When Moses followed Yahweh's pattern and set up the Tabernacle in the Wilderness, it was one of the most amazing times this Earth has ever known, because, for a season, it was "on earth as it is in heaven." The assembling of all the pieces of the Tabernacle happened on the New Moon of the first month, called Aviv or as it is known today, Nissan. It was a new time and a new season in history. All the tribes of the Children of Israel were together, and Yahweh was their King seated on His throne in their midst. The Tabernacle in the Wilderness displayed to all the world Yahweh's desired order and service. The daily, monthly and yearly sacrifices, along with the prayers and worship, were all done for our King's pleasure according to the principles of His Kingdom. Remember that the tribe of Levi was set apart at that time from the other tribes and didn't dwell in the camp that surrounded the Tabernacle. They dwelt near the Tabernacle and gave their life to the service of Yahweh alone, reflecting His heart's desire to all the people.

> *The children of Israel shall pitch their tents, every man by his*
> *own camp, and every man by his own standard, according*

to their divisions.But the Levites shall encamp around the Tabernacle of the Testimony, that there may be no wrath on the congregation of the children of Israel: and the Levites shall be responsible for the Tabernacle of the Testimony." Num.1: 52,53

When we see the Moon as the bride, we can also see that it is a 'type and shadow' of the tribe of Levi. The Moon travels through its eight phases giving varying degrees of light to the Earth as an analogy of the varying degrees of service the priesthood brings to the people. The Moon, like the priests of Levi, is a picture of those willing to serve as the royal priesthood within the brightness of Yahweh's presence in the Holy Place and ultimately the Holy of Holies. In Yahweh's presence, the bride or priesthood is hidden in His light, washed in His Word and renewed for service just as it is declared in the final verses of Psalm 19.

The law of the Lord is perfect, converting the soul;
The testimony of the Lord is sure, making wise the simple;
The statutes of the Lord are right, rejoicing the heart;
The commandment of the Lord is pure, enlightening the eyes;
The fear of the Lord is clean, enduring forever;
The judgments of the Lord are true and righteous altogether.
More to be desired are they than gold,
Yea, than much fine gold;
Sweeter also than honey and the honeycomb.
Moreover by them Your servant is warned,
And in keeping them there is great reward.
Who can understand his errors?
Cleanse me from secret faults.
Keep back Your servant also from presumptuous sins;
Let them not have dominion over me.
Then I shall be blameless,
And I shall be innocent of great transgression.
Let the words of my mouth and the meditation of my heart
Be acceptable in Your sight,
O Lord, my strength and my Redeemer. Ps.19:7-14

The New Moon, for those who faithfully follow Yahshua and desire to become His spotless bride, is the time of being hidden in the glorious light of the Bridegroom just as the Sun and Moon travel through the heavens together on the day of conjunction. As we saw revealed in the Hebrew word codesh for New Moon, this glorious day is when the bride is in perfect echad or oneness with her Beloved and the entire Earth is unified by a dark moonless sky.

I would like to take a moment now to touch on the topic of women wearing head coverings. In our western culture, women's head coverings are not common, yet we cannot dismiss the picture that Yahweh wants us to see and understand within it. By Yahweh's design, there is an order of protection and authority through covering. The design begins when a man chooses to walk with Yahweh and has His covering over his life. Then when that man takes a wife, the woman has the covering of her husband. If you look at this from Yahweh's perspective, you can also see that Yahweh is the covering for Yahshua our Bridegroom, (for Yahshua did nothing without Yahweh's leading) and when we accept Yahshua as our Savior, He becomes our covering.

For a man indeed ought not to have his head covered, because he is the image and glory of God, but the woman is the glory of the man. For man is not from woman, but woman from man; for man wasn't created for the woman, but woman for the man. For this cause the woman ought to have authority on her head, because of the angels. 1 Cor. 11:7-10

When Yahweh's order is in place, there is shalom and safety. The true bride of the Messiah will gratefully accept the covering and protection of her Beloved. His covering will be her comfort for she will trust Him with all her heart. Her love and trust will manifest in her willingness to submit to the ways of His household and be lead by His wise, loving authority. Never is this a position that is abusive or mean. On the contrary, proper covering for a woman is displayed in the way Yahshua loves His bride and laid down His life for her. Only love covers in Yahweh's Kingdom, and the bride shows that she is honored to come under her Beloved's Name and His household by wearing a veil or head cover.

Husbands, love your wives, even as Christ also loved the assembly, and gave himself up for it; that he might sanctify it, having cleansed it by the washing of water with the word, that he might present the assembly to himself gloriously, not having spot or wrinkle or any such thing; but that it should be holy and without blemish. Even so husbands also ought to love their own wives as their own bodies. He who loves his own wife loves himself. Eph.5:25-28

In the story of Isaac and Rebekah, found in Genesis 24, there is a stirring picture of this Biblical truth. Let's now recount how Rebekah beautifully foreshadows Yahshua's bride. The story begins with Abraham sending out his servant Eliezer, (who is a shadow picture of the Holy Spirit), to seek a fair maiden for his son. Eliezer is told that the woman he seeks must be willing to leave her country to live under Isaac's covering, for Abraham did not want Isaac to have a wife from among the Canaanite people where he lived. Abraham's final requirement was so vital that even if the woman was kind, beautiful and wanted to marry Isaac, her refusal to follow Eliezer would release him from his oath to Abraham.

"If the woman isn't willing to follow you, then you shall be clear from this oath to me. Only you shall not bring my son there again." Gen.24:8

Eliezer then leaves and journeys to Mesopotamia. There he comes to a well, where the daughters daily draw water. To be completely sure that he makes the right choice, Eliezer prays that Yahweh would bring him success and reveal the maiden by her willingness to serve him water and also offer to serve water to the camels. It should be noted that camels are known to drink many gallons of water when they are thirsty and that an offer to water the camels would reveal rare character qualities of kindness and service. Soon a beautiful woman comes to the well and Eliezer watches as she fills her pitcher with water. Eliezer asks her for a drink. Rebekah immediately and unselfishly gives him the water that she had drawn for herself. Then she fulfills Eliezer's prayer to Yahweh by offering to water all of Eliezer's camels.

She said, "Drink, my lord." She hurried, and let down her pitcher on her hand, and gave him drink. When she had done giving him drink, she said, "I will also draw for your camels, until they have done drinking." She hurried, and emptied her pitcher into the trough, and ran again to the well to draw, and drew for all his camels. Gen. 24:18-20

Eliezer silently watches, as Rebekah makes sure each of the camels are watered. He is delighted and now sure that she is the one for Isaac. He then approaches Rebekah, gives her gifts and tells her about Isaac. Rebekah brings her family to meet Eliezer. They listen to his story and how he wants Rebekah to go with him to become Issac's wife. At first, Rebekah's family hesitates to let her go, but Rebekah settles Eliezer's heart, by agreeing to leave her family and go with him to become Isaac's wife.

They said, "We will call the young lady, and ask her." They called Rebekah, and said to her, "Will you go with this man?"

She said, "I will go." Gen.24:57,58

Yahweh's engaging story comes to a close with a very touching scene that displays Rebekah's willingness to come under Isaac's covering. Eliezer leaves Mesopotamia with Rebekah riding on a camel with him. They arrive home as the Sun is setting. Isaac is out in the open field, bent down in meditation. Perhaps he is praying and longing for Eliezer's return. Something breaks his concentration and draws his attention to the horizon.

Isaac went out to meditate in the field at the evening. He lifted up his eyes, and saw, and, behold, there were camels coming. Gen.24:63

As he lifts his eyes to gaze across the open field, he sees in the distance Eliezer returning at last and beside him …? Yes, it is the silhouette of someone riding with him. Isaac rises to his feet and walks toward them. Rebekah also lifts her eyes to look out to the horizon. Suddenly she sees

Isaac walking toward them. Her heart begins to race as Isaac draws near. Quickly Rebekah dismounts the camel.

"Who is this man walking in the field?" she asks.

"It is Isaac, my master," Eliezer replies.

Without hesitation, Rebekah takes her veil and covers herself.

> Rebekah lifted up her eyes, and when she saw Isaac, she dismounted from the camel. She said to the servant, "Who is the man who is walking in the field to meet us?"
>
> The servant said, "It is my master."
>
> She took her veil, and covered herself. Gen.24: 64,65

We have been given this beautiful picture of Rebekah's willingness to follow Eliezer and come under her husband's covering as a wonderful revelation and foreshadow of Yahshua's bride. The ones who will be the bride of Yahshua will be those willing to follow the leading of the Holy Spirit and willing to leave all to serve and follow their Betrothed. She will be made up of those who understand that it is a privilege and honor to be one with Yahshua and dwell in His household all the days of her life.

> He (Yahshua) said to them, "Most certainly I tell you, there is no one who has left house, or wife, or brothers, or parents, or children, for God's Kingdom's sake, who will not receive many times more in this time, and in the world to come, eternal life." Luke 18:29,30
>
> So therefore whoever of you who doesn't renounce all that he has, he can't be my disciple. Luke 14:33

Are we willing to leave the world behind and take our privileged place under Yahshua's covering, where we are protected and renewed? No matter what the world has to offer, it will never compare to the awesome relationship Yahshua is calling us to have with Him.

Another piece to this picture is that the word translated as covered in the phrase "covered herself" is again, Strong's #H3680 keseh, the same word used for full or appointed time in Psalm 81. The pattern of the bride covered at the New Moon in the presence of the bridegroom is beautifully brought into focus in this story. Isaac is the shadow of the Messiah and Rebekah the shadow of His bride. The attributes of the bride that we see in the Moon are the same as those seen in Rebekah. These are the attributes Yahweh is looking for in women because as women we have the privilege of displaying the qualities of Yahshua's bride. We see this in many honorable women found in Scripture who feared Yahweh and were willing to submit to their bridegroom or husband.

Wives, submit to your own husbands, as to the Lord. For the husband is head of the wife, as also Christ is head of the church; and He is the Savior of the body. Therefore, just as the church is subject to Christ, so let the wives be to their own husbands in everything. Eph.5: 22-24

As Yahshua's bride we will love our Bridegroom with humble submission, welcoming His covering and dwelling with Him in the secret place of His Tabernacle. Yahshua came to Earth in human flesh and paid the most extravagant price for us to be free from our sin. He has sent His Spirit to comfort us, guide us and keep us as we leave this world behind on our journey home to Him, just as Rebekah left all behind to journey home to Isaac.

Evening is now upon us and the time of our journey home is coming to a close. Yahweh has displayed His pictures all around us. His magnificent love story has been declared faithfully before every generation from the beginning of time. Our part is to see it and hear what He is saying to us in these last days, for He is calling us to play the most wonderful part of returning to Him as His bride. As we accept His Covenant terms, it will be to us as it was with Rebekah when she came to Issac; He will take us under His covering and protection. We have seen the picture of the chuppah and how it relates to the secret place. This combined with the story of Isaac and Rebekah is where we find the mystery of our future home revealed. When Rebekah came to Isaac, he took her into his secret place, which was Sarah's tent. This foreshadows the New Jerusalem where Yahshua will take us when we go home to Him.

Isaac brought her into his mother Sarah's tent, and took Rebekah, and she became his wife. He loved her. Gen.24: 67a

But the other woman, Sarah, represents the heavenly Jerusalem. She is the free woman, and she is our mother. Gal.4: 26(NLT)

Behold the most intimate picture of the pattern of life! When a man takes his beloved bride into the secret place of his chamber, and together they become one or echad. Hidden from all the eyes of the world in their secret place, their new life of oneness begins. This, beloved of the Most High, is the awesome picture that the New Moon displays for us each month. For one glorious day, we will see our Beloved Bridegroom face to face and bow before Him in awe and submission to His glorious majesty! Then He will take us into His secret chamber away from the eyes of all the world, and we will become one in Spirit with Him as He is one with His Father.

So that they are no more two, but one flesh. What therefore God has joined together, don't let man tear apart. Matt.19:6

I am no more in the world, but these are in the world, and I am coming to you. Holy Father, keep them through your name which you have given me, that they may be one, even as we are. John 17:11

Not for these only do I pray, but for those also who believe in me through their word, that they may all be one; even as you, Father, are in me, and I in you, that they also may be one in us; that the world may believe that you sent me. John 17:20,21

Now that we have seen how the Moon was designed to reveal so many amazing things to Yahweh's people about His bride let's look at what it reveals about Yahweh's heart to protect her.

PROTECTION

The Secret Place

I REMEMBER AS A YOUNG CHRISTIAN, HOW THE THOUGHT OF GOD HAVING a secret place was such a mysterious concept. "How could we hope to know the secret place of Almighty God?" Naturally, if Yahweh wanted a place to be kept secret, it was likely I may never be able to find it, or so I thought. I was naive then and didn't understand Yahweh's heart as I do now. Now that He has graciously revealed His patterns in the heavens and in the Tabernacle, I *can* see the secret place. Through a process of time and trial, Yahweh allows us to see many things from His perspective. Just as with a child, it takes time and growth to see things as an adult. Yahweh's pattern of concealing something in darkness first, and then bringing light and life to it, is throughout Scripture. His secret place is hidden to those who do not accept Yahshua for they have no reverence for His treasures. As we seek Yahweh with all our heart, He rewards us with the things of His heart and the privilege of being hidden with Him. We see this in the protocol of the Tabernacle and the order of the royal priesthood. Once we are born again and allow Yahweh to purify our hearts and submit to His ways, we then can have access into His holy presence.

Create in me a clean heart, O God. Renew
a right spirit within me. Ps.51:10

Blessed are the pure in heart, for they shall see God. Matt.5:8

The sacrifices and offerings of the Tabernacle teach us Yahweh's protocol for entering into His presence. The same protocol was later seen in the Temple. In spite of all that was required of the High Priest to be clean and walk in righteousness, he was still not allowed to enter through the veil into the Holy of Holies, except once a year, on Yom Kippur or the Day of Atonement. If he entered on his own accord any other day … he would die. The veil that separated the Holy Place from the Holy of Holies was the covering for the secret place of Yahweh.

You shall hang up the veil under the clasps, and shall bring the ark of the testimony in there within the veil: and the veil shall separate the holy place from the most holy for you. Ex.26:33

Solomon's Temple was thirty cubits high. Then later when Herod rebuilt the Temple it was increased to forty cubits, making the veil of separation up to sixty feet high. This amazing veil, for both the Tabernacle and Solomon's Temple, had woven images of cherubim as symbols of Yahweh's warning and protection. Though Herod's Temple does not record these images in the curtains, two large cherubim were built with the same purpose, to guard the Holy of Holies and separate sinful man from Yahweh's holy presence. The images of the two cherubim served as a reminder of the two cherubim that were stationed at the entry of the Garden of Eden, guarding the way to the original Holy of Holies on Earth. After Adam and Eve sinned, they could no longer enter the Holy Garden, and the cherubim guarded the way back. Though separation from Yahweh is heartbreaking, it is for our protection. Our sin will bring instant death in His presence! It is also Yahweh's mercy that separates us from His wrath. We see this sign of protection displayed through the cherubim that cover the mercy seat on the Ark of the Covenant.

So he drove out the man; and he placed cherubim at the east of the garden of Eden, and a flaming sword which turned every way, to guard the way to the tree of life. Gen.3:24

You shall make a veil of blue, and purple, and scarlet, and fine twined linen, with cherubim. Ex.26:31

He made the veil of blue, and purple, and crimson, and fine linen, and ornamented it with cherubim. 1Kings 6:14

For thousands of years, our sin has separated man from Yahweh, and we could never make a way for ourselves to return. Each year the High Priest would make atonement for the people on Yom Kippur by taking the blood of a goat through the veil and sprinkling it on the mercy seat, but this was a temporary atonement that needed to be done every year, allowing only the High Priest into Yahweh's presence. Though it satisfied Yahweh for a time, it did not release us from our sin or the separation we had from Him.

The Tabernacle gives us pictures that reveal our sinful nature, and that there was no way into the secret place of Yahweh except by sacrifice. We are in a perpetual state of sin and always in need of a Savior. This is the awesome reality of who Yahshua is and how the veil of separation or covering represents Him ... for He stands between the Father and us. Our only way to the heavenly Father is through Yahshua.

Jesus said to him, "I am the way, the truth, and the life. No one comes to the Father, except through me." John 14:6

When Yahweh's appointed time had come, He sent His only Son to Earth to make a way for us. At the appointed time of Passover, Yahshua died for our sin and shed His blood for us, making a way for us to enter the Holy of Holies. That most fearful and awesome day that the great veil of separation was torn; was not by human hands, but by the mighty hand of Yahweh Himself ... for it was torn from the top down.

Jesus cried again with a loud voice, and yielded up his spirit. Behold, the veil of the temple was torn in two from the top to the bottom. The earth quaked and the rocks were split. Matt.27:50,51

The sun was darkened, and the veil of the temple was torn in two. Luke 23:45

Halleluyah! The separation between Yahweh and man is no more! That is of course if we do not live out life in our own flesh. We must be hidden in Yahshua's covering and allow Yahweh to test us and cleanse us of our old ways by His Spirit.

For you died, and your life is hidden with Christ in God. When Christ, our life, is revealed, then you will also be revealed with him in glory. Col.3:3,4

Again we see that Yahweh's covering, which comes to us through the shed blood of Yahshua brings new life and protection. With Yahshua as our covering, we now have favor and access to the throne of grace in the secret place of the Most High.

Let us therefore draw near with boldness to the throne of grace, that we may receive mercy, and may find grace for help in time of need. Heb.4:16

Yahshua is the manifestation of Yahweh's mercy and grace. As High Priest, in the order of Melchizedek, Yahshua came to atone for our sin once and for all. He sprinkled His own blood on the mercy seat of heaven's throne.

So also Christ didn't glorify himself to be made a high priest, but it was he who said to him,

"You are my Son.

Today I have become your father."

As he says also in another place,

"You are a priest forever,

after the order of Melchizedek."

He, in the days of his flesh, having offered up prayers and petitions with strong crying and tears to him who was able to save him from death, and having been heard for his godly fear, though he was a Son, yet learned obedience by the things which he suffered. Having been made perfect, he became to all of those who obey him the author of eternal salvation, named by God a high priest after the order of Melchizedek. Heb.5:5-10

For such a high priest was fitting for us: holy, guiltless, undefiled, separated from sinners, and made higher than the heavens; who doesn't need, like those high priests, to offer up sacrifices daily, first for his own sins, and then for the sins of the people. For he did this once for all, when he offered up himself. Heb.7:26,27

But Christ having come as a high priest of the coming good things, through the greater and more perfect tabernacle, not made with hands, that is to say, not of this creation, nor yet through the blood of goats and calves, but through his own blood, entered in once for all into the Holy Place, having obtained eternal redemption. For if the blood of goats and bulls, and the ashes of a heifer sprinkling those who have been defiled, sanctify to the cleanness of the flesh: how much more will the blood of Christ, who through the eternal Spirit offered himself without defect to God, cleanse your conscience from dead works to serve the living God? Heb.9:11-14

When Yahshua said, "I am the Way," He was referring to this, for He made a way to the secret place. We no longer will die in the presence of Yahweh for Yahshua our High Priest has become the sacrifice for our sin, and His blood gives us covering and entry into the Holy of Holies.

For Christ hasn't entered into holy places made with hands, which are representations of the true, but into heaven itself, now to appear in the presence of God for us; nor yet that he should offer himself often, as the high priest enters into the

*holy place year by year with blood not his own, or else he must
have suffered often since the foundation of the world. But now
once at the end of the ages, he has been revealed to put away
sin by the sacrifice of himself. Inasmuch as it is appointed
for men to die once, and after this, judgment, so Christ also,
having been offered once to bear the sins of many, will appear
a second time, without sin, to those who are eagerly waiting for
him for salvation. Heb.9:24-28*

Now we have become a part of the Covenant found within the Ark, which
is covered by the cherubim wings over the mercy seat.

*Blessed are they whose iniquities are forgiven, whose sins are
covered. Rom.4:7*

In the safety of the Holy of Holies under the shadow of Yahweh's wing,
we have refuge and joy. This is the awesome place where the pattern of life
is revealed, for we are covered in the blood of Yahshua and hidden in Him,
away from the eyes of all the world in His secret place.

*Show your marvelous loving kindness,
you who save those who take refuge by your
right hand from their enemies.
Keep me as the apple of your eye.
Hide me under the shadow of your wings,
from the wicked who oppress me,
my deadly enemies, who surround me. Ps. 17:7-9*

The New Moon is revealing this breathtaking picture to us every conjunction. Yahweh's loving kindness and His mercy compels us to seek the
refuge of Yahweh's throne room and the power of His life-giving presence.

*You are my hiding place and my shield.
I hope in Your word. Ps.119:114*

*You are my hiding place.
You will preserve me from trouble.
You will surround me with songs of deliverance. Ps.32:7*

For in the day of trouble he will keep
me secretly in his pavilion.
In the covert of his tabernacle he will hide me.
He will lift me up on a rock. Ps.27:5

Notice how Psalm 27 gives us amazing insight into the pattern of life that we have seen displayed in the New Moon. Daily we are called to seek Yahweh, as His mercy welcomes us every morning. Each day He molds us and prepares us for the privilege of dwelling with Him in the secret place. While in His presence we may inquire of His wisdom in prayer and behold His majestic beauty in worship. Then as we align our walk with His cycles and the things of His heart He secures us and hides us upon the Rock within His Tabernacle. We saw this pictured in the word levana for Moon and the few rare frankincense trees that grow out of rock. When we choose a life of dwelling in the secret place, just as Moses chose to climb the mountain into Yahweh's presence, we too become hidden and secured on the Rock of our salvation.

"Yahweh is my rock,
my fortress,
and my deliverer, even mine;
God is my rock in whom I take refuge;
my shield, and the horn of my salvation,
my high tower, and my refuge.
My savior, you save me from violence. 2 Sam.22:2,3

The Hebrew word translated as 'secret place' is Strong's #H5643 סתר sether, which also means; a cover, hiding place, protection, secret. Sether comes from Strong's #5641 satar (same spelling) which means; conceal, keep close, covering, protection, hiding or secret place. Notice that these words carry the same meaning as keseh and that each of the word's descriptions are related to intimacy and safety. Looking back to Psalm 81 and how all of these words and pictures knit together with one message, we can see that Psalm 81 is a prophetic warning for us to hear the voice of Yahweh and to take refuge in Him at the time of the New Moon. Each New Moon prepares us for Yom Teruah and the coming of our King! Psalm 81 also speaks of Joseph, who like the Moon, was hidden away from his family to serve Potiphar until he was imprisoned. There in the prison chamber under Yahweh's care, Joseph was protected and restored to become the man Yahweh had called him to be. At the appointed time he was brought forth to serve Yahweh in Pharaoh's house. He was then able to restore his relationship with his father and brothers while supplying food to many during a severe famine.

> *It happened, when his master heard the words of his wife, which she spoke to him, saying, "This is what your servant did to me," that his wrath was kindled. Joseph's master took him, and put him into the prison, the place where the king's prisoners were bound, and he was there in custody. But Yahweh was with Joseph, and showed kindness to him, and gave him favor in the sight of the keeper of the prison. The keeper of the prison committed to Joseph's hand all the prisoners who were in the prison. Whatever they did there, he was responsible for it. The keeper of the prison didn't look after anything that was under his hand, because Yahweh was with him; and that which he did, Yahweh made it prosper. Gen. 39: 19-23*

Esther, was also hidden away from her family and all the world to serve as queen within King Ahasuerus' palace. At the appointed time she was called to intercede for her people. Her fasting, prayers, and obedience to Yahweh prepared her to go before the king. When she entered the king's throne room on her own accord, she received favor instead of death. The time that she had spent hidden in the secret place brought grace and protection to her, and the result was that all Israel was saved. Esther's calling is also our calling! We must find refuge in the secret place of the King of the Universe, bringing our prayers and petitions to Him.

> *I love you, Yahweh, my strength.*
> *Yahweh is my rock, my fortress, and my deliverer;*
> *my God, my rock, in whom I take refuge;*
> *my shield, and the horn of my salvation, my high tower.*
> *I call on Yahweh, who is worthy to be praised;*
> *and I am saved from my enemies.*
> *Hear my cry, God.*

Listen to my prayer.
From the end of the earth, I will call to
you, when my heart is overwhelmed.
Lead me to the rock that is higher than I.
For you have been a refuge for me,
a strong tower from the enemy.
I will dwell in your tent forever.
I will take refuge in the shelter of your wings. Ps.61:1-4

You will find that there are many Hebrew words that have a similar meaning to keseh and sether, too many to mention here, but clearly, Scripture is showing us that Yahweh desires to hide, cover, conceal and protect that which is precious to Him ... especially His bride. His desire is to cover her during times of intimacy and hide her during times of trouble. Yahweh longs to gather His people into His secret place and renew them, protect them and speak His words of life to them. This has been His desire from the very beginning of time for His people are His treasure.

For the Lord hath chosen Jacob unto himself,
and Israel for his peculiar treasure.
Ps.135:4(KJV)

Our responsibility is to seek Yahweh and the desires of His heart so that we will find favor and refuge with Him. As His special treasure, He longs to have time with us that is set apart with no distractions. Yahshua exhorted his followers to this, according to Isaiah.

Come, my people, enter into your rooms, and shut your doors
behind you. Hide yourself for a little moment, until the
indignation is past. Is.26:20

But you, when you pray, enter into your inner room, and
having shut your door, pray to your Father who is in secret, and
your Father who sees in secret will reward you openly. Matt.6:6

When we are hidden with Yahweh, the enemy has no power over us. This is critical to remember and understand, for the times of intimacy we develop with Yahweh in the secret place now, will equip us with the wisdom and understanding we need to discern the times we are in. One day soon, no matter what you believe, every knee will bow, and every tongue will confess that Yahshua is the King of kings.

For it is written,

"'As I live,' says the Lord, 'to me every knee will bow.
Every tongue will confess to God.'"

So then each one of us will give account of himself to God. Rom 14:11,12

Therefore God also highly exalted him, and gave to him the name which is above every name; that at the name of Jesus every knee should bow, of those in heaven, those on earth, and those under the earth, and that every tongue should confess that Jesus Christ is Lord, to the glory of God the Father. Phil.2:9-11

We now rehearse this as the Day of Atonement or Yom Kippur. When Yahshua returns to judge us all, we will stand before His throne and give an answer for our life choices. Our love for Him through the keeping of His Commandments and our love for those around us, especially the least of them, will be accounted for on this awesome day. If we have lived a life of dwelling in the secret place with Him, this will be a blessed day. But if we have ignored Him and turned away from His commands we will be righteously judged and receive the consequences.

I command you therefore before God and the Lord Jesus Christ, who will judge the living and the dead at his appearing and his Kingdom: preach the word; be urgent in season and out of season; reprove, rebuke, and exhort, with all patience and teaching. 2 Tim.4:1,2

I saw a great white throne, and him who sat on it, from whose face the earth and the heaven fled away. There was found no place for them. I saw the dead, the great and the small, standing before the throne, and they opened books. Another book was opened, which is the book of life. The dead were judged out of the things which were written in the books, according to their works. Rev.20:11,12

For those who know the King, their name will be found in the Book of Life, and they will enter into eternal joy. For those who have followed satan, the antiChrist or the false prophets this will be a day with eternal consequences. This is so vitally important to see!

If anyone was not found written in the book of life, he was cast into the lake of fire. Rev.20:15

There will in no way enter into it anything profane, or one who causes an abomination or a lie, but only those who are written in the Lamb's book of life. Rev.21:27

We are in a time of testing and rehearsing to prepare us to dwell with the King for all eternity. Our choices now will bring us the protection and provision we need during troubled times in the future, and teach us how to walk as children of the Light. Can we expect Yahweh to dwell with us, protect us or provide for us if we have disregarded Him and His voice on a daily basis? We cannot disregard Him before the trouble comes and then cry out to Him for help.

Seek Yahweh, all you humble of the land, who have kept his ordinances. Seek righteousness. Seek humility. It may be that you will be hidden in the day of Yahweh's anger. Zeph.2:3

You therefore, beloved, knowing these things beforehand, beware, lest being carried away with the error of the wicked, you fall from your own steadfastness. 2 Pet. 3:17

We need to separate ourselves from the many voices of the world to hear His voice alone. The New Moon at conjunction is designed to be a sign for us to come into the secret place and be prepared for His return. Just as the Moon slips eastward into the glorious light of the Sun, we too are called into the presence of our King. There we will find new life and the wisdom to go out into the world and reflect all that He has imparted to us.

Therefore don't be afraid of them, for there is nothing covered that will not be revealed; and hidden that will not be known. What I tell you in the darkness, speak in the light; and what you hear whispered in the ear, proclaim on the housetops. Matt. 10:26:27

Yahshua urged people to heed the call of His Father and draw near to Him. He exposed the condition of their hearts and called them to repent and return to the ways of Yahweh, but they would not hear Him. His desire was to protect and cover them, but they refused Him. Yahshua grieved over this when He said;

Jerusalem, Jerusalem, who kills the prophets, and stones those who are sent to her! How often I would have gathered your children together, even as a hen gathers her chicks under her wings, and you would not! Matt.23:37

Even during the time of Yahshua dwelling directly the midst of people's lives, He could not change the consequences of their choices. He could not make them listen or obey if they were not willing to come under the shadow of His wings. The cry of Yahweh has gone out to His people over and over throughout history with the same message.

And I have put My words in your mouth;
I have covered you with the shadow of My hand,
That I may plant the heavens,
Lay the foundations of the earth,
And say to Zion, 'You are My people.'" Is. 51:16

Draw near to God and He will draw near to you. James 4:8

If we do not heed the call and draw near now, we will be left exposed and vulnerable when trouble comes. We will then suffer the consequences of our disobedience, just as they did when Yahshua was here. We see this pictured in the way Yahweh designed a family. When a man and woman are married, they enter into a covenant together. Their covenant holds promises and commitments to care for and protect one another in every circumstance of life. If a child is born to them, that child becomes covered by the loving commitment of their parent's covenant. As a part of their family, the children too are cared for and protected. But if that child desires to experience the world and runs away from home, they consequently remove themselves from the benefits they had within their parent's protection and care. Yahshua expressed this in His parable of the prodigal son. The younger son left the benefits of living in his father's household and squandered his inheritance for the pleasures of the world. When he realized his mistake, he returned home willing to be a servant under his father's care and protection.

When we accept Yahshua and become Abraham's seed, we become sons and daughters of Yahweh and heirs to the promises He made to Abraham. If we dwell with Him in the secret place, we have the privilege of all the care and protection of a loving Father. Still, like the prodigal son, we often run away to the world in search of freedom and acceptance. For a time we may enjoy the pleasures of the world, but ultimately we lose Yahweh's covering and protection. People still think that they can somehow make it on their own or that the ways of the world are more desireable. In many cases, they believe they can hide themselves during the times of trouble that are coming and don't need to walk toward the Holy Place of Yahweh. The truth is man can only hide from man, never from Yahweh or His judgment on this world. Adam tried to hide from Yahweh in the Garden of Eden, but it was no use. We also see this in the story of Jonah, who thought he could run and hide from Yahweh, but Yahweh was with Him even in his running.

> But Jonah rose up to flee to Tarshish from the presence of Yahweh. He went down to Joppa, and found a ship going to Tarshish; so he paid its fare, and went down into it, to go with them to Tarshish from the presence of Yahweh. Jonah 1:3

From the beginning of time until the end, the safest place in all the world is in the will and presence of Yahweh.

Can any hide himself in secret places so that I shall not see him? says Yahweh. Don't I fill heaven and earth? says Yahweh. Jer.23:24

The kings of the earth, the princes, the commanding officers, the rich, the strong, and every slave and free person, hid themselves in the caves and in the rocks of the mountains. They told the mountains and the rocks, "Fall on us, and hide us from the face of him who sits on the throne, and from the wrath of the Lamb, for the great day of his wrath has come; and who is able to stand?" Rev.6: 15-17

The pattern of life is real and cannot be avoided! In Yahweh's timing, it will play out as the end draws near. Darkness will cover the earth before the manifestation of life and restoration, just as we saw foreshadowed when Yahweh rescued His people from Egypt. Yahweh exposed His greatness and power to Pharaoh and his empire by bringing forth His plagues, to reveal to them W*ho* it was that had come to rescue the Hebrew people from Pharaoh's grip, and take them back to Himself. With the ninth plague, Yahweh put the pattern of life in motion and horrible darkness covered the land; darkness so thick you could feel it. True to Yahweh's pattern those who knew Yahweh had His light within the darkness.

They didn't see one another, neither did anyone rise from his place for three days; but all the children of Israel had light in their dwellings. Ex.10:23

Throughout history this pattern remains. We can choose to be in Covenant with the King and covered by His mighty hand of protection or exposed to the consequences. Those who refuse the terms of Yahweh's Covenant suffer loss and are unprotected. This reality may not seem relevant while things are going along seemingly smooth from day to day, but when trouble comes, the consequences will also come and then it will be too late. Psalm 91 brings this truth to life!

He who dwells in the secret place of the Most High
will rest in the shadow of the Almighty.

I will say of Yahweh, "He is my refuge and my fortress;
my God, in whom I trust."
For he will deliver you from the snare of the fowler,
and from the deadly pestilence.
He will cover you with his feathers.
Under his wings you will take refuge.
His faithfulness is your shield and rampart.
You shall not be afraid of the terror by night,
nor of the arrow that flies by day;
nor of the pestilence that walks in darkness,
nor of the destruction that wastes at noonday.
A thousand may fall at your side,
and ten thousand at your right hand;
but it will not come near you.
You will only look with your eyes,
and see the recompense of the wicked.
Because you have made Yahweh your refuge,
and the Most High your dwelling place,
no evil shall happen to you,
neither shall any plague come near your dwelling. Ps.91:1-10

How beautifully this Psalm reveals the truth about Yahweh's pattern of life. Notice that it speaks to us of the way it was in Egypt for those who listened to Yahweh, "no plague will come near your dwelling." Each year at Passover we remember this awesome truth. Passover is designed to remind us of Yahweh's Covenant and give us sure footing for the year's cycle that lies ahead. When we hear or shema Yahweh's voice and obey His Covenant terms revealed in Passover, we begin our yearly walk under Yahweh's protection. If we refuse ... the consequences can be fatal. Yahweh's pattern could not be more crucial than it is now in these last days. Jeremiah tells us that one day there will be another great rescue mission.

Therefore behold, the days come, says Yahweh, that it shall no
more be said, As Yahweh lives, who brought up the children
of Israel out of the land of Egypt; but, As Yahweh lives, who
brought up the children of Israel from the land of the north,
and from all the countries where he had driven them. I will

bring them again into their land that I gave to their fathers.
Jer. 16:14,15

It is not uncommon in this generation for people to speak of the days
we live in as 'the last days.' I believe that the signs we are seeing confirm
that we truly are in the final chapters and verses of Yahweh's great Love
Story. How long will it take for the last days to unfold in their fullness
remains to be seen, but we must not lose our anticipation or hope. Often
our hopes are dashed if our expectations of how things should go do not
come to pass. Yet, more than knowing which day or year the Messiah will
return, we need to focus on our heart's condition, our daily walk and how
to be a light to the world. It is our responsibility to keep Yahweh's cycles
alive and prayerfully watch.

He said to them, "It isn't for you to know times or seasons
which the Father has set within his own authority. But you will
receive power when the Holy Spirit has come upon you. You
will be witnesses to me in Jerusalem, in all Judea and Samaria,
and to the uttermost parts of the earth."Acts 1:7,8

Yahshua is exhorting us in the above verse to be ready to receive the
power of the Holy Spirit into our lives so that we will be His children
of light and witnesses of who He is. As we walk out His Word in Spirit
and Truth, our lives will proclaim *WHO* the one true God or Elohim is.
Yahshua is coming to take His bride home at the appointed time. A time
designed within Yahweh's story before the foundations of the Earth were
set in place. His story's ending will parallel the pattern of life seen in the
heavens, the Exodus and as revealed throughout Revelation. That is why
it is so important to understand Yahweh's pattern, watch the heavens and
learn from those who went before us as examples.

Now I would not have you ignorant, brothers, that our fathers
were all under the cloud, and all passed through the sea; and
were all baptized into Moses in the cloud and in the sea; and
all ate the same spiritual food; and all drank the same spiritual
drink. For they drank of a spiritual rock that followed them,
and the rock was Christ. However with most of them, God was

not well pleased, for they were overthrown in the wilderness. Now these things were our examples, to the intent we should not lust after evil things, as they also lusted. Don't be idolaters, as some of them were. As it is written, "The people sat down to eat and drink, and rose up to play." Let us not commit sexual immorality, as some of them committed, and in one day twenty-three thousand fell. Let us not test Christ,as some of them tested, and perished by the serpents. Don't grumble, as some of them also grumbled, and perished by the destroyer. Now all these things happened to them by way of example, and they were written for our admonition, on whom the ends of the ages have come. Therefore let him who thinks he stands be careful that he doesn't fall. 1 Cor.10:1-12

Paul's letter to the Corinthians is also a warning to Yahweh's people in these last days. May we never forget the examples of those who went before us and learn from their mistakes.

The Children of Israel were fearful, doubting and rebelled against Yahweh in the Wilderness. Sadly they suffered the consequences of their selfishness and lack of trust, and we are at risk of doing the same.

Yahweh's desire is to be in an everlasting Covenant with His people. When Yahweh rescued His people from Egypt and took them to a special place away from the world's eyes, it was to show them His design for life. This was Yahweh's set-apart time of betrothal or the giving of His Covenant to His treasured people.

All the people perceived the thunderings, the lightnings, the sound of the trumpet, and the mountain smoking. When the people saw it, they trembled, and stayed at a distance. They said to Moses, "Speak with us yourself, and we will listen; but don't let God speak with us, lest we die."

Moses said to the people, "Don't be afraid, for God has come to test you, and that his fear may be before you, that you won't sin." The people stayed at a distance, and Moses came near to the thick darkness where God was. Ex.20:18-21

Yahweh's presence came down upon Mount Sinai, in a covering of thick darkness. In fact, the description of Yahweh's presence resembles that of an intense storm. A shofar cries out, lightening flashes, thunder rolls, and a dark cloud covers the mountain. The response of the people was fear ... the wrong kind of fear! The fear most of the people felt kept them away from Yahweh's presence instead of drawing them closer to Him. Somehow the reality that Yahweh had rescued them with love was forgotten, for they feared Him as though they needed to preserve their own lives. They acted as though they we concerned for their own comforts more than desiring to face the One who had just saved them. In their fear, they chose to keep a "safe" distance from Him. What they didn't realize was that each time Yahweh spoke to them or brought before them a challenging situation it was designed to test their heart ... and they were failing.

Moses was different though. He saw all that was happening through Yahweh's love. He had a deep understanding of Yahweh's heart and he feared Him more than his own life or what anyone else thought. With loving fear, Moses desired to serve Yahweh unto death. When he heard Yahweh's voice call his name from within the dark cloud, he willingly climbed into the midst of the fierce storm to be with Him. This picture is so important for us to see! These two completely different perspectives of the same event are examples for us today! The people stood back from Yahweh in selfish fear, while Moses climbed the mountain directly toward Yahweh in loving fear. There Moses was enveloped in the awe of Yahweh's presence.

At the bottom of the mountain, the people were left to wait for Moses to return. It wasn't long before their impatience and imagination of what was happening took over. For Moses on the other hand, all time as we know it would have ceased and even become irrelevant in Yahweh's presence. Days would seem like fleeting moments as He sat before the King and listened to His Mighty Words. I wonder if it would be like Scripture declares; a thousand years feeling like a day in the presence of Yahweh. In stark contrast, it would have been the opposite for the people below! Time would have dragged on; a day like a thousand years or minutes seeming like hours, as they waited for Moses to return. In their impatience, they chose to make things more interesting. Taking things into their own hands, they decided to have a celebration and make something to remind them of Yahweh. Moses was, after all, taking such a long time to return and talk to them.

When the people saw that Moses delayed to come down from the mountain, the people gathered themselves together to Aaron, and said to him, "Come, make us gods, which shall go before us; for as for this Moses, the man who brought us up out of the land of Egypt, we don't know what has become of him."

All the people took off the golden rings which were in their ears, and brought them to Aaron. He received what they handed him, and fashioned it with an engraving tool, and made it a molten calf; and they said, "These are your gods, Israel, which brought you up out of the land of Egypt."

When Aaron saw this, he built an altar before it; and Aaron made a proclamation, and said, "Tomorrow shall be a feast to Yahweh."

They rose up early on the next day, and offered burnt offerings, and brought peace offerings; and the people sat down to eat and to drink, and rose up to play. Ex.32:1-6

If we are honest with ourselves, we will admit that there are times when we have had similar experiences. When things do not happen the way we hope or anticipate we often become lonely or bored in the waiting. Impatience grows quickly, and soon we are tempted to take things into our own hands to satisfy the crowd and ourselves. Louder and stronger opinions usually take precedence for the sake of peace, as we fill our lives with good ideas and the desires of people and their needs. From a worldly perspective, this is simply the way life goes. When it comes to peer pressure some may even call it survival, but from Yahweh's perspective, it is lack of trust. When this happens, we run the risk of drifting away from intimacy with Yahweh and miss the joy of waiting for His presence and seeing His miracles.

Abraham's wife, Sarah went through the same experience. Yahwch had given her and Abraham the promise of a child, but when the promise was delayed and became what seemed impossible in their minds, Sarah began to doubt. Her body was far beyond the natural age of child bearing, and she could not see beyond her physical reality. In Sarah's impatience and doubt she devised a practical way for Yahweh's promise to come to pass ... or we could say that she took things into her own hands.

Sarah approaches her maidservant Hagar and asks her to take her place with Abraham. Abraham agrees with her plan, and Hagar becomes pregnant with Ishmael. These are stirring and even frightening pictures of how our impatience can have life long affects! Choosing to not draw near to Yahweh and trust Him during the waiting, even when all seems impossible produces a selfish perspective. Sarah through her impatience initiated the bringing forth of Ishmael, who was a replacement for Isaac, Yahweh's promise. The people at the bottom of Mount Sinai, through their impatience, brought forth a golden calf (by Aaron's hand), which was a replacement for Yahweh. Even though they had all encountered Yahweh's power and judgment they still wanted His promises in their time, according to their own understanding, on their terms ... not His.

Be patient therefore, brothers, until the coming of the Lord. Behold, the farmer waits for the precious fruit of the earth, being patient over it, until it receives the early and late rain. You also be patient. Establish your hearts, for the coming of the Lord is at hand. James 5:7,8

Trust in Yahweh with all your heart, and don't lean on your own understanding.

In all your ways acknowledge him, and he will make your paths straight. Prov. 3:5,6

Here the difference in Moses' heart compared to the rest of the people is revealed, and we see why Yahweh chose to speak to him so intimately. He knew the power of Yahweh and could see the motivation of His heart. Moses chose to serve and worship Yahweh according to His terms alone. Consequently, the time Moses spent on the mountain with Yahweh was unlike anything anyone had ever experienced and in a place, no one dared to go.

> *Moses went up on the mountain, and the cloud covered the mountain. Yahweh's glory settled on Mount Sinai, and the cloud covered it six days. The seventh day he called to Moses out of the middle of the cloud. The appearance of Yahweh's glory was like devouring fire on the top of the mountain in the eyes of the children of Israel. Ex.24:15-17*

Yahweh's awesome presence came to them in a cloud, just as they had seen with the pillar of cloud that led them out of Egypt, and would later see in the cloud above the Tabernacle. In earlier chapters, we saw how the Torah is like the casting forth of rain. Yahweh designed the rain to come forth from a dark cloud cover that pours forth life to the earth. Likewise, when Moses was under the dark cloud covering of Yahweh's presence, the Torah was poured out to him like wonderful rain, designed to bring forth life. Yahweh is so awesome!! ... even a simple, rainy day declares His glory! Look at these lyrics from the song, Word of God Speak, by Mercy Me, with this picture in mind.

Word of God speak

Would you pour down like rain

Washing my eyes to see

Your majesty

To be still and know

That you're in this place

Please let me stay and rest

In your holiness

Word of God speak

Over and over, whether in Creation or Scripture, Yahweh's patterns hold true and align together to reveal the fingerprints of the One True Elohim!

For the invisible things of him since the creation of the world are clearly seen, being perceived through the things that are made, even his everlasting power and divinity; that they may be without excuse. Rom. 1:20

Yes, he loads the thick cloud with moisture.
He spreads abroad the cloud of his lightning.
It is turned around by his guidance,
that they may do whatever he commands them
on the surface of the habitable world,
Whether it is for correction, or for his land,
or for loving kindness, that he causes it to come.
"Listen to this, Job.
Stand still, and consider the wondrous
works of God. Job 37:11-14

The date of Moses's remarkable encounter with Yahweh on the mountain is not recorded, but the way it played out gives us the pattern of one week including the Sabbath day. Moses dwelt on the cloud-covered mountain six days listening to Yahweh's voice, and then on the seventh day, something amazing happened ... Yahweh invited Moses to come even higher into the center of the cloud and directly into His presence. Moses' ascent was on the seventh day or Sabbath ... no other day! Remember too, that Yahweh is a consuming fire, and the people below could see His fire, but they could not see Moses; for he was hidden within Yahweh's covering and enveloped in His light. We find the same picture during the New Moon at conjunction and in the wonder and majesty of the secret place.

Have you ever thought of how little Moses would have talked during this time or thought of himself? Truly this was Yahweh's time ... set apart with the one person He trusted to share the things of His heart. Moses did not question, complain or need to add to the conversation. One might say that Moses didn't 'add or take away' from any of the Words that Yahweh was speaking. He didn't give Yahweh a list of his plans or ideas for the future. Instead with reverence Moses chose to be still and listen or shema to all Yahweh spoke to him.

"Be still, and know that I am God. I will be exalted among the nations. I will be exalted in the earth." Ps.46:10

I'm sure there are no words to describe the awesome experience Moses had with the King, listening to the pattern for His dwelling place with them, the order of how to serve Him, and how to live in His presence and show our love to Him and others. We have so much to learn from this, for it gives us pictures of what a Shabbat and a New Moon are to be like. Though we can pray and seek Yahweh at anytime during the six days, Yahweh has given us one day a week and one day a month, to sit at His feet and listen to the things of His heart.

It shall happen that from one new moon to another, and from one Sabbath to another, all flesh will come to worship before me," says Yahweh. Is. 66:23

How precious these times are meant to be for each of us, and how much they mean to Yahweh. If we will be still in the awesome presence of our King and listen (shema) to the things of His heart, the things of this world will no longer be what we hunger for. As the familiar hymn, by Helen Lemmel, says;

Turn your eyes upon Jesus,
Look full in His wonderful face,
And the things of earth will grow strangely dim,
In the light of His glory and grace.

The alternative, of course, is displayed in the people who chose to stay at the bottom of the mountain. Their refusal to listen to Yahweh kept them from experiencing the great joy of knowing His loving heart. They longed for worldly things that appeased their hunger and desired the comforts they were familiar with. Consequently, their thoughts quickly turned to all that they were used to in Egypt. The very things they had just been rescued from!

Yahweh spoke to Moses, "Go, get down; for your people, who you brought up out of the land of Egypt, have corrupted themselves! They have turned aside quickly out of the way which I commanded them. They have made themselves a molten calf, and have worshiped it, and have sacrificed to it, and said, 'These are your gods, Israel, which brought you up out of the land of Egypt.'" Ex. 32:7,8

When Yahweh heard the noise of their adulteress ways, He was so hurt and outraged that He considered wiping them off the face of the Earth right then and there. Moses then makes a phenomenal move to stand in the gap for both the people and for Yahweh. He begs Yahweh to reconsider. At that moment Moses foreshadowed Yahshua and the intercession that He brings before the throne on our behalf. For we are like the people at the bottom of the mountain and in great need of a Savior and intercessor.

Who could bring a charge against God's chosen ones? It is God who justifies. Who is he who condemns? It is Christ who died, yes rather, who was raised from the dead, who is at the right hand of God, who also makes intercession for us. Rom.8:33,34

Therefore he is also able to save to the uttermost those who draw near to God through him, seeing that he lives forever to make intercession for them. Heb. 7:25

We too, as those who are called to serve and dwell in the secret place carry the responsibility to align ourselves with our High Priest and Bridegroom and intercede for those who are going astray and do not know Yahweh.

Confess your offenses to one another, and pray for one another, that you may be healed. The insistent prayer of a righteous person is powerfully effective. James 5:16

Moses' relationship with Yahweh teaches us so much about Yahweh's heart and gives us a wonderful picture of how we are to receive the Torah into our lives. The first time Yahweh spoke to Moses, He gave Moses tablets of stone where He had written His Covenant Words or Commandments to His people. Before Moses had delivered the Words of Yahweh's heart to the people, they had created an image of Yahweh and started to worship Him their own way. Moses rushed down the mountain with the stone tablets in hand, but when he came to them, he was so filled with anger and grief, that he smashed the tablets of the Covenant Words. Moses then intercedes for them forty days and makes new tablets of stone to replace the ones he had broken. He takes the renewed tablets before Yahweh in worship and repentance, asking Him to rewrite the Words of His heart that He had written on the first set.

He chiseled two tablets of stone like the first; and Moses rose up early in the morning, and went up to Mount Sinai, as Yahweh had commanded him, and took in his hand two stone tablets. Yahweh descended in the cloud, and stood with him there, and proclaimed Yahweh's name. Yahweh passed by before him, and proclaimed, "Yahweh! Yahweh, a merciful and gracious God, slow to anger, and abundant in loving kindness and truth, keeping loving kindness for thousands, forgiving iniquity and disobedience and sin; and that will by no means clear the guilty, visiting the iniquity of the fathers on the children, and on the children's children, on the third and on the fourth generation."

Moses hurried and bowed his head toward the earth, and worshiped. He said, "If now I have found favor in your sight, Lord, please let the Lord go among us; although this is a stiff-necked people; pardon our iniquity and our sin, and take us for your inheritance." Ex.34:4-9

Yahweh's pattern of darkness first and then life is powerfully played out here. Moses rises early and takes empty tablets (symbolizing our hearts) into the darkness that covered the mountain and the glorious presence of the King of the Universe. There he worships in Yahweh's presence as

Yahweh declares to Moses Who He is, reaffirming His Name and then graciously restoring the Words of the Covenant and instructions for life on the new tablets. This amazing picture of true restoration is Yahweh's desire for all of us today.

> But this is the covenant that I will make with the house of Israel after those days, says the Lord: I will put My law in their minds, and write it on their hearts; and I will be their God, and they shall be My people. Jer. 31:33

Having Yahweh's Covenant words written on our hearts just as they were written on the tablets of stone is our point of renewal and rebirth. Our hearts cannot be filled with our own desires, dreams or even the best of other teacher's words. We must have clean hearts to receive the Word of Yahweh alone.

> Who may ascend to Yahweh's hill?
> Who may stand in his holy place?
> He who has clean hands and a pure heart;
> who has not lifted up his soul to falsehood,
> and has not sworn deceitfully.
> He shall receive a blessing from Yahweh,
> righteousness from the God of his salvation.
> This is the generation of those who seek Him,
> who seek your face—even Jacob. Ps.24: 3-6

Yahweh's pattern of covering and life comes to us during our intimate times with Him. Who may ascend to Yahweh's hill? Those who have cleansed their hearts and hands and desire His Covenant Words to be written on their hearts in the secret place of darkness.

> He made darkness his hiding place, his pavilion around him, darkness of waters, thick clouds of the skies. Ps. 18:11

> I will give you the treasures of darkness
> And hidden riches of secret places,
> That you may know that I, the Lord, Who
> call you by your name,

Remember, this moving picture plays out for us in the heavens each month at the New Moon, when the Moon returns to the all-consuming light of the Sun at conjunction. Moses, like the Moon, was hidden beneath a dark cloud on the mountain, in the glory of Yahweh's light. Each month at conjunction, Yahweh's set apart people or bride are also called to the secret place, hidden with Yahshua in His glorious light where we see Him for Who He truly is! As we bow before Him in worship and allow His presence to renew us ... the results are phenomenal! Let's look again at this amazing time Moses had with Yahweh and the breathtaking consequences!

When Moses came down from Mount Sinai with the two tablets of the testimony in Moses' hand, when he came down from the mountain, Moses didn't know that the skin of his face shone by reason of his speaking with him. When Aaron and all the children of Israel saw Moses, behold, the skin of his face shone; and they were afraid to come near him. Ex 34:29,30

Can you see that Moses' time with Yahweh is a picture of the glory that the heavens are declaring? When Moses returned from being in Yahweh's presence on the mountain his face shone like the Sun, and He carried in his hands the renewed Covenant or the Brit Chadashah written on renewed tablets. I am convinced that this awesome picture is revealing Yahweh's heart for us on the New Moon. Each month we are to be hidden away in His presence just as the Moon is hidden in the presence of the Sun. While in His presence, we repent of our ways and give thanks to our King for His ways; dying to ourselves and becoming renewed in His glorious presence. As we worship Him in Spirit and Truth and listen to the desires of His heart, we will be refreshed, renewed and ready to face the month that lies ahead, reflecting His light to a dark world.

Even so, let your light shine before men; that they may see your good works, and glorify your Father who is in heaven. Matt.5:16

Then the righteous will shine like the sun in the Kingdom of their Father. He who has ears to hear, let him hear. Matt.13:43

For we don't preach ourselves, but Christ Jesus as Lord, and ourselves as your servants for Jesus' sake; seeing it is God who said, "Light will shine out of darkness," who has shone in our hearts, to give the light of the knowledge of the glory of God in the face of Jesus Christ. 2 Cor.4:5,6

The time that Moses spent in the presence of the King of the Universe is also a picture of the High Priest's duty before the Ark of the Covenant. Now we too have been called to follow Yahshua and serve Yahweh as a royal priesthood. Our key to understanding the secret place is found here, for by the work of Yahshua's shed blood we are cleansed and covered, which gives us access to the presence of our King. What a great and fearful privilege! The Tabernacle was Yahweh's dwelling place on Earth, patterned after the Tabernacle in the heavens and designed for the presence of our almighty King.

I rejoice at Your word
As one who finds great treasure. Ps.119:162

The overhanging part that remains of the curtains of the tent, the half curtain that remains, shall hang over the back of the tabernacle. The cubit on the one side, and the cubit on the other side, of that which remains in the length of the curtains of the tent, shall hang over the sides of the tabernacle on this side and on that side, to cover it. Ex.26:12,13

In the above verse, the word translated as cover is keseh, the same word used for New Moon in Psalm 81. All that was in the Tabernacle, including the secret place, was covered or concealed from the eyes of the world. As Yahshua's bride, this is our hope and our longing, to dwell with Yahweh in His Tabernacle forever.

Surely goodness and loving kindness shall
follow me all the days of my life,
and I will dwell in Yahweh's house forever. Ps.23: 6

For we know that if the earthly house of our tent is dissolved, we have a building from God, a house not made with hands, eternal, in the heavens. 2 Cor.5:1

The New Moon is our rehearsal for dwelling in the secret place with our King, now and in the future when His Kingdom is restored.

You shall hide them in the secret place of Your presence
From the plots of man;
You shall keep them secretly in a pavilion
From the strife of tongues. Ps.31:20

The word translated as pavilion in the above verse is Strong's #H5521, sukkah, which means tent or tabernacle. In our journey through Yahweh's cycles and appointed days, this picture will culminate when the final feast days, which is Tabernacles or Sukkot (plural for sukkah) is fulfilled. The feast of Tabernacles is our rehearsal for the time when we will dwell with Yahshua forever. When the fullness of time has come, and Yahshua returns, dwelling in Yahweh's sukkah or Tabernacle (that we saw revealed in Sarah's tent) will be the reward for those who are counted worthy to live and reign with Him forever.

All the angels were standing around the throne, the elders, and the four living creatures; and they fell on their faces before his throne, and worshiped God, saying, "Amen! Blessing, glory, wisdom, thanksgiving, honor, power, and might, be to our God forever and ever! Amen."

One of the elders answered, saying to me, "These who are arrayed in white robes, who are they, and from where did they come?"

I told him, "My lord, you know."

He said to me, "These are those who came out of the great tribulation. They washed their robes, and made them white in the Lamb's blood. Therefore they are before the throne of God, they serve him day and night in his temple. He who sits on the throne will spread his tabernacle over them. Rev.7:11-15

Over and over, whether in Creation or Scripture, Yahweh's patterns hold true. May Yahweh give us ears to hear what the Spirit is revealing to us in these last days and hearts that are willing to follow Yahshua. May we accept the discipline of our loving, heavenly Father so that we will become worthy of the royal priesthood and found dwelling in the secret place at the appointed time of Yahshua's return!

His Glorious Coming

WHAT DO YOU THINK THE PHRASE, *the Day of the Lord*, MEANS TO THE average person alive today? Does it stir up joy and anticipation, or fear and dread? Is it a reason for scoffing and doubt, or serious soul searching? There are many people who have never given the Day of the Lord any thought at all or even heard of it. Those who claim to follow Yahshua often sing of it and speak of it, yet how does 'the Day of the Lord' affect our daily lives?

> *The great day of Yahweh is near. It is near, and hurries greatly, the voice of the day of Yahweh. The mighty man cries there bitterly. That day is a day of wrath, a day of distress and anguish, a day of trouble and ruin, a day of darkness and gloom, a day of clouds and blackness, a day of the trumpet and alarm, against the fortified cities, and against the high battlements. Zeph.1:14-16*

Generations have come and gone throughout the courses of time and with them many speculations about the return of the Messiah. As seasons turn and years pass, so do the many signs in the heavens, bringing awe and wonder to all who witness them. Still, once the signs pass, their message fades away with the cares of life. People return to their busy schedules, and the skeptics laugh at the excitement that the signs brought, especially during these last days.

> *This is now, beloved, the second letter that I have written to you; and in both of them I stir up your sincere mind by reminding you; that you should remember the words which were spoken before by the holy prophets, and the commandments of us, the apostles of the Lord and Savior: knowing this first, that in the last days mockers will come, walking after their own lusts, and saying, "Where is the promise of his coming? For, from the day that the fathers fell asleep, all things continue as they were from the beginning of the creation." For this they willfully forget, that there were heavens from of old, and an earth formed out of water and amid water, by the word of God; by which means the world that then was, being overflowed with water, perished. But the heavens that now are, and the earth, by the same word have been stored up for fire, being reserved against the day of judgment and destruction of ungodly men. 2 Peter 3:1-7*

The above verses are warning us about promise, for when Yahweh promises something…it will happen. The problem lies with our sense of timing, interpretation, and response to what Yahweh is doing. As we read this and other warnings in Yahweh's Word about His return, each of us will experience a different response depending on our heart's condition and our relationship with Yahweh. One common response is, 'No matter what happens; God knows my heart.' As we discussed earlier, Yahweh's foremost concern is our heart, and He knows our hearts very well. With fear and trembling we can be assured of Yahweh's omnipotent, omnipresent and omniscient power and in the end, everything will be judged by our heart's condition, for out of our hearts flows all matters of life.

> *Yahweh, you have searched me,*
> *and you know me.*
> *You know my sitting down and my rising up.*
> *You perceive my thoughts from afar.*
> *You search out my path and my lying down,*

and are acquainted with all my ways.
For there is not a word on my tongue,
but, behold, Yahweh, you know it altogether. Ps.139:2-4

Keep your heart with all diligence,
for out of it is the wellspring of life. Prov. 4:23

How we live and what we do shapes our thoughts, which in turn affects our hearts. We are all creatures of patterns and habits, no matter where we live or what our social status is. Patterns as we have seen can be very good; helping us to stay on Yahweh's path of righteousness, but most of man's patterns are not so good. Many of the patterns and habits we have developed over time, we are not even aware of because they simply are a part of daily life, especially our thought patterns. Have you ever rearranged something in your home, only to return to where it was over and over before you break the pattern of looking for it in the place it was originally? Every moment of every day is filled with our preset, expectations and responses. Each of them then affects us emotionally and physically, shaping our heart and mind daily. Our thought patterns are especially powerful because what we think about others and ourselves is manifested in our words, actions and life choices. As we have seen, if we spend time with people who speak negative words or gossip, we have to consciously fight against those words, so that we don't develop negative thoughts. When we think negatively or with fear, it becomes the pattern that we view the world and those around us. Thankfully this is also true for the positive and why Scripture tells us to edify one another.

Let no corrupt speech proceed out of your mouth, but such as is good for building up as the need may be, that it may give grace to those who hear. Eph.4:29

A gentle tongue is a tree of life, but deceit in it crushes the spirit. Prov. 15:4

The truth behind this is found in the way Yahweh designed us from the very beginning. Our brains are designed with cells that scientists call, 'mirror neurons.' These intriguing little cells were designed to affect us by our environment. Below is a quote from Psychology today:

Buried deep inside your skull are special brain cells that read the minds of others and know their intentions.

Dubbed mirror neurons, these cells fire in response to the "reflection" of another person. Whether you lift your coffee cup or watch your coworker lift his, the neurons respond to both actions as if they were the same. Neuroscientists believe these cells are what allow humans— and some primates—to feel empathy and compassion for others.

It is interesting to note that these mirror neurons respond to the reflection of another. Can you see why it is so important for those who believe in Yahshua to follow Him, pattern themselves after Him and reflect His Light? If we don't, we may find that we are reflecting a light, through our words and patterns that is of the world. As followers of the Messiah, we must be careful as Scripture says, to keep good company and be a good example for others to follow, especially if you are an elder on any level.

> Don't be deceived! "Evil companionships corrupt good morals." 1 Cor.15:33

> Don't befriend a hot-tempered man, and don't associate with one who harbors anger: lest you learn his ways, and ensnare your soul. Prov.22:24,25

> Have no fellowship with the unfruitful works of darkness, but rather even reprove them. Eph.5:11

> Now we command you, brothers, in the name of our Lord Jesus Christ, that you withdraw yourselves from every brother who walks in rebellion, and not after the tradition which they received from us. 1Thess.3:6

If we spend time in the company of the enemy's darkness, we risk being like that darkness. This amazing reality confirms the pictures we have seen of us being reflectors of light, like the Moon. As we follow Yahshua and apply His Word to our lives, spending time with like-minded friends in who also love Yahshua, we become mirrors of our Master and only source of light. The way Yahweh created us reveals the reason it is so vitally important to know Yahweh and seek His light alone. Like the Moon, we are meant to reflect His light to those around us, so that they will have the light of the true Messiah in their lives.

This I say therefore, and testify in the Lord, that you no longer walk as the rest of the Gentiles also walk, in the futility of their mind, being darkened in their understanding, alienated from the life of God, because of the ignorance that is in them, because of the hardening of their hearts; who having become callous gave themselves up to lust, to work all uncleanness with greediness. But you did not learn Christ that way; if indeed you heard him, and were taught in him, even as truth is in Jesus: that you put away, as concerning your former way of life, the old man, that grows corrupt after the lusts of deceit; and that you be renewed in the spirit of your mind, and put on the new man, who in the likeness of God has been created in righteousness and holiness of truth. Eph.4:17-24

As Yahshua's return draws near the enemy is working at an accelerated rate to draw people away from the truth. What is being declared as truth is often a twisted lie, and we must be so careful not to get caught or snared by it.

The wicked have laid a snare for me,
yet I haven't gone astray from your precepts. Ps.119:110

Scripture tells us that the day of Yahweh will come suddenly while people are wrapped up in life and savoring the ways of the world, just as it was in the days of Noah.

"As the days of Noah were, so will be the coming of the Son of Man. For as in those days which were before the flood they were eating and drinking, marrying and giving in marriage, until the day that Noah entered into the ship, and they didn't

know until the flood came, and took them all away, so will be
the coming of the Son of Man" Matt.24: 37-39

I think it is safe to say that Noah was not a popular guy. He had been called by Yahweh to endure preparing for a disaster that was decades away. In the face of ridicule and scoffing, he believed Yahweh with all his heart and chose to obey His voice alone.

> *I am a reproach among all my enemies,*
> *But especially among my neighbors,*
> *And am repulsive to my acquaintances;*
> *Those who see me outside flee from me.*
> *I am forgotten like a dead man, out of mind;*
> *I am like a broken vessel.*
> *For I hear the slander of many;*
> *Fear is on every side;*
> *While they take counsel together against me,*
> *They scheme to take away my life.*
> *But as for me, I trust in You, O Lord;*
> *I say, "You are my God."*
> *My times are in Your hand;*
> *Deliver me from the hand of my enemies,*
> *And from those who persecute me.*
> *Make Your face shine upon Your servant;*
> *Save me for Your mercies' sake. Ps.31:11-16 (NKJ)*

How difficult it must have been for Noah and his family to give their lives to something that no one believed was possible. Still Noah's heart remained fixed on obeying the words that Yahweh had spoken to him ... no matter how men scorned him.

> *Let your eyes look straight ahead. Fix*
> *your gaze directly before you.*
> *Make the path of your feet level. Let all*
> *of your ways be established.*
> *Don't turn to the right hand nor to the*
> *left. Remove your foot from evil.*
> *Prov.4:25-27*

Finally, brethren, whatever things are true, whatever things are noble, whatever things are just, whatever things are pure, whatever things are lovely, whatever things are of good report, if there is any virtue and if there is anything praiseworthy— meditate on these things. Phil.4:8

Our hearts must also be separated from man's ways even when people turn against us. Yahshua rebuked the Pharisees for living their lives according to the traditions and habits of men.

He said to them, "You are those who justify yourselves in the sight of men, but God knows your hearts. For that which is exalted among men is an abomination in the sight of God." Luke 16:15

If we wholeheartedly believe that the time of Yahshua's return is drawing near, then we are faced with a heart response that reflects our belief and manifests itself in our words and actions, just as it did with Noah. Wrong behavior is embraced and tolerated in today's culture, while a vast array of personal opinions and beliefs impact our lives daily. Now the words Yahshua, spoken two thousand years ago grow more relevant to us than ever before.

"Behold, I come quickly. Blessed is he who keeps the words of the prophecy of this book." Rev.22:7

'Behold, I come quickly,' is a statement that Yahshua spoke to convey an urgency of time. Does it seem that people are conducting themselves as though the Messiah's return is quickly approaching? More and more our minds are filled with what the media entices us with; like the next movie, the next phone, car, etc.

You are probably familiar with the 'frog in the pot' analogy. The picture is that of a frog being placed in a pot of cold water, which the frog is obviously used to and so he is content to stay. Everything is fine until the temperature under the pot is gradually increased while the frog happily swims around. Because the change in the water's temperature is so slow and subtle the frog adjusts to it without noticing the change. Sadly, the frog that was once *only* content with cold water, naively adjusts to the warming water. Instead of trying to escape the pot, the frog happily swims around in the heating water until it's hot enough to cook him to death.

Scripture refers to this as 'falling asleep.' If we are honest, we will agree that this is exactly what is happening to people in our world today, and the 'frog in the pot' scenario is not only playing out in the secular world but in the spiritual world as well. What used to be considered unacceptable has slowly crept into our lives to become accepted and often embraced. The mainstream religions claim salvation through Yahshua or Jesus's death on the cross, but 'little by little' they have walked away from Yahweh's Covenant and let the world's ways and the traditions of man rule their lives. The water is heating up, and they don't see that they are embracing sinful activity under a false banner of love and acceptance.

Many others who can see the dangers of what is happening to our morals and our walk have left the mainstream religions to seek Yahweh in truth. Some have found that separation from the religious institutions to be an incredible blessing filled with revelation and joy. For others though, their hunger for truth has led them down a path of seeking knowledge above all else. Yes, it is true that without knowledge we will perish, but there is a danger of seeking knowledge to the point of stripping Yahweh's Word apart. Then like a frog, not in a pot but a science lab, they dissect Yahweh's Word over and over until the original message is lost. They forget that Yahweh's Word was spoken from His heart for life and for beauty, and the very purpose for which He wrote His Word is lost or distorted. Here is a quote that explains this process.

"Explaining a joke is like dissecting a frog. You understand it better but the frog dies in the process." E.B. White

I am not speaking of a joke, but if we carefully dissect Yahweh's Word in an attempt to over explain it and answer every question we can think of, we risk killing the wonder, beauty, and life that it was designed to bring.

For the time is coming when people will not endure sound teaching, but having itching ears they will accumulate for themselves teachers to suit their own passions, and will turn away from listening to the truth and wander off into myths. 2 Tim.4:3 (ESV)

May we never loose sight of our goal, which is to know Yahweh and to trust Him when we don't understand. Our searching must be balanced, always seeing Him as the Potter and ourselves as the clay. Clay was never meant to question the Potter, especially not to the point of walking away from Him.

You turn things upside down! Should the potter be thought to be like clay; that the thing made should say about him who made it, "He didn't make me;" or the thing formed say of him who formed it, "He has no understanding?" Is.29:16

"Woe to those who quarrel with their Maker, those who are nothing but potsherds among the potsherds on the ground. Does the clay say to the potter, 'What are you making?' Does your work say, 'The potter has no hands'? Is.45:9

But indeed, O man, who are you to reply against God? Will the thing formed ask him who formed it, "Why did you make me like this?" Rom. 9:20

If we over analyze everything, we will eventually remove the life out of it; sometimes even turning people away from the truth rather than drawing them closer. People are becoming weary with the literal smorgasbord of beliefs, gatherings, and institutions that all claim to follow the one true God, while ignoring the cares and needs of those around them.

…making void the word of God by your tradition, which you have handed down. You do many things like this." Mark 7:13

For those who are on the outside looking in, the hypocrisy they see and experience can be very disheartening. Where is forgiveness, repentance, honor and love? I pray that Yahweh will wake us from our slumber to see that the water is getting hot. No matter where you are in your walk with

Yahshua, it is time to shake off the indifference and hear the voice of the Holy Spirit calling out to warn us!

But all things, when they are reproved, are revealed by the light, for everything that reveals is light. Therefore he says, "Awake, you who sleep, and arise from the dead, and Christ will shine on you." Eph.5:13,1

Notice that the verse above proclaims the pattern of life. After we rise from the dead, that is death to ourselves and the ways of man, then Yahshua shines on us. The Moon's faithful role is to remind us of our new life in Yahshua, reflecting His light; a light that is rooted in truth and motivated by love.

A new commandment I give to you, that you love one another. Just as I have loved you, you also love one another. By this everyone will know that you are my disciples, if you have love for one another." John 13:34,35

So then, my beloved, even as you have always obeyed, not only in my presence, but now much more in my absence, work out your own salvation with fear and trembling. For it is God who works in you both to will and to work, for his good pleasure. Do all things without murmurings and disputes, that you may become blameless and harmless, children of God without defect in the middle of a crooked and perverse generation, among whom you are seen as lights in the world, holding up the word of life; that I may have something to boast in the day of Christ, that I didn't run in vain nor labor in vain. Phil.2:12-16

The *'KING OF THE UNIVERSE'* is returning on a New Moon of the seventh Hebrew month for a bride who is anxiously waiting and watching for Him. A bride that has no spot or wrinkle from the world, but has been washed in His Word and reflects her Bridegroom's love, power, and majesty to all those around her. Her light will bring the reality of who He is and His soon return.

Husbands, love your wives, even as Christ also loved the assembly, and gave himself up for it; that he might sanctify it, having cleansed it by the washing of water with the word, that he might present the assembly to himself gloriously, not having spot or wrinkle or any such thing; but that it should be holy and without blemish. Eph.5:25-27

The anticipation we have for our Bridegroom's return will ultimately be revealed in the way we live our lives. How do we love Yahweh and others in our words and actions, each and every day?

For the grace of God has appeared, bringing salvation to all men, instructing us to the intent that, denying ungodliness and worldly lusts, we would live soberly, righteously, and godly in this present world; looking for the blessed hope and appearing of the glory of our great God and Savior, Jesus Christ; who gave himself for us, that he might redeem us from all iniquity, and purify for himself a people for his own possession, zealous for good works. Titus 2:11-14

Notice that we are redeemed from all iniquity and purified so that we will be a people, zealous for good works. If we live each day with the thought of Yahshua's return at the forefront of our mind, we will touch many lives. Unfortunately, Yahshua's return is often portrayed as a random moment in the distant future; a moment in time that no one can foresee or anticipate. Often misunderstanding comes from the following verse.

But no one knows of that day and hour, not even the angels of heaven, but my Father only. Matt.24: 36

If no one can know the day and hour … then why try? Right? Imagine if someone you loved very much was away from you for many years. To comfort you, they send you a message telling you that they will come in the fall, at the time of the trumpet's call, but they couldn't reveal the exact, year, day or hour they would arrive. What would your response be? If you truly loved them, would you stop watching or waiting? No, you would not. As in every true love story, a betrothed bride or bridegroom would never stop hoping that this was the year that they would finally see their beloved's face again.

Our faithful anticipation of our Beloved's return is revealed when we rehearse that great day. The mainstream religions that have left Yahweh's commandments and appointed days for the ways of the world, have removed the timing and rehearsals for Yahshua's return from their lives altogether. When we remove His patterns, signs and seasons from our lives, it is like removing the loving instructions of a Father who wants to guide His children safely home. Without them, we loose our way of hope and anticipation, while placing emphasis on *this* life's joy more than the joy of the eternal life that is to come. If we see Yahweh's story as His great Masterpiece with patterns, signs and seasons embedded in all of His Creation, to learn from and walk in, it changes everything! Instead of not knowing the times or season, we have before us the map and guide we need to discern them.

> But he answered them, "When it is evening, you say, 'It will be fair weather, for the sky is red.' In the morning, 'It will be foul weather today, for the sky is red and threatening.' Hypocrites! You know how to discern the appearance of the sky, but you can't discern the signs of the times! Matt.16:2,3

When someone says that we cannot know the day or the hour as a reason to not be concerned about Yahshua's return, they are missing the bigger picture and isolating Scripture to suit their own comforts. When Yahshua said, 'no one knows the day or hour,' He was lovingly giving His bride a clue to the very season He would return. The phrase "no one knows the day or the hour" is an idiom used when referring to the only feast day that falls on a New Moon, which is Yom Teruah or the Feast of Trumpets.

> But concerning the times and the seasons, brethren, you have no need that I should write to you. For you yourselves know perfectly that the day of the Lord so comes as a thief in the night. For when they say, "Peace and safety!" then sudden destruction comes upon them, as labor pains upon a pregnant woman. And they shall not escape. But you, brethren, are not

in darkness, so that this Day should overtake you as a thief. You are all sons of light and sons of the day. We are not of the night nor of darkness. Therefore let us not sleep, as others do, but let us watch and be sober. 1 Thess. 5:1-6

The great day of Yahweh ... the day when Yahshua will return as King is described over and over in Scripture as a terrible day. The 'Day of the Lord' stands alone in its severity and will be the climax that strikes after the crescendoing events of the tribulation.

> *"Woe to you who desire the day of Yahweh!*
> *Why do you long for the day of Yahweh?*
> *It is darkness, and not light. Amos 5:18*

But the day of the Lord will come as a thief in the night; in which the heavens will pass away with a great noise, and the elements will be dissolved with fervent heat, and the earth and the works that are in it will be burned up. 2 Pet. 3:10

These fearful words are beyond our imagining! Often we breeze over them because we cannot comprehend how devastating that day will be, but to ignore them is foolish. We must take them to heart just as Noah did. Yahweh is the Almighty, and soon He will bring righteous judgment upon the Earth for our every word and deed.

But according to your hardness and unrepentant heart you are treasuring up for yourself wrath in the day of wrath, revelation, and of the righteous judgment of God; who "will pay back to everyone according to their works:" to those who by patience in well-doing seek for glory, honor, and incorruptibility, eternal life; but to those who are self-seeking, and don't obey the truth, but obey unrighteousness, will be wrath and indignation, oppression and anguish, on every soul of man who does evil, to the Jew first, and also to the Greek.

But glory, honor, and peace go to every man who does good, to the Jew first, and also to the Greek. For there is no partiality with God. Romans 2:5-11

For those who love Yahweh and long to be with Him, this breathtaking reality demands a response. Nothing in all the world is more important than Yahshua's bride being ready for Him. The nations are stirring, violence is rising, and the earth is groaning. Yahshua said when He rose into heaven that He was going to prepare a place for us in His Father's house. If we desire to dwell with Him there, as His beloved bride, we need to return to the Father's ways, which are the ways of His kingdom and household.

> *"Don't let your heart be troubled. Believe in God. Believe also in me. In my Father's house are many homes. If it weren't so, I would have told you. I am going to prepare a place for you. If I go and prepare a place for you, I will come again, and will receive you to myself; that where I am, you may be there also. John 14:1-3*

> *So then you are no longer strangers and foreigners, but you are fellow citizens with the saints, and of the household of God, Eph.2:19*

> *For many walk, of whom I told you often, and now tell you even weeping, as the enemies of the cross of Christ, whose end is destruction, whose god is the belly, and whose glory is in their shame, who think about earthly things. For our citizenship is in heaven, from where we also wait for a Savior, the Lord Jesus Christ; who will change the body of our humiliation to be conformed to the body of his glory, according to the working by which he is able even to subject all things to himself. Phil.3:18-21*

What is this place that Yahshua is preparing for us? It is the place, where we will be citizens not of Earth, but of heaven! ... a place unlike any earthly mansion. As we saw pictured when Isaac took Rebekah into Sarah's tent, Yahshua is preparing our eternal home ... the New Jerusalem! Those who endure and overcome to the end will have the privilege of being taken there to serve Yahweh and reign with Him.

Jesus said to them, "Most certainly I tell you that you who have followed me, in the regeneration when the Son of Man will sit on the throne of his glory, you also will sit on twelve thrones, judging the twelve tribes of Israel. Matt. 19:28

Nevertheless, hold that which you have firmly until I come. He who overcomes, and he who keeps my works to the end, to him I will give authority over the nations. He will rule them with a rod of iron, shattering them like clay pots; as I also have received of my Father: and I will give him the morning star. He who has an ear, let him hear what the Spirit says to the assemblies. Rev. 2:25–29

These ones will sit with Him in His Holy Temple just as Yahshua sits at the right hand of the Father now. When Yahweh's story reaches its finale, the things of this world will no longer be needed; all things will be made new and the New Jerusalem will descend upon the Earth as Revelation declares.

One of the seven angels who had the seven bowls, who were loaded with the seven last plagues came, and he spoke with me, saying, "Come here. I will show you the wife, the Lamb's bride." He carried me away in the Spirit to a great and high mountain, and showed me the holy city, Jerusalem, coming down out of heaven from God, having the glory of God. Rev.21: 9,10

Hallelujah! The same Tabernacle pattern that is displayed in the heavens and was given to Moses in the Wilderness, is the same pattern that will come down to Earth in unmatched glory.

For if that which passes away was with glory, much more that which remains is in glory. 2 Cor.3:11

Beloved, Yahweh's pattern is the reward that awaits us for all eternity. I cannot emphasis this enough because it is so important for those who desire to be His bride to understand.

We need to be lead by Yahweh's Spirit in preparation to become His spotless bride and royal priesthood. In the parable of the ten virgins, only five had truly prepared to be in the presence of their Bridegroom and King. Yahweh's appointed times are designed to teach us of our Bridegroom. They reveal so much of *Who* He is, and the timing of His soon return. They create in us heavenly patterns, instead of worldly patterns and develop in us a walk that is in His likeness. One day soon it will not be a potluck at someone's house or even a gathering at the western wall in Jerusalem that we will participate in. At His appointed time, the time He designed before the foundations of the Earth, the day of the Lord will arrive and our Messiah will shake this world with His presence. He will then walk us through every detail of what we have rehearsed and all that His appointed days foreshadow. His bride must prayerfully consider the consequences of her actions now, for what we choose and how we live today, will determine where we will be on the great day of Yahshua return!

The New Moon is our key to preparing for His return. The Moon moves faithfully through the night sky like a magnificent time piece setting all the other days of a Biblical month in order, but as we have seen in Yahweh's pattern it is so much more than simply a time piece. The New Moon gives us understanding of the bride hidden in the secret place on the great day of Yahweh's return. We will now look at Yahshua's glorious return through the perspective of the New Moon and Yom Teruah and how they compliment one another.

Yom Teruah

HERE WE ARRIVE AT YAHWEH'S HEIGHTENED MOMENT, THE CLIMAX AND reward of all that we have been looking at. Yom Teruah commences the concluding scenes of Yahweh's Love Story and grande finale. The day that Yahshua's bride has been longing for, and all Creation is groaning for. Yahweh's great day, when the trumpets resound and joyful shouts fill the air, the fulfillment of the New Moon will unfold into one breathtaking moment. Yom Teruah is the soon coming day when the true meaning of echad or oneness, found in the words and pictures we have seen within the New Moon will come into beautiful fruition as Yahshua gathers His bride to Himself.

> *Then he will send out his angels, and will gather together his chosen ones from the four winds, from the ends of the earth to the ends of the sky. Mark 13:27*

At this set apart time in Yahweh's masterful, love story many applications of two joining together as one, will be fulfilled. Just as the Sun and the Moon become one in the heavens revealing Yahweh's glory, so Yahshua, our Bridegroom will join together as one with His bride as He meets her in the heavens.

Behold, I tell you a mystery. We will not all sleep, but we will all be changed, in a moment, in the twinkling of an eye, at the last trumpet. For the trumpet will sound, and the dead will be raised incorruptible, and we will be changed. 1 Cor. 15:51,52

For the Lord himself will descend from heaven with a shout, with the voice of the archangel, and with God's trumpet. The dead in Christ will rise first, then we who are alive, who are left, will be caught up together with them in the clouds, to meet the Lord in the air. 1 Thess. 4:16,17

As we look at all the word pictures and meanings behind Yom Teruah, we will see that it is a day of double blessing and abundant joy for Yahweh's bride. I also believe that part of the double blessing that Jacob gave to Joseph's son Ephraim will be experienced on this day. When Yahweh told Abraham that his descendants would be like the stars of the heavens and the sand of the sea, He was speaking of the many who come into Covenant with Him through His Son Yahshua. The name Ephraim comes from Strong's # H669, which means double fruit or fruitfulness. Ephraim's fruitfulness will be made manifest through the firstborn blessing that Jacob prayed over him, who was the younger of Joseph's sons and not the older.

His father (Jacob) refused, and said, "I know, my son, I know. He also will become a people, and he also will be great. However, his younger brother (Ephraim) will be greater than he, and his offspring will become a multitude of nations." Gen.48:19

The phrase, 'a multitude of nations' in the above verse, is translated from the Hebrew 'melo ha goyim' which could also be translated as 'the fullness of the Gentiles.' The double portion blessing is the reward that comes to those of us across the world, who faithfully love Yahweh with all their heart and are being restored to the Covenant or grafted into the olive tree.

But if some of the branches were broken off, and you, being a wild olive, were grafted in among them, and became

*partaker with them of the root and of the richness of the olive
tree; Rom.11:7*

Yahweh's plan of salvation fulfills what was promised to Abraham and
spoken to the prophets. Ezekiel saw it in two groups of people revealed as
sticks in Yahweh's hand, one as Joseph revealed in Ephraim and the other
as Judah.

*Thus says the Lord Yahweh: Behold, I will take the stick of
Joseph, which is in the hand of Ephraim, and the tribes of
Israel his companions; and I will put them with it, with the
stick of Judah, and make them one stick, and they shall be one
in my hand. Ez.37:19*

*For I don't desire you to be ignorant, brothers, of this mystery,
so that you won't be wise in your own conceits, that a partial
hardening has happened to Israel, until the fullness of the
Gentiles has come in, Rom.11:25*

A double portion blessing is reserved for those who will follow Yahshua,
who was the firstfruits of many. Be aware though, that the blessing also
comes with a caution. We have no merit of our own, and there is only
ONE way to be joined to Yahweh, and that is through the shed blood
of Yahshua!

*But if you boast, it is not you who support the root, but the
root supports you. You will say then, "Branches were broken off,
that I might be grafted in." True; by their unbelief they were
broken off, and you stand by your faith. Don't be conceited,
but fear; for if God didn't spare the natural branches, neither
will he spare you. Rom.11:18-21*

As we saw earlier, the Moon is our reminder of the fear we are to have
before Yahweh. We have nothing of our own to offer, and without Him, we
can do nothing! Yahweh's two appointed days, the New Moon and Yom
Teruah come together each year to join as one and herald the coming of

the Messiah! Soon the world will stand in awe as the truth about Yahshua is revealed and all the wondering and mystery will finally be exposed.

> *The fear of the Lord is clean, enduring for ever: the judgments of the Lord are true and righteous altogether. More to be desired are they than gold, yea, than much fine gold: sweeter also than honey and the honeycomb. Moreover by them is thy servant warned: and in keeping of them there is great reward. Ps.19:9-11*

The name Yom Teruah found in Leviticus 23, comes from two Hebrew words; yom for day and teruah for blowing. Today, Yom Teruah is most commonly known as the Feast of Trumpets or Rosh Hashanah. The blowing of the shofar and much celebration is usually how Yom Teruah is observed. As we look deeper at the word teruah though, we find that there is an intensity to this day that cannot be overlooked. Teruah is Strong's #H8643, תרועה which means; an acclamation of joy or a battle cry; especially a clangor of trumpets. The root word for teruah, is Strong's, #7321 רעה, rua, which means; to mar, especially by breaking; to split the ears with sound, that is shout for alarm or joy. The contrast of the two meanings for teruah, joy and alarm, reveal that when the fulfillment of this day arrives it will be a terrifying a day for some and a joyous day for others.

> *The great day of Yahweh is near. It is near, and hurries greatly, the voice of the day of Yahweh. The mighty man cries there bitterly. That day is a day of wrath, a day of distress and anguish, a day of trouble and ruin, a day of darkness and gloom, a day of clouds and blackness, a day of the trumpet and alarm, against the fortified cities, and against the high battlements. Zeph.1:14-16*

> *For you yourselves know well that the day of the Lord comes like a thief in the night. For when they are saying, "Peace and safety," then sudden destruction will come on them, like birth pains on a pregnant woman; and they will in no way escape. 1Thess. 5:2,3*

All of the pictures of two becoming one and the two meanings behind the trumpet's call are beautifully displayed in the two Silver Trumpets that Yahweh commanded Moses to make.

> *Yahweh spoke to Moses, saying, "Make two trumpets of silver. You shall make them of beaten work. You shall use them for the calling of the congregation, and for the journeying of the camps. When they blow them, all the congregation shall gather themselves to you at the door of the Tent of Meeting. If they blow just one, then the princes, the heads of the thousands of Israel, shall gather themselves to you. When you blow an alarm, the camps that lie on the east side shall go forward. When you blow an alarm the second time, the camps that lie on the south side shall go forward. They shall blow an alarm for their journeys. But when the assembly is to be gathered together, you shall blow, but you shall not sound an alarm.*

> *"The sons of Aaron, the priests, shall blow the trumpets. This shall be to you for a statute forever throughout your generations. When you go to war in your land against the adversary who oppresses you, then you shall sound an alarm with the trumpets. Then you will be remembered before Yahweh your God, and you will be saved from your enemies.*

> *"Also in the day of your gladness, and in your set feasts, and in the beginnings of your months, you shall blow the trumpets over your burnt offerings, and over the sacrifices of your peace offerings; and they shall be to you for a memorial before your God. I am Yahweh your God." Num. 10:1-10*

These remarkable instruments were made of hammered silver, which speaks of the redemption price that our Bridegroom paid for His bride. Their hammered work is also a picture of the trials that come to those who faithfully take up their cross to follow Yahshua. Their voice was a signal and a declaration to the people of the camp. The people had the responsibility to know the difference in their sound so that they would know how to respond to their different calls. Though the voice of the Silver Trumpets resounding together cannot be heard today in the natural, the voice of those who are redeemed and walk as Yahweh's royal priesthood through the trials of life can be. Their voice like the cry of the trumpets is calling to the people to be ready for the return of the King and High Priest.

Below is an excerpt from Batya Wootten's article called Yom Teruah and the Two Silver Trumpets.

On the New Moon, and thus on Yom Teruah, Israel is to blow two hammered silver trumpets (Numbers 10:1-10). Listening with the ears of the Spirit to a brief outline of the instructions for this time will help us to see Yom Teruah in its coming glory.

YHVH said Israel was to make two trumpets of silver hammered work and priests were to blow them. The united sound of the trumpets would then be used to summon all Israel, and to have the camps set out. Two trumpets were to be sounded when going to war in the land, that we might be remembered before our God, and by Him, be saved from our enemies.

Note that the two silver trumpets of Numbers chapter 10 were used to:

Gather the assembly (vs. 2)
move the camp (vs. 5)
prepare for war (vs. 9)
celebrate the feasts (vs. 10)

We also note that silver depicts our being refined (Malachi 3:3), and that trumpets depict voices (Revelation 1:10). "Cry loudly, do not hold back; raise your voice like a trumpet, and declare to My people their transgression and to the house of Jacob their sins" (Isaiah 58:1).

Scripture tells us that the silver trumpets were to be sounded at Yom Teruah and the New Moon. Together their voices join as one in purpose; to warn people of Yahweh's timing and bring unity; preparing the camp for war and to usher in the long-awaited time when Yahshua will be united with His bride. You can see in the use and purpose of the silver trumpets the full meaning behind the Hebrew word teruah; the sound of warning and the sound of joy. When Yom Teruah is fulfilled, the separation of those who know Yahweh and those who do not will have an overwhelming effect on the entire world.

Let's now look at the Scripture commands for Yom Teruah and the New Moon and how they reveal to us the heart behind keeping the New Moon.

> *When you go to war in your land against the adversary who oppresses you, then you shall sound an alarm with the trumpets. Then you will be remembered before Yahweh your God, and you will be saved from your enemies.*

> *"Also in the day of your gladness, and in your set feasts, and in the beginnings of your months, you shall blow the trumpets over your burnt offerings, and over the sacrifices of your peace offerings; and they shall be to you for a memorial before your God. I am Yahweh your God."Num.10:9,10*

> *Yahweh spoke to Moses, saying, "Speak to the children of Israel, saying, 'In the seventh month, on the first day of the month, shall be a solemn rest to you, a memorial of blowing of trumpets, a holy convocation. You shall do no regular work; and you shall offer an offering made by fire to Yahweh.'" Leviticus 23:24-25*

The New Moon and Yom Teruah, both call for trumpets to be blown and both are to be a memorial. The verse in Numbers 10 also confirms that the sound of the trumpets will be a memorial not only to us but to Yahweh. This appointed time is a time of sweet reflection, both for our Beloved and us. As we join together to recall our faithfulness to Yahweh's Covenant, He then lovingly protects us from our enemies. All that we have looked at concerning being kept safe under the shadow of the Most High, culminates on this day for those who chose to abide with Him in His secret place. The New Moon is designed as a day for remembering Yahweh's goodness to us; His provision, His protection and of course, His unfailing love. As we remember all the wonderful ways Yahweh has cared for us each month, our hearts will overflow with thanksgiving, worship, and praise to Him. As we humble ourselves in His presence, He will mercifully restore us to new life.

He has caused His wonderful works to be remembered.
Yahweh is gracious and merciful. Ps.111:4

Praise Yahweh, my soul!
All that is within me, praise his holy name!
Praise Yahweh, my soul,
and don't forget all his benefits;
who forgives all your sins;
who heals all your diseases;
who redeems your life from destruction;
who crowns you with loving kindness and tender mercies;
who satisfies your desire with good things,
so that your youth is renewed like the eagle's. Ps.103:1-5

These appointed times of remembering also help us remember our human nature. We are prone to sinful weaknesses no matter how much we desire to be holy. For, like the Moon, we have no light at all. The light we need, the only light that will ever make a difference in this world, is the light we receive from the Father of lights.

For I know that in me, that is, in my flesh, dwells no good thing. For desire is present with me, but I don't find it doing that which is good. For the good which I desire, I don't do; but the evil which I don't desire, that I practice. But if what I don't desire, that I do, it is no more I that do it, but sin which dwells in me. I find then the law, that, to me, while I desire to do good, evil is present. For I delight in God's law after the inward man, but I see a different law in my members, warring against the law of my mind, and bringing me into captivity under the law of sin which is in my members.What a wretched man I am! Who will deliver me out of the body of this death? I thank God through Jesus Christ, our Lord! So then with the mind, I myself serve God's law, but with the flesh, the sin's law. Rom.7:18-25

Our time of soul searching will bring us to repentance before Yahweh. With humility and death to ourselves Yahweh will restore right order in our hearts and minds, cleansing our spirits with gratitude, adoration, honor and love for our King.

Create in me a clean heart, O God.
Renew a right spirit within me. Ps.51:10

Recorded for us in Nehemiah, is a remarkable and stirring account of Yahweh's people being brought into a time of remembering, one very special Yom Teruah long ago.

All the people gathered themselves together as one man into the wide place that was in front of the water gate; and they spoke to Ezra the scribe to bring the book of the law of Moses, which Yahweh had commanded to Israel. Ezra the priest brought the law before the assembly, both men and women, and all who could hear with understanding, on the first day of the seventh month. Neh.8:1,2

There are a few important things to notice here. First, the people were assembled as one man or echad; again, this is the goal and heart of the New Moon which we saw revealed in the word codesh. Secondly, the people had not heard Yahweh's Word for a very long time. Could we say that they were experiencing a drought or famine of Yahweh's Word? We see evidence of the people's hunger and thirst for it when they asked Ezra to read the Torah out loud to them.

Behold, the days come," says the Lord Yahweh,
"that I will send a famine in the land,
not a famine of bread, nor a thirst for water,
but of hearing Yahweh's words. Amos 8:11

God, you are my God.
I will earnestly seek you.
My soul thirsts for you.
My flesh longs for you,

in a dry and weary land,
where there is no water. Ps.63;1

Blessed are those who hunger and thirst after righteousness,
for they shall be filled. Matt.5:6

The last thing I would like you to notice in Nehemiah's account is that those who heard Yahweh's Words on that day were those with understanding. Knowledge of Torah is good ... if it is sought with the right motivation and understanding. When we attempt to know everything and seek for knowledge without wanting to know Yahweh's heart, it can become an overwhelming stream of facts, information, and rules. We must never loose sight of the Author. When we search for knowledge with the intention of knowing Yahweh, we can then gain understanding of His heart and apply it to our lives. The word for knowledge in Hebrew is Strong's #1847 da'at, which means; cunning or aware. This word comes from the Hebrew word yada; which has a long list of words to describe its meaning, but is summed up in this; to know someone intimately, as with a close friend or loved one. One can research and know many facts about someone, but as we have discovered you won't truly know one another until you desire to spend time with them and see them for who they truly are. Likewise, understanding the words that an author chooses to write comes from knowing the author's heart and reason for writing their words. Consider this quote from Mortimer J. Alder and Charles Van Doran, authors of 'How to Read a Book.'

Perhaps we know more about the world than we used to, and in sofar as knowledge is a prerequisite to understanding, that is all to the good. But knowledge is not as much a prerequisite to understanding as is commonly supposed. We do not have to "know" everything about something in order to understand it; too many facts are often as much of an obstacle to understanding as too few. There is a sense in which we moderns are inundated with facts to the detriment of understanding.

In other words, if we choose to fill ourselves with information without considering the motivation of the author, we risk the potential of ruining the heart of the writing. This is where a childlike attitude and faith in our heavenly Father need to come into practice. Knowledge with the purpose of understanding and building relationships has the potential to impact our lives for good. But, as we saw in the picture of the frog being dissected in a science class, we must not loose the wonder of Yahweh's original purpose, which is for us to have abundant life. We will only have true understanding when we see Him, *the Author*, for who He truly is.

> *For I desire mercy, and not sacrifice; and the knowledge of God more than burnt offerings. Hos.6:6*

Our eyes are opened to this when we hear and understand that each one of Yahweh's Words were written with love. Then our hearts can receive them with understanding. In the Garden of Eden, Adam and Eve were forbidden to eat from the Tree of the knowledge of Good and Evil. Why? … when Scripture also says that we will perish for lack of knowledge?

> *My people are destroyed for lack of knowledge. Because you have rejected knowledge, I will also reject you, that you may be no priest to me. Because you have forgotten your God's law, I will also forget your children. Hosea 4:6*

The key is in knowing Yahweh and trusting Him above the information we seek, for we run the risk of knowing to the point of trusting our own judgment. Yahweh's Word does not tell us that the fruit of the Tree of the knowledge of Good and Evil would cause Adam and Eve to know Him better. On the contrary! Knowing Yahweh in the context of the Hebrew word 'yada' comes only from the Tree of Life! Daily spending time with Yahweh and talking with Him as they did in the Garden. The desire for self-sufficiency, self-reliance, and self-promotion is at the root of the Tree of the knowledge of Good and Evil.

> *The serpent said to the woman,"You won't surely die, for God knows that in the day you eat it, your eyes will be opened, and you will be like God, knowing good and evil."Gen. 3:4*

Our world today is filled with knowledge, and it increases daily. We have become a people obsessed with knowing and having access to information, literally at our fingertips. Yet in a world filled with, may I say tech-knowl-edgey, the knowledge of Yahweh and who He truly is, is being lost.

> *Hear Yahweh's word, you children of Israel; for Yahweh has a charge against the inhabitants of the land: "Indeed there is no truth, nor goodness, nor knowledge of God in the land. Hos.4:1*

Could it be that we live in 'the time of the end' that Daniel spoke of?

> *But you, Daniel, shut up the words, and seal the book, even to the time of the end: many shall run back and forth, and knowledge shall be increased. Dan.12:4*

We must wonder then, if there is more knowledge in this age than ever before, why does it seem that we have less time than ever before? Why are we more apathetic than ever before? As quoted above; **There is a sense in which we moderns are inundated with facts to the detriment of under-standing.** In these last days, when Daniel's words are playing out before us, we must be very discerning about what we receive as knowledge. With humble hearts, we must seek to know Yahweh and understand His heart. For the way to have abundant life, is by eating from the Tree of *Life*.

> *Oh the depth of the riches both of the wisdom and the knowledge of God! How unsearchable are his judgments, and his ways past tracing out! Rom.11:33*

When Yahweh's Word is received with open hearts and understanding ... it is all powerful!

> *Your testimonies are righteous forever.*
> *Give me understanding, that I may live.Ps.119:144*

With these verses in mind, let's continue with Nehemiah's account;

> *Ezra opened the book in the sight of all the people; (for he was above all the people;) and when he opened it, all the people stood up: and Ezra blessed Yahweh, the great God. All the people answered, "Amen, Amen," with the lifting up of*

their hands. They bowed their heads, and worshiped Yahweh with their faces to the ground. Also Jeshua, and Bani, and Sherebiah, Jamin, Akkub, Shabbethai, Hodiah, Maaseiah, Kelita, Azariah, Jozabad, Hanan, Pelaiah, and the Levites, caused the people to understand the law: and the people stayed in their place. They read in the book, in the law of God, distinctly; and they gave the sense, so that they understood the reading. Nehemiah, who was the governor, and Ezra the priest the scribe, and the Levites who taught the people, said to all the people, "Today is holy to Yahweh your God. Don't mourn, nor weep." For all the people wept, when they heard the words of the law. Neh. 8:5-9

On this profound Yom Teruah, the Words of Yahweh's Torah were received into people's hearts with such understanding for the Author, that their hearts broke. Overwhelmed with love for the One who wrote the Torah, they bowed their heads in worship to Yahweh. Yahweh was referring to this in Hosea when He said that people perish for the lack of knowledge. He explains what He means when He says, "because you have forgotten God's law" or Torah. In other words, they perish because they lack knowledge of Yahweh.

> *Give me understanding, and I will keep your law.*
> *Yes, I will obey it with my whole heart. Ps.119:34*

The knowledge of the Holy One is understanding. Prov.9:10b

The remarkable thing about this particular Yom Teruah, is that there was no controversy, no disagreement and no competition in the midst the people. They were one in heart, and together they realized that they had walked away from Yahweh and the desires of His heart. Immediately they responded with humility and regret. What an awesome picture of the power of Yahweh's Word! His preeminent Word deeply touches the hearts of those who openly receive it, bringing the revelation of Yahweh's holiness and the wretchedness of our sin and depravity.

For the word of God is living and active, and sharper than any two-edged sword, piercing even to the dividing of soul and spirit, of both joints and marrow, and is able to discern the thoughts and intentions of the heart. Heb. 4:12

As Yahweh's Words pierced the people's hearts, they wept in repentance. Ezra then comforted them and exhorted them not to weep, but to savor the presence of Yahweh while they had time. He explained to them that the joy Yahweh had in seeing their hearts return to Him, should strengthen them to praise Him for His goodness, especially while the appointed time of celebration was at hand!

Then he said to them, "Go your way. Eat the fat, drink the sweet, and send portions to him for whom nothing is prepared; for today is holy to our Lord. Don't be grieved; for the joy of Yahweh is your strength."

So the Levites stilled all the people, saying, "Hold your peace, for the day is holy; neither be grieved."

All the people went their way to eat, and to drink, and to send portions, and to make great mirth, because they had understood the words that were declared to them. Neh.8:10-12

These stirring verses in Nehemiah, paint a wonderful picture of the future fulfillment of the New Moon and Yom Teruah together as one. The New Moon exhorts us each month to remember Yahweh, His Covenant and His goodness to us. It also compels us to remember all that we have done to serve our King and show our love to Him. When the purpose of these two days come together as one on 'the great Day of the Lord,' it will be the awesome day that Yahshua our Messiah, Yahweh's Living Word in the flesh, will come in power. Yahweh's Word will then be revealed as never before! Above and beyond all that is recorded in Nehemiah, one Yom Teruah in the near future, our hearts will be overwhelmed as Yahweh's truth pierces through every lie. The enemy may try to bring controversy and confusion to the truth of the New Moon and Yom Teruah, yet with Yahweh's patterns as our foundation and our knowledge of the Author's magnificent love story before us, we can look to Yom Teruah with great anticipation, joy and understanding.

... for God is not a God of confusion, but of peace. 1Cor.14:33

On an average, calendar Yom Teruah comes in September or October as Rosh Hashanah and is celebrated by many as the beginning of a year, just as most people celebrate New Year's Eve. Usually, the celebration holds a party atmosphere with good wishes for God to bring us a prosperous new year. Scripture does not support this perspective. The only mention of the beginning of a year in Scripture is found regarding the Hebrew month, Aviv or Nissan, which comes in the spring, when the barley is ripe, and the preparations for Passover begin, as seen in the verse below.

This month shall be to you the beginning of months. It shall be the first month of the year to you. Ex.12:2

When Yahshua returns He will make all things new, but until that magnificent day, the truth remains for us now that Yom Teruah is not the beginning of a year, but rather the New Moon or Rosh Chodesh of the seventh month, known today as Tishri. As we have seen, seven is used throughout Scripture as the number that signifies wholeness and completion and when Yahshua returns this will become astoundingly evident as the completion or grande finale of Yahweh's glorious story and song comes upon the world. For Yahshua will then return to fulfill each and every detail of Yahweh's feast days and bring wholeness and completion to Yahweh's seven thousand year story.

But don't forget this one thing, beloved, that one day is with the Lord as a thousand years, and a thousand years as one day. 2 Pet.3:8

As we walk with Yahweh through the cycle of each year, we come to Yom Teruah as the fifth appointed day on His path. You will find this quite intriguing as we take a deeper look at the significance of the number five from Yahweh's perspective. The meaning of the number five in Hebrew brings the significance of Yom Teruah and the New Moon together. I have inserted below a portion of a teaching on the number five by Brad Scott from Wildbranch Ministries:

Every source I have concerning this number associates the idea of God's grace and life to it. The 5th word of scripture is shamayim, or heaven. There are not many bad things to say about heaven, and there is probably alot of grace and life there. The 5th day of restoration of the creation is the first appearance of life. The idea of preparation is also seen in the Hebrew word chamash, the word for five. Chamash means to prepare or be ready. Five is an expression of preparedness as a result of receiving his mercy and grace. Is it just a coincidence that we denotatively call Torah, the FIVE books of Mosheh? Grace prepares you for Torah and Torah prepares you for life. David, in preparing for Goliath, took up FIVE smooth stones. To prepare and perfect the saints for ministry we are given FIVE GIFTS, apostles, prophets, evangelists, pastors and teachers (Ephesians 4:11-12). The narration of the preparation and building of the tabernacle in Sh'mot is filled with fives and multiples of fives that are too numerous to mention. In Mattityahu 25, there are FIVE virgins who are PREPARED when their Master comes. Noach found GRACE in the eyes of YHVH, and then PREPARED an ark, in which few, that is eight souls, were saved by water (1 Kefa 3:20). The anointing oil was prepared with FIVE ingredients in Sh'mot 30:23-25. God's unearned gift of grace is given to prepare us for our ultimate glorification. This process of glorification happens from YHVH's point of view in FIVE steps. For whom He did FOREKNOW, He also did PREDESTINATE, and whom he did predestinate, them He also CALLED; and whom He called, them He also JUSTIFIED, and whom He justified, them He also GLORIFIED (Romans 8:29-31).

Brad is showing us that the number five has great importance to Yahweh. The number five puts into perspective all that Yom Teruah and the New Moon are preparing us for. When we see Yahshua's bride in the parable of the *five* virgins, we can see that the preparations she will make for her Beloved's return are also filled with the significance of the number *five*. First she is saved by grace, renewed by the baptism of the Holy Spirit and shows her love for Him by keeping His Covenant Commandments, revealed to her in the *five* books of instruction, which is the Torah. While Yahshua's bride waits and watches for Him, she fulfills her calling within the *five* ministry gifts (apostle, prophet, evangelist, pastor and teacher) with humility and love, so that she may grow in wisdom and be prepared as a royal priesthood. Each year she anticipates and rehearses for her Beloved's return on the fifth appointed day, faithfully walking through His cycle laid out for her from the beginning time and worshipping Yahweh in spirit and truth.

One Yom Teruah, the trumpet's call will pierce through the chaos of the world ... but not everyone will hear the same sound. This will be the day when the truth of what we believe is revealed. For those who love and follow Yahshua, the trumpet's call will be a familiar sound and a welcome shout of joy and victory! For those who have loved the world and rejected the Words of Yahweh, the trumpet's call will sound as a battle cry, as the wrath of Yahweh falls upon the nations.

The reality of two different messages coming from one sound may seem odd at first, but it plays out for each of us in our daily lives. Most often you see it in a parent, child relationship, especially with an older child. If the child has a good and respectful relationship with their parents, they will hear their parent's words of instruction as good, loving counsel. On the other hand, if they have a disrespectful relationship with their parents, those same words may sound judgmental or controlling. We also find this in other scenarios that come between an employer and an employee, or a coach and a team player. In the end, the saddest example of this comes with the Heavenly Father and His children. When we are humble and teachable, we hear Yahweh's Words with love and accept His caring judgments into our lives. With wisdom and discernment, motivated by love and understanding we will have the ears to hear our all of our heavenly Father's Words with love.

How I love your law!
It is my meditation all day. Ps.119:97

As we develop an intimate relationship with Yahweh, He then allows us to dwell intimately with Him in His secret place; daily learning the ways of Yahshua until our ears become attuned to what the Spirit is saying to the assemblies in these last days. In the glorious presence of our King, each New Moon, our ears also become familiar with the trumpet's sound and the call to remember all that Yahweh has done with joy and thanksgiving.

Blessed are the people who know the joyful sound!
They walk, O Lord, in the light of Your countenance. Ps.89:15

The phrase "joyful sound" in this Psalm is translated from the Hebrew word teruah! The above verse could have been translated as, "Blessed are the people who know the teruah! They will walk, O Yahweh, in the light of Your countenance." This verse expresses the awesome hope and longing of the bride of Messiah! For on the fast approaching Yom Teruah of Yahshua's return, Yahweh's great trumpet will resound throughout all the earth and those who love Yahshua and are prepared will hear with understanding the call of their Beloved. They will then be gathered into the glorious light of His countenance, as we have seen in the pattern of the New Moon. On that great day Yahweh's voice will resonate as the sound of His great shofar, just as it did on Mount Sinai … thundering through the heavens.

> *On the third day, when it was morning, there were thunders and lightnings, and a thick cloud on the mountain, and the sound of an exceedingly loud trumpet; and all the people who were in the camp trembled. Ex.19:16*

Yahweh's voice is also described as a shofar again in Revelation when John is given a vision of Yahshua in all His glory.

> *I was in the Spirit on the Lord's day, and I heard behind me a loud voice, like a trumpet saying, "What you see, write in a book and send to the seven assemblies : to Ephesus, Smyrna, Pergamum, Thyatira, Sardis, Philadelphia, and to Laodicea."*

> *I turned to see the voice that spoke with me. Having turned, I saw seven golden lamp stands. And among the lamp stands was one like a son of man, clothed with a robe reaching down to his feet, and with a golden sash around his chest. His head and his hair were white as white wool, like snow. His eyes were like a flame of fire. His feet were like burnished brass, as if it had been refined in a furnace. His voice was like the voice of many waters. He had seven stars in his right hand. Out of his*

mouth proceeded a sharp two-edged sword. His face was like the sun shining at its brightest. When I saw him, I fell at his feet like a dead man. Rev.1:10-17

Yahweh's voice is so powerful! It is described as thunder, rushing waters or a shofar blast! The command to blow the shofar is symbolic of the presence of Yahweh's voice or authority in our midst. You see it used in many places throughout Scripture for warning, victory, and command. Both the Shofar and the Silver Trumpets are to be blown on the New Moon, and Yom Teruah and each serves their purpose to declare truth and call out to Yahweh's people. Our responsibility is to recognize and understand their sound. Yom Teruah, as the rehearsal for Yahshua's coming, prepares us to hear and know the sound of both the Shofar and Silver Trumpets and how we are to respond to their call. On the appointed night of Yahshua's return, Yahweh's shofar will call out in response to the many shofars and trumpets that will cry out across the world. Those that know the sound will be prepared and waiting. They will be the remnant who will follow Yahshua as His firstfruits bride, and will be raised to His side to live in His glorious Light forever.

For this we tell you by the word of the Lord, that we who are alive, who are left to the coming of the Lord, will in no way precede those who have fallen asleep. For the Lord himself will descend from heaven with a shout, with the voice of the archangel, and with God's trumpet. The dead in Christ will rise first, then we who are alive, who are left, will be caught up together with them in the clouds, to meet the Lord in the air. So we will be with the Lord forever. Therefore comfort one another with these words. 1Thess. 4:15-18

But each in his own order: Christ the first fruits, then those who are Christ's, at his coming. Then the end comes, when he will deliver up the Kingdom to God, even the Father; when he will have abolished all rule and all authority and power. 1 Cor. 15:23,24

Scripture warns us that the last days will be filled with deception, false teachers, and even delusion. The warning is rooted in who the Messiah truly is, and our belief in the truth. Our perception of the one we claim to follow will affect our daily choices and the way we live life.

> And Jesus answered and said to them: "Take heed that no one deceives you. For many will come in My name, saying, 'I am the Christ,' and will deceive many. Matt.24:4,5(NKJ)

> For false christs and false prophets will rise and show great signs and wonders to deceive, if possible, even the elect. See, I have told you beforehand. Matt.24:24,25(NKJ)

> The coming of the lawless one is according to the working of Satan, with all power, signs, and lying wonders, and with all unrighteous deception among those who perish, because they did not receive the love of the truth, that they might be saved. And for this reason God will send them strong delusion, that they should believe the lie, that they all may be condemned who did not believe the truth but had pleasure in unrighteousness. 2 Thess. 2:9-12(NKJ)

It's important to understand that the delusion is not sent by satan, but by Yahweh! Why would He do such a thing? Because people took pleasure in unrighteousness! This needs to deeply touch the heart of each and every one of us. When Yahshua walked the Earth two thousand years ago, there were many opinions of who He was, as there are today. Even His own disciples were rattled when He confronted them, asking, "Who do you say that I am?"

> Now Jesus and His disciples went out to the towns of Caesarea Philippi; and on the road He asked His disciples, saying to them, "Who do men say that I am?"

> So they answered, "John the Baptist; but some say, Elijah; and others, one of the prophets."

He said to them, "But who do you say that I am?" Mark 8:27-29

Yahshua's question to His disciples is even more urgent for us today. As His disciple and follower, "Who do you say that He is?" Our answer is vital to our walk, and eventually, our salvation, for our answer will, in turn, establish our course of action and our faith. What and *who* we believe in guides each and every decision we make daily.

Beloved, don't believe every spirit, but test the spirits, whether they are of God, because many false prophets have gone out into the world. 1John 4:1

Test all things, and hold firmly that which is good. 1 Thess. 5: 21

Who has ascended up into heaven, and descended?
Who has gathered the wind in his fists?
Who has bound the waters in his garment?
Who has established all the ends of the earth?
What is his name, and what is his son's name, if you know?
"Every word of God is flawless.
He is a shield to those who take refuge in him.
Don't you add to his words,
lest he reprove you, and you be found a liar. Prov.30:4-6

Scripture tells us that Yahshua is our High Priest and King according to the order of Melchizedek, which means 'King of Righteousness!' Our journey through life *must* reflect His light and all that He stands for, or we need to examine our faith.

This hope we have as an anchor of the soul, a hope both sure and steadfast and entering into that which is within the veil; where as a forerunner Jesus entered for us, having become a high priest forever after the order of Melchizedek. Heb.6:19,20

Through the foundations that Yahweh has laid out in His Word and His Creation, we *can* test the patterns and traditions that have been passed down through the ages, and discern if they are based on the truth of Yahweh's Word or man's ideals and systems. Yahshua challenged the

Pharisees on this all the time. The traditions of the Pharisees were not always based on Yahweh's Word, and often they held their tradition even higher than His Word. When they walked out their faith against the ways of Yahweh, Yahshua rebuked them. He exposed their hearts and revealed that their ideals were filled with selfish pride ... not humility and love. In contrast, Yahshua walked out Yahweh's Word according to the will and ways of His Father ... faithfully!

> The Pharisees and the scribes asked him, "Why don't your disciples walk according to the tradition of the elders, but eat their bread with unwashed hands?"
>
> He answered them, "Well did Isaiah prophesy of you hypocrites, as it is written,
> 'This people honors me with their lips,
>   but their heart is far from me.
> But they worship me in vain,
>   teaching as doctrines the commandments of men.' Mark 7:5-7
>
> Be careful that you don't let anyone rob you through his philosophy and vain deceit, after the tradition of men, after the elements of the world, and not after Christ. Col.2:8

The world is watching all those who claim to be believers, no matter what name we call ourselves by, and they are aware of our religious hypocrisy. If we are to be a light in the darkness and take the good news of Yahshua to a lost world, we must challenge man's traditions and ask," Do the traditions align with Yahweh's Word and bring glory to His Name and character?" Some of man's traditions are good and give us righteous patterns to follow bringing unity and focus to the body of Messiah. Still, many other of man's traditions simply follow the ways of the world and take our focus away from Yahweh's Word and heart.

> "For you set aside the commandment of God, and hold tightly to the tradition of men—the washing of pitchers and cups, and you do many other such things." He said to them, "Full well do

you reject the commandment of God, that you may keep your tradition." Mark 7:8,9

This testimony is true. For this cause, reprove them sharply, that they may be sound in the faith, not paying attention to Jewish fables and commandments of men who turn away from the truth. To the pure, all things are pure; but to those who are defiled and unbelieving, nothing is pure; but both their mind and their conscience are defiled. They profess that they know God, but by their deeds they deny him, being abominable, disobedient, and unfit for any good work. Titus 1:13-16

Often the traditions of men are taught as though they are as important as Yahweh's Word. This is where we must use discernment and prayer. Traditions of value will follow Yahweh's Word and teach us about Yahweh, not going against His patterns or design. Good traditions help keep us together as one and cause us to be a blessing to those around us. Paul exhorted new believers to follow the traditions that his fellowship was keeping so that those coming to the faith had a positive pattern to follow without mixing the ways of the world into their midst. The most important thing is that all we do is done with sincere love for Yahweh and others.

So then, brothers, stand firm, and hold the traditions which you were taught by us, whether by word, or by letter. 2Thess.2:15

This is his commandment, that we should believe in the name of his Son, Jesus Christ, and love one another, even as he commanded. John 3:23

Seeing you have purified your souls in your obedience to the truth through the Spirit in sincere brotherly affection, love one another from the heart fervently: 1 Pet.3:23

I have brought this to your attention because I would like to show you four names that are traditionally used by Jewish sages to reference Yom Teruah. Though they are not found as names for Yom Teruah in Scripture, each name aligns with the events surrounding that great day. Can it be a coincidence that these names that have been handed down for centuries, align perfectly with the patterns that we have seen in the New Moon and consequently Yom Teruah? I believe it is not a coincidence at all, but the sovereign hand of the Master, who has left us pieces to put together, and as we lay the pieces out upon the foundation of His patterns we will see His Masterpiece!

The first name I would like to look at is Yom Hakeseh. Once again we are brought back to Psalm 81:3 and the word for full, which is the Hebrew word, keseh.

Blow the trumpet at the time of the New Moon,
At the full moon, on our solemn feast day.

Keseh, as we have already seen, means to conceal or cover for hiding period Yom HaKeseh could then be translated as; The Hidden or Concealed Day connecting us to Yahweh's purpose and pattern of the New Moon. Each year the New Moon gives us eleven rehearsals for this one Great day. Each month or codesh we are called to watch and anticipate the Moon's last waning sliver in the eastern sky, in contrast to those who watch for the sliver in the western sky. Though we are to seek Yahweh at all times, the approaching of the New Moon will be seen by those who rise early, just before dawn to seek Him and watch the eastern sky.

Yahweh, in the morning you shall hear my voice.
In the morning I will lay my requests before
you, and will watch expectantly. Ps. 5:3

I rise before dawn and cry for help.
I put my hope in your words.
My eyes stay open through the night watches,
that I might meditate on your word. Ps. 119:147,148

Early in the morning, while it was still dark, he rose up and went out, and departed into a deserted place, and prayed there. Mark 1:35

For as the lightning flashes from the east, and is seen even to the west, so will be the coming of the Son of Man. Matt. 24:27

As the last of the Moon's sliver slips away from our sight on the eastern horizon, the Sun and the Moon join as one or become echad in the heavens. The Moon is then lost in the light of the Sun, declaring the glory of the future Yom Teruah when Yahshua's bride will be lost in the glorious light of her Bridegroom. As we have seen repeated over and over in Scripture and throughout Yahweh's Creation, life comes after a time of being concealed and covered in darkness. Once again we see that the Moon is our faithful witness to this each month as it becomes concealed from our sight for up to three days. The Moon gives testimony to our goal as Yahshua's bride, which is to be hidden with Him.

> *For you died, and your life is hidden with Christ in God. When Christ, our life, is revealed, then you will also be revealed with him in glory. Col.3:3,4*

Those who are hidden from the world and safe in the presence of Yahweh on that day will rise to be renewed in the likeness of their Beloved for all eternity. Repeatedly we see that this is the steadfast message the heavens are declaring! The verses from Jeremiah below tell us that if the ordinances or message set in the heavens ever ceases then the offspring of Israel would also cease.

> *Yahweh, who gives the sun for a light by day, and the ordinances of the moon and of the stars for a light by night, who stirs up the sea, so that its waves roar; Yahweh of Armies is his name, says: If these ordinances depart from before me, says Yahweh, then the offspring[a] of Israel also shall cease from being a nation before me forever. Jer.31:35,36*

Yahweh's relentless desire to rescue His beloved and cover her in His presence, is the same yesterday, today and forever, just as He is the same yesterday and today and forever.

> *"When I passed by you again and looked upon you, indeed your time was the time of love; so I spread My wing over you and covered your nakedness. Yes, I swore an oath to you and*

entered into a covenant with you, and you became Mine," says the Lord God. Ez.16:8 (NKJ)

Those who have not been faithful in rehearsing Yom Teruah through the keeping of the New Moon, will not understand what the heavens are proclaiming, and will be caught off guard as the trumpets call out on that great day.

> *Seek Yahweh, all you humble of the land, who have kept his ordinances. Seek righteousness. Seek humility. It may be that you will be hidden in the day of Yahweh's anger. Zeph.2:3*

The ones, who are *not* hidden with Yahweh as their Rock of refuge, will then seek to find refuge in the rocks of the Earth.

> *Enter into the rock,*
> *and hide in the dust,*
> *from before the terror of Yahweh,*
> *and from the glory of his majesty.*
> *The lofty looks of man will be brought low,*
> *the haughtiness of men will be bowed down,*
> *and Yahweh alone will be exalted in that day. Is.2:10,11*

It is so important to see the fullness of Yom Teruah as Yom HaKeseh. Obviously the word keseh is worthy of more of our attention. So with humble hearts, let's now take a deeper look at the Hebrew word keseh, and it significance on the glorious day of Yahshua's return.

As we have seen, the Hebrew language is a language of pictures, which is not surprising when we see how our Father in Heaven has created all things through pictures and stories. The word keseh is one of His beautiful storytelling words. It is spelled in Hebrew כסה, which from right to left are the Hebrew letters kaph, samech and hey. In Frank Seekins' book, 'Hebrew Word Pictures,' we find insight to each of the Hebrew letters in their original picture form, and how each individual picture is a player in His story. The first Hebrew letter in the word keseh is the kaph כ; meaning the palm of a hand or the wing of a bird, for covering or to open a way. The next Hebrew letter is the samech ס; meaning a prop, which supports, upholds or helps someone or something. The final Hebrew letter is the hey ה; meaning a man lifting his arms to reveal or behold something. When we put these smaller pictures and meanings of each letter of keseh together, the whole picture unfolds to become, "The revelation of our support and help, is the covering of a hand or wing over us." This little Hebrew word keseh confirms all that Yahweh is telling us in His Word! Yahweh desires for us to be hidden under the shadow of His wing or outstretched hand, for He is our only hope and true support in times of trouble.

> *Keep me as the apple of your eye.*
> *Hide me under the shadow of your wings,*
> *from the wicked who oppress me,*
> *my deadly enemies, who surround me. Ps.17:8,9*

> *For you have been my help.*
> *I will rejoice in the shadow of your wings.*
> *My soul stays close to you.*
> *Your right hand holds me up. Ps.63:7,8*

> *Be merciful to me, God, be merciful to me,*
> *for my soul takes refuge in you.*
> *Yes, in the shadow of your wings, I will take refuge,*
> *until disaster has passed. Ps.57:1*

> *How precious is your loving kindness, God!*
> *The children of men take refuge under the*
> *shadow of your wings. Ps.36:7*

> *He will cover you with his feathers.*
> *Under his wings you will take refuge.*
> *His faithfulness is your shield and rampart. Ps.91:4*

Is there a more secure place in all the world than under the shadow of Yahweh's wing? No, not in all the world! Man may build bunkers, shelters or run to caves, but the only true place of safety is hidden in the presence of Yahweh. His glorious light casts the shadow of His wing over us, and we are comforted and concealed in the protection of the Almighty. When the great day of Yahshua's return comes upon the world, it will be too late to understand this. You must seek Him and develop an intimate relationship with Him now, dwelling in the secret place, to ensure your protection and covering in the future. Yahshua's life was hidden in His Father's, and He died to give us a life likened to His. Now we must die, take up our cross and have our life hidden in Him. If we are hidden in Yahshua, our High Priest, we are covered in His redemptive blood and have acceptance and entry to the awesome throne room of the Father.

> *You have forgiven the iniquity of your people.*
> *You have covered all their sin. Ps.85:2*

> *Let us therefore draw near with boldness to the throne of grace,*
> *that we may receive mercy, and may find grace for help in time*
> *of need. Heb.4:16*

When Yahshua said, "I am the Way," He was telling us that He is the *only* way to the secret place with his Father. The enemy and the spirit of the antichrist are bringing false teachings and twisting the truth to keep us from knowing the Way. These lies bring a false sense of security.

> *When the overflowing scourge passes through, it won't come*
> *to us; for we have made lies our refuge, and we have hidden*
> *ourselves under falsehood. Is.28:15b*

Nevertheless, when Yahshua returns, He will be revealed for who He truly is. Halleluyah! Those who know Him and have endured to the end, will find their names written in the Book of Life. They will then receive the crown of life and dwell with their Beloved forever!

> *Blessed is the man who endures temptation, for when he has*
> *been approved, he will receive the crown of life, which the Lord*
> *promised to those who love him. James 1:12*

> *Jesus answered him, "If a man loves me, he will keep my word.*
> *My Father will love him, and we will come to him, and make*
> *our home with him. John 14:23*

How lovely are your dwellings,
Yahweh of Armies!
My soul longs, and even faints for the courts of Yahweh.
My heart and my flesh cry out for the living God. Ps.84:2

The word 'longs' in Psalm 84, is Strong's #H3700 כסף kasaph, which is a cognate or family word for keseh. Strong's definition of kasaph is simply, 'to yearn or long after,' but in Ernest Klein's, Etymological Dictionary of the Hebrew Language, there is another intriguing description for kasaph. Ernest Klein describes kasaph as colorless, obscured, eclipsed; as the Sun or Moon. Wow! Once again we see another piece to the picture of Yahshua's bride and the Moon! Even the pale colorless face of the Moon, and the eclipses that the Sun and Moon share, tell of the longing that the bride has for her Beloved. As the Moon has no light of its own and longs for the light of the Sun, so the bride of the Messiah with no light of her own, longs to dwell in the brilliant presence of her Bridegroom.

While I am in the world, I am the light of the world. John 9:5
You will show me the path of life.
In your presence is fullness of joy.

In your right hand there are pleasures forever more. Ps.16:11

Kasaph as a cognate word to keseh brings an intriguing dimension to a solar eclipse. When we consider the meanings of keseh and kasaph we find something special that we may not have considered before. As you know a solar eclipse can only happen at the time of the New Moon, which ties the 'hidden and concealed' meaning of keseh with the 'color-less, obscured, eclipsed' meaning of kasaph. At all other New Moons, the Moon is lost in the brightness of the Sun, but at a solar eclipse, something different happens. Instead of being hidden, the Moon moves in front of the Sun, and for a few magnificent moments, the Moon faces the glory of the Sun. From a spiritual perspective, this may seem like the Moon or bride is taking center stage and blocking the light of the Sun, but indeed, quite the opposite is taking place. As the Moon moves in front of the Sun, those beneath the path of totality are able to gaze in awe and wonder at the extraordinary Sun. They cannot do this at any other time without special equipment! In fact, the Moon's spectacular alignment in front of the Sun causes people to celebrate the rare opportunity to discover more about the Sun. A total solar eclipse is a miraculous picture of Yahshua's bride humbly making way for her Beloved to be seen in all His majesty! ... Just as it will be on the New Moon of Yahshua's return!

Behold, he is coming with the clouds, and every eye will see him, including those who pierced him. All the tribes of the earth will mourn over him. Even so, Amen. Rev.1:7

Therefore God also highly exalted him, and gave to him the name which is above every name; that at the name of Jesus every knee should bow, of those in heaven, those on earth, and those under the earth, and that every tongue should confess that Jesus Christ is Lord, to the glory of God the Father. Phil.2:9-11

On that glorious day, every person alive will tremble. Those who know Him will tremble with joyful awe when they finally hear the sound of Yahweh's shofar, for they will have been waiting and watching for Him. Those who do *not* know Yahweh or have rejected His Word will tremble with fear and regret because they will be shocked as the trumpets declare the battle cry of Yahweh pouring out His wrath upon the nations.

Now we will look at another name used for Yom Teruah, which is Yom HaMelech or the day of the King. Yom Teruah is also known as the day when Yahshua will be crowned as 'Conquering King.' I find it fascinating that Yahshua's coronation day is a memorial of trumpet blowing and a hidden day. When Yahshua came to us two thousand years ago, as a humble King, He allowed men to mock Him as King of the Jews and to shove a crown of thorns onto His head. In that day, even though He was in the midst of throngs of people, He was hidden from their sight. Few people had the eyes to see Him for who He truly was. Of course this was Yahweh's design, for *had* they seen Him ... they would not have scourged the very King they had prayed would come to them.

Rejoice greatly, daughter of Zion!
Shout, daughter of Jerusalem!
Behold, your King comes to you!

He is righteous, and having salvation;
lowly, and riding on a donkey,
even on a colt, the foal of a donkey. Zech.9:9

They stripped him, and put a scarlet robe on him. They braided a crown of thorns and put it on his head, and a reed in his right hand; and they kneeled down before him, and mocked him, saying, "Hail, King of the Jews!" Matt. 27:28,29

Some historians say that in ancient times when a king came to a country on a donkey he was declaring peace. One then could ask, 'When Yahshua entered Jerusalem on a donkey, was He declaring peace?' If He was, His declaration of peace was not as the people expected. On the contrary, many were frustrated with His steadfast composure in the midst of the political uproar of the day. His peaceful composure irritated them because they wanted Him to rise up with them and take a stand against the Roman rule. Yahshua challenged them and their way of seeking peace when He said:

I came to throw fire on the earth. I wish it were already kindled. But I have a baptism to be baptized with, and how distressed I am until it is accomplished! Do you think that I have come to give peace in the earth? I tell you, no, but rather division. Luke 12:49-51

Did our King come to bring peace at that time? The answer is of course, 'Yes!' Yahshua did come to bring peace as Isaiah declares;

For to us a child is born. To us a son is given; and the government will be on his shoulders. His name will be called Wonderful, Counselor, Mighty God, Everlasting Father, Prince of Peace. Is.9:6

His mission of peace was to restore, reconcile, and renew the Covenant promises on behalf of His Father. He walked as our example of how to respond to the challenges of life and to those who revile us. Yahshua's peaceful composure showed us that the way of peace is to trust His Father with all our heart, especially when everything around us is in turmoil. Our amazing King humbly submitted to the authorities and did not return reviling for reviling. Instead with quiet confidence, He did the will of His Father.

> He was oppressed, yet when he was afflicted he didn't open his mouth. As a lamb that is led to the slaughter, and as a sheep that before its shearers is silent, so he didn't open his mouth Is.53:7.

> For thus said the Lord Yahweh, the Holy One of Israel, "You will be saved in returning and rest. Your strength will be in quietness and in confidence." Is.30:15

> The work of righteousness will be peace; and the effect of righteousness, quietness and confidence forever. Is.32:17

Yahshua's statement of not bringing peace but division is directed to us. Peace is determined by our trust in Him and responding to the One who is our ultimate authority. Each of us, at some time in our life, will make a choice of whether to trust and follow Yahweh completely or not. Our choice will determine our future and whether we will truly have peace. Remember that the word for peace in Hebrew is shalom, which holds the meaning of wholeness and completion. Yahshua had shalom in the assurance of His Father's will and that there was a reward set before Him in the completion of His Father's Word.

The longer one walks with Yahweh, the more they can see and understand that all things in Yahweh's Kingdom have a positive and negative application to them. Just as it is with the sound of the trumpets or with words of counsel, so it is with the Words of Yahweh. When we are submitted to Yahweh, we hear the right rulings of His Kingdom in a positive, loving way and it brings peace to our hearts. On the other hand, when we are not obeying Yahweh, we can hear the same right rulings as judgmental and legalistic. If we do not submit to Yahweh, the same words that were designed for peace will agitate and frustrate us. Yahweh brings difficult situations and trials to us to test our hearts and our response. Our daily walk and the trials of life need to be seen from this perspective, to help us overcome our selfishness and strengthen us to trust in Yahweh completely.

He will guide the humble in justice. He will
teach the humble his way. Ps.25:9

Take my yoke upon you, and learn from me, for
I am gentle and humble in heart; and you
will find rest for your souls. Matt.11:29

But even as we have been approved by God to be entrusted with the Good News, so we speak; not as pleasing men, but God, who tests our hearts. 1Thess. 2:4

Oh let the wickedness of the wicked come to an end,
but establish the righteous;
their minds and hearts are searched
by the righteous God. Ps.7:9

Yahshua showed us that when we fully surrender our lives to Yahweh, and trust Him alone, we *can* have peace; even when turmoil surrounds us … or when our family and closest friends turn against us. When we are secured to Yahshua the Rock, we can overcome the hurtful and difficult storms of this world, just as we saw in the word levana for Moon. Then and only then, will we have the peace or shalom that surpasses all understanding and protect our hearts from becoming hard and bitter.

In nothing be anxious, but in everything, by prayer and petition with thanksgiving, let your requests be made known to God. And the peace of God, which surpasses all understanding, will guard your hearts and your thoughts in Christ Jesus. Phil.4:6,7

Peace I leave with you. My peace I give to you; not as the world gives, give I to you. Don't let your heart be troubled, neither let it be fearful. John 14:27

We must learn the way of meekness and humility that Yahshua gave us as an example. If we harbor pride in our life, we will not have peace, because Yahweh resists the proud.

Likewise, you younger ones, be subject to the elder. Yes, all of you clothe yourselves with humility, to subject yourselves to one another; for "God resists the proud, but gives grace to the humble." 1 Pet.5:5

Again, this is pictured in the Moon that has no light of its own, but humbly serves to reveal the light of the Sun. I have inserted an excerpt from Andrew Murray's book, Humility, which speaks of the importance of being humble.

Brother, have we not here the reason that our consecration and our faith have availed so little in the pursuit of holiness? It was by self and its strength that the work was done under the name of faith; it was for self and its happiness that God was called in; it was, unconsciously, but still truly, in self and its holiness that the soul rejoiced. We never knew that humility, absolute, abiding, Christ-like humility and self-effacement, pervading and marking our whole life with God and man, was the most essential element of the life of the holiness we sought for.

It is only in the possession of God that I lose myself. As it is in the height and breadth and glory of the sunshine that the littleness of the mote playing in its beams is seen, even so humility is the taking our place in God's presence to be nothing but a mote dwelling in the sunlight of His love.

"How great is God! how small am I! Lost, swallowed up in Love's immensity! God only there, not I."

May God teach us to believe that to be humble, to be nothing in His presence, is the highest attainment, and the fullest blessing of the Christian life. He speaks to us: "I dwell in the high and holy place, and with him the is of a contrite and humble spirit." Be this our portion!

"O, to be emptier, lowlier,

Mean, unnoticed, and unknown,

And to God a vessel holier,

Filled with Christ, and Christ alone!"

Above all, our greatest depths of peace or shalom will come to us when we let go of ourselves and allow Yahshua full reign in our lives as King and High Priest. After all is 'said and done' according to Yahweh's great story, Yahshua *will* come, and He will judge each one of us and return all things to righteous order. When Yahshua returns, He is not coming upon a donkey. No! At Yahweh's appointed time Yahshua will split open the heavens riding a white horse as our Warrior King. Hallelujah!

> *I saw the heaven opened, and behold, a white horse, and he who sat on it is called Faithful and True. In righteousness he judges and makes war. His eyes are a flame of fire, and on his head are many crowns. He has names written and a name written which no one knows but he himself. He is clothed in a garment sprinkled with blood. His name is called "The Word of God." The armies which are in heaven followed him on white horses, clothed in white, pure, fine linen. Out of his mouth proceeds a sharp, double-edged sword, that with it he should strike the nations. He will rule them with an iron rod. He treads the wine press of the fierceness of the wrath of God, the Almighty. He has on his garment and on his thigh a name written, "KING OF KINGS, AND LORD OF LORDS." Rev. 19: 11-16*

The New Moon of Yom Teruah is the glorious day when Yahshua will be crowned King of all kings. On that magnificent day, all the wondering will cease and He will be seen for Who He truly is!

> *For nothing is hidden, that will not be revealed; nor anything secret, that will not be known and come to light. Luke 8:17*

As we continue to seek the fullness of Yahweh's Masterpiece, there is one more piece to this picture found in another of keseh's cognate words.

The Hebrew word kisseh is, Strong's #H3678, כסה, which as you can see has the same spelling as the keseh, for covered or concealed. Kisseh is a remarkable piece when we see Yom Teruah as Yahshua's coronation day, because this cognate word kisseh means; a throne, seat, stool! As we look deeper at these two meanings for keseh, we will see how they join together to reveal the truth about Yom Teruah and the awesome events that will take place on that Great Day!

To understand kisseh, we must consider the revelation of Yahweh's throne given to Moses in the wilderness. The Holy of Holies or secret place was hidden from the eyes of man and reserved only for the High Priest. If you were the High Priest at that time, you would find a single piece of furniture there, known as the Ark of the Covenant. This awesome vessel is the very throne of Yahweh! As we saw earlier, Yom Teruah is filled with pictures of two becoming one and here we see again, the two understandings of keseh coming together to give us revelation of the Ark of the Covenant. The first meaning for keseh,(to cover or conceal) compliments the second meaning, kisseh or throne. Yahweh's throne (kisseh) is designed so that the mercy seat *covers* or conceals (keseh) the things of His heart. These precious things are the Covenant written on tablets of stone, a vessel filled with Manna and Aaron's budding rod. Yahweh's throne is a testimony of His loving character and the things that He treasures. These two meanings from the spelling of keseh bring us to an even deeper understanding than before, for they hold the key to our hope for the future and reveal the double blessing that comes from dwelling in the secret place or Holy of Holies. The first blessing we receive comes when we have entry to the throne room of the King by Yahshua's atonement or blood covering that is upon us and the mercy seat of Yahweh's throne. The Hebrew word for atonement is kaphar, which also means; *to cover*, forgive, reconcile.

The second blessing comes to us when we choose to become His royal priesthood and adhere to the ways of Yahshua as our High Priest and dwell with Him in the secret place. Below is a portion of an article written by Aurthur Pink, about Yahweh's throne.

Suppose an Ark with no Mercy-seat: the Law would then be uncovered: there would be nothing to hush its thunderings, nothing to arrest the

execution of its righteous sentence. The law expresses God's righteousness, and demands the death of its violator: "Cursed is everyone that continueth not in all things which are written in the book of the Law to do them" (Gal. 3:10). Such is the inevitable judgment pronounced on all sinners by the inexorable sentence of the law. The only man who could stand before God on the basis of having kept that law was the Man Christ Jesus. He could have been justified by it, enthroned upon it, and from it have pronounced sentence of just doom on all of Adam's guilty race. But He did not do so. No; blessed be His name, instead of coming to earth as the Executioner of the law, He bared His holy bosom to its righteous sword. The same heart which held the law unbroken (Ps. 40:8) received the penalty which was due His people for having broken it. The storm of wrath having spent itself upon Him, the law can no longer touch those who have fled to Him for refuge. It is of this that the blood-sprinkled Mercy-seat, covering the tables of stone within the Ark, so blessedly speaks.

How beautifully this expresses the wonder of our King and Savior, and all that He has done for us! I am in awe of how the little Hebrew word keseh holds so much of Yahweh's work of redemption. The power of Yahweh's love and grace was established through Yahshua's atoning blood covering upon the mercy seat! Praise Yah! There in the secret place of the Most High, upon the throne of Yahweh, is the everlasting memorial of the price Yahshua paid for His bride. Amazingly, this truth and pattern was revealed to the world in the Tabernacle in the Wilderness as a shadow picture of the very throne room or Holy of Holies of heaven where Yahweh is majestically seated forever.

After these things I looked and saw a door opened in heaven, and the first voice that I heard, like a trumpet speaking with me, was one saying, "Come up here, and I will show you the things which must happen after this."

Immediately I was in the Spirit. Behold, there was a throne set in heaven, and one sitting on the throne that looked like a jasper stone and a sardius. There was a rainbow around the throne, like an emerald to look at. Around the throne were twenty-four thrones. On the thrones were twenty-four elders sitting, dressed in white garments, with crowns of gold on their heads. Out of the throne proceed lightnings, sounds, and thunders. There were seven lamps of fire burning before his throne, which are the seven Spirits of God.Rev.4:2-5

Notice in this description of Yahweh's throne room that the sound of a trumpet is what calls John to come up into the heavenly realm. There, he witnesses heaven's throne radiating with flashes of lightening and the sound of thunder; before Yahweh's throne stands a Menorah surrounded with the colors of a rainbow! Can you see how this magnificent picture is strikingly similar to the account of Moses being called by Yahweh to go up into what appears to be a storm at the top of Mount Sinai? This captivating parallel leads us to believe that Moses was going before the very throne of Yahweh. Here again, we see that Yahweh's glorious presence is enveloped in cloud, darkness, and lightening and thundering noise!

Yahweh reigns!
Let the earth rejoice!
Let the multitude of islands be glad!
Clouds and darkness are around him.
Righteousness and justice are the foundation of his throne.
A fire goes before him,
and burns up his adversaries on every side.
His lightning lights up the world.
The earth sees, and trembles
The mountains melt like wax at the presence of Yahweh,
at the presence of the Lord of the whole earth.
The heavens declare his righteousness.
All the peoples have seen his glory. Ps. 97:1-6

I believe that Moses was fully aware that he was being summoned to stand before the throne of Yahweh. In obedience and awe, he was compelled to climb up Mount Sinai into frightening conditions. Yahweh's throne emanates His glory, majesty, and power. For those who do not adhere to His righteous judgments, being before the throne of the King can and will be a frightening experience. Even the earthly High Priests, who were trained in righteousness risked death when they went before Yahweh's throne on Yom Kippur. But now, Praise Yah! ... because of Yahshua's sacrifice, there could be no safer place in all the Universe! The veil that once separated us from Yahweh's presence has been torn in heartfelt victory at the moment of Yahshua's death upon the cross. Now we have access to Yahweh's throne through the shed blood of our Redeemer!

The sun was darkened, and the veil of the temple was torn in two. Luke 23:45

Jesus cried again with a loud voice, and yielded up his spirit. Behold, the veil of the temple was torn in two from the top to the bottom. The earth quaked and the rocks were split. Matt. 27:50,51

When the sixth hour had come, there was darkness over the whole land until the ninth hour. At the ninth hour Jesus cried with a loud voice, saying, "Eloi, Eloi, lama sabachthani?" which is, being interpreted, "My God, my God, why have you forsaken me? Mark 15:33,34

True to Yahweh's pattern of life, on the day of Yahshua's sacrifice, Yahweh covered the world in darkness and the Earth trembled. As Yahweh's only Son bore the Covenant conditions on our behalf, Yahweh tore the veil of the Temple from top to bottom, making a way for those who would believe on Yahshua to have access into His presence. Now all those who love Yahweh and follow Yahshua, have a place of covering, comfort and refuge in the secret place or Holy of Holies. By grace, it is our humble privilege to enter into Yahweh's presence and have life. We cannot take this privilege for granted. We must seek Yahweh now, with meekness and repentance before the day of Yahshua's return is upon us. If we wait it may be too late.

Seek Yahweh while he may be found.
Call on him while he is near.
Let the wicked forsake his way,

and the unrighteous man his thoughts.
Let him return to Yahweh, and he will have mercy on him;
and to our God, for he will freely pardon. Is.55:6,7

Seek Yahweh, all you humble of the land, who have kept his ordinances. Seek righteousness. Seek humility. It may be that you will be hidden in the day of Yahweh's anger. Zeph.2:3

The Yom Teruah of Yahshua's return will set in motion a process that will change the world as we know it forever. All of the principalities and powers that have had a lying grip on this world will be exposed, and the truth revealed. Scripture tells us that after Yahshua rose from the dead, He sat down at the right hand of His Father and there He is waiting for the blessed day when He will return as conquering King.

From now on, the Son of Man will be seated at the right hand of the power of God. Luke 22:69

The fulfillment of this day and it's timing is in the hands of Yahshua's Father and according to His Word. As we see prophecy fulfilled and the fullness of time unfold before us, we must prepare to be a light to the lost, for it is Yahweh's will that none should perish. Remember too, that even to this day, Yahshua is interceding on your behalf.

The Lord is not slow concerning his promise, as some count slowness; but is patient with us, not wishing that any should perish, but that all should come to repentance. 2 Pet.3:9

Who could bring a charge against God's chosen ones? It is God who justifies. Who is he who condemns? It is Christ who died, yes rather, who was raised from the dead, who is at the right hand of God, who also makes intercession for us. Rom.8:33,34

As High Priest of the Kingly order of Melchizedek, Yahshua serves the needs of the Tabernacle in heaven. He was born as Yahweh's spotless Lamb to become our redemptive sacrifice. He delivered His blood to the heavenly mercy seat, and He now attends to the Altar of Incense and the prayers that rise before Yahweh's Throne.

I turned to see the voice that spoke with me. Having turned, I saw seven golden lamp stands. And among the lamp stands was one like a son of man, clothed with a robe reaching down to his feet, and with a golden sash around his chest. His head and his hair were white as white wool, like snow. His eyes were like a flame of fire. His feet were like burnished brass, as if it had been refined in a furnace. His voice was like the voice of many waters. He had seven stars in his right hand. Out of his mouth proceeded a sharp two-edged sword. His face was like the sun shining at its brightest. When I saw him, I fell at his feet like a dead man. Rev. 1: 12-17

Notice again, that John's description of Yahshua is with eyes like a flame and a face like the Sun at its brightest. John's vision gives us much detail about what Yahshua is wearing, but does not record Him wearing a crown. Could this be revealing that there will be a Coronation day in the future? Daniel, like John was given a terrifying vision of Yahweh. His vision revealed the great day when Yahweh's Books will be opened, and the Son of Man is given authority over all.

"I watched till thrones were put in place,
And the Ancient of Days was seated;
His garment was white as snow,
And the hair of His head was like pure wool.
His throne was a fiery flame,
Its wheels a burning fire;
A fiery stream issued
And came forth from before Him.
A thousand thousands ministered to Him;
Ten thousand times ten thousand stood before Him.
The court was seated,
And the books were opened.
"I was watching in the night visions,
And behold, One like the Son of Man,
Coming with the clouds of heaven!
He came to the Ancient of Days,
And they brought Him near before Him.

Then to Him was given dominion and glory and a kingdom,
That all peoples, nations, and languages should serve Him.
His dominion is an everlasting dominion,
Which shall not pass away,
And His kingdom the one
Which shall not be destroyed. Dan.7:9,10,13,14(NKJ)

It appears that Daniel's vision reveals the Yom Teruah of Yahshua's return, when all those who worship Yahweh in spirit and truth, will be gathered to a place of protection and covering to behold Yahshua being crowned King of kings. Time will reveal all that we are not able to fully see now, but we must prepare for all that Yahweh has designed. Only those worthy to enter the Holy of Holies and stand before the Throne or the Ark of the Testimony will see their Beloved face to face. Those who are saved by grace and choose to show their love to Yahweh according to the conditions of the Covenant, and have submitted to the service of the royal priesthood, will be gathered to their Beloved that day. Halleluyah!

But you are a chosen race, a royal priesthood, a holy nation,
a people for God's own possession, that you may proclaim
the excellence of him who called you out of darkness into his
marvelous light: who in time past were no people, but now
are God's people, who had not obtained mercy, but now have
obtained mercy.1 Pet. 2:9,10

Beloved of the King, just as the Moon is keseh or concealed in the glorious light of the Sun at the New Moon, so we will be concealed in the glorious Light of Yahshua as He is crowned King of all kings upon His throne, on the New Moon when Yom Teruah is fulfilled. As we have seen through Yahweh's pattern, the Moon dances across the heavens beside the Sun, lost in its brilliant light each New Moon. Likewise, on the day of Yahshua's return, His bride will take her place beside Him and be lost in His glorious light. At that moment, in the twinkling of an eye, we will be changed and a sudden, overwhelming revelation of who the sons of Yahweh truly are, will finally come to fruition. At last Creation's waiting will be over! Those who have followed Yahshua, will understand all that is unfolding on that great day, for they will have rehearsed it many times.

These will be the royal priesthood, prepared to be clothed in eternal glory, and ready to walk through all they have rehearsed as the final choruses of Yahweh's Song resound throughout the Universe!

For the creation waits with eager expectation for the children of God to be revealed. Romans 8:19

I will greatly rejoice in Yahweh, my soul shall be joyful in my God; for he has clothed me with the garments of salvation, he has covered me with the robe of righteousness, as a bridegroom decks himself with a garland, and as a bride adorns herself with her jewels. Is. 61:10

Behold, I tell you a mystery. We will not all sleep, but we will all be changed, in a moment, in the twinkling of an eye, at the last trumpet. For the trumpet will sound, and the dead will be raised incorruptible, and we will be changed. 1Cor.15:51,52

On that day, when Yahweh opens His Books, the truth of our hearts and deeds will be revealed. Then all who have walked away from Yahweh will have ten days of awe to reconsider their ways and return to Him in repentance. These days are when the wrath of Yahweh will be poured out on the Earth to prepare for Yom Kippur or the Day of Atonement. Those who are not gathered to the Messiah at this time will be thrust into a time of sorrow. The parable of the ten virgins gives a heart-wrenching picture of these events.

But at midnight there was a cry, 'Behold! The bridegroom is coming! Come out to meet him!' Then all those virgins arose, and trimmed their lamps. The foolish said to the wise, 'Give us some of your oil, for our lamps are going out.' But the wise answered, saying, 'What if there isn't enough for us and you? You go rather to those who sell, and buy for yourselves.' While they went away to buy, the bridegroom came, and those who were ready went in with him to the marriage feast, and the door was shut. Matt.25:6-10

The unsettling message of this parable is that all ten were virgins and all ten had lamps, yet only five *knew* the Bridegroom and were *known* by Him. Only five of the virgins had truly prepared to be with their Beloved and gain entry into His chamber ... the other five virgins are left outside grieving the error of their ways.

> *Afterward the other virgins also came, saying, 'Lord, Lord, open to us.' But he answered, 'Most certainly I tell you, I don't know you.' Matt.25:11,12*

The five virgins who crossed the threshold into the chamber of their Beloved, were those who were wise and known by their Beloved. We will take a detailed look at these five virgins later, but for now, it is important to see that some were ready and gained entry to their Beloved's chamber, and some were left outside weeping with regret.

> *Then I will tell them, 'I never knew you. Depart from me, you who work iniquity.' Matt.7:23*

Now we come to the last two names used for Yom Teruah. One is Yom HaZikkaron or the Day of Remembrance, and the other is Yom HaDin or the Day of Judgement. These last two names tie together the awesome events that will unfold on the 'Day of the Lord.' Over the course of a year, the New Moon prepares us for Yom Teruah through the importance of remembering. The New Moon and Yom Teruah share the common purpose of being a memorial of blowing the trumpet, and a set apart time of remembering Yahweh and all the attributes of His Name and His faithfulness to His people. We all have memories of the ways Yahweh has touched our lives; to save us, to protect us, provide for our needs and to graciously give us gifts. Without question His lovingkindness and mercy is unmatched!

> *Give thanks to Yahweh! Call on his name!*
> *Make his doings known among the peoples.*
> *Sing to him, sing praises to him!*
> *Tell of all his marvelous works.*
> *Glory in his holy name.*

Let the heart of those who seek Yahweh rejoice.
Seek Yahweh and his strength.
Seek his face forever more.
Remember his marvelous works that he has done;
his wonders, and the judgments of his mouth,
you offspring of Abraham, his servant,
you children of Jacob, his chosen ones. Ps.105:1-6

The Hebrew word for remember is Strong's #H2142, zakar, which means; to mark so as to be recognized, to remember, make mention of, recount, record. The name Yom HaZikkaron, used for Yom Teruah, is realized through the importance of remembering Yahweh, especially when we remember Him with grateful hearts. As we remember all that Yahweh has done for us, and consider all that He requires us do for Him, it will be a sign of our love and faithfulness to Him and His Covenant. The New Moon and Yom Teruah are designed to bring memories of Yahweh's goodness to our hearts and minds in praise and worship. They are also set apart times for Yahweh to remember the love that we have shown Him in our faithfulness in word and deed.

Praise Yahweh, my soul, and don't forget all his
benefits; who forgives all your sins; who heals all your
diseases; who redeems your life from destruction; who
crowns you with loving kindness and tender mercies;
who satisfies your desire with good things, so that
your youth is renewed like the eagle's. Ps.103:2-5

When the great day of Yom Teruah is fulfilled, Yahweh will give full authority to Yahshua to reign over the Earth and judge each of us for our response to all He has done for us. The weightiness of this reality is behind the name Yom HaDin, or the Day of Judgment for Yom Teruah.

For we must all appear before the judgment seat of Christ,
so that each one may be recompensed for his deeds in the
body, according to what he has done, whether good or bad.
2 Cor. 5:10

But now he commands that all people everywhere should repent, because he has appointed a day in which he will judge the world in righteousness by the man whom he has ordained; of which he has given assurance to all men, in that he has raised him from the dead. Acts 17:30,31

Yahweh's Books hold records of all that we have said and done, both the good and the bad. Thankfully at the time when we accept Yahshua as our Savior, Yahweh blots out our transgressions and remembers them no more. After that day though, we are accountable for our actions because we are now ambassadors of Yahweh's love, mercy, and grace. When Yahshua comes, His Books will be opened, and we will be reminded of all our choices and responses. That day, there will be no excuses, only truth.

Have I any pleasure in the death of the wicked? says the Lord Yahweh; and not rather that he should return from his way, and live? But when the righteous turns away from his righteousness, and commits iniquity, and does according to all the abominations that the wicked man does, shall he live? None of his righteous deeds that he has done shall be remembered: in his trespass that he has trespassed, and in his sin that he has sinned, in them shall he die. Ez.18:23,24

But this is the covenant that I will make with the house of Israel after those days, says Yahweh: I will put my law in their inward parts, and in their heart will I write it; and I will be their God, and they shall be my people: and they shall teach no more every man his neighbor, and every man his brother, saying, Know Yahweh; for they shall all know me, from their least to their greatest, says Yahweh: for I will forgive their iniquity, and their sin will I remember no more. Jer.31:33,34

This wonderful truth is the reason that we are called to walk on the path of righteousness and become holy. Once our sins of the past have been blotted out and forgotten, we cannot continue in them or any other sin, for we will give an account for how we lived as those who have been redeemed.

"I tell you that every idle word that men speak, they will give account of it in the day of judgment. For by your words you will be justified, and by your words you will be condemned."Matt.12:36,37

So then each of one us will give account of himself to God. Romans 14:12

Therefore also we make it our aim, whether at home or absent, to be well pleasing to him. For we must all be revealed before the judgment seat of Christ; that each one may receive the things in the body, according to what he has done, whether good or bad. 2 Cor. 5:9,10

Yahweh wants and deserves to be remembered for all the awesome ways He has loved and protected us, for He is *always* mindful of us. He watches over us daily and patiently waits for us to seek after Him.

Yahweh, you have searched me,
and you know me.
You know my sitting down and my rising up.
You perceive my thoughts from afar.
You search out my path and my lying down,
and are acquainted with all my ways.
For there is not a word on my tongue,
but, behold, Yahweh, you know it altogether. Ps.139:1-4

Sing, heavens; and be joyful, earth;
and break out into singing, mountains:
for Yahweh has comforted his people,
and will have compassion on his afflicted.
But Zion said, "Yahweh has forsaken me,
and the Lord has forgotten me."
"Can a woman forget her nursing child,
that she should not have compassion on the son of her womb?
Yes, these may forget,
yet I will not forget you!

Behold, I have engraved you on the palms of my hands.
your walls are continually before me. Is.49:13-16

Have you ever been blessed by someone who did something for you without having to ask them to? We are mere reflections of Yahweh's heart. He desires to be apart of our lives in every way and remembered for His loving-kindness and faithfulness. He does not desire that we only respond to Him out of command. Yahweh wants us to remember Him and His Covenant out of love. When we do, it is a blessing to Him.

Beware lest you forget Yahweh your God, in not keeping
his commandments, and his ordinances, and his
statutes, which I command you today. Deut.8:11
Praise Yah!
I will give thanks to Yahweh with my whole heart,
in the council of the upright, and in the congregation.
Yahweh's works are great,
pondered by all those who delight in them.
His work is honor and majesty.
His righteousness endures forever.
He has caused his wonderful works to be remembered.
Yahweh is gracious and merciful. Ps.111:1-4

Seek Yahweh and his strength.
Seek his face forever more.
Remember his marvelous works that he has done,
his wonders, and the judgments of his mouth,
you offspring of Israel his servant,
you children of Jacob, his chosen ones.
He is Yahweh our God.
His judgments are in all the earth.
Remember his covenant forever, 1 Chron.16: 11-15

Yahweh wants us to remember His faithfulness to us and for us to be faithful to Him. This is His heartfelt reason behind the tassels or tzitzit. Yahweh asks His people to make them as a sign of remembrance, proclaiming that we are in a Covenant with Him. A wedding ring holds the same purpose; to remember and declare a covenant commitment.

And you shall have the tassel, that you may look upon it and remember all the commandments of the Lord and do them, and that you may not follow the harlotry to which your own heart and your own eyes are inclined, and that you may remember and do all My commandments, and be holy for your God. Num. 15:39,40

One last thing I will mention about Yahweh's books that we often forget, is that each of us were designed for a purpose before we were even born. Psalm 139 says;

For you formed my inmost being.
You knit me together in my mother's womb.
I will give thanks to you,
for I am fearfully and wonderfully made. Ps.139: 13,14

Psalm 139 continues to tell us that our lives and how Yahweh designed them, through our gifts, etc., were recorded in His Book before we were even born.

Your eyes saw my body.
In your book they were all written,
the days that were ordained for me,
when as yet there were none of them.Ps. 139:16

In the end, when Yahweh opens His books, He will compare His desire for our lives, to the path we chose to take. Did we choose His heart's desire for our life or the leading of man and the world? Did we use the gifts that He knit into our DNA, to serve Him or to serve ourselves? These personal choices that we face each day need our prayerful consideration, for one day we will stand face to face before Him and give an answer.

The call to repent and live abundantly is always before us, and Yahweh's mercy is new every morning. Each day holds the opportunity to love Him and others with all our heart, soul and strength. Our goal when all is said and done should be to have our names written in the most precious book of all, the Lamb's Book of Life.

They don't consider in their hearts that I
remember all their wickedness.

Now their own deeds have engulfed them.
They are before my face. Hosea 7:2

"At that time shall Michael stand up, the great prince who stands for the children of your people; and there shall be a time of trouble, such as never was since there was a nation even to that same time: and at that time your people shall be delivered, everyone who shall be found written in the book. Dan. 12:1

The city has no need for the sun, neither of the moon, to shine, for the very glory of God illuminated it, and its lamp is the Lamb. The nations will walk in its light. The kings of the earth bring the glory and honor of the nations into it. Its gates will in no way be shut by day (for there will be no night there),and they shall bring the glory and the honor of the nations into it so that they may enter. There will in no way enter into it anything profane, or one who causes an abomination or a lie, but only those who are written in the Lamb's book of life. Rev. 21:23-27

Spending eternity with our beloved Bridegroom and serving with Him in His Holy City is the glorious reward for remembering Yahweh, and all that Yahshua sacrificed and accomplished for us. Again, Yahshua's bride will be made up of those who seek Him with all their heart, keep His Covenant and abide with Him in the secret place. There they will dwell before His throne praying, serving and keeping His commandments by the leading of His Spirit. Each of these ones will be remembered by name and written in the Lamb's Book of Life forever.

For he will never be shaken. The righteous will be remembered forever. Ps. 112:6

Like them, the one who is victorious will be clothed in white garments. And I will never blot out his name from the book of life, but I will confess his name before My Father and His angels. Rev. 3:5

When we are taken home to dwell with Yahshua, we will live a life that is governed by the principles and patterns we see pictured in the Tabernacle or Yahweh's dwelling place. The life we have gained in Yahshua is paralleled to a walk through Yahweh's Tabernacle in preparation for our future home. Yahshua washed His disciple's feet at Passover, to prepare them to enter into Covenant with Him and become a part of the royal priesthood; fit to serve the elements of the Tabernacle or Temple.

Now we too, embark on a journey in preparation for the royal priesthood, when we accept Yahshua as our Savior. The first stop in the Tabernacle is in the courtyard at the Brazen Altar, where we meet Yahshua and except His sacrifice that makes atonement for our sin. We experience this when we keep Passover and encounter, the sacrifice Yahshua made for us allowing us to walk towards the Holy Place. Again, this is what Yahshua was referencing when He said, "I am the Way," for He has made 'the Way' for us walk into the secret place and the presence of His Father. Next, we come to the Laver; the place of washing which represents baptism and the washing of Yahweh's Word in our lives. The laver is the place where He cleanses our hearts of our old life, and we become a new creature. Each of these stops are vital and sanctify us for entry into the Holy place as priests ready to serve Yahweh.

When we accept Yahshua as our Savior, we are accepting a life called to holiness, for we are called to learn the service in the Tabernacle, and how it applies to our lives. As we take up our cross and follow Yahshua daily, we learn day by day how to become sons and daughters of the King. Taking up our cross cannot truly happen unless we are humble and teachable; willing to receive Yahweh's Word and Covenant into our hearts, letting it change us into the likeness of Yahshua. Our willingness takes us down what Yahshua called a narrow and difficult path that few are able to find, which is the path of righteousness. Many who accept the sacrifice Yahshua made for us, quickly fall away like the seeds in the parable of the sower that encounter bad growing conditions: not accepting the terms of Yahweh's Covenant and service in the Holy Place of the Tabernacle.

The ones by the road are the ones where the word is sown; and when they have heard, immediately Satan comes, and takes away the word which has been sown in them. These in the same way are those who are sown on the rocky places, who, when they have heard the word, immediately receive it with joy. They have no root in themselves, but are short-lived. When oppression or persecution arises because of the word, immediately they stumble. Others are those who are sown among the thorns. These are those who have heard the word, and the cares of this age, and the deceitfulness of riches, and the lusts of other things entering in choke the word, and it becomes unfruitful. Mark 4:15-19

Enter in by the narrow gate; for wide is the gate and broad is the way that leads to destruction, and many are those who enter in by it. How narrow is the gate, and restricted is the way that leads to life! Few are those who find it. Matt.7:13,14

Nevertheless, the very Earth that we have the privilege of living on, yearns and mourns for the ways of the Creator to be restored, and until Yahshua returns, it is our responsibility to be a light and an ambassador of the truth.

The earth mourns and fades away. The world languishes and fades away. The lofty people of the earth languish. The earth also is polluted under its inhabitants, because they have transgressed the laws, violated the statutes, and broken the everlasting covenant. Is.24:4,5

The Tabernacle gives us a deeper understanding of Yahshua's words. When He said, 'I am the Light,' He was referencing the Menorah. When He said, 'I am the Bread,' He was referencing the Manna. When He intercedes for us and calls us to prayer and intercession for those who are lost, He is referencing the Altar of Incense. The earthly Tabernacle gives us the picture and pattern of the Heavenly Tabernacle, which is the same pattern that will be restored during Yahshua's Millennial reign. The pattern in the Wilderness, revealed the blueprint of Heaven, and the order of Yahweh's service for all those who desire to follow His heart and serve with Him. Many people come to Yahweh hoping to serve Him from what they feel is a safe distance, outside the Tabernacle. They give their life to serving Him according to worldly ideals that are dictated by the ways of man.

"The Lord said, "Because this people draws near with their mouth and with their lips to honor me, but they have removed their heart far from me, and their fear of me is a commandment of men which has been taught; Isaiah 29:13*

> *There is a way which seems right to a man,*
> *but in the end it leads to death. Prov.14:12*

> *Every way of a man is right in his own eyes,*
> *but Yahweh weighs the hearts. Prov.21:2*

As we has seen, in the end there is no protection in the ways of man and Yahshua is coming as our Righteous Judge! Overwhelming evidence of prophecy is unfolding before our eyes, and we must examine our motives and test all things against the Word that we will be judged by. I believe it is no mistake that Yom Teruah has been called by names that reference remembering and judgment. Our responsibility is to align our hearts with Yahweh's heart; to know Him and remember His Mighty works, especially as deception and lies creep into every area of our lives through an onslaught of media.

The need to be prepared for what is looming on the horizon has swept the world, both practically and spiritually. The question we must all consider is, 'what are we preparing for?'... one world government? ... third world war? ... aliens? I have seen a spectrum of preparation in the world that spans, preparing for a zombie apocalypse, to believers becoming fully armed troopers, ready to escape to the wilderness. Our preparations as believers for the final events in Yahweh's magnificent Love Story are personal. Each of us must humbly ask Yahweh for wisdom and understanding to know His heart and follow the patterns He has laid out for us. May our hearts and minds be ready to respond to the sound of the Silver Trumpets and Yahweh's Great Shofar on that great and fearful Yom Teruah of Yahshua's return! In a sea of voices and opinions, it has never been so important to hear the leading of Yahweh's Spirit and to be found safe in His presence.

No matter what we do to physically prepare for the future, real preparedness for the return of the Messiah begins in our hearts.

> *See that you don't refuse him who speaks. For if they didn't escape when they refused him who warned on the Earth, how much more will we not escape who turn away from him who warns from heaven, Heb.12:25*

PREPARATION

The Wedding

IF YOU ARE MARRIED OR HAVE HELPED PREPARE FOR A WEDDING, YOU know that there is little else that compares to the excitement it brings. The bride and groom want the day to hold the uniqueness of their love for each other and so they spend many hours choosing their venue, colors, music, food, etc. In western tradition, the bride typically does most of the planning, and the groom oversees her choices. From Yahweh's perspective though a wedding is quite the opposite. The preparations for Yahshua's wedding are in the Bridegroom's hands, and His Father is the overseer of it all ... especially the timing. Yahshua reassured us of this before He rose to sit at the right hand of His Father.

> *"Don't let your heart be troubled. Believe in God. Believe also in me. In my Father's house are many homes. If it weren't so, I would have told you. I am going to prepare a place for you. If I go and prepare a place for you, I will come again, and will receive you to myself; that where I am, you may be there also. John 14:1-3*

> *But of that day or that hour no one knows, not even the angels in heaven, nor the Son, but only the Father. Watch, keep alert, and pray; for you don't know when the time is. Mark 13:32*

These precious words were spoken to those who desire to be Yahshua's bride. In stark contrast to our western ways, the bride of Yahshua is not required to plan the details of the wedding. Yahshua's bride is to be focused on waiting, watching, serving and preparing her heart for His soon return. Her ideas of the wedding details are not needed because His wedding was planned before the foundations of the world were set in motion. Even the wedding garment for the bride has been taken care of; for there is only one type of wedding garment that will please Yahshua, and He has saved it as a reward for those who have made themselves ready by walking in holy righteousness.

Let us rejoice and be exceedingly glad, and let us give the glory to him. For the marriage of the Lamb has come, and his wife has made herself ready." It was given to her that she would array herself in bright, pure, fine linen: for the fine linen is the righteous acts of the saints. Rev.19:7,8

Here Scripture also confirms that Yahshua's bride will be made up of those who are familiar with the elements of the Tabernacle. She will love by keeping His Commandments, and her good works will reflect the light of her High Priest and Bridegroom Yahshua.

This is how we know that we know him: if we keep his commandments. One who says, "I know him," and doesn't keep his commandments, is a liar, and the truth isn't in him. But whoever keeps his word, God's love has most certainly been perfected in him. This is how we know that we are in him: he who says he remains in him ought himself also to walk just like he walked. 1 John 2:4-6

The bride of the Messiah will be faithful to prepare herself to be adorned in Yahweh's linen wedding garment and it will be for glory and for beauty, pleasing to Yahweh.

You shall make holy garments for Aaron your brother, for glory and for beauty. Ex.28:2

Just as all priests who served Yahweh had to purify themselves before putting on the linen garments for service to Him, so we too must purify ourselves by the washing of His Word and living a life separate from the filth of this world.

Husbands, love your wives, even as Christ also loved the assembly, and gave himself up for it; that he might sanctify it, having cleansed it by the washing of water with the word, that he might present the assembly to himself gloriously, not having spot or wrinkle or any such thing; but that it should be holy and without defect. Eph.5:25-27

Know this for sure, that no sexually immoral person, nor unclean person, nor covetous man, who is an idolater, has any inheritance in the Kingdom of Christ and God. Eph. 5:5

Who may ascend to Yahweh's hill? Who
may stand in his holy place?
He who has clean hands and a pure heart;
who has not lifted up his soul to falsehood, and
has not sworn deceitfully.Ps.24:3,4

Why linen as the chosen wedding garment? First and foremost we are to be a bride prepared as His royal priesthood, and linen represents righteousness for service in the Tabernacle. From a practical perspective, linen and wool hold an amazing frequency of 5,000. Other fibers such as cotton, silk, etc., only carry a frequency of 100 or less, making linen and wool the best fabric for our health. Yahweh told us to not mix linen and wool together because their frequencies collapse and cancel each other out when bound together, losing their wonderful properties.

The most obvious difference between linen and wool is that linen comes from seed and wool comes from an animal. Could it be that the wool represents redemption compared to the linen representing righteous acts? Let's take a moment to look at a few unique characteristics about linen that create a picture for us, and help us see the beauty of the garment we hope to be adorned in one day.

Flax linen is grown in a short hundred-day period, beginning with planting in early spring and harvesting in mid-summer. The seeds are sown close together so that the stalks grow tall and don't fall over. When harvest time draws near, the flax plants blossom for a brief, beautiful week. During that week small blue, purple and white five-petalled flowers appear early in the morning to grace the fields. Their beauty quickly fades after a few hours and their small delicate petals fall. After that week, there is only thirty days until harvest. Then the plants are gathered up by pulling them out of the ground with their roots, and bundling them together to dry in the Sun.

You can see that the life of a flax plant holds lovely pictures symbolic of our life as children of Yahweh. Just like the flax, we are to grow up in righteousness beside our brothers and sisters in the Messiah; encouraging each other to become strong and keeping each other from falling. Like the blossoms that come near harvest, we too are to rise early each morning before Yahweh and remember all that the number five (displayed in the petals) means to our daily lives. Then, at the end Yahshua will come to gather us up together before His Presence.

An interesting reference to bundled flax is found when Joshua was in the Promised Land and faced with overcoming the city of Jericho. The King of Jericho heard that Joshua had sent spies into his city and he so he sent out soldiers to kill them.

> *Joshua the son of Nun secretly sent two men out of Shittim as spies, saying, "Go, view the land, including Jericho." They went and came into the house of a prostitute whose name was Rahab, and slept there.*
>
> *The king of Jericho was told, "Behold, men of the children of Israel came in here tonight to spy out the land."*
>
> *Jericho's king sent to Rahab, saying, "Bring out the men who have come to you, who have entered into your house; for they have come to spy out all the land." Josh.2:1-3*

Though Rahab was a harlot, she was aware of the powerful God that these men served. When the soldiers came to Rahab's place in search of the spies, she hid the men in the bundles of linen flax on her roof to protect them.

The woman took the two men and hid them. Then she said, "Yes, the men came to me, but I didn't know where they came from. About the time of the shutting of the gate, when it was dark, the men went out. Where the men went, I don't know. Pursue them quickly. You may catch up with them." But she had brought them up to the roof, and hidden them under the stalks of flax which she had laid in order on the roof. Josh.2:4-6

The kindness Rahab showed the two men by hiding them under the bundles of flax, was rewarded. A scarlet thread hanging from Rahab's window became the reminder of her righteous acts, and she and her family were saved from the destruction of Jericho. Rahab's story gives us an intriguing picture of linen, for even in its raw flax form, it appears to represent righteous acts. Note that two men were *hidden* in the walls of Jericho which, as we saw earlier, is also known as the *City of the Moon*. Here is another picture of how being hidden brings protection as it is with the secret place of Yahweh.

There is one last attribute of linen that I would like to point out. Linen, unlike wool, has a natural luster that reflects light...like the Moon! The glory that the Sun and Moon are declaring in the heavens about a groom and his bride will come to reality when Yahshua's true bride is adorned in a white linen garment reflecting His light. What a marvelous reward to anticipate ... to be arrayed in fine linen and standing before our Beloved Bridegroom reflecting the glory of His Light! Scripture tell us that in the end there will be no need of the Sun and Moon any longer. Yahshua, the Light of the World will be the only light needed, and His bride will reflect His Light in everything that she does as her garment will reveal. May we never loose sight of this awesome goal set before us and strive to be worthy of the white linen that represents our acts of righteousness.

Until that blessed day when we will be a bride without spot or wrinkle, there is another garment that we are admonished to wear. As the days grow darker we are called to put on the garments of a warrior priest. A true priest is always conscious of Yahweh's holiness and the righteous requirements of serving Him in holy obedience. We too must stand as Yahweh's priesthood and perform the acts of righteousness that His Holy Spirit is calling us to. Our call is to humbly walk as people of service and light in a lost and dark world; overcoming the ploys of the enemy and responding to our circumstances according to Yahweh's Word and not man's words.

Finally, be strong in the Lord, and in the strength of his might. Put on the whole armor of God, that you may be able to stand against the wiles of the devil. For our wrestling is not against flesh and blood, but against the principalities, against the powers, against the world's rulers of the darkness of this age, and against the spiritual forces of wickedness in the heavenly places. Therefore put on the whole armor of God, that you may be able to withstand in the evil day, and, having done all, to stand. Stand therefore, having the utility belt of truth buckled around your waist, and having put on the breastplate of righteousness, and having fitted your feet with the preparation of the Good News of peace; above all, taking up the shield of faith, with which you will be able to quench all the fiery darts of the evil one. And take the helmet of salvation, and the sword of the Spirit, which is the word of God; with all prayer and requests, praying at all times in the Spirit, and being watchful to this end in all perseverance and requests for all the saints; Eph.6:10-18

Often the armor of Yahweh is depicted as knight's armor, but in Paul's letter to the Ephesians he was actually reminding and encouraging them to walk as warrior priests that stand against the schemes of the enemy. When we allow Yahshua to be our example and follow the leading of His Spirit, then we too will learn the heavenly way of becoming warrior priests.

Righteousness will be the belt of his waist,
and faithfulness the belt of his waist. Is. 11:5

Therefore his own arm brought salvation to him;

and his righteousness sustained him.
He put on righteousness as a breastplate,
and a helmet of salvation on his head. Is.59:16,17

For the word of God is living and active, and sharper than
any two-edged sword, piercing even to the dividing of soul
and spirit, of both joints and marrow, and is able to discern
the thoughts and intentions of the heart. Heb. 4:12

Every word of God is flawless.
He is a shield to those who take refuge in him. Prov.30:5

Yahweh tells us that the days before our Bridegroom's return will unfold through great darkness. He will appear as a thief in the night unannounced and ready to judge the world for its wickedness. Those who do not know Him will bear the shock and fear of being in His presence ... exposed and unprepared.

Be silent at the presence of the Lord Yahweh, for the day of
Yahweh is at hand. For Yahweh has prepared a sacrifice. He has
consecrated his guests. It will happen in the day of Yahweh's
sacrifice, that I will punish the princes, the king's sons, and
all those who are clothed with foreign clothing. In that day, I
will punish all those who leap over the threshold, who fill their
master's house with violence and deceit.

The great day of Yahweh is near. It is near, and hurries greatly,
the voice of the day of Yahweh. The mighty man cries there
bitterly. That day is a day of wrath, a day of distress and
anguish, a day of trouble and ruin, a day of darkness and
gloom, a day of clouds and blackness, a day of the trumpet
and alarm, against the fortified cities, and against the high
battlements. I will bring distress on men, that they will walk
like blind men, because they have sinned against Yahweh, and
their blood will be poured out like dust, and their flesh like
dung. Zeph.1:7-9,14-17

Those who are alive during this time will have come through a season of great darkness, trial, and tribulation. Notice in the above verse of Proverbs 30 that those who take refuge and are hidden with Yahweh are shielded by Him. This is so important! We have seen that Yahweh's pattern of life is the same for birth, for a day, for a seed, for a month and it will be the same for the new millennium. The world will go through deep darkness, as it was in the days of Noah before we experience the long awaited new life at the end. The preordained way that Yahweh designed from the beginning of time is the magnificent theme that He has woven into all of Creation to display His heart.

I saw a new heaven and a new earth: for the first heaven and the first earth have passed away, and the sea is no more. I saw the holy city, New Jerusalem, coming down out of heaven from God, prepared like a bride adorned for her husband. I heard a loud voice out of heaven saying, "Behold, God's dwelling is with people, and he will dwell with them, and they will be his people, and God himself will be with them as their God. He will wipe away from them every tear from their eyes. Death will be no more; neither will there be mourning, nor crying, nor pain, any more. The first things have passed away."

He who sits on the throne said, "Behold, I am making all things new." He said, "Write, for these words of God are faithful and true." Rev. 21:1-5

How will we discern the difference between those who choose to follow the Messiah and those who do not during this time? Again, I believe it was foreshadowed for us in the account of the Children of Israel being gathered at Mount Sinai in the Wilderness.

One would have to wonder if those who feared Yahweh's presence and the Words He wanted to speak, had truly prepared their heart? Did they simply go through the motions? Moses, on the other hand, was humble and moved with righteous fear. He knew the heart of His Master and was very familiar with His power and might. He loved Yahweh with all his heart, and without hesitation, Moses willingly climbed the mountain into the darkness and storm. Could this foreshadow a time that Yahshua's bride will face in the last days? Surely she will see darkness of all kinds. She must have her eyes fixed on her Beloved as Moses did. Then with Yahweh's wisdom and discernment, and through time spent with Him, she will be equipped to discern between the deceptive darkness of this world, and the awesome presence of Yahweh and His voice. Nothing could be more important than knowing whom to fear and where to go as the tribulation unfolds. How we prepare for this will determine our response when the time comes.

> *He sent Moses His servant,*
> *And Aaron whom He had chosen.*
> *They performed His signs among them,*
> *And wonders in the land of Ham.*
> *He sent darkness, and made it dark;*
> *And they did not rebel against His word. Ps.105:28*

The important line in the above verse is that Moses and Aaron did not rebel against Yahweh's Word. Moses was willing to risk his life for Yahweh and walked directly into the fierce fire of Yahweh's presence. Yahweh's fire on Mount Sinai was also covered in the darkness of a thick cloud, because Yahweh reveals Himself through fire and cloud. His fearful presence is a consuming fire and His glory an overwhelming cloud.

> *I love you, Yahweh, my strength.*
> *Yahweh is my rock, my fortress, and my deliverer;*
> *my God, my rock, in whom I take refuge;*
> *my shield, and the horn of my salvation, my high tower.*
> *I call on Yahweh, who is worthy to be praised;*
> *and I am saved from my enemies.*
> *The cords of death surrounded me.*
> *The floods of ungodliness made me afraid.*
> *The cords of Sheol[a] were around me.*
> *The snares of death came on me.*
> *In my distress I called on Yahweh,*
> *and cried to my God.*
> *He heard my voice out of his temple.*
> *My cry before him came into his ears.*

Then the earth shook and trembled.
The foundations also of the mountains
quaked and were shaken,
because he was angry.
Smoke went out of his nostrils.
Consuming fire came out of his mouth.
Coals were kindled by it.
He bowed the heavens also, and came down.
Thick darkness was under his feet. Ps. 18:1-9

The Children of Israel that gathered at the base of the mountain were not willing to walk toward Yahweh's fire or give up their own ways, and so they kept their distance. I believe it was their distance from Yahweh that made it so easy for them to commit adultery with the golden calf so soon after their Covenant agreement. In contrast, Moses trusted Yahweh with all his heart and laid down his ways to obey Yahweh's voice. All that was seen and experienced in Egypt, including the final destruction of Pharaoh in the Red Sea, declared that Yahweh's righteousness demands righteousness in return. Yes, His grace and mercy are always making a way for us, but there does come a moment in time when our neglect in responding to His outstretched arm brings the consequences of our choices. Our choices in life must reflect the way of righteousness that Yahweh has made for us. In other words, we need to follow our Shepherd in every area of life and to heed His Spirit's voice, for the journey ahead will be heaped with deception and trials.

Wail; for the day of Yahweh is at hand! It will come as destruction from the Almighty. Therefore all hands will be feeble, and everyone's heart will melt. They will be dismayed. Pangs and sorrows will seize them. They will be in pain like a woman in labor. They will look in amazement one at another. Their faces will be faces of flame. Behold, the day of Yahweh comes, cruel, with wrath and fierce anger; to make the land a desolation, and to destroy its sinners out of it. For the stars of the sky and its constellations will not give their light. The sun will be darkened in its going out, and the moon will not cause its light to shine. Is.13:6-10

Where will we be and what will we be doing if we live to see this day fulfilled? These important questions should be on everyone's mind in some way. Not simply from the perspective of preparing food and supplies, but from the perspective of caring for the things of our Master's heart and preparing our hearts to stand strong and faithful to our Beloved in the face of trial. Yahshua exhorted us with parables about servants that were given the responsibility of taking care of their master's household while he was away. The servants were called to keep their master's things safe and watch diligently for his return.

> *"Let your waist be dressed and your lamps burning. Be like men watching for their lord, when he returns from the marriage feast; that, when he comes and knocks, they may immediately open to him. Blessed are those servants, whom the lord will find watching when he comes. Most certainly I tell you, that he will dress himself, and make them recline, and will come and serve them. They will be blessed if he comes in the second or third watch, and finds them so. But know this, that if the master of the house had known in what hour the thief was coming, he would have watched, and not allowed his house to be broken into. Therefore be ready also, for the Son of Man is coming in an hour that you don't expect him." Luke 12:35-40*

When you think of a thief coming to your house, what do you think of? Most often you do *not* think of someone being loud and obvious. Typically you think of someone coming quietly and secretly into a home; usually with the purpose of stealing the owner's valuables while they are unaware. In the parable of the servant, we find servants given the responsibility of caring for Yahshua's household, which can be paralleled to the Temple or Tabernacle. As those who are called to be in service to Yahweh, we are to see ourselves as those servants. We are to show our love for Him by caring for His things and loving those around us until His return.

> *Take heed, therefore, to yourselves, and to all the flock, in which the Holy Spirit has made you overseers, to shepherd the assembly of the Lord and God which he purchased with his*

own blood. For I know that after my departure, vicious wolves will enter in among you, not sparing the flock. Men will arise from among your own selves, speaking perverse things, to draw away the disciples after them. Therefore watch, remembering that for a period of three years I didn't cease to admonish everyone night and day with tears. Acts 20:28-31

The word overseer is described in Thayer's Greek Lexicon as; a man charged with the duty of seeing the things needing to be done by others, and making sure they are done rightly. This was also the duty of the priesthood. Now that we are Yahweh's children in training, we hold the responsibility of proving to the world what matters to Yahweh's heart as servants that care for His household. But, if Yahweh's own children (His servants) lose heart waiting for His return and indulge in their own pleasures and succumb to the ways of the world, they also loose their testimony... or as Yahshua put it, their saltiness.

"You are the salt of the earth, but if the salt has lost its flavor, with what will it be salted? It is then good for nothing, but to be cast out and trodden under the feet of men. Matt. 5:13

Losing our saltiness is seen when we become lacks in our compassion and service to Yahweh. He sees it as lukewarm as Yahshua said.

I know your works, that you are neither cold nor hot. I wish you were cold or hot. So, because you are lukewarm, and neither hot nor cold, I will vomit you out of my mouth. Rev.3:15,16

In a lukewarm state, our guard goes down and we stop watching. Those who are distracted, impatient and lose heart in the waiting and watching are the ones who will be caught off guard. For these ones, there will come a night when Yahshua's return will come upon them as a thief. Consequently, we must consistently anticipate and watch for the return of the Master; making sure that everything is done according to our Master's Word and enduring all things to the very end.

If we endure, we will also reign with him. If we deny him, he also will deny us. 2 Tim.2:12

For it is commendable if someone endures pain, suffering unjustly, because of conscience toward God. 1 Pet.2:19

You have perseverance and have endured for my name's sake, and have not grown weary. Rev.2:3

The above verse from Revelation confirms that our endurance is for His Name sake. The Greek word for 'my name' is Strong's #3686, onoma and it means; the manifestation or revelation of someone's character. This concept is not as common today as it used to be, especially in western culture, but it is very important to Yahweh. Thayer's Greek Lexicon describes 'onoma' or the meaning behind 'His Name sake' like this;

By a usage chiefly Hebraistic the name is used for everything which the name covers, everything the thought or feeling of which is roused in the mind by mentioning, hearing, remembering, the name, i. e. for one's rank, authority, interests, pleasure, command, excellences, deeds.

Our calling and service to our Beloved is to uphold His Name or character in a world that has forgotten who He is. At the time of the Temple, the High Priest was given watch over the duties of the other priests. Now Yahshua, our High Priest watches over us and gives us guidance in our duties as those in training as priests. One important duty of the priests within Yahweh's house or Tabernacle was to keep the fire on the altar burning. Of course during the daylight hours, this is not a difficult task because you are alert and rested. But during the night watch, when it is dark, quiet and you are tired, this task becomes very trying. Consequently, the night watch was extremely important, for the fire was never to go out!

Fire shall be kept burning on the altar continually; it shall not go out. Lev.6:13

The High Priest would make his rounds during the night watch to see if the priest on duty was slacking on his responsibility. Often the High Priest would come at a time when the priest would not expect, to see if the priest had fallen asleep or taken any intoxicating drink, jeopardizing the fire on the altar. If the priest had become distracted or had fallen asleep, the High Priest would then take some of the hot coals from the altar and place them on the priest's garments. The priest would wake up in shock and horror, stripping off his burning clothes.

"Behold, I come like a thief. Blessed is he who watches, and keeps his clothes, so that he doesn't walk naked, and they see his shame." Rev.16:15

But concerning the times and the seasons, brothers, you have no need that anything be written to you. For you yourselves know well that the day of the Lord comes like a thief in the night. For when they are saying, "Peace and safety," then sudden destruction will come on them, like birth pains on a pregnant woman; and they will in no way escape. But you, brothers, aren't in darkness, that the day should overtake you like a thief. You are all children of light, and children of the day. We don't belong to the night, nor to darkness, so then let's not sleep, as the rest do, but let's watch and be sober.1 Thess.5:1-6

Our duty as Yahshua's servants and priestly bride is to be sober in our service to Him and to watch and pray. We are never to let the fire of Yahweh to go out in our lives!

He came to the disciples, and found them sleeping, and said to Peter, "What, couldn't you watch with me for one hour? Watch and pray, that you don't enter into temptation. The spirit indeed is willing, but the flesh is weak."Matt.26:40,41

Watch therefore, for you don't know when the lord of the house is coming, whether at evening, or at midnight, or when the rooster crows, or in the morning; lest coming suddenly he might find you sleeping. What I tell you, I tell all: Watch." Mark13:35-37

Therefore he says, "Awake, you who sleep, and arise from the dead, and Christ will shine on you." Eph.5:14

Staying watchful and serving Yahweh in the secret place is one way that Yahshua's bride will make herself ready. Most of the Brit Chadasha or New Testament was written to restore and warn those who would accept Yahshua as their Savior and the terms of the Covenant. Our response is to prepare ourselves for all that must take place before the end comes.

You will hear of wars and rumors of wars. See that you aren't troubled, for all this must happen, but the end is not yet. For nation will rise against nation, and kingdom against kingdom; and there will be famines, plagues, and earthquakes in various places. But all these things are the beginning of birth pains. Matt.24: 6-8

The important words to remember are 'see that you are not troubled.' They challenge us to ignore the enemy's attempts to sensationalize everything in hopes of bringing fear and worry upon us. Our trust in Yahweh and the leading of His Spirit's voice must be at the heart of all our preparation.

I am sure most people have experienced, in some way, the thrill and anticipation of a pregnancy whether it was your own or someone you know. The excitement for the "soon to be" parents and their families is all consuming. The mom is filled with quiet awe as she contemplates the reality of a little one growing and kicking inside her. As the months pass and the anticipation mounts, mom and dad become eager to meet their son or daughter. Then, when the final days approach, their focus changes and the delivery process comes to the forefront of their thoughts.

For the mom, especially a first time mom, the realization that pain must come before the baby is in her arms is often intimidating. If her focus is on the pain alone, it will only make the delivery more difficult for her. After nine months of waiting to meet their little one, to now focus on the pain would rob the parents, (especially the mother) of the joy of bringing forth their baby. Focusing more on the joy, on the other hand, can greatly reduce the difficulty of delivery.

You will be sorrowful, but your sorrow will be turned into joy. A woman, when she gives birth, has sorrow, because her time has come. But when she has delivered the child, she doesn't remember the anguish any more, for the joy that a human being is born into the world. Therefore you now have sorrow, but I will see you again, and your heart will rejoice, and no one will take your joy away from you. John 16: 20-22

We tend to anticipate the coming of the Messiah in a similar way. Yahshua tells us in the above verse that it will not be easy to see and experience the trials that are to come, but we must trust Him and focus on the joy that is coming. The enemy wants to woo us with false security, peace, and entertainment. His scheme is to keep us asleep, entertained, intoxicated and distracted. Yet the trials and tribulation that we will face are meant to keep us awake, alert and prepared to bring forth the new life that awaits those who endure to the end.

For when they are saying, "Peace and safety," then sudden destruction will come on them, like birth pains on a pregnant woman; and they will in no way escape. 1 Thess.5:3

As we have seen in earlier chapters, those who follow Yahweh and dwell with Him in the secret place are not overwhelmed by the tribulation. On the contrary, they are secured on the Rock and covered by His presence. They have learned through the trials of life to trust Yahweh in the storms and to find solace in knowing that His plans are perfect. The joy on the other side of our trials must rise above the difficulties to motivate and drive our speech and actions. Yes, there will be pain and testing, but just as pain is needed to bring forth a child, it is also needed to bring forth the true bride and ready her for the future. We also see this when someone trains for a race. The hard work and discipline that it takes to achieve the prize at the end, does cause pain. It is interesting to note though that the pain that comes from training is often considered satisfying, because the one who is in training knows that the pain is a sign that they are making progress, and getting stronger. In the end, they will be more capable to compete and finish well; anticipating the prize that awaits them at the end. There is a saying in athletic circles that goes, "No pain, no gain." We find this is also true in our lives. As followers of the Messiah we should count it all joy, for every trial and heartbreak is strengthening us to endure to the end.

Count it all joy, my brothers, when you fall into various temptations, knowing that the testing of your faith produces endurance. Let endurance have its perfect work, that you may be perfect and complete, lacking in nothing. James1: 2-4

Don't you know that those who run in a race all run, but one receives the prize? Run like that, that you may win. Every man who strives in the games exercises self-control in all things. Now they do it to receive a corruptible crown, but we an incorruptible. I therefore run like that, as not uncertainly. I fight like that, as not beating the air, but I beat my body and bring it into submission, lest by any means, after I have preached to others, I myself should be rejected. 1 Cor.9: 24-27

The joy of being with our Beloved Messiah forever needs to rise to the forefront of all we face.

Therefore let us also, seeing we are surrounded by so great a cloud of witnesses, lay aside every weight and the sin which so easily entangles us, and let us run with patience the race that is set before us, looking to Jesus, the author and perfecter of faith, who for the joy that was set before him endured the cross, despising its shame, and has sat down at the right hand of the throne of God. Heb.12:1,2

Our preparation for Yahshua's return must begin with seeking Him with all our heart and learning to trust Him in every situation so that we too can endure all things for Him until the end. May our anticipation of the unspeakable joy of His presence, be the motivation for us to be overcomers in this world!

As examples to us, the Children of Israel were delivered from Egypt and experienced Yahweh's might and power, yet they did not make it to the end. When they were faced with trial, they quickly lost sight of who Yahweh truly was to them. Even from the start of their journey, they forgot His power and the promises that He had just spoken to them. When their comfort was compromised in any way, they longed for the ways of Egypt that they were used to. Ironically, it was Yahweh who set the trials before them as a test for their hearts. He wanted to expose their true motivation for following Him. Sadly they proved their hearts to be unfaithful, by complaining and continually using Egypt as a reference point for their needs. When they grew impatient, hungry or scared, they wanted what Egypt had given them and grumbled when they didn't get it. The Children of Israel were no different from any of us.

Yahweh is looking for a people that will love Him faithfully to the end. Unfortunately, as we get older and more experienced we become set in our ways and very comfortable with our lifestyle; no matter what our lives are like. Little children, on the other hand, look to the world as a place of discovery and experience. They are full of wonder and trust their parents or loving caregiver, as we should trust Yahweh.

> *Then Jesus called a little child to Him, set him in the midst of them, and said, "Assuredly, I say to you, unless you are converted and become as little children, you will by no means enter the kingdom of heaven. Therefore whoever humbles himself as this little child is the greatest in the kingdom of heaven. Whoever receives one little child like this in My name receives Me. Matt. 18:2-5*

> *Little children, these are the end times, and as you heard that the Antichrist is coming, even now many antichrists have arisen. By this we know that it is the final hour. 1 John 2:18*

Once we are born again, Yahweh calls us to accept our new life as one of His children. As a child, we should be willingly to accept the ways of our Father and trust Him above all else. Still, there are many influences in our lives even from an early age; caregivers, teachers, peers and the many voices of media. We are not in this world long and a parent's voice becomes one in a sea of voices. Unless there is a strong parent-child relationship, the child's trust may fade. The difficulty with trust comes from the world's hold on us today. The overriding ploy is to induce fear and rob us all of any sense of trust or security we may have. It benefits marketers and all types of business to convince us that we need to buy or insure their product for a myriad of potential problems. The enemy's agenda is to make us feel that nothing is trustworthy or secure … not even our heavenly Father.

Insecurity has profoundly influenced all aspects of our lives especially our relationships; including marriage, parent and child, friendships, partnerships, and many others. Much too often a breech of trust or a broken promise gives way to broken hearts, rebellion and loss. Ultimately, these negative experiences affect how we trust Yahweh. When difficult times come, or things don't go as we had hoped and planned, our perception of a loving God is altered. When others hurt or deceive us, we question His love and care for us. Usually during these times of questioning God, is when trusting our own judgment seeps into our lives. This is very subtle and seemingly wise, but we must keep our belief and trust in Yahweh at the center of all we do. Trust in Him is the only solid hope we have in this world. If we don't trust Yahweh, we risk loosing our relationship with Him.

Now I desire to remind you, though you already know this, that the Lord, having saved a people out of the land of Egypt, afterward destroyed those who didn't believe. Jude 1:5

Yahweh became angry when the Children of Israel lost their trust in Him, and began whining and begging for the things of Egypt. People forget that though Yahweh is extremely patient, He does not accept being tested or slighted. We will suffer the consequences if we choose to not listen to Him or trust Him in all things. In His great love and mercy He has given us everything, and yet we often treat His love and provision as not enough. Remember it is this same attitude that the Children of Israel had with the manna that came to them each day from Heaven.

*They tempted God in their heart
by asking food according to their desire.
Yes, they spoke against God.*

They said, "Can God prepare a table in the wilderness?
Behold, he struck the rock, so that waters gushed out,
and streams overflowed.
Can he give bread also?
Will he provide flesh for his people?"
Therefore Yahweh heard, and was angry.
A fire was kindled against Jacob,
anger also went up against Israel,
because they didn't believe in God,
and didn't trust in his salvation.
Yet he commanded the skies above,
and opened the doors of heaven.
He rained down manna on them to eat,
and gave them food from the sky.
Man ate the bread of angels.
He sent them food to the full. Ps.78:18-25

The above verse reveals how the attitude of the Children of Israel in the Wilderness disappointed Yahweh. The consequences were devastating; all perished except those who fully trusted Yahweh and were devoted to serving Him on His terms. In the end, it was only two; Joshua and Caleb who saw the Promised Land. Now we have the greater manna, the Manna from Heaven! … the Bread of Life that has come to give us life everlasting!

They said therefore to him, "What then do you do for a sign, that we may see, and believe you? What work do you do? Our fathers ate the manna in the wilderness. As it is written, 'He gave them bread out of heaven to eat.'"

Jesus therefore said to them, "Most certainly, I tell you, it wasn't Moses who gave you the bread out of heaven, but my Father gives you the true bread out of heaven. For the bread of God is that which comes down out of heaven, and gives life to the world." John 6:30-33

Is Yahshua enough to satisfy... or will we seek for more of what the world has? He has given us His all and provides for our needs each day. When we pray the Father's prayer "Give us this day our daily bread," we are crying out for Yahshua our Bread of Life. He is our manna and our sufficiency, and when we trust in Him, He protects, keeps and covers us.

The Lord is good, A stronghold in the day of trouble;
And He knows those who trust in Him. Nahum 1:7 (NKJ)

Yahweh will also be a high tower for the oppressed;
a high tower in times of trouble.
Those who know your name will put their trust in you,
for you, Yahweh, have not forsaken
those who seek you.Ps.9: 9,10

How precious is your loving kindness, God!
The children of men take refuge under
the shadow of your wings.
They shall be abundantly satisfied with
the abundance of your house.
You will make them drink of the river
of your pleasures.Ps.36:7,8

All of Scripture exhorts us to trust Yahweh and see the trials of life as Yahweh's training ground for us to learn to be overcomers; able to endure all hardships with His help. He is testing our hearts to refine them and purge out our selfishness and pride. As we align ourselves with the heart of Yahweh and trust Him fully, He blesses us with all we need to flourish, and be the bride that the Messiah is coming for.

"Blessed is the man who trusts in the Lord,
And whose hope is the Lord.
For he shall be like a tree planted by the waters,
Which spreads out its roots by the river,
And will not fear when heat comes;
But its leaf will be green,
And will not be anxious in the year of drought,
Nor will cease from yielding fruit. Jer. 17:7,8

In today's world, the phrase 'trusting like a child' could be misunderstood to mean that we can relax to the point of letting go of our responsibilities. You may have seen this attitude in action when a child stays on the couch and the parent does everything for them. In our relationship with Yahweh, a complacent attitude is expressed like, "He is powerful, and I am weak, and so there is nothing I can do to truly make a difference. I am content to be saved, to be one of His children and wait until I go to heaven." We see this attitude is seen in the parable of the talents, through the servant with the one talent, who buried his talent in the ground until his Master's return.

"He also who had received the one talent came and said, 'Lord, I knew you that you are a hard man, reaping where you did not sow, and gathering where you did not scatter. I was afraid, and went away and hid your talent in the earth. Behold, you have what is yours.'

"But his lord answered him, 'You wicked and slothful servant. You knew that I reap where I didn't sow, and gather where I didn't scatter. You ought therefore to have deposited my money with the bankers, and at my coming I should have received back my own with interest. Take away therefore the talent from him, and give it to him who has the ten talents. For to everyone who has will be given, and he will have abundance, but from him who doesn't have, even that which he has will be taken away. Throw out the unprofitable servant into the outer darkness, where there will be weeping and gnashing of teeth.' Matt. 25:24-30

Yahweh desires us to be like the servants with the two and five talents, who worked diligently in preparation for His return. Our trust in Yahweh is to be as wholehearted as a child who knows the desires of his Father's heart and with honor upholds the standard of His household even while He is away. As we are faithful in the responsibilities entrusted to us, we grow and mature, becoming more like Yahshua who showed us the way to love and obey.

Now after a long time the lord of those servants came, and reconciled accounts with them. He who received the five talents came and brought another five talents, saying, 'Lord, you delivered to me five talents. Behold, I have gained another five talents besides them.'

"His lord said to him, 'Well done, good and faithful servant. You have been faithful over a few things, I will set you over many things. Enter into the joy of your lord.'

"He also who got the two talents came and said, 'Lord, you delivered to me two talents. Behold, I have gained another two talents besides them.'

"His lord said to him, 'Well done, good and faithful servant. You have been faithful over a few things, I will set you over many things. Enter into the joy of your lord.' Matt. 25:19-23

Our actions are to be as vigilant as a soldier, yet always motivated by love to bring honor and glory to our Master's Name. May we come to love the work of our Father's heart and listen for the leading of His Spirit's voice in all we do. May the fire in our hearts for Him never go out as we make ourselves ready for our Beloved's return; always alert, sober and watching so that His return could never come upon us as a thief.

"Behold, I come quickly. My reward is with me, to repay to each man according to his work." Rev.22 :12

Watching

WE HAVE SEEN THAT YAHSHUA'S BRIDE WILL CONSIST OF THOSE WHO follow Yahweh in the ways of the royal priesthood; daily serving Him and rehearsing the things of His heart. The more she endures and learns to follow in His steps, the closer her walk will align with His Word until eventually, she will be able to keep pace with Him. As she walks with Him on His path of righteousness, she will learn to watch and see more clearly what Yahweh sees. With each step, whether down into a valley or up a steep ascent, she learns to trust Him for what she cannot see.

... for we walk by faith, not by sight. 2Cor.5:7

As the seasons take their turn, year after year, Yahshua's bride will anticipate the desires of His heart even before He tells her what they are. When this happens His bride will be most radiant. For then she will be able to prepare in advance to serve Him and respond to the needs of others on the path.

For you were once darkness, but are now light in the Lord. Walk as children of light, Eph.5:8

The journey of the bride of the Messiah reminds me of when I was young girl, and my Dad would take me on walks through woodland trails. As I grew, the trails he chose became increasingly more difficult until I could climb mountain trails. In my Dad's quiet way he showed me the many wonders of Yahweh's Creation each step of the trail. I remember well his steady, rhythmic footsteps and his gentle manner. When I was a little girl, I could not keep pace with him though. Often I would lag behind, and he would have to wait for me to catch up. Other times I would get distracted by my selfish desires and whine because I was hungry, tired or simply too impatient to walk all the way to our destination. Still, he waited for me, fed me snacks from his pack and encouraged me to keep going to the end. Along the way, he would faithfully point out the many treasures hidden on the trail that I would have otherwise missed. Time passed, and I walked many trails with him. As I grew up, I began to match his stride and trade my selfish desires for the joy of walking with him and the anticipation of the final resting place. With experience, I could now spot dangers and look for treasures on the trail for myself. The repeated walks with him, helped me to remember all that he had shown me as a child and to carefully watch and listen. As an adult, I then shared the joy of the trail with him in a new way. We talked and watched together as we walked the trail to our destination.

Our walk with Yahweh on the path of righteousness is the same. We begin our walk with Him as children. The first time down His path is difficult because we have never been on it before and we aren't able to keep pace with Yahweh. The path of righteousness is also very narrow, and we can easily stumble. Often it feels overwhelming to stay on the path and take in all that Yahweh wants to show us. Sometimes we become distracted by our selfish desires; our flesh grows weary, our hearts get discouraged, and we lag behind. Other times we may feel a surge of zealous energy, and with confidence, we run ahead. Yet if we are not careful we risk making a wrong turn and losing our way. As a loving Father, Yahweh is always guiding us and bringing us back to His side by His Spirit so that we will learn to keep pace with Him. As we stay by Him and listen to His voice, we will grow wise, strong and mature.

Oh that my people would listen to Me, that
Israel would walk in My ways! Ps.81:13

Teach me your way, Yahweh; I will
walk in your truth; Ps.86:11a

Yahweh's cycles are designed to keep us on His path of righteousness. They help our feet to find the steady pace of our Father's steps. Some people say that repetition is burdensome, confining and restricts the Holy Spirit. This way of thinking is inconsistent with the patterns that Yahweh has placed in Creation. On the contrary, His faithful patterns were designed with the purpose of showing us His narrow way. In Hebrew, the word 'way' is derekh, Strong's #H1870 and it literally means a road or path. This way or path is mapped out for us in Torah and confirmed in the rest of Scripture. I have inserted below, a description of the way or path that Yahweh has designed for us by Jeff Benner, from the Ancient Hebrew Research Center.

When traveling the wilderness it is important to stay on course in order to find the next landmark as well as the pastures and water sources. If one was to lose their way they will become lost and may die if they do not return to the proper route. The idea of being on course and lost from the course is found in two Hebrew words, צדיק (tsadiyq, Strong's #6662) and רשע (rasha, Strong's #7563). The word tsadiyq literally means to stay on course, to remain on the path while rasha means to be lost from the path. Tsadiyq is usually translated as righteous and rasha as wicked but, these English words do not convey the original meaning behind the Hebrew very well. One who is tsadiyq remains on the road, following God's directions but on the other hand, one who is rasha is lost and is in jeopardy of death. Consider Proverbs 10:11 which states, The mouth of the tsadiyq is a source of life but the violence covers the mouth of the rasha. Once one realizes that he has become lost (rasha) his goal is to turn around and return to the correct path. This idea is expressed in the Hebrew verb שוב (shuv, Strong's #7725). This same verb is used in the context of repenting (returning to the path) from wrongdoing (lost from the path) and returning to the commands (directions) of God - And thou shalt return and obey the voice of the LORD, and do all his commandments which I command thee this day or, from a more Hebraic perspective - and you will return to the path and you

will listen to the voice of Yahweh and you will follow all his directions which I have pointed out to you today (Deuteronomy 30:8). In ancient times the stars would guide one on their journey. The Hebrew verb הלל (halal, Strong's #7725) is the shining light of these stars - For the stars of the heavens and their constellations will not give their light הלל (Isaiah 13:10). This same word is also translated as "praise" but Hebraicly means to "look toward another as a shining light." When the Psalms say, Praise Yah (halelu-Yah) (Psalm 135:3) it is literally saying "Look to Yah as the light that will guide you on your journey.»

How beautifully this confirms all that we have seen in the way of the heavens and our journey with Yahweh! Just as the Moon faithfully stays on its orbital path looking to the Sun for light and direction, we too are stay on our heavenly Father's path that takes us through His cycles of righteousness. The Moon's journey is steady and unchanging and never turns away from its source of light. For those who choose to follow Yahshua (the Way) on the path of righteousness it will be the same. They will stay on the steady, unchanging path of Yahweh, and never turn away from Yahshua, their source of light. The repetition will not be a burden, but an overwhelming delight. In fact, the repetition will be a comfort and an assurance that we are not lost! Psalm 23 states that, 'Your rod and staff comfort me.' The rod and staff of Yahshua, the Good Shepherd represent Yahweh's Word that keeps us from straying off the path and getting lost.

> *"Come to Me, all you who labor and are heavy laden, and I will give you rest. Take My yoke upon you and learn from Me, for I am gentle and lowly in heart, and you will find rest for your souls. For My yoke is easy and My burden is light."Matt.11:28-30*

The picture Yahshua was portraying for us in this verse was that of a young ox coming under the yoke of a seasoned, stronger ox that was trained to thresh the grain in a circle. The older, stronger ox knows the way and bears the weight of the work, as the young ox follows along learning the manner of the mighty one. The burden for the young ox is therefore light, for he simply needs to follow the well-worn path of the mighty one. This is Yahweh's plan for us. By living a life that is consistent in following Yahshua's steps, we like a young ox are being trained and transformed, step by step, into His likeness. The patterns of our Master become our patterns, His desires become our desires, and eventually we become strong enough to walk the circle or path alone. Then we will become a reflection of our One and Only true source of Light.

But we all, with unveiled face, beholding as in a mirror the glory of the Lord, are being transformed into the same image from glory to glory, just as by the Spirit of the Lord. 2 Cor. 3:18

Each year Yahweh's cycle is set before us as His path to follow. Each year that we walk with Him, His path becomes more familiar and easier to walk. As we learn to trust His leading, we are able to manage the difficult places on the path and keep pace with His steps. Each cycle He lovingly reveals more treasures to us than the year before. As His path becomes more familiar we will anticipate His signs and see more of what He sees. Our journey upon Yahweh's path teaches us to have a keen eye that watches and discerns all that is around us as we sojourn home to our resting place. Thankfully, there are frequent stops along the way, to be still with our Beloved, to savor the beauty of His Creation that surrounds us and to worship Him for His faithfulness. Take a moment now to read Psalm 23 with this picture in mind.

Yahweh is my shepherd: I shall lack nothing.
He makes me lie down in green pastures.
He leads me beside still waters.
He restores my soul.
He guides me in the paths of righteousness for his name's sake.
Even though I walk through the valley of the shadow of death,
I will fear no evil, for you are with me.
Your rod and your staff,
they comfort me.
You prepare a table before me
in the presence of my enemies.
You anoint my head with oil.
My cup runs over.

Surely goodness and loving kindness shall
follow me all the days of my life,
and I will dwell in Yahweh's house forever.

How beautifully this reflects our walk with Yahshua, our Good Shepherd, Who always makes sure we are safe as He leads us to the waters where He restores our soul. He uses His rod and staff to see that we stay on the path and don't wander off. He teaches us His instructions by the washing of His Word and prepares a banquet for us in the face of our enemies.

The Hebrew word for path in the phrase 'paths of righteousness' is Strong's #H4570 magal, which means; a track as circular. Magal comes from the Hebrew word agol, meaning; to revolve in a circle. Magal can only be referring to the path of righteousness, which does not change; it is constant and true. The narrow path is where we are to faithfully walk each year, just as the Moon faithfully follows the same path in the heavens. Then just as we saw earlier, we will grow ever brighter on our journey until we are seen shining like Sun.

But the path of the righteous is like the dawning light,
that shines more and more until the perfect day. Prov.4:18

Yahshua is our shining example of how to walk the path of righteousness. As we walk with Him we become familiar with our Beloved's heart and learn to shine as He shines, reflecting His light to those around us. Our walk of faith, strengthens us to stand strong no matter what the enemy may use to taunt or distract us. For the enemy surrounds us, hoping to lure us off the path of righteousness onto his path of destruction. Proverbs warns us of the terrible danger of leaving Yahweh's path.

I have taught you in the way of wisdom.
I have led you in straight paths.
When you go, your steps will not be hampered.
When you run, you will not stumble.
Take firm hold of instruction.
Don't let her go.
Keep her, for she is your life.
Don't enter into the path of the wicked.
Don't walk in the way of evil men.

Avoid it, and don't pass by it.
Turn from it, and pass on.Prov.4:11-15

When we walk with our Shepherd we learn to watch for His signs and discern danger along the way.

Be sober and self-controlled. Be watchful. Your adversary, the devil, walks around like a roaring lion, seeking whom he may devour. 1Pet. 5:8

Therefore watch carefully how you walk, not as unwise, but as wise; redeeming the time, because the days are evil. Therefore don't be foolish, but understand what the will of the Lord is. Eph. 5:15,16

Each day ... even each moment, we must listen to the Shepherd's voice and learn to watch as He watches and see what He sees.

Watch, keep alert, and pray; for you don't know when the time is. Mark13:33

Remember therefore how you have received and heard. Keep it, and repent. If therefore you won't watch, I will come as a thief, and you won't know what hour I will come upon you. Rev.3:3

Scripture admonishes us to watch as a vital part of our walk. So, what does watching look like in our everyday life? The Greek word used for watch in the New Testament is, gregoreuo, Strong's #G1127, which means; to be awake and have your wits about you. When you look for words related to watching in the Hebrew, you will find that many words used for watching that give us deeper insight into the meaning behind watching. Each word builds upon the other to help us see what the action of watching truly looks like. We will look at a few of these words to help us put into perspective how we can apply watching to our lives.

The first word we will look at is Strong's # H6822 צָפָה tsaphah, which means to lean forward and peer into the distance. Tsaphan is most often translated as watchman, which paints the picture of someone on a lookout peering out onto the horizon to see what is approaching. Watchman duty is given to us to warn people so that they are not taken off guard. This is why it is so important to recognize the signs on the horizon and discern what they mean.

> *Son of man, I have made you a watchman (H6822) to the house of Israel: therefore hear the word from my mouth, and give them warning from me. Ez. 3:17*

There is a cognate word to tsaphah which has the same spelling, which is Strong's #H6823, צפה. This version of tsaphah is used to describe the gold overlay for the vessels in the Tabernacle. At first glance, this meaning doesn't seem related to watching, but there is a connection. The cognate use of tsaphah is related to the first use of this word by taking our watching out to the horizon in an act of awareness. Let me explain. The vessels of the Tabernacle were things prepared to be useful in displaying the heart of Yahweh. The gold overlay was to be a hammered work that took the gold through a process of making it into a thin sheet. The gold was then laid over the vessels as a protective and reflective covering. The duty of a watchman is summed up in this picture. We must endure the process of being refined as gold and hammered out to be fit to watch over His things and reflect His light. Also, as we conform to His image, we become worthy to watch out for His people and discern what we are seeing on the horizon. Here again, we see the imagery of the Moon; reflecting His light and giving signs for His people.

> *I will bring the third part into the fire, and will refine them as silver is refined, and will test them like gold is tested. They will call on my name, and I will hear them. I will say, 'It is my people;' and they will say, 'Yahweh is my God.'" Zech. 13:9*

> *But he knows the way that I take. When he has tried me, I shall come forth like gold. Job 23:10*

We now come us to another intriguing Hebrew word used for watch, which is Strong's #H8245 שקד, shaqad, meaning; to be alert, awake, on the lookout. Shaqad is the word translated as watching in the following Proverb.

> *Blessed is the man who hears me,*
> *watching daily at my gates,*
> *waiting at my door posts.*
> *For whoever finds me, finds life,*
> *and will obtain favor from Yahweh. Prov.8:34,35*

The Hebrew word shaqad brings the action of watching to that of wide-eyed, anticipation. A watchman may stand guard to protect the camp from the enemy, but he must also stay alert and watch for signs of the return of those who are away, especially his master. As Yahshua's bride in preparation for her Husband's return, we can never forsake watching for our Beloved. Shaqad shares an interesting cognate word with the same spelling, which is the Hebrew word for almond. We will look at this word more in the last chapter of this section about 'The Five Wise,' but at a glance, one can see that an almond is shaped like an eye to remind us of the need to watch. Yahweh also designed the Menorah; the only source of light in the Holy Place with almond shapes, bringing the call to watch and the call to be a light together in one vessel within the Tabernacle. With hopeful, longing Yahshua's bride watches over all that is in the household of her Beloved (the Tabernacle), bringing light to the darkness as she daily watches for His return.

The English word circumspect, used in Ephesians 5 in some translations helps reveal the actions of the Hebrew words for watch. The 1928 American Dictionary describes circumspect as; looking on all sides, as to look all around; cautious; prudent; watchful on all sides; examining carefully all the circumstances that may affect a determination or a measure to be adopted. The root of the word circumspect is circum, which means; around in a circle or to surround something. Isn't that amazing! The word circumspect takes us back to the Hebrew word magal for the path of righteousness, which is displayed in the Moon's orbit of the Earth. The Moon faithfully faces the Sun and travels circumspectly on its path giving light and signs to a dark and lost world. The Moon's phases, in turn, help us walk circumspectly on Yahweh's path of righteousness and through

Yahweh's appointed days by giving us the times and seasons to keep pace with Him.

> *Therefore He says:*
> *"Awake, you who sleep,*
> *Arise from the dead,*
> *And Christ will give you light."*

See then that you walk circumspectly, not as fools but as wise, redeeming the time, because the days are evil. Eph.5:14-16 (NKJ)

In the King James Version, you will find a Hebrew word translated as circumspect in one verse in Exodus.

And in all things that I have said unto you be circumspect: and make no mention of the name of other gods, neither let it be heard out of thy mouth. Ex.23:13

Here the Hebrew word translated as circumspect is Strong's #H8104 שמר shamar. Throughout Scripture shamar is also translated as guard, beware, observe, take heed, preserve, save, regard, be circumspect, watch, wait and keep. All of these meanings for shamar knit together the bride's call to watch and be circumspect while caring for the things of her Beloved's heart.

> *I wait for the Lord, my soul waits,*
> *And in His word I do hope.*
> *My soul waits for the Lord*
> *More than those who watch (H1804) for the morning—*
> *Yes, more than those who watch for the*
> *morning. Ps.130:5,6(NKJ)*

Shamar is a great example of how the same Hebrew word is translated in different ways to give us the fullness of the word's meaning. In one verse it is used to speak of how our hearts wait for Yahshua, and in the other, it is used to warn us to watch our words and attitude toward other gods. The word shamar takes the call to watch into the many duties of a servant or priest of Yahweh. Shamar gives the bride understanding and revelation of her responsibility as part of the royal priesthood, for it is the bride's privilege and honor, to watch over and care for all the things of Yahshua's heart.

Therefore keep (shamar) the words of this covenant and do them, that you may prosper in all that you do. Deut.29:9

Behold, I have taught you statutes and ordinances, even as Yahweh my God commanded me, that you should do so in the middle of the land where you go in to possess it. Keep therefore and do them; for this is your wisdom and your understanding in the sight of the peoples, who shall hear all these statutes, and say, "Surely this great nation is a wise and understanding people." Deut.4:5,6

> *Give me understanding, and I will keep (shamar) your law.*
> *Yes, I will obey it with my whole heart.Ps.119:34*

The bride of the Messiah as a good steward of Yahweh's household will keep or shall I say guard and protect what her Bridegroom cherishes. She will diligently rehearse His coming each Rosh Chodesh, longing for that great and blessed day when she will be by His side. Yahshua's bride will also shamar or keep all of His appointed days, New Moons, and Sabbaths, as well as the principles and patterns of His Word or Torah. She will allow the His Holy Spirit to show her the way of holiness, so that she may know her Bridegroom and be known by Him. Then, at the appointed time, she will be worthy of and adorned in the priestly wedding garments of fine linen.

I have heard it said that we cannot *truly* keep or obey the Commandments of Yahweh in the times that we live, especially the feast days. If we adhere to this perspective we are misunderstanding the word 'keep or shamar.' I would ask those who feel that this is true, how they would keep or care for a valuable heirloom? For though it may not be able to fully function at this time, its value is only increasing if it is well kept. When we implement the meanings for the Hebrew word shamar into the action of keeping some-thing, our actions honor and protect the person and the things of their heart. The way we keep or shamar Yahweh's commands including His feast days is meant to bring honor to Yahweh. As we observe, guard, watch, wait and keep all of Yahweh's Commandments we are actively representing His Name and the things of His heart until Yahshua returns and restores all things. The Torah, revealed in Yahshua is our standard of how we love Him and those around us, as Yahshua said;

If you love me, keep my commandments. John 14:15

By this we know that we love the children of God, when we love God and keep his commandments. For this is the love of God, that we keep his commandments. His commandments are not grievous. 1John 5:2,3

Each of Yahweh's Commandments are important because they lay the foundation for knowing Yahshua. Each one builds upon the other to complete the fullness of Yahweh's love story. Though we are unable to perform each one; our actions and words must honor and uphold their meaning for our attitude and efforts toward them speaks volumes of our heart. Would it not be contradicting for Yahweh to tell us to do something that is impossible? Yahshua is the revelation of all that the Torah requires, and now our hearts hold the seed of Him, (Yahweh's Word) and the writing of His Covenant Words.

Is the law then against the promises of God? Certainly not! For if there had been a law given which could make alive, most certainly righteousness would have been of the law. But the Scriptures imprisoned all things under sin, that the promise by faith in Jesus Christ might be given to those who believe. But before faith came, we were kept in custody under the law, confined for the faith which should afterwards be revealed. So that the law has become our tutor to bring us to Christ, that we might be justified by faith. Gal.3:21-24

Yahshua came to reveal the heart of Torah, for the Torah was designed to keep (preserve, save, guard) those who were waiting and watching for the coming of the Messiah. The written Torah reveals the standard of Yahweh's heart in our actions, Yahshua, who is the Torah in the flesh, raised the bar to the point of our thoughts and attitude. If you are a parent, you will see this principle in action all the time. As a child grows up, they discover through rules and discipline what is important to their parents. They learn to listen and copy what their parents express to them. A toddler observes what his or her parents do and say and then in innocence tries to imitate them; even though it is impossible for them to do it in the same way as the parents. Should the parents chastise them for trying? Of course not ... because it is out of a pure heart of love that they are putting into action the ways of the household. With consistent, daily training the child learns and understands how to keep things as their parents do. Just as we saw pictured in walking a trail, Yahweh's path of righteousness teaches us how to walk with Him and see as He sees. Soon we will find that there is always something of Yahweh's entire Word that applies to our lives each day. The patterns and attitude we develop as we walk Yahshua's path of righteousness then trains our minds and hearts to think like Yahshua, and reflect His light through our loving words and actions.

Train up a child in the way he should go,
And when he is old he will not depart from it.
Prov.22:6

For the commandment is a lamp,
And the law a light;
Reproofs of instruction are the way of life, Prov.6:23

As we walk by faith, our words and actions are cleansed of our selfish ambition and devoted to loving Yahweh and our neighbors. Then our hearts, like Yahweh's will be motivated by selfless love; for without His love as the motivation for our actions and words... all our efforts mean nothing and ultimately destroy the beauty of being in harmony with Yahweh.

If I speak with the languages of men and of angels, but don't have love, I have become sounding brass, or a clanging cymbal. If I have the gift of prophecy, and know all mysteries and all knowledge; and if I have all faith, so as to remove mountains, but don't have love, I am nothing. If I dole out all my goods to feed the poor, and if I give my body to be burned, but don't have love, it profits me nothing. 1 Cor. 13:1-3

In this the children of God are revealed, and the children of the devil. Whoever doesn't do righteousness is not of God, neither is he who doesn't love his brother. 1 John 3:10

A new commandment I give to you, that you love one another. Just as I have loved you, you also love one another. By this everyone will know that you are my disciples, if you have love for one another." John 13:34,35

The lack of love in people who claimed to follow Yahweh, but do not show it in their actions is what broke Yahshua's heart while He was here with us. He rebuked the Pharisees; for they were filled with words about Yahweh, but their deeds did not reflect a love toward Yahweh or His Word. The same is true in many cases today. Often we become filled with knowledge, competition and the desire to be right, forgetting the weightier things of loving Yahweh with all our heart, loving one another and reaching the lost. Yahweh is calling out to us to return to Him with love, forgiveness, and repentance. We must edify and build one another up in the love of our Messiah and stop tearing each other down. Those who are on the outside see very clearly the state the body of the Messiah is in. The time has come for us to stand for all that honors our Beloved and become a people that declares our love for the King in unity and love for another, so that when Yahshua comes we are found caring for His household as He would. As we take our place as watchmen and servants, may we begin to see as Yahshua sees, never forgetting to tell those who are lost that there is a heavenly Father who loves them, and caring for others with His love until He comes.

His lord said to him, 'Well done, good and faithful servant; you were faithful over a few things, I will make you ruler over many things. Enter into the joy of your lord.' Matt. 25:21

Standing guard and looking out onto the horizon for what is coming is a challenge in this busy, distracted world. We need set apart time to dwell in the secret place, to be renewed and refreshed in our commitment to our Beloved. Those who do will be given the love, faith and hope they need to be prepared for the return of their Beloved Master.

Watch! Stand firm in the faith! Be courageous! Be strong!
Let all that you do be done in love. 1Cor. 16:13,14

Elul

ELUL IS THE SIXTH NEW MOON THAT COMES TO US AS WE WALK ALONG Yahweh's path of righteousness and is the final month before Yahweh's appointed fall feast days. For those who are watching it is a time of joyful anticipation for one year, their Beloved's return will appear at the end of Elul on the seventh New Moon. Elul usually begins on the Gregorian calendar during August, which for many people is the busy time when summer is ending. These last days of summer bring to my mind an intriguing fable accredited to Aesop called, 'The Ant and the Grasshopper.' It is a short fable, but it has been told countless times in many forms across the world, generation after generation. As we take a closer look at this fable though, it appears to have Biblical roots. The characters and their attitudes surprisingly apply to those who will live during last days before Yahshua's return; which will unfold during Elul.

Remember with me the setting of this fable. The story takes place in the country during the last days of summer, with two small creatures having different responses to the approaching winter. One of the creatures is an ant, who works diligently to store the abundance of summer's harvest before its gone. The other creature is a grasshopper, who spends his time playing music and leisurely enjoying the summer days. The grasshopper sees the ant laboring in the hot sun and invites him to come away from his work and join him in his fun. The ant boldly refuses the invitation and continues to work hard in spite of the heat. Indignant, the grasshopper scoffs at the ant's busy-ness and inability to 'live a little.' Then the grasshopper continues on his way, singing and playing in the Sun.

You know the rest of the fable, the seasons take their turn as seasons faithfully do and soon a bitter, cold winter covers the land. The ant then reaps the fruit of his labor and spends the winter safe, warm and content with plenty of food to last him the winter. The forlorn grasshopper on the other hand, has only his memories of 'fun in the Sun' to keep him warm and he spends the winter cold, hungry and suffering the consequences of his foolish behavior. The obvious moral of this little fable? ... 'be prepared for the future.'

Now, with these intriguing images in mind, let's take a deeper look at this fable and its players; the grasshopper and the ant through Yahweh's Word.

It is He who sits above the circle of the earth,
And its inhabitants are like grasshoppers,
Who stretches out the heavens like a curtain,
And spreads them out like a tent to dwell in. Is.40:22(NKJ)

The ants are a people not strong,
Yet they prepare their food in the summer; Prov.30:25

Long before Aesop's fable was penned, Scripture has used the grasshopper and the ant to teach us about work and our attitude toward preparedness. Each year we experience the examples seen through the actions and attitude of these little creatures in our own lives, as we rehearse for the time of Yahshua's return. Each year the long beautiful days of summer come to us after the completion of the spring feast days. If you have a farm or garden, summer is a busy time of planting and maintaining what you have in the ground, so that you don't miss the full benefit of the season. Biblically the crops that will come forth from the summer are for the fall harvest, food for the winter and to fulfill the needs of the fall feast days.

If you do not have land for planting or a small garden to maintain, summer is still a very busy time. Most children are out of school, and so many outdoor activities fill a family's days. Those who work outdoors also have an extra workload to get done before the rain and cold sets in. In general, there is limited free time and a limited amount of suitable weather for outdoor work. Consequently most people are kept running in some way until the long, warm days begin to cool, the harvest is in, and school begins again.

As we walk through these times each year, there is a practical and spiritual application to consider. From a practical perspective, it is prudent to prepare for winter, whatever that may look like in your area. For many people, the seasons are not distinct and so the practical perspective of seeing the seasons will vary depending on where you live, but the spiritual perspective is worldwide. The spiritual perspective of summer includes the preparation of our hearts for the fall feasts, so that we may stand before our King with a pure heart on His appointed days. There are plans to be made for the needs of our family and for the needs of others who will gather with us to celebrate. Summer is a time that requires focused and sincere attention, for just as we bring in the harvest in the natural, we also need to mindful of the harvest of souls in the spiritual. For as the day of Yahshua's return quickly approaches, those who are lost, need to hear the truth and see His light.

> *Don't you say, 'There are yet four months until the harvest?' Behold, I tell you, lift up your eyes, and look at the fields, that they are white for harvest already. He who reaps receives wages, and gathers fruit to eternal life; that both he who sows and he who reaps may rejoice together. John 4:35,36*

> *Then he said to them, "The harvest is indeed plentiful, but the laborers are few. Pray therefore to the Lord of the harvest, that he may send out laborers into his harvest. Luke 10:2*

The story of the ant and the grasshopper should not be taken lightly. Biblically the grasshopper represents those who are caught up in the 'fun-seeking' ways of the world, and the ant represents those who have the wisdom and perseverance to do what was right in preparation for the times ahead ... whatever the cost. Yahshua told us that there would be few workers willing to bring in the harvest of souls. As we prepare ourselves for what lies ahead, we must be ready to reach out to others and be mindful of Yahweh's harvest. One problem with people vs. ants is that people have a harder time working together for a common goal than ants do. Our world is not an easy environment for building working relationships that include putting others first and edifying one another. Yet for an ant it is instinctive. In an anonymous online article, an author records his observation of how ants live and work together.

Ants are self-motivated

Ants are extremely organized

Ants run away fast when something harmful is around

Ants understand their gifts and work within their specific abilities

Ants build together

Ants have single focus

Ants help and share with others

Ants are team players

Ants are hard workers

Ants take rest seriously

Ants understand timing

The characteristics and attributes Yahweh created in ants reveal a wonderful picture of unity. Together a colony of ants care for each another, stay true to their goals and prepare for what is coming. Obviously, there are many different species of ants, and they are considered pests to most people, but there is still a lot we can learn from them. The attributes of a grasshopper, on the other hand, are not so industrious, or group focused. They do not have a nest or home of their own and migrate from place to place. They are most commonly known for their destruction, especially of what someone else has planted. In Aesop's fable, the grasshopper despises the preparation the ants were working for and bore the serious consequences of his carefree, lazy attitude. The grasshopper's alluring and distracting words do not win in the end, and the ant stands firm to the task set before him.

> *Go to the ant, you sluggard!*
> *Consider her ways and be wise,*
> *Which, having no captain,*
> *Overseer or ruler,*
> *Provides her supplies in the summer,*
> *And gathers her food in the harvest. Prov.6:6-8*
>
> *Laziness casts one into a deep sleep,*
> *And an idle person will suffer hunger.Prov.19:15*

Now notice in the account of the twelve spies, in Numbers 13 the attitude of the spies with these pictures in mind. Twelve spies were sent into the Promised land to assess its worth and condition. Ten of the spies come back with a bad, fearful report which included seeing themselves as grasshoppers.

> *And they gave the children of Israel a bad report of the land which they had spied out, saying, "The land through which we have gone as spies is a land that devours its inhabitants, and all the people whom we saw in it are men of great stature. There we saw the giants(the descendants of Anak came from the giants); and we were like grasshoppers in our own sight, and so we were in their sight."Num. 13:32,33*

Those with the bad report saw things from their own fleshly abilities and not from Yahweh's perspective. His power and His promises were not considered in how they viewed the Promised Land. Their negative report of hopelessness, fear, and laziness cost them everything because they saw themselves through their own doubting eyes and all those who believed their report suffered along with them.

> *Tell them, 'As I live, says Yahweh, surely as you have spoken in my ears, so will I do to you. Your dead bodies shall fall in this wilderness; and all who were numbered of you, according*

to your whole number, from twenty years old and upward, who have murmured against me, surely you shall not come into the land, concerning which I swore that I would make you dwell therein, except Caleb the son of Jephunneh, and Joshua the son of Nun. But your little ones, that you said should be captured or killed, them I will bring in, and they shall know the land which you have rejected. Num.14:28-31

Only two of the spies, Joshua and Caleb, saw the land from Yahweh's perspective. They saw the beauty of the Promised Land in spite of its inhabitants, and they knew that with Yahweh's help they could overcome all obstacles that stood in their way. Consequently, they were the ones to lead the few people who were left of the Children of Israel into the Promised Land. This story gives us insight to those who are like grasshoppers. They are the ones not willing to see Yahweh in all His power and glory or to trust in His Word. They are lazy, fearful, and their negative perspective and lack of belief is infectious, breaking down the morale of the people who listen to them.

In contrast, we are called to persevere in spiritual prudence and prayerful preparation. The work of the tiny ant, no matter how overwhelming, is never enough to stop them. They are renowned for their strength, speed and willingness to do whatever is needed to bring in the harvest. Proverbs also refers to the ant as one of the four small creatures who is exceedingly wise.

> *There are four things which are little on the earth,*
> *But they are exceedingly wise:*
> *The ants are a people not strong,*
> *Yet they prepare their food in the summer; Prov. 30:24,25*

Some say, 'there is nothing we can do to be prepared for what is coming.' Others say, 'Yahweh will take care of everything, for we have freedom in Him.' The only element of truth to these perspectives is that we can do nothing without Yahshua.

I am the vine. You are the branches. He who remains in me, and I in him, the same bears much fruit, for apart from me you can do nothing. John 15:5

A languid perspective as we saw in the servant with one talent is dangerous, especially in a world that is compelling us to seek entertainment and to live for today just as the grasshopper did. Yahshua was telling us in the picture of the vine, that bearing fruit apart from Him was impossible. All that we need to do in preparation for Yahshua's return, will require separation from the world and its ways, just as it was for Noah. Separation is difficult though and often brings ridicule as it did for Yahshua.

If the world hates you, you know that it has hated me before it hated you. If you were of the world, the world would love its own. But because you are not of the world, since I chose you out of the world, therefore the world hates you. John 15:18,19

We are called to serve Yahweh and uphold the things of His heart as good servants. He came to make a way for us to be apart of His family and enjoy a relationship with His Father. We are to serve Yahweh out of love, as sons and daughters. The work of Yahweh's house or Tabernacle is the work of love that reflects our Father's Name. As His sons and daughters, we willingly put our hands to the work of His heart ... which is to bring in a harvest of souls and prepare for Yahshua's return.

He who gathers in summer is a wise son;
He who sleeps in harvest is a son who causes shame. Prov.10:5

The fruit of the righteous is a tree of life.
He who is wise wins souls.
Prov. 11:30

Are we to be likened to an ant? No, we are people, and as we saw earlier, creatures of habit driven by emotions. Yahweh asks us to look to the ways of the ant to see their diligence. He knows that in order for us to have direction we need a Shepherd and leader, which of course is Yahshua. Instead of referring to us as ants, He graciously calls us His sheep, for we are far more like sheep and naturally prone to distraction and being led astray than focusing on a task like the ants. Like sheep, our tendency is to follow the crowd and be driven by our selfish desires, which leads us away from the safety and covering of the Good Shepherd. Therefore it is vital that we learn the voice of our Shepherd.

I am the good shepherd. I know my own, and I'm known by my own; even as the Father knows me, and I know the Father. John 10:14,15

My sheep hear My voice, and I know them, and they follow Me. John 10:27

The sheep who know the voice of their Shepherd will delight in following Him wherever He goes, for they trust Him with all their heart and know that He will keep them on the path of righteousness that leads to green pastures. They are also the ones who are training for the royal priesthood in preparation to be His bride. As they adhere to their Shepherd's voice they will learn the ways of the ant and their days will be filled with the duties that please and honor Yahshua and His Father Yahweh.

Now this is the commandment, the statutes, and the ordinances, which Yahweh your God commanded to teach you, that you might do them in the land where you go over to possess it; that you might fear Yahweh your God, to keep all his statutes and his commandments, which I command you; you, and your son, and your son's son, all the days of your life; and that your days may be prolonged. Hear therefore, Israel, and observe to do it; that it may be well with you, and that you may increase mightily, as Yahweh, the God of your fathers, has promised to you, in a land flowing with milk and honey. Hear, Israel: Yahweh is our God. Yahweh is one. You shall love Yahweh your God with all your heart, with all your soul, and with all your might. These words, which I command you today, shall be on your heart; and you shall teach them diligently to your children, and shall talk of them when you sit in your house, and when

you walk by the way, and when you lie down, and when you
rise up. Deut: 6:1-8

You may know this familiar Scripture as the *Shema*. Earlier we saw how
the Hebrew word shema means more than to simply listen, also holds the
meaning of obedience. To shema, is to listen with understanding and then
move into action. When we shema the voice of the Shepherd, and then
show our faith in His words by our actions we will reflect His light. These
pictures always take us back to the faithful witness of the Moon that has
no light of its own.

For you were once darkness, but are now light in the Lord. Walk
as children of light, for the fruit of the Spirit is in all goodness
and righteousness and truth, Eph.5:8,9

Each piece of Yahweh's story knits together as one! Each part of His
Creation and Word play their part in His love story! Elul is the time for us
to consider the ant and its ways. It is a time to prepare our hearts to stand
before Him; taking stock of all we have done for our Beloved in the past.
In Hebrew, Elul is understood to be an acronym for "I am my beloved's,
and my beloved is mine." To see the acronym you need to first see Elul
spelled in Hebrew, which is אלול and then you can see the acronym in
Hebrew which is, אני לדודי ודודי לי pronounced "Ani ledodi v'dodi li."
The beauty of this meaning behind Elul puts into perspective the reason
for the preparations of those who follow the Messiah. Elul is the month
when the bride's heart fills with the anticipation of her Beloved's soon
return, as the climax of Yahweh's love story plays out before her. The true
bride of the Messiah will be busy with the activities and prayers that
prepare her for the greatest and most longed for day in all history!

Now let's turn our attention to Proverbs 31 to see how it weaves together
the shema, a busy little ant, and the Moon. I have included the Hebrew
letters with their verses, as they would be in the original text.

10 א
Who can find a virtuous wife?
For her worth is far above rubies.

11 ב

The heart of her husband safely trusts her;
So he will have no lack of gain.

12 ג

She does him good and not evil
All the days of her life.

13 ד

She seeks wool and flax,
And willingly works with her hands.

14 ה

She is like the merchant ships,
She brings her food from afar.

15 ו

She also rises while it is yet night,
And provides food for her household,
And a portion for her maidservants.

16 ז

She considers a field and buys it;
From her profits she plants a vineyard.

17 ח

She girds herself with strength,
And strengthens her arms.

18 ט

She perceives that her merchandise is good,
And her lamp does not go out by night.

19 י

She stretches out her hands to the distaff,
And her hand holds the spindle.

20 כ

She extends her hand to the poor,
Yes, she reaches out her hands to the needy.

21 ל

She is not afraid of snow for her household,
For all her household is clothed with scarlet.

22 מ

She makes tapestry for herself;
Her clothing is fine linen and purple.

23 נ

Her husband is known in the gates,
When he sits among the elders of the land.

24 ס

She makes linen garments and sells them,
And supplies sashes for the merchants.

25 ע

Strength and honor are her clothing;
She shall rejoice in time to come.

26 פ

She opens her mouth with wisdom,
And on her tongue is the law of kindness.

27 צ

She watches over the ways of her household,
And does not eat the bread of idleness.

28 ק

Her children rise up and call her blessed;
Her husband also, and he praises her:

29 ר

"Many daughters have done well,
But you excel them all."

30 ש

Charm is deceitful and beauty is passing,
But a woman who fears the Lord, she shall be praised.

31 ת

Give her of the fruit of her hands,
And let her own works praise her in the gates. (NKJ)

Isn't this woman amazing?! Have you ever wondered how she could accomplish so much? She appears to do a daunting amount of daily work in the same manner as the ant. She approaches each day's work with strength, purpose, and compassion. She rises early to care for the needs of her household, and she fears Yahweh with all her heart. Many have wondered how any woman could compare to this woman of virtue, for she outshines us all. Who is this woman … this woman of virtue? She is Yahshua's bride! The one who follows the leading of her Shepherd with wisdom, caring for her husband's needs, the needs of her house and the needs of the poor. The pictures we have seen in the heavens and in Yahweh's Word find their fullness here. The attributes we see in the life of the ant, the faithful Moon and the virtuous woman, compel us to diligently serve our Beloved Yahshua and others with fervent love. As we work together as one, serving and loving Yahweh with all our heart, soul and strength, our light will be the reflection of His light alone. As His bride, we will naturally seek to understand our Husband's heart first and foremost, and then prepare to serve and meet His needs.

Yahshua is the Word of Yahweh, and He declared that He is the Alpha and the Omega ' the beginning and the end.' As we looked at earlier, Yahshua would have said that He is the Aleph and Tav because He is the consummation and revelation of Yahweh's entire Word which was origi-nally Hebrew. Those who understand the beauty of the Hebrew language know that it is a language of life. Remember that the Hebrew aleph-bet has 22 letters that make up the entire Word of Yahweh. Each of the 22 letters are applied in many intriguing ways in Scripture; the most common is in acrostic form, as we saw laid out in Proverbs 31. Probably the most famous acrostic though is Psalm 119, where each stanza and verse begins with the corresponding letter of the Hebrew aleph-bet. These set-apart pieces of Scripture are designed to convey the fullness of Yahweh's heart on a topic. That is why it is so fitting that Yahshua, who is the Aleph and the Tav, the Beginning and the End, would have His bride described through an acrostic from the aleph to the tav. Proverbs 31 reveals to us that the way we are to reflect Yahshua's light is by keeping the Word of Yahweh in every aspect of our daily life.

The Proverb of the virtuous woman and the pictures portrayed for us in the ways of the Moon and the life of an ant, tell us that those who work diligently to do Yahweh's will receive a reward.

Remember also that in Proverbs 6, the sluggard is told to go to the ant to learn how to become wise.

Laziness casts one into a deep sleep,
And an idle person will suffer hunger.
He who keeps the commandment keeps his soul,
But he who is careless of his ways will die. Prov.19:15,16

The sluggard will not plow by reason of the winter;
therefore he shall beg in harvest, and have nothing. Prov.20;4

Will our good works save us? Most certainly not, but our good works will train us and be evidence of the love we have for our King and our faith in Him. In the end, all that we do and say will be judged by Yahweh's Word.

You believe that God is one. You do well. The demons also
believe, and shudder. But do you want to know, vain man,
that faith apart from works is dead? Wasn't Abraham our
father justified by works, in that he offered up Isaac his son
on the altar? You see that faith worked with his works, and
by works faith was perfected; and the Scripture was fulfilled
which says, "Abraham believed God, and it was accounted to
him as righteousness"; and he was called the friend of God.
James 2:19-23

May our hearts and hands be strengthened so that we don't fall into the snare of laziness and pleasure seeking. Let us not grow weary in doing good for the time of the great harvest is at hand. Yahshua gave us many pictures and parables of the ingathering of wheat and the harvest of fruit in the latter days.

For this cause, we also, since the day we heard this, don't cease praying and making requests for you, that you may be filled with the knowledge of his will in all spiritual wisdom and understanding, that you may walk worthily of the Lord, to please him in all respects, bearing fruit in every good work, and increasing in the knowledge of God; strengthened with all power, according to the might of his glory, for all endurance and perseverance with joy; giving thanks to the Father, who made us fit to be partakers of the inheritance of the saints in light. Col.1:9-12

Again, therefore, Jesus spoke to them, saying, "I am the light of the world. He who follows me will not walk in the darkness, but will have the light of life." John 8:12

As Yahshua's bride, we are called to respond to His voice with love and diligence, pressing in to do His work, especially as we walk through the sixth month of Elul. Yahweh's Word will then shine through every area of our life, giving light to those around us. Just as the Moon is a faithful witness in the heavens, so the bride of the Messiah will faithfully reflect the light of Yahshua as a testimony of her love for Yahweh.

You are the light of the world. A city located on a hill can't be hidden. Neither do you light a lamp, and put it under a measuring basket, but on a stand; and it shines to all who are in the house. Even so, let your light shine before men; that they may see your good works, and glorify your Father who is in heaven..Matt. 5:14-16

The opening line of Proverbs 31, asks, "Who can find a woman of virtue?" This question is impling that she is rare and not easily found, just as it is with the gems of this world and so her worth is "far above rubies!" Have you ever thought about the worth of a ruby? Most often when we think of a valuable gem in today's world, we think of a diamond even though there are many other gems that are more rare and valuable. One of the most valuable diamonds in the world today is the 'Pink Star Diamond,' which is a wapping 59.6 carats and was sold for over 83 billion US dollars. In comparison, the ruby in today's world that even comes close to this in value is the 'Sunrise Ruby' which is less than half its size and sold for 30 million US dollars. These prized and rare gems are graded on their size, perfection and how difficult it is to seek for them. The more rare and challenging it is to find the gem, the more it is valued.

Rubies, diamonds and the many other rare gems of this world, as beautiful as they are, are not at the heart of what Yahweh is trying to reveal to us in Proverbs 31. A ruby in Scripture is translated as a sardius in most English translations, but in Hebrew, it is odem, Strong's #H124; meaning to be red or blood colored. In Proverbs 31, the Hebrew word most often translated as rubies, is actually Strong's #H6443 פְּנִי paniy (panee). Paniy comes from the Hebrew root word, Strong's #H6437 פָּנָה panah, which means, to turn, to face, look; tide, dawning, go away, pass away, prepare and respect. The meaning behind paniy, displays again the attributes of the bride as we saw in the Moon; always facing the Sun, effecting the tides, preparing to be a light, etc. But it gets even better. The Hebrew word used for rubies, paniy is a cognate word to paniym, Strong's #6440, which also has many words listed in its description, but its main meaning is face, before and presence. Paniym is used over two thousand times in the Tanach (Torah, Writings, and Prophets) and is most often translated as face or before; as being in someone's presence or referring to the countenance of someone. Paniym is used when referencing Yahweh showing His face toward us or His favor upon us, as it is written in the Aaronic blessing.

> 'Yahweh bless you, and keep you.
> Yahweh make his face to shine on you,
> and be gracious to you.
> Yahweh lift up his face toward you,
> and give you peace.' Num. 6:24-26

We could then say, that to have the face or countenance of Yahweh shine upon us, is to be in His light for He is the LIGHT! The Hebrew word paniy and its relationship to the word paniym, is very intriguing because it is also translated as shew or show as in shewbread.

And you shall set the showbread on the table before Me always. Ex.25:30(NKJ)

In this verse paniym is used twice; for shew and before. In Hebrew the shewbread could also be called 'the face bread' or 'bread of presence.' This is fascinating because of the location of the Table of Shewbread in the Tabernacle. If you were to walk through the curtains into the Holy Place, you would find the Menorah on your left, which again is the only source of light in the dwelling of Yahweh and represents the Messiah, the Light of the world. If you then looked to your right you would see the Table of Shewbread in the light or face of the Menorah, just as it says in Numbers 6, 'Yahweh make His face shine upon you.' The Table of Shewbread and its twelve loaves are symbolic of the twelve tribes of Israel, set before or in the presence of the Messiah.

Bear with me, for there is a beautiful reason that I am telling you all of this. Yahweh's masterful design brings all things together in His Word for His glory, and I hope that I can convey the wonder and fullness of His work. Man makes Yahweh's Word appear abstract and random because they have missed the Master's overall heartfelt story and Masterpiece. The truth seen in the picture that Yahweh displayed through the Moon is seen in this word paniym; for just as the Table of Shewbread always faces the Menorah, the Moon always faces the Sun reflecting its light. Israel, displayed in the twelve tribes is meant to dwell in the presence of Yahweh and be a light to all other nations. We also see this displayed and confirmed in Proverbs 31, with the faithfulness of the virtuous woman, who loves Yahweh and others in all the work that she faithfully does each day. She lives to shed the light of her Master to all those around her. Together these pictures reveal the duty and characteristics of the Messiah's radiant bride, and how valuable she is to Him.

Now let's return to the question of a ruby's worth. The answer is found in the true meaning of the Hebrew word translated as rubies, which again is Strong's # H6443 פְּנִי paniy. Her worth is not related rubies, for the true meaning of paniy is pearl. The worth of Yahshua's virtuous bride is 'far above a pearl!' This remarkable piece to Yahweh's Masterpiece gives us understanding of what Yahshua meant when He referred to a precious pearl in this parable statement;

"Again, the Kingdom of Heaven is like a man who is a merchant seeking fine pearls, who having found one pearl of great price, he went and sold all that he had, and bought it. Matt.13:45,46

Here Yahshua is revealing to us that His Kingdom is likened to a man who is seeking for a treasure and that treasure is a pearl! When he finds the pearl, he sells or gives up everything he has to buy it. What a breath-taking picture of what Yahshua did for His bride! He sought those who would be like the woman of virtue, more precious than a pearl and then gave up everything, His throne, His reputation, His life ... to pay the price for her, even before she had become luminous like a pearl! It would not be until after He had paid the price for her that she would learn to reflect His light and become His pearl. How do we become Yahshua's pearl ... His woman of virtue …His treasure? The answer lies in the making of a real pearl.

Unlike the gems of the world which are typically mined from the earth and cut into shapes by man, a pearl is found beneath the water and hidden within a mollusk.

Natural (or wild) pearls, formed without human intervention, are very rare. Many hundreds of pearl oysters or mussels must be gathered and opened, and thus killed, to find even one wild pearl; for many centuries, this was the only way pearls were obtained, and why pearls fetched such extraordinary prices in the past. Pearl; Wikipedia

Being found in water was also true of the stones used for the altar; which like a pearl are not shaped by man's sharp instruments but by Yahweh's creative hand alone.

If you make me an altar of stone, you shall not build it of cut stones; for if you lift up your tool on it, you have polluted it. Ex.20:25

Take twelve men out of the people, a man out of every tribe, and command them, saying, 'Take from out of the middle of the Jordan, out of the place where the priests' feet stood firm, twelve stones, and carry them over with you, and lay them down in the place where you'll camp tonight.'"Josh.4:2,3

The stones for the altar were taken out of the water just as a pearl is taken out of the water. A genuine pearl is found hidden away in an oyster's shell and formed by a single grain of sand. That grain of sand is an irritant to the oyster, and so the oyster makes a coating over the grain of sand until it is smooth and does not irritate it any longer. As Abraham's seed, we too are likened the sand of the sea.

You said, 'I will surely do you good, and make your offspring as the sand of the sea, which can't be numbered because there are so many.' Gen.32:12

Wow! ... another awesome piece to Yahweh's Masterpiece. Yahshua knew that eventually there would come a remnant of people willing to be His bride. These few, like grains of sand hidden in the world, which is likened to an oyster shell, would willingly go through various trials because of their love and faithfulness to Him. The world does *not* love Yahweh's remnant, and in many ways they are an irritant and often suffer trial because of it.

You will be hated by all men for my name's sake, but he who endures to the end will be saved. Matt.10:22

If the world hates you, you know that it has hated me before it hated you. If you were of the world, the world would love its own. But because you are not of the world, since I chose you out of the world, therefore the world hates you. John 15:18,19

Over time the trials, the training and the enduring causes those who have been bought with the precious blood of the Messiah to become luminous like a pearl. The most valuable pearls are never found in pearl farms but in the natural waters. They are rare, and the coating they develop within the oyster is soft and able to absorb and reflect light! How beautifully this describes Yahshua's bride! She is scattered among the nations (waters) and submits herself to the work and trials of life, gaining the wisdom of her Beloved each day until she becomes humble, loving (soft), and wise … reflecting His light!

> *Behold, You desire truth in the inward parts,*
> *And in the hidden (part) You will make*
> *me to know wisdom. Ps.51:6*

I have inserted brackets around the word part because it is not in the original text. It should read, "And in the hidden You will make me to know wisdom." Those who are hidden away in secret with their Beloved will humbly come to know Him and His ways and with time, will become His treasured bride and pearl of great price.

> *You are not your own, for you were bought with a price. Therefore glorify God in your body and in your spirit, which are God's. 1Cor.6:20*

> *You were bought with a price. Don't become bondservants of men. 1 Cor.7:23*

Yahshua's words now come alive! He came seeking a fine pearl for His Kingdom and paid the highest price possible for her. As those who desire to become Yahshua's bride there can be no other response to the price He paid for us, but to become all that He desires us to be. Yahweh's moving picture brings us back to the patterns and pictures that we saw in the Moon and the glory that the heavens are declaring. Every attribute seen in the description of the Moon is seen in the description of the virtuous woman. All the trials we face and each heartache we experience trains us to overcome and become His pearl of great price.

I urge you, beloved of Yahweh, the next time there is a clear night in the middle of the Moon's faithful cycle, step outside and look up, for there you will see the glory that the heavens are declaring. Many have referred to the face of the Moon as the 'man in the moon,' but I believe that the face you see, is a stirring reminder of Yahshua's bride. As a faithful witness to the love of our Savior, the luminous Moon, like a great pearl glows against the backdrop of Yahweh's glorious story. Just as Proverbs 31:15 and 18 tell us, this is the image of the virtuous woman up in the night hours shedding the light of her Beloved; her lamp does not go out for she is faithful to Him, His household and to the needs of her family and friends.

15 ‎י

She also rises while it is yet night,
And provides food for her household,
And a portion for her maidservants.

18 ‎ט

She perceives that her merchandise is good,
And her lamp does not go out by night.

Who is she who looks out as the morning,
beautiful as the moon, clear as the sun,
and awesome as an army with banners? Song of Songs 6:10

Who is she who looks forth as the morning, fair as the Moon, clear as the Sun? Yes, it is Yahshua's bride … His pearl of great price. She is the company of those who are trained as His royal priesthood; a trusted army of those who serve, work and fight for their Beloved. Just as it is with the order of the priesthood, Yahshua's bride will move through His cycles each day, week, month and year, serving Him alone and reflecting His light into a dark, lost world. She will bring continual offerings to her King as she watches, stands firm on His Word and cares for those who are in need. Yahshua's bride will be like the frankincense that was revealed in the word levana for the Moon; found in prayerful worship to her King and secured on the Rock through every storm. She will celebrate the appointed times of her Beloved and dance in a circular motion before Him in praise and joyful adoration.She is the remnant of those who walk as the virtuous woman, with love, fear, wisdom and obedience.

If there ever was a question of what we should be doing as we wait for our Bridegroom's return, all we need to do is prayerfully study Proverb 31 and see how it reveals the works of Yahweh's Word in our lives. As James exhorts us "faith without works is dead." May we then say, that faith *with* works is life? I believe we can, for it is the way of bearing fruit. We must learn to abide in Yahshua as a branch that has been grafted into the vine and then patiently allows the root and vine to transform it into its likeness. Over time, if we allow Yahweh to prune us, His fruit will come forth in our lives.

> *Be patient therefore, brothers, until the coming of the Lord. Behold, the farmer waits for the precious fruit of the earth, being patient over it, until it receives the early and late rain. You also be patient. Establish your hearts, for the coming of the Lord is at hand. James 5:7,8*

> *"I am the true vine, and my Father is the farmer. Every branch in me that doesn't bear fruit, he takes away. Every branch that bears fruit, he prunes, that it may bear more fruit. You are already pruned clean because of the word which I have spoken to you. Remain in me, and I in you. As the branch can't bear fruit by itself, unless it remains in the vine, so neither can you, unless you remain in me. I am the vine. You are the branches. He who remains in me, and I in him, the same bears much fruit, for apart from me you can do nothing. John 15:1-5*

Each year as Elul rolls around farmers and gardeners are found harvesting the fruit of their labor before winter. If you have kept a garden or field of grain, you know that this is a very rewarding time of year; the time when you take inventory of all that your crops have yielded. From a spiritual perspective, it is the time when you take inventory of all your heart and hands have yielded. Have we laid down our agendas to allow the fruit of the Spirit to grow and flourish in our lives? Have we contributed to Yahweh's harvest of souls? Will our Beloved say, 'Well done' or will He say, 'Depart?' We must ask ourselves these questions daily, but even more, as we see His day approaching.

There is a tradition of blowing the shofar once every day during Elul to wake people from worldly slumber. We must not be like the grasshopper and ignore the warnings. Just as the priest prepared to go before Yahweh in the Tabernacle, we too must examine ourselves as His royal priestly bride and regard the requirements of becoming holy that are laid out for us in Yahweh's Word. Then we will be ready to enter the chamber of the King.

The final verse of Proverbs 31 is marked with the letter tav ת. Remember that this is the letter of the Hebrew aleph-bet that symbolizes, a mark or a sign of a covenant. You can see in the commonly printed form above, that it looks like a door frame reminding us of the blood on the door-post at Passover; which was a sign of the covenant with Yahweh. The tav's original pictograph form looks like a cross ✗, which takes us to Yahshua's fulfillment of Passover and the renewed Covenant. The cross is a reminder that those who are in Covenant with Yahshua must also take up their cross to follow Him, for this is His bride's way of bearing fruit and shedding His light.

If anyone desires to come after me, let him deny himself, take up his cross, and follow me. For whoever desires to save his life will lose it, but whoever will lose his life for my sake, the same will save it. Luke 9:23,24

We see this in the final verse of Proverb's 31 which is marked with the tav ת or cross ✗, for the work of the virtuous woman's enduring heart proves that she is in Covenant with Yahshua. Yahshua said that He was the Aleph and the Tav, the beginning and the end and at the end He will reward all those who followed His heart.

ת 31
Give her of the fruit of her hands,
And let her own works praise her in the gates.

The Hebrew word for gates in the above verse is sha'ar, Strong's #H8179 שער, meaning an opening, door or gate. On the New Moon of the seventh month on Yahweh's Calendar, the trumpet will resound across the heavens. Many who claim to love Yahweh will be found anxiously waiting for Him, but at that moment a heart-wrenching reality will play out. Yahshua's true bride will flourish with the fruit of her works, having clean hands and a pure heart from her faithful service to her King. Her life of prayer, humility, and commitment to guarding the Covenant commands, will have developed an intimate relationship with her Beloved and she will be well known by Him.

Afterward the other virgins also came, saying, 'Lord, Lord, open to us.' But he answered, 'Most certainly I tell you, I don't know you.' Matt.25: 11,12

At that moment Yahshua's bride will be taken through the gate into the wedding chamber as foreshadowed in the Feast of Tabernacles, when the fruit of the land is gathered with joyful celebration under Yahweh's covering, His Tabernacle or Sukkah. Spiritually, this will be the time when the fruit of the Messiah's bride will be gathered before Him and she will be given the reward for her labors.

Blessed are those who do his commandments, that they may have the right to the tree of life, and may enter in by the gates into the city. Rev.22:14

When the fulfillment of Yahweh's fall feast days are completed, the gates of His glorious city will give entry into the King's chamber; this is the heavenly Jerusalem, our final destination. Remember too, that each of the gates to the heavenly Jerusalem is made of a single pearl! How fitting that Yahshua's pearl of great price would find entry into the Great City of the King through a gate made of one pearl!

The twelve gates were twelve pearls. Each one of the gates was made of one pearl. Rev. 21:21a

What a breathtaking finale to Yahweh's awesome Love Story! One day in the near future Yahshua and His bride will reign together in His radiant City. As a royal priesthood in training, this is the goal and reward that we press on to receive. Halleluyah! The characteristics of the ant and the Proverb of the virtuous woman, teach us that we must be diligent in preparing for our Beloved. Yes, there will be obstacles, trials and deception, but we must overcome and endure all that is set before us. From the New Moon of Elul to the New Moon of Tishri, we are given a set apart time to turn our attention to our Beloved Bridegroom, repent of our ways and stand ready to meet Him face to face.

Therefore prepare your minds for action, be sober, and set your hope fully on the grace that will be brought to you at the revelation of Jesus Christ 1Pet.1:13

A Woman of Virtue

THE MORE WE SEE OF YAHWEH'S MASTERPIECE, THE MORE CLEAR IT IS that He is the most amazing and masterful Artist, Composer and Designer of all! His love is so extraordinary that all He created by His Word speaks and resonates of His heart. The wonder of His Love Story reaches out to the deepest longings of our hearts. How can we hope to be worthy of being called the bride of One so magnificent? We have seen how Proverbs 31 gives us a picture of the heartfelt work of Yahshua's bride. Now we need to take steps to understand how to become that, 'woman of virtue'. The character qualities Yahshua is looking for in a bride are not common in our culture. The words virtue and virtuous are hardly ever spoken anymore, much less strived for in life application. In the past though, the concepts of virtue and honor were well known, especially during the time that the Scriptures were translated from Hebrew into English. In Noah Webster's 1828 Dictionary virtuous is described this way:

-Morally good; acting in conformity to the moral law.

Being in conformity to the moral or divine law.

Moral excellence. Chaste.

As the character qualities of virtue and honor fade away under the guise of old-fashioned ideals in our world today, we see a rise in selfishness. There is a shift towards self-promotion and self-improvement that is taking center stage; just as Scripture prophesied that it would. The generation coming is being trained by every type of media to become lovers of self.

But know this, that in the last days, grievous times will come. For men will be lovers of self, lovers of money, boastful, arrogant, blasphemers, disobedient to parents, unthankful, unholy, without natural affection, unforgiving, slanderers, without self-control, fierce, not lovers of good, traitors, headstrong, conceited, lovers of pleasure rather than lovers of God; holding a form of godliness, but having denied its power. Turn away from these, also. 2Tim. 3:1-5

And because lawlessness will abound, the love of many will grow cold. Matt. 24:12(NKJ)

The bride of the Messiah must not be seduced by the ways of the world. In stark contrast to the world, she must become humble and selfless like her Beloved. As a woman of virtue, she will be morally excellent and con-forming to the divine law. You can search the world over, but you will find that there is only one moral law. Of course many attempts have been made to distort the original, that Yahweh established in His Torah, but in the end, His Kingdom will be ruled by it. When every knee has been made to bow before His throne it will be Yahweh's moral standard found in His Covenant Torah that He will judge us by, as Yahshua said;

"Don't think that I will accuse you to the Father. There is one who accuses you, even Moses, on whom you have set your hope. For if you believed Moses, you would believe me; for he wrote about me. But if you don't believe his writings, how will you believe my words?" John 5:45-47

A man who disregards Moses' law dies without compassion on the word of two or three witnesses. How much worse punishment do you think he will be judged worthy of who has trodden under foot the Son of God, and has counted the blood of the covenant with which he was sanctified an unholy thing, and has insulted the Spirit of grace? For we know him who said, "Vengeance belongs to me," says the Lord, "I will repay." Again, "The Lord will judge his people." It is a fearful thing to fall into the hands of the living God. Heb.10:28-31

Yahshua's bride will have no greater joy than to serve her King according to His moral standard, because the life described for her in His Word, is the abundant life that He paid for her to have. The key is to not bear it on our own, or to try and live it in our flesh, but to abide in our Master as He walks the path of righteousness as we saw pictured in the mighty ox yolked to the younger. The life He paid for us to have is a life of walking with Him and keeping His commandments by the leading of His Spirit. Yahshua came to earth to bring the truth of keeping His Torah to a more glorious level, even more glorious than Moses knew.

But if the ministry of death, written and engraved on stones, was glorious, so that the children of Israel could not look steadily at the face of Moses because of the glory of his countenance, which glory was passing away, how will the ministry of the Spirit not be more glorious? For if the ministry of condemnation had glory, the ministry of righteousness exceeds much more in glory. For even what was made glorious had no glory in this respect, because of the glory that excels. For if what is passing away was glorious, what remains is much more glorious. 2 Cor. 3:7-11(NKJ)

Let's now look at how the first steps on the path with Yahshua also reveal the woman of virtue. As we have seen, the first steps of our walk begin with Passover where we are born again. At the first Passover Yahweh required that each home put the blood of a spotless lamb on their lintel and door-posts. Then at midnight, the 'angel of death' passed through Egypt and something remarkable happened. Remember that the blood of the lamb on the doorposts became a sign to Yahweh, a sign that those inside the house were agreeing to His Covenant conditions. When Yahweh saw the sign, He then protected the firstborns of that household from the angel of death. That first Passover foreshadowed the Covenant requirements that would be fulfilled by Yahshua once and for all. When we accept the death and shed blood of Yahweh's only Son, Yahshua, the spotless Lamb and partake of the Passover cup, we are agreeing to be in Covenant with Yahweh. We have seen this in Yahshua's name, which is a combination of 'Yah' and 'shua' meaning, "Yah's salvation!" Yahweh's spotless lamb, Yahshua is our blood covering and saves us from death into everlasting life. We are then grafted in to become a part of Israel, His firstborn and protected by Yahweh's Covenant conditions.

> *He is the head of the body, the assembly, who is the beginning, the firstborn from the dead; that in all things he might have the preeminence. Col.1:18*

> *For whom he foreknew, he also predestined to be conformed to the image of his Son, that he might be the firstborn among many brothers. Rom.8:29*

I am repeating this because this is where the picture of what virtuous truly means to Yahweh begins to take shape. The life we have through Yahshua is seen in the familiar Hebrew word for life or living, which is חי chai. This word is made up of the letter chet ח, which in its picture form symbolizes the wall of a home and the yod י which symbolizes a hand. From a childlike perspective, we can see that Yahweh's picture letters tell a story. Yahweh's word for life is made of one letter that looks like a wall or door frame ח (chet) joined with a hand י (yod). These letters make a story picture that is remarkably similar to the Passover picture, of a hand placing the blood of a lamb on the doorposts and lintel of a home. In Yahweh's masterful design the word 'chai' for living חי, appears to be a constant reminder of our redemption and the true life that comes from Yahweh's only Son, our spotless Lamb. The word חי chai is also a reminder that Yahshua, our source of life and light, is the door for His sheep or people.

> *I am the door. If anyone enters in by me, he will be saved, and will go in and go out, and will find pasture. The thief only*

comes to steal, kill, and destroy. I came that they may have life, and may have it abundantly. I am the good shepherd. The good shepherd lays down his life for the sheep. John 10:9-11

Yahshua is the way or door for us to return to the Covenant that Yahweh originally made with Abraham. Now we, as Abraham's seed are able to share in those same Covenant conditions as we have seen in all we have looked at in Yahweh's Masterpiece. By grace we are freed from our debt of sin and safe under His care.

After these things Yahweh's word came to Abram in a vision, saying, "Don't be afraid, Abram. I am your shield, your exceedingly great reward."Gen.15:1

Jesus said to him, "I am the way, the truth, and the life. No one comes to the Father except through Me." John 14:6

Once we have accepted Yahshua as our Passover Lamb and Savior and come under His Covenant conditions, we are free to follow Yahshua through all of Scripture with hearts of love.

"Most certainly, I tell you, one who doesn't enter by the door into the sheep fold, but climbs up some other way, the same is a thief and a robber. But one who enters in by the door is the shepherd of the sheep. The gatekeeper opens the gate for him, and the sheep listen to his voice. He calls his own sheep by name, and leads them out. Whenever he brings out his own sheep, he goes before them, and the sheep follow him, for they know his voice. They will by no means follow a stranger, but will flee from him; for they don't know the voice of strangers."John 10:1-5

We see Yahshua as a Shepherd calling His sheep and leading them on the path of righteousness into safety expressed so wonderfully in the beloved Psalm 23, as we looked at earlier. King David had spent many years as a shepherd, and I believe that is why he was considered a man after Yahweh's heart; he had such joy in seeing Yahweh as his Shepherd. He was familiar with a shepherd's rod and staff and understood how they were a comfort and not a threat, because they keep us (the sheep) from wandering away and getting lost.

Let's now look again at the picture of life in the Hebrew word chai, with the addition of a shepherd's staff. In Hebrew the letter lamed ל is the picture for a shepherd's staff. In fact, in the original pictograph Hebrew looks just like an inverted shepherd's staff ∠. The name lamed is where we get the Hebrew word for disciple, which as we saw earlier is talmid. The word talmid or disciple literally means to learn by goading. The Webster's dictionary defines goading as; to put pressure on, urge, excite, provoke, etc. This is fascinating because sheep are notorious for getting lost and so a shepherd has to teach them by goading to keep them safe. The lamed or shepherd's staff is revealing to us that the life that Yahshua bought for us brings us into His family or flock, which, in turn, brings us under the leading and learning of that new life. A disciple is one who willingly submits to the provoking, urging and leading of the Good Shepherd and His staff. Unfortunately, if there is one in the flock that refuses to stay under the care of the shepherd and runs off, it puts itself and all the other sheep in danger. Yes, the shepherd would leave the ninety-nine to fetch the lost one, but a truly good shepherd, would have to potentially use his staff to break the legs of a lamb that persistently wanders away into danger. Once the leg of a disobedient lamb was broken, the shepherd would then lovingly take the lamb into his arms and carry it to a safe place. There the shepherd would teach the lamb to obey his voice, and care for it until its leg was fully restored. There in a set apart place of healing, the wayward lamb would learn to love and trust the shepherd, never to run away again. To some this may sound like harsh discipline but the alternative is death for the lamb.

The staff that a shepherd carries symbolizes authority and leadership, just as Moses' staff declared that Moses was under Yahweh's authority to Pharaoh and all Egypt. Yahweh also used Aaron's staff to declare that He had given authority to Aaron, as His chosen High Priest. The important thing to remember is that a shepherd's staff or lamed is a picture of being under the care and protection of the Shepherd and willingly submitting to His leading.

Now let's put these pictures together to understand Yahweh's bride or woman of virtue. We have seen that Yahweh's people have life or chai חי because they were bought with the precious blood of the Lamb. Those who choose to become the bride of the Messiah seek *'the life'* or chai that was bought for her, by following her Beloved (the Good Shepherd) wherever He goes. She is led and taught by Him each day ... as pictured in the lamed ל. Now when we add the lamed or shepherd's staff to the word for life or living, we find the Hebrew word for virtue ... חיל chayil! In other words, to become Yahshua's virtuous bride, one must have the foundations of life, found in the blood of the Lamb, and then follow the ways of Yahweh seen in Yahshua, our Good Shepherd. With patience and perseverance she will become His disciple, or more importantly His chayil; humbly taking her place as the bride of Messiah. In His leading, she will learn to die to herself and become the virtuous woman that Proverbs 31 is speaking of and Yahshua's "pearl of great price!"

The Strong's Concordance definition of chayil חיל #2428 is ; virtue, a force, an army, strength, and valor. Here the fullness of who we are to become as the bride of the Messiah comes together. Chayil is translated many times throughout the Old Testament as; active, valor, valiant, strength, power, army, forces, might, wealth, riches and substance, bringing us back to the verse in the Song of Songs that reveals Yahshua's bride;

> *Who is she who looks out as the morning,*
> *beautiful as the moon, clear as the sun,*
> *and awesome as an army with banners? Song of Songs 6:10*

All of Yahweh's pictures come together and confirm one another in His Masterful design. Yahshua's bride will be as beautiful as the Moon and a strong company of people, like an army with banners that overcomes the trials of life and submits to the leading of her Master Shepherd!

The word chayil or valor is used by Boaz in the story of Ruth, when he praises Ruth for faithfully gleaning the fields and being devoted to her mother in-law, Naomi. These same attributes are what is pictured in the Proverbs 31 woman. As Yahshua's bride, we too must see ourselves through these glorious pictures. Yahshua's bride is not a timid damsel in constant need of help; on the contrary, she is a valiant woman whose fear and trust is rooted in her mighty King. Her confidence in Him makes her a force to be reckoned with, like a worthy company of soldiers as Timothy exhorts us to be.

> *You therefore, my child, be strengthened in the grace that is in Christ Jesus. The things which you have heard from me among many witnesses, commit the same to faithful men, who will be able to teach others also. You therefore must endure hardship, as a good soldier of Christ Jesus. No soldier on duty entangles himself in the affairs of life, that he may please him who enrolled him as a soldier. 2Tim.2:1-4*

As a watchful member of the royal priesthood, Yahshua's bride will welcome Yahweh's leading, training or 'goading' to show her the way of being an overcomer, for Revelation tells us that it will be those who overcome that will be blessed at the end.

> *He who overcomes will be arrayed in white garments, and I will in no way blot his name out of the book of life, and I will confess his name before my Father, and before his angels. He who has an ear, let him hear what the Spirit says to the assemblies. Rev.3:5,6*

> *He who overcomes, I will give to him to sit down with me on my throne, as I also overcame, and sat down with my Father on his throne. He who has an ear, let him hear what the Spirit says to the assemblies. Rev. 3:21,22*

Here again we see those who shema or hear what Yahweh's Spirit is saying, are the ones being led to overcome, have eternal life and are arrayed in white garments, just as Yahshua said:

> *Jesus answered them, "I told you, and you don't believe. The works that I do in my Father's name, these testify about me. But you don't believe, because you are not of my sheep, as I told you. My sheep hear my voice, and I know them, and they*

follow me. I give eternal life to them. They will never perish, and no one will snatch them out of my hand. John 10:25-28

There is one more beautiful picture related to chayil or virtuous that I would like to share with you. The picture is seen through a cognate or family word of chayil. The word chayil, חיל, as we have discovered is spelled with the small Hebrew letter yod י that comes between the chet and the lamed. In the cognate spelling of chayil, we find the middle letter changed to a vav ו, which looks like an extended yod י. The vav's ו picture meaning is just the way it looks; like a nail. When we add the nail to the meaning of virtuous, it takes us into a more intimate picture of the virtuous woman. Remember that the picture of the yod or hand by the doorpost reflects the first Passover, which foreshadowed Yahweh's ultimate redemptive work to be fulfilled by His only Son. Yahshua then came to fulfill Passover by taking the nail or vav into His hands for us. When chayil is spelled with the yod or picture of a hand, it means virtue or valor. The cognate word which is spelled with the vav or nail picture, is Strong's #H2342 חול kheel, which means; to twist or whirl in a circle, that is to dance, to fear or writhe in pain, and to wait longingly! When we put the meaning of these two words together, we find another wonderful picture of Yahshua's bride. The Hebrew word kheel חול, spelled with a vav ו or nail, reflects the bride's fullness of life (chai) that she receives through Yahshua's death on the cross. The truth of how much He suffered to save her, brings her such overwhelming joy that she is compelled to dance in a circle before her King, just as David danced before Yahweh.

David danced before Yahweh with all his might; and David was clothed in a linen ephod. 2 Sam.6:14

She rejoices in knowing that her King is mighty and victorious and that He has become her Salvation.

Praise him with tambourine and dancing!
Praise him with stringed instruments and flute! Ps.150:4

The writhing in pain description for kheel, is related to the bride dying to self daily. This is the way of bringing forth fruit in her life; as she humbles herself, repents and overcomes the trials set before her. We have seen overwhelming evidence that this is the message of the New Moon. There in the secret place, before her King Yahshua's bride travails in intercession for the lost.

Most certainly I tell you, that you will weep and lament, but the world will rejoice. You will be sorrowful, but your sorrow will be turned into joy. John 16:20

Lament and mourn and weep! Let your laughter be turned to mourning and your joy to gloom. Humble yourselves in the sight of the Lord, and He will lift you up. James 4:9,10

As we saw in the Hebrew word yarach for Moon Yahshua's bride is one that fears Yahweh above all else, for she knows He is a righteous judge and that He is worthy to be praised with fear and trembling.

Serve Yahweh with fear, and rejoice with trembling. Ps.2:11

The final meaning for kheel is to wait longingly. Waiting for the Bridegroom's return and His timing, requires trust and faith. Those who grow impatient often loose heart and fall into sin in their frustration, like Aaron and the Children of Israel. Instead of waiting for Moses to return from the mountain, they made a golden calf to take the place of Yahweh. In the end times this will be revealed in those who accept the antichrist or the "instead of Messiah." On the other hand, those who wait for the true Messiah will be lifted up on eagles wings and renewed, just as it was when Yahweh delivered His people from Egypt.

Yahweh is good to those who wait for
him, to the soul that seeks him.
It is good that a man should hope and quietly wait
for the salvation of Yahweh. Lam.3:25,26

But those who wait for Yahweh will renew their strength.
They will mount up with wings like eagles.
They will run, and not be weary.
They will walk, and not faint. Is.40:31

*'You have seen what I did to the Egyptians, and how I bore
you on eagles' wings, and brought you to myself. Ex.19:4*

Those who wait for Yahweh to bring forth the final events of His story in
His timing will be rewarded, for they will have acquired the wisdom and
strength to persevere through the darkness to the end.

*For since the beginning of the world
Men have not heard nor perceived by the ear,
Nor has the eye seen any God besides You,
Who acts for the one who waits for Him. Is.64:4(NKJ)*

*Show me your ways, Yahweh.
Teach me your paths.
Guide me in your truth, and teach me,
For you are the God of my salvation,
I wait for you all day long. Ps.25:4,5*

*Yahweh is good to those who wait for him, to
the soul that seeks him.Lam.3:25*

*Inasmuch as it is appointed for men to die once, and after this,
judgment, so Christ also, having been offered once to bear the
sins of many, will appear a second time, without sin, to those
who are eagerly waiting for him for salvation. Heb.9:27,28*

The call to wait can be discouraging, and at times we can get weary of
the hype and many predictions of when the end will come. The excitement has come and gone over the years like waves upon the shore. Still no
matter how long we wait or how many days you have been given, your life
is important. We must not grow slack or disheartened with the deception
that Yahshua's return is too far off to matter in our lives today.

*This is now, beloved, the second letter that I have written to you;
and in both of them I stir up your sincere mind by reminding
you; that you should remember the words which were spoken
before by the holy prophets, and the commandments of us, the*

apostles of the Lord and Savior: knowing this first, that in the last days mockers will come, walking after their own lusts, and saying, "Where is the promise of his coming? 2Pet.3:1-4

Wherever you are, the light of Yahshua reflected through you is touching the lives of those around you. Let us not forget to edify and encourage one another in our gifts so that we do not loose heart. You and the gifts Yahweh placed within you are important to the body of the Messiah.

Don't be deceived. God is not mocked, for whatever a man sows, that he will also reap. For he who sows to his own flesh will from the flesh reap corruption. But he who sows to the Spirit will from the Spirit reap eternal life. Let us not be weary in doing good, for we will reap in due season, if we don't give up. So then, as we have opportunity, let's do what is good toward all men, and especially toward those who are of the household of the faith. Gal.6:7-10

Finally, be strong in the Lord, and in the strength of his might. Put on the whole armor of God, that you may be able to stand against the wiles of the devil. For our wrestling is not against flesh and blood, but against the principalities, against the powers, against the world's rulers of the darkness of this age, and against the spiritual forces of wickedness in the heavenly places. Therefore put on the whole armor of God, that you may be able to withstand in the evil day, and, having done all, to stand. Eph.6:10-13

From the beginning of time, when Yahweh called to the vast array of elements within the darkness and the Universe was whirled into an orchestrated existence, the pattern of darkness first and then the revealing of life has been His ordained order. His pattern is woven throughout all He made, displaying His glorious love story. As we learn to keep pace with Him and follow Yahshua's example; submitting to His ways as His chayil or virtuous bride, this pattern becomes an important part of our lives, and will prepare us for His presence. Those alive at the end, will witness this pattern as the world goes into great darkness before Yahweh's breathtaking finale and the revealing of His Light. We see this same pattern in the everyday lives of people when they return home from their labors at the setting of the Sun. Remember that the physical Creation lays the foundation for the spiritual because the same Artist has designed all things. Peter is exhorting us to remember this as we watch for Yahshua's return.

But, beloved, do not forget this one thing, that with the Lord one day is as a thousand years, and a thousand years as one day. 2 Pet.3:8

All of time is designed according to Yahweh's pattern of a week, making the seven-thousandth day the time of being in Yahweh's presence; as it is with His Sabbath day. The seventh thousand day will be the time of His millennial reign when the Kingdom will be restored. Each day closes and begins in darkness as we turn homeward for rest and restoration in the darkness. As the six-thousandth day closes, Scripture tells us that the darkness will be overwhelming. The darkness will come upon us slowly, just as the light slowly fades at the end of a day and mixes with the enveloping darkness. From a spiritual point of view, it is obvious that the mix of light and darkness, or good and evil is already upon us. In the natural, evening or twilight is the time when it is the most difficult to see clearly. Now spiritual twilight is coming upon us, as the lines of right and wrong are becoming blurred and even reversing.

Woe to those who call evil good, and good evil;
Who put darkness for light, and light for darkness;
Who put bitter for sweet, and sweet for bitter!
Woe to those who are wise in their own eyes,
And prudent in their own sight! Is.5: 20,21

The darkness is coming, like the heating water for the frog in the pot, as the six-thousandth day begins to close and we enter the seven-thousandth day. Can you hear Yahweh's people being called home from their labors to enter into the promise of His presence and rest?

The Lord is not slack concerning His promise, as some count slackness, but is longsuffering toward us, not willing that any should perish but that all should come to repentance.

But the day of the Lord will come as a thief in the night, in which the heavens will pass away with a great noise, and the elements will melt with fervent heat; both the earth and the works that are in it will be burned up. Therefore, since all these things will be dissolved, what manner of persons ought you to be in holy conduct and godliness, looking for and hastening the coming of the day of God, because of which the heavens will be dissolved, being on fire, and the elements will melt with fervent heat? Nevertheless we, according to His promise, look for new heavens and a new earth in which righteousness dwells. 2Peter 3:9-13

Remember, those who do not know Yahweh and His ways are in danger of listening to and believing a lie. We cannot stop our work! On the contrary, we must endure like the ant. As Yahweh's final chapters play out, it is not a time to be slack, but to persevere, for there has never been a more critical time to hold on to Yahshua and be steadfast in our walk with Him.

Therefore, beloved, seeing that you look for these things, be diligent to be found in peace, without defect and blameless in his sight. Regard the patience of our Lord as salvation; even as our beloved brother Paul also, according to the wisdom given to him, wrote to you; as also in all of his letters, speaking in them of these things. In those, there are some things that are hard to understand, which the ignorant and unsettled twist, as they also do to the other Scriptures, to their own destruction. You therefore, beloved, knowing these things beforehand, beware, lest being carried away with the error of the wicked, you fall from your own steadfastness. But grow in the grace and knowledge of our Lord and Savior Jesus Christ. To him be the glory both now and forever. Peter 3:14-18

If you look at Scripture as a whole, you see that most of it was written to exhort, guide and warn those who would be alive during the latter days. As Yahweh's people, we naturally will rehearse His appointed days through His New Moon, Sabbaths and Feast Days. The monthly rehearsal of the New Moon is especially designed to teach us how to watch and prepare us for the greatest moment in all history. Soon the day that all Creation groans and waits for will come to pass as the trumpet of Yahweh sounds on the New Moon of Yom Teruah, and we are gathered into our Beloved's Presence. Will we be ready to hear and respond to Yahshua's call?

Search me, God, and know my heart.
Try me, and know my thoughts.
See if there is any wicked way in me,
and lead me in the everlasting way. Ps. 139:23,24

When we willingly humble ourselves and pray, giving our attention to the voice of Yahweh's Spirit, then we will be safe under His covering as the New Moon is revealing to us. On the New Moon of Elul, one month before Yom Teruah, Yahshua's bride will begin her preparations and press into prayer and repentance. Just as the priests prepared to go before Yahweh in the Holy of Holies in the Tabernacle, we must examine ourselves and regard the requirements of a priest laid out for us in Torah, so that we will be ready to enter the chamber of the King. I have found only one place in Scripture that names the month of Elul and it is in the book of Nehemiah.

So the wall was finished in the twenty-fifth day of Elul, in fifty-two days. Neh. 6:15

Amazingly, the story that follows this verse records a strong company of people, like Yahshua's chayil, fighting to restore the walls of Jerusalem, and overcome the enemy before the approaching Yom Teruah. Their enemies mock and threaten them, but they work through the night with tools in one hand and weapons in the other. Nehemiah's story foreshadows Yahshua's bride as a strong chayil or woman of virtue, working in the night and fighting the good fight in the face of adversity. His story like so many others in Scripture is about restoration and safety. Jerusalem as you know, is Yahweh's City, and its name sums up His heart for His people. Jerusalem is Strong's Concordance #H3389 ירושלם and is a compound of two words. The first word is yarah, which we spoke of earlier when we looked at yarach for Moon. If you remember yarah is the root word for Torah, and it means to cast forth like rain or to hit a target. The second word is shalem, which is related to the familiar and beloved Hebrew word shalom. Shalom is often translated as peace, but peace is so misunderstood in our world. For many today 'peace' is understood as; the absence of war, tolerance and acceptance. Peace is promoted as the ability to get along with all belief systems. From Yahweh's perspective, this is not the way of peace. Shalom for peace is not tolerance, but the fulfillment of a preordained plan, which is seen when something is finished or completed. Shalem carries the same meaning; to be safe, restored, and whole. If we accommodate someone's conflicting ideals, the fullness of the original plan must be aborted. To have true peace, we must fight to see Yahweh's original plan and purpose fulfilled. Hence the meaning for Jerusalem, 'the place where Yahweh's Word keeps us whole, safe and prospering.' When we pray for the peace of Jerusalem, we are praying for its restoration and fulfillment at the end. Though many world leaders want to control Jerusalem, claiming peace and security as their mandate, it is not in the name of restoration and safety.

But concerning the times and the seasons, brothers, you have no need that anything be written to you. For you yourselves know well that the day of the Lord comes like a thief in the night. For when they are saying,"Peace and safety," then sudden destruction will come on them, like birth pains on a pregnant woman; and they will in no way escape. 1Thess. 5:1-3

Yahweh's peace comes when His order, design, and restoration is completed. That is why we are called to pray for the peace of Jerusalem.

Pray for the peace of Jerusalem. Those who love you will prosper. Ps.122:6

Our responsibility is to align ourselves with Yahweh's original plan and look forward to the future when Jerusalem will be completely restored and new. In Nehemiah's story, the wall of Jerusalem was miraculously restored in fifty-two days against all odds.

Our adversaries said, "They shall not know, neither see, until we come in among them, and kill them, and cause the work to cease."

When the Jews who lived by them came, they said to us ten times from all places, "Wherever you turn, they will attack us." Therefore set I in the lowest parts of the space behind the wall, in the open places, I set the people after their families with their swords, their spears, and their bows. I looked, and rose up, and said to the nobles, and to the rulers, and to the rest of the people, "Don't be afraid of them! Remember the Lord, who is great and awesome, and fight for your brothers, your sons, and your daughters, your wives, and your houses."

When our enemies heard that it was known to us, and God had brought their counsel to nothing, all of us returned to the wall, everyone to his work. From that time forth, half of my servants worked in the work, and half of them held the spears, the shields, and the bows, and the coats of mail; and the rulers were behind all the house of Judah. They all built the wall and those who bore burdens loaded themselves; everyone with one of his hands worked in the work, and with the other held his weapon; and the builders, everyone wore his sword at his side, and so built. He who sounded the trumpet was by me. I said to the nobles, and to the rulers and to the rest of the people, "The work is great and large, and we are separated on the wall, one far from another. Wherever you hear the sound of the trumpet, rally there to us. Our God will fight for us." Neh.4:11-20

As Yahshua's chayil, we too must have the strength and courage to rebuild the walls of Yahweh's kingdom. If we ignore the fact that the walls around Jerusalem from a spiritual perspective are broken down, we are also ignoring all that the enemy wants to bring upon Yahweh's City and His people. We are called to stand firm in prayer, preparation and purpose as we wait for the return of our King. This is part of our training as the royal priesthood of the New Jerusalem that will come down and be our future home.

But you have come to Mount Zion, and to the city of the living God, the heavenly Jerusalem, and to innumerable multitudes of angels, to the general assembly and assembly of the firstborn

who are enrolled in heaven, to God the Judge of all, to the
spirits of just men made perfect, to Jesus, the mediator of a
new covenant, and to the blood of sprinkling that speaks better
than that of Abel. Heb.12:22-24

We are the generation called to live with Godly fear and bring honor and
restoration back to Yahweh. Like those that worked to restore the walls of
Jerusalem with Nehemiah, we must encourage and support one another
to overcome and press on in the face of difficulty. When we do, we will be
safe and our names will be written in Yahweh's book.

Then those who feared Yahweh spoke one with another; and
Yahweh listened, and heard, and a book of memory was written
before him, for those who feared Yahweh, and who honored his
name. They shall be mine," says Yahweh of Armies, "my own
possession in the day that I make, and I will spare them, as a
man spares his own son who serves him. Mal.3:16,17

In Nehemiah, it is recorded that those who had worked to restore the
broken wall, gathered as one (echad) at its completion, on the New Moon
of the seventh month, which is Yom Teruah or the memorial of blowing-
Trumpets. They were united in heart for they had worked hard together
and completed their goal. Then, together they listened as Ezra read the
Torah out loud to them. Yahweh's Word pierced their hearts that day, and
they wept.

Ezra opened the book in the sight of all the people; (for he
was above all the people;) and when he opened it, all the
people stood up: and Ezra blessed Yahweh, the great God. All
the people answered, "Amen, Amen," with the lifting up of
their hands. They bowed their heads, and worshiped Yahweh
with their faces to the ground. Also Jeshua, and Bani, and
Sherebiah, Jamin, Akkub, Shabbethai, Hodiah, Maaseiah,
Kelita, Azariah, Jozabad, Hanan, Pelaiah, and the Levites,
caused the people to understand the law: and the people
stayed in their place. They read in the book, in the law of God,
distinctly; and they gave the sense, so that they understood the

reading. Nehemiah, who was the governor, and Ezra the priest the scribe, and the Levites who taught the people, said to all the people, "Today is holy to Yahweh your God. Don't mourn, nor weep." For all the people wept, when they heard the words of the law. Neh.8:5-9

The people heard all that Ezra read from the Torah and those who had the ears to hear, obeyed Yahweh's Command and kept the Feast of Tabernacles for the first time since Joshua, the son of Nun.

So the people went out, and brought them, and made themselves booths, everyone on the roof of his house, and in their courts, and in the courts of God's house, and in the wide place of the water gate, and in the wide place of Ephraim's gate. All the assembly of those who had come again out of the captivity made booths, and lived in the booths; for since the days of Jeshua the son of Nun to that day the children of Israel had not done so. There was very great gladness. Also day by day, from the first day to the last day, he read in the book of the law of God. They kept the feast seven days; and on the eighth day was a solemn assembly, according to the ordinance. Neh. 8:16-18

Wow, the Torah had not been kept since the time of Joshua! Similarly, the majority of people have not kept the Torah since the time of Yahshua. Some have tried, but in a general sense, the true Covenant understanding of the Torah, that Yahshua came to restore, has been misunderstood for centuries. If man attempts to keep the Torah without Yahshua, it is all in vain and subject to bondage. Yahshua came to make a way for us to return to the Father. He came to restore the walls of Yahweh's Kingdom City, and reveal His Father's heart to us so that our hearts would be convicted, and we too would weep at His Words and come to repentance. Yahshua, as the Word made flesh, came to remove the veil from our eyes, so that we could see the Torah and all of Scripture through Yahweh's great Love Story.

Having therefore such a hope, we use great boldness of speech, and not as Moses, who put a veil on his face, that the children of Israel wouldn't look steadfastly on the end of that which was passing away. But their minds were hardened, for until this very day at the reading of the old covenant the same veil remains, because in Christ it passes away. But to this day, when Moses is read, a veil lies on their heart. But whenever one turns to the Lord, the veil is taken away. Now the Lord is the Spirit and where the Spirit of the Lord is, there is liberty. But we all, with unveiled face seeing the glory of the Lord as in a mirror, are transformed into the same image from glory to glory, even as from the Lord, the Spirit. 2 Cor. 3:12-18

The above Scripture is often misunderstood. The Old Testament has a veil upon it because it was designed to reveal the coming of the Messiah and to be fulfilled by Him. Even though it was glorious when Moses first received it, without our Savior, its requirements were unattainable in the flesh and could only bring death. In Yahweh's mercy and grace, when we turn to Yahshua as our Savior and Light, the veil is lifted. Now, with unveiled faces, when we look at the Torah or Old Testament we see that it brings to life the fullness of Who our Beloved is. Again, just as Moses became glowing with Yahweh's light when receiving the Covenant on tablets of stone, we like the Moon will become even more glorious as we are transformed into the image of Yahshua from glory to glory.

And we all, with unveiled face, beholding the glory of the Lord, are being transformed into the same image from one degree of glory to another. For this comes from the Lord who is the Spirit. 2 Cor.3:18(ESV)

Evening is upon us, and soon we will be called to work through the dark of night, as the twilight fades. We are Yahshua's chayil and called to restore His ways, rebuilding the walls that have been torn down through lies and deception. As we abide with our Master, we are hidden in the secret place of the Most High and no evil can touch us. The wonder and awe of all that Yahweh has done to show His love for us, compels us to press on to the goal and seek Yahweh with all our heart. As the days grow darker, physically and spiritually, we will be challenged as never before, and the words given to Joshua before he journeyed into the Promised Land will come alive for us now.

> *Haven't I commanded you? Be strong and courageous.*
> *Don't be afraid. Don't be dismayed, for Yahweh your*
> *God[b] is with you wherever you go. Jos.1:9*

I would like now to review some key points of what we have shared together. We have seen how the One and Only Creator, the most wonderful and brilliant Artist and King of all the Universe has masterfully woven His heart into all of His Creation. He has woven words and pictures together so that we, His children, would see the fullness of His story and His foundational patterns. Under His covering, we find refuge and restoration. There, the light of His presence brings us His wisdom by His Spirit. As our Beloved Bridegroom, He hides us under His wings, and secures us to the Rock within His Tabernacle just as the few tenacious frankincense or levana trees are secured on the rock. The fullness of these pictures are confirmed in Psalm 27, which ties together many of the patterns and pictures we have looked at together.

> *Yahweh is my light and my salvation.*
> *Whom shall I <u>fear</u>?*
> *Yahweh is the strength of my life.*
> *Of whom shall I be afraid?*
> *When evildoers came at me to eat up my flesh,*
> *even my adversaries and my foes, they stumbled and fell.*
> *Though an army should encamp against me,*
> <u>*my heart shall not fear*</u>*.*
> *Though war should rise against me,*
> *even then I will be confident.*
> *One thing I have asked of Yahweh, that I will seek after,*
> <u>*that I may dwell in Yahweh's house all the days of my life,*</u>
> <u>*to see Yahweh's beauty,*</u>
> *and to inquire in his temple.*
> <u>*For in the day of trouble he will keep*</u>
> <u>*me secretly in his pavilion.*</u>
> <u>*In the covert of his tabernacle he will hide me.*</u>

He will lift me up on a rock.
Now my head will be lifted up above my enemies around me.
I will offer sacrifices of joy in his tent.
I will sing, yes, I will sing praises to Yahweh.
Hear, Yahweh, when I cry with my voice.
Have mercy also on me, and answer me.
When you said, "Seek my face,"
my heart said to you, "I will seek your face, Yahweh." Ps.27:1-8

All that we have seen in the way of the Moon is summed up in this Psalm! Just as it is tradition to blow the shofar each day of Elul, it is also tradition for Psalm 27 to be read each day, starting on the New Moon of Elul and continuing to Yom Teruah. Each day of Elul, this Psalm admonishes the bride to be prepared to stand before her Beloved King. For the bride of the Messiah, these traditions are not foreign. She will have rehearsed them many times at each New Moon of the year and her sacrifices of joy will declare it. The 'sacrifices of joy' in Psalm 27 are not what we may think at first glance. In Psalm 27 the word translated as joy in referencing a sacrifice of something quite different from simchah. The sacrifices that Psalm 27 is referring to, is 'teruah' as in Yom Teruah! Remember, teruah holds the meaning of shouts of joy, as well as trumpet blasts and alarm. So the verse in Psalm 27 could also read, "I will offer sacrifices of teruah!" To those who are waiting, watching and preparing to be Yahshua's bride, this will be one of the offerings made in His Tabernacle, as the great day of His return approaches. We saw this in the two Silver Trumpets that are to be blown at the time of the New Moon. This is confirmed in Psalm 89:

Blessed is the people that know the
joyful sound: they shall walk,
O Lord, in the light of thy countenance. Ps. 89:15(NKJ)

The word translated as joyful sound in this Psalm is also teruah, the same Hebrew word found translated as 'sacrifices of joy' in Psalm 27. In other words, those that know the sound of teruah, those who are familiar with it because of rehearsing it at the New Moon and throughout Elul, will walk in the light of Yahweh's countenance, just as the Moon journeys in the light of the Sun. Psalm 27 also confirms that the secret place is where Yahshua's bride will find joy and refuge, even though her enemies surround her, *'Now my head will be lifted up above my enemies around me.'* Remember this picture is found in the beloved Psalm 23;

You prepare a table before me
in the presence of my enemies.

In the safety of Yahweh's presence, the enemy has no power over us. As we dwell in the secret place with Yahweh, He reveals the treasures of His heart, renews our spirits and protects us from the onslaught of evil. How awesome! Yahshua's royal priesthood and bride has become part of the same Covenant conditions that were promised to Abraham.

After these things Yahweh's word came to Abram in a vision, saying, "Don't be afraid, Abram. I am your shield, your exceedingly great reward. Gen. 15:1

You are my hiding place and my shield;
I hope in Your word. Ps. 119:114

I will give you the treasures of darkness,
and hidden riches of secret places,
that you may know that it is I, Yahweh,
who call you by your name,
even the God of Israel. Is. 45:3

I pray that these compelling pictures have encouraged you to endure and press on to the end. The journey of becoming Yahshua's chayil or 'pearl of great price' is worth everything. May it become our delight to set apart our time and our hearts to rehearse for our Beloved's return with longing and great anticipation!

He who overcomes will be arrayed in white garments, and I will in no way blot his name out of the book of life, and I will confess his name before my Father, and before his angels. Rev. 3:5

Let us rejoice and be exceedingly glad, and let us give the glory to him. For the marriage of the Lamb has come, and his wife has made herself ready." It was given to her that she would *array herself in bright, pure, fine linen: for the fine linen is the righteous acts of the saints. Rev.19:7,8*

Many will attend Yahshua's wedding as guests, but only a few will be worthy of the wedding garments. Many will be in the Kingdom, but not all will have the privilege of serving Him and ruling with Him as His bride. May it burn in our hearts to be worthy, ready and waiting for our Beloved when His trumpet calls.

The Five Wise

THE PARABLE OF THE TEN VIRGINS HAS STIRRED PEOPLE'S HEARTS FOR centuries. As one of the most compelling parables that Yahshua told, many artists have attempted to depict the heart-wrenching scene. Typically, they portray the five foolish virgins outside the closed chamber door, crying in anguish because the door is not being opened to them. Another similarly unsettling story that Yahshua told, is that of a poor beggar named Lazarus. In desperate hunger, he begged outside a rich man's mansion gate for a few crumbs of his food. In the end, both Lazarus and the rich man die, but like the five wise and the five foolish virgins, their destinies are dramatically different.

"Now there was a certain rich man, and he was clothed in purple and fine linen, living in luxury every day. A certain beggar, named Lazarus, was laid at his gate, full of sores, and desiring to be fed with the crumbs that fell from the rich man's table. Yes, even the dogs came and licked his sores. It happened that the beggar died, and that he was carried away by the angels to Abraham's bosom. The rich man also died, and was buried. In Hades, he lifted up his eyes, being in torment, and saw Abraham far off, and Lazarus at his bosom. He cried and said, 'Father Abraham, have mercy on me, and send Lazarus,

that he may dip the tip of his finger in water, and cool my tongue! For I am in anguish in this flame.' Luke16:19-24

In both of these stories, the ten virgins and Lazarus, we find people in circumstances of choice that include attitude, and in both stories, there is an outcome of regret. Once the consequences of bad choices or a complacent attitude come to pass, a desperate desire to correct it follows. As the old saying goes, "Hindsight is 20/20." Just as with the story of the grasshopper and the ant, the message or moral is, that those who have a complacent, selfish attitude are the ones who suffer in the end. The rich man enjoyed the pleasures of life while all seemed good to him. In his selfish pleasure, he overlooked or ignored the poor suffering beggar at his gate. In the end … not even Abraham could reach out to sooth his torment.

"But Abraham said, 'Son, remember that you, in your lifetime, received your good things, and Lazarus, in the same way, bad things. But now here he is comforted and you are in anguish. Besides all this, between us and you there is a great gulf fixed, that those who want to pass from here to you are not able, and that none may cross over from there to us.' Luke 16:25,26

A similar attitude is revealed in Yahshua's parable of the wedding feast. This parable reads as a specific warning to those who desire to attend the Marriage Supper of the Lamb.

The Kingdom of Heaven is like a certain king, who made a marriage feast for his son, and sent out his servants to call those who were invited to the marriage feast, but they would not come. Again he sent out other servants, saying, 'Tell those who are invited, "Behold, I have prepared my dinner. My cattle and my fatlings are killed, and all things are ready. Come to the marriage feast!"' But they made light of it, and went their ways, one to his own farm, another to his merchandise, and the rest grabbed his servants, and treated them shamefully, and killed them. Matt.22:2-6

Once again, we see attitude coming into play. A king sends out invitations to his friends to come to his son's wedding. The people who receive the invitation are shockingly apathetic! Can you imagine a king inviting people to his son's wedding and they turn down the invitation…because they are too busy?! I believe this is why Yahshua repeatedly says in Revelation, *"He who has an ear, let him hear what the Spirit says to the assemblies."* He is mercifully reminding Yahweh's assemblies to hear or shema His call. The King of the Universe *HAS* sent out His invitation! Each one of us has received it. What is the Spirit saying to the assemblies? DON'T TURN DOWN THE INVITATION!!… accept Yahshua as your Savior and *BE READY for HIM*! In Yahweh's relentless love and mercy He calls to the lost, lonely and hurting people all over the world to come to Him while there is time.

"Come, everyone who thirsts, to the waters! Come, he who has no money, buy, and eat! Yes, come, buy wine and milk without money and without price.

Why do you spend money for that which is not bread? and your labor for that which doesn't satisfy? listen diligently to me, and eat you that which is good, and let your soul delight itself in fatness.

Turn your ear, and come to me; hear, and your soul shall live: and I will make an everlasting covenant with you, even the sure mercies of David. Is.55:1-3

"Behold, I come quickly. My reward is with me, to repay to each man according to his work. I am the Alpha and the Omega, the First and the Last, the Beginning and the End.

Blessed are those who do his commandments, that they may have the right to the tree of life, and may enter in by the gates into the city. Outside are the dogs, the sorcerers, the sexually immoral, the murderers, the idolaters, and everyone who loves and practices falsehood. Rev.22:12-15

Sadly most of us in today's culture are distracted with the multiple ways technology keeps us entertained and attached to the world. As a result, it becomes harder and harder to give undivided attention to Yahweh, or anyone for that matter. Today's lackadaisical hearing reminds me of the word Yahweh spoke to Ezekiel. These people hear Yahweh's Words as a lovely sound and even agree with them, but they don't care to do them. These ones like the five foolish, love Yahweh and His Word, but don't do the works of the woman of virtue or Yahshua's pearl of great price.

> *As for you, son of man, the children of your people talk of you by the walls and in the doors of the houses, and speak one to another, everyone to his brother, saying, Please come and hear what is the word that comes forth from Yahweh. They come to you as the people come, and they sit before you as my people, and they hear your words, but don't do them; for with their mouth they show much love, but their heart goes after their gain. Behold, you are to them as a very lovely song of one who has a pleasant voice, and can play well on an instrument; for they hear your words, but they don't do them. When this comes to pass, (behold, it comes), then shall they know that a prophet has been among them. Ez.33:30-33*

Of course we want to *hear* the voice of our Beloved, but His Words need to pierce our daily lives to the point of action. To be identified with the five *wise* virgins, we must pay the price for the oil, which will include knowing the heart of our Bridegroom and being known by Him. Notice that when the appointed time finally came, the five wise could not give away the oil that they had acquired ... especially at the last minute.

> *"Then the Kingdom of Heaven will be like ten virgins, who took their lamps, and went out to meet the bridegroom. Five of them were foolish, and five were wise. Those who were foolish, when they took their lamps, took no oil with them, but the wise took oil in their vessels with their lamps. Now while the bridegroom delayed, they all slumbered and slept. Matt.25:1-5*

At the onset of Yahshua's parable, the ten virgins appear to have no visible difference between them; they are all virgins, they are all waiting for their beloved, they all have lamps, and they all rise from their sleep to diligently trim their lamps. Somehow along the way, there is a crucial misunderstanding for five of them. Only when the midnight cry was heard, and the lamps of the foolish virgins begin to run out of oil did the revelation of the wise become shockingly clear.

> But at midnight there was a cry, 'Behold! The bridegroom is coming! Come out to meet him!' Then all those virgins arose, and trimmed their lamps. The foolish said to the wise, 'Give us some of your oil, for our lamps are going out." Matt.25:6-8

Some may ask, "Where is the compassion of the wise?" After all, the five foolish had come far enough along to be standing there with them at the midnight cry. Could the five wise not give away some of their oil? This is an important piece to see. If the five wise had given up their precious oil at that moment, then all that they had prepared for, worked for, and longed for, would have been lost. Like we saw in the story of the Ant and the Grasshopper, the wise had been diligent and they could not give away what they had acquired. It was simply too late for those who had not prepared. We see a similar outcome in the story of Lazarus. Once the rich man found himself in Hades, he was filled with deep regret and cries out to Abraham to cool his tongue and warn his *five* brothers ... but again, it was too late.

> "He said, 'I ask you therefore, father, that you would send him to my father's house; for I have five brothers, that he may testify to them, so they won't also come into this place of torment.' "But Abraham said to him, 'They have Moses and the prophets. Let them listen to them.' "He said, 'No, father Abraham, but if one goes to them from the dead, they will repent.' "He said to him, 'If they don't listen to Moses and the prophets, neither will they be persuaded if one rises from the dead.'» Luke 16:27-31

These stirring pictures are meant to warn us that there is a time for responding followed by the consequences for our response. For us to understand the five wise fully though, we need to also understand what led the five foolish into being deceived. How could the foolish virgins make such a devastating mistake? What could they have overlooked? I believe that there are two possibilities; one, that the foolish virgins did not see an urgent need for the oil and so they naively enjoyed worldly pleasures; or two, they had acquired something they thought was as good or even better!

> But the wise answered, saying, 'What if there isn't
> enough for us and you? You go rather to those
> who sell, and buy for yourselves.'Matt.25:9

Most of us have studied or heard teachings on the oil of the virgin's lamps. The most common understanding is that the oil represents the Holy Spirit. Though the Holy Spirit is vital for leading us into all truth, there is a problem with this perspective. Each person, teacher, denomination or culture perceives the Holy Spirit in a different way. If we adhere to the understanding of the Holy Spirit being the oil, there is a huge risk of the oil for the lamps being interpreted in many different ways. Not to mention the many ideas of what truth is. As a result, if we hold this understanding, we will be in danger of getting an abstract view of what the oil is or how to acquire it. The most significant factor about the oil is that it was bought with a price. The wise respond to the foolish by telling them to go and *buy* oil for themselves. Their response reveals the reason that the Holy Spirit cannot qualify as the oil for the lamps. The Holy Spirit is a free gift from Yahweh and cannot be bought.

> Peter said to them, "Repent, and be baptized, every one of you,
> in the name of Jesus Christ for the forgiveness of sins, and you
> will receive the gift of the Holy Spirit. Acts 2:38

So ... where *do* we buy this treasured oil? As it is with Yahweh and most things of worth, we must seek for them. Do you remember the thrill of a treasure hunt as a child? ... or the excitement in playing 'hide and seek?' There is something intriguing and even exhilarating about searching for something that is hidden. As we have found in our search for answers to the New Moon, Yahweh's pattern of life reveals that things need to be hidden for safety and life to come forth. Also, when someone takes the time to search for someone or something it shows that they have a deep desire and concern for what they are searching for. Imagine how heart breaking it would be if you were lost or hidden and no one came to find you. Yahweh conceals and hides things from us to entice us to search them out, which, as we have seen, includes Himself. When we seek Yahweh with all our heart it is an expression of our love for Him.

Truly, you are a God who hides himself,
O God of Israel, the Savior. Is.45:15(ESV)

I will wait for Yahweh, who hides his
face from the house of Jacob,
and I will look for him. Is.8:17

You shall seek me, and find me, when you shall
search for me with all your heart. Jer.29:13

For thus says Yahweh to the house of Israel:
"Seek me, and you will live;Amos5:4

Those who are serious about seeking are those who invest time, money and energy to hunt for what is lost or hidden. Just as we saw earlier, in the garden pattern, there are different levels of searching. Remember, the d'rash level is seen when our search is driven by love, like the search for a lost child or spouse. Here we find the way to seek for Yahweh and for the precious oil needed for our lamp. Once we have found the treasure, we then go to the sod level of seeking. Again, this is the level where we seek what is hidden from the eyes of the world and those who want to steal it.

The picture of concealing treasure was was best seen with kings of long ago. They were known for keeping their valuables in a special treasury with guards to watch over it. It is said though, that there was usually a portion of a king's treasure that was so valuable to him that he would not even allow his trusted guards to watch over it. This portion of his treasure was guarded by the king himself and hidden with him. The origin of this picture comes from our King. Yahweh has always guarded and concealed His most valuable treasures with Himself. He revealed this to us at the building of the Tabernacle in the wilderness and the care of the Ark of the Covenant, which is His throne.

When we seek for Yahweh with all our heart, as seen in the d'rash level, Yahweh takes us into His secret place, as seen in the sod or hidden level of our search. This is the Holy of Holies, where we will find Yahweh seated on His throne (kisseh) or Ark of the Covenant, which holds His treasures; the Covenant tablets, the manna and Aaron's rod! As we have discovered, the secret place is where Yahweh protects all the treasures of His heart, including us. If we want to find Yahweh and His treasured things, including the oil for our lamps, we must seek to walk according to His patterns and find Him in His secret place.

May we never forget what an incredible honor and privilege it is to have entry into the secret place by the shed blood of Yahshua and to know the things of Yahweh's heart. This is the deeper meaning behind this verse in Proverb 25.

It is the glory of God to conceal a matter;
it is the glory of kings to search out a matter. Prov.25;1

When we find the treasures of Yahweh's heart and apply them in our lives as preparation to become the spotless bride of the Messiah, our treasure will also be stored in the secret place safe from the destruction of this world.

"Don't lay up treasures for yourselves on the earth, where moth and rust consume, and where thieves break through and steal; but lay up for yourselves treasures in heaven, where neither moth nor rust consume, and where thieves don't break through and steal; for where your treasure is, there your heart will be also. Matt.6:19-21

There is one more intriguing factor that we will encounter in your search for oil, and where to buy it, and that is that many times the things which we are searching for are not far from us. In fact, sometimes the most difficult things to find … are actually right before our eyes. Have you ever experienced one of those epiphany moments, when you scratch your head and ask yourself, "Why didn't I see that before?" Our search for oil will be like this in many ways. Yahshua's disciples experienced it one morning after they had fished all night long and returned to shore with nothing in their nets. As they reach the shore someone (Yahshua) calls to them, asking if they had anything to eat. The disciples reply to Him, "No," not recognizing their risen Master. He then tells them to throw their nets out of the right side of the boat.

> But when day had already come, Jesus stood on the beach, yet the disciples didn't know that it was Jesus. Jesus therefore said to them, "Children, have you anything to eat?" They answered him, "No." He said to them, "Cast the net on the right side of the boat, and you will find some." They cast it therefore, and now they weren't able to draw it in for the multitude of fish. John 21:4-6

Can you imagine what they may have thought after so many hours of trying? "Right..the other side, why didn't I think of that." Nevertheless, when they listened to Yahshua, and did what He said, even though it may have gone against all their logic, their nets were filled to overflowing with fish. Often we simply don't have the eyes to see or the heart to understand what Yahweh has placed right before us. Like Abraham said to the rich man when he cried out for someone to warn his five brothers, 'If they don't listen to Moses and the prophets, neither will they be persuaded if one rises from the dead.' In other words, 'If they didn't get it, when it was right before their eyes, they are not going to get it just because someone says they are back from the dead.' The same could be said to us about Yahshua. If all that He did to show us the way back to the Father, to work miracles and to pay the price for our sins isn't enough for us, then the consequences will come because there simply isn't anymore to be done.

> For if we sin willfully after we have received the knowledge of the truth, there remains no more a sacrifice for sins, but a certain fearful expectation of judgment, and a fierceness of fire which will devour the adversaries. A man who disregards Moses' law dies without compassion on the word of two or three

witnesses. How much worse punishment, do you think, will he be judged worthy of, who has trodden under foot the Son of God, and has counted the blood of the covenant with which he was sanctified an unholy thing, and has insulted the Spirit of grace? Heb.10:26-29

Yahshua was here right in front of people's eyes. Many could have reached out and touched the King of the Universe, but only a few had the eyes to see Him for Who He was. We could say He was hidden in plain sight. Could this is also true for the oil that we seek? Though many have wondered what the oil of the five wise may be, it has always been right before our eyes. The precious oil that we need for our lamps to give light ... is wisdom!

Get wisdom.
Get understanding.
Don't forget, neither swerve from the words of my mouth.
Don't forsake her, and she will preserve you.
Love her, and she will keep you.
Wisdom is supreme, Get wisdom.
Yes, though it costs all your possessions,
get understanding. Prov.4:5-7

He lays up sound wisdom for the upright. He
is a shield to those who walk in integrity;
that he may guard the paths of justice, and
preserve the way of his saints.

"But where shall wisdom be found? Prov.2:7,8

Just as there are different levels of searching out Yahweh and His treasures, so it is with His wisdom. The writer of Proverbs even puts an urgency to our search, as we see expressed in the d'rash level of seeking; telling us that, no matter what the cost, *if it costs us all our possessions,* ... get wisdom and understanding. Once we find it, we can then apply the sod level of seeking wisdom allowing our hearts and minds to be fully surrendered to Yahshua and His leading. The deep work that Yahshua's Spirit does within us, transforms us into the image of our Beloved. The sod level goes beneath the surface to reveal the foolishness of our flesh and show us Yahweh's wisdom. Precious gems are sought out of the earth in this way; the deeper the search, the more valuable and rare the find, and so it is for the oil of wisdom.

> *So as to turn your ear to wisdom, and*
> *apply your heart to understanding;*
> *Yes, if you call out for discernment, and lift*
> *up your voice for understanding;*
> *if you seek her as silver, and search for*
> *her as for hidden treasures:*
> *then you will understand the fear of Yahweh, and*
> *find the knowledge of God. Prov.2:2-5*

> *With God is wisdom and might. He has*
> *counsel and understanding. Job 12:13*

Our desire to seek after Yahweh and His wisdom reflects how much we value and believe in Him. That is why it is called the glory of kings to seek out a matter, especially the matters of Yahweh's kingdom.

> *We speak wisdom, however, among those who are full grown;*
> *yet a wisdom not of this world, nor of the rulers of this world,*
> *who are coming to nothing. But we speak God's wisdom in*
> *a mystery, the wisdom that has been hidden, which God*
> *foreordained before the worlds for our glory, which none of the*
> *rulers of this world has known. For had they known it, they*
> *wouldn't have crucified the Lord of glory. 1Cor. 2:6-8*

In other words, our love for Yahweh is what compels us to seek after His wisdom, which in turn will enable our faith to become works of worth or the bearing of fruit. We saw this revealed through the woman of virtue or Yahshua's pearl of great price. Yahshua was willing to pay the highest price for His pearl, and now she must pay the price for the oil of wisdom needed to shed His light. The initial cost will come as we separate ourselves from the world and choose to follow Yahshua.

Now great multitudes were going with him. He turned and said to them, "If anyone comes to me, and doesn't disregard his own father, mother, wife, children, brothers, and sisters, yes, and his own life also, he can't be my disciple. Whoever doesn't bear his own cross, and come after me, can't be my disciple. For which of you, desiring to build a tower, doesn't first sit down and count the cost, to see if he has enough to complete it? Or perhaps, when he has laid a foundation, and is not able to finish, everyone who sees begins to mock him, saying, 'This man began to build, and wasn't able to finish.' Or what king, as he goes to encounter another king in war, will not sit down first and consider whether he is able with ten thousand to meet him who comes against him with twenty-thousand? Or else, while the other is yet a great way off, he sends an envoy, and asks for conditions of peace. So therefore whoever of you who doesn't renounce all that he has, he can't be my disciple.
Luke 14:25-33

As one of Yahshua's disciples in training for the royal priesthood, we *must* hear His voice alone. People all over the world are being swept away with ideas and beliefs that are not grounded in truth. Taking a stand for Yahweh and His truth, will soon bear a higher price than ever before in history because you will potentially be seen as an extremist. The basis of our faith is being challenged, while other beliefs are taking the spotlight. Even simply believing that Yahweh created the heavens and the Earth, as it is recorded in the first chapters of Genesis is becoming uncommon. Nevertheless, when we see that all of Creation is declaring the unfathomable wisdom of Yahweh, we can then understand how awesome He truly is and that there is none compared with Him.

Oh the depth of the riches both of the wisdom and the knowledge of God! How unsearchable are his judgments, and his ways past tracing out! Rom.11:33

Each of the patterns that we have looked at, confirm the character and majestic hand of the One who designed them. When we look outside and see the wonders of His Creation, we are seeing evidence of what is hidden, for all things were created to praise the One and Only Creator, Who is unseen. The wisdom of Yahweh is so awesome, that the author of Proverbs personifies it as one who was with Yahweh at the very beginning. His Masterful works of wisdom are beyond our ability to fully grasp and they praise Him and bring glory to His Name each and every day.

Yahweh, how many are your works!
In wisdom have you made them all.
The earth is full of your riches. Ps.104:24

"Yahweh possessed me in the beginning of his work,
before his deeds of old.
I was set up from everlasting, from the beginning,
before the earth existed.
When there were no depths, I was brought forth,
when there were no springs abounding with water.
Before the mountains were settled in place,
before the hills, I was brought forth;
while as yet he had not made the earth, nor the fields,
nor the beginning of the dust of the world.
When he established the heavens, I was there;
when he set a circle on the surface of the deep,
when he established the clouds above,
when the springs of the deep became strong,
when he gave to the sea its boundary,
that the waters should not violate his commandment,
when he marked out the foundations of the earth;
then I was the craftsman by his side.
I was a delight day by day, always
rejoicing before him, Prov.8:22-30

Once we establish how magnificent and wise Yahweh is, as Creator and King of the Universe, there is no choice but to approach Him with fear and trembling. As we saw in the word, yerach for the Moon, our fear of Yahweh will bring rightful order to our perspective and keep us humble. Fear is the key that opens the door for our search, for it was with wisdom that all of Creation was set in place.

Where is the place of understanding?
Man doesn't know its price;
Neither is it found in the land of the living.
The deep says, 'It isn't in me.'
The sea says, 'It isn't with me.'Job 28:12-14

The fear of Yahweh is the beginning of wisdom.
The knowledge of the Holy One is understanding. Prov.9:10

The fear of Yahweh is the beginning of wisdom.
All those who do his work have a good understanding.
His praise endures forever! Ps.111:10

These Scriptures are foundational because they reveal how a healthy fear of Yahweh will lead us to His wisdom. Our fear of Him will put into proper order how much we need to trust His leading and not trust in our own understanding.

Trust in Yahweh with all your heart,
and don't lean on your own understanding.
In all your ways acknowledge him,
and he will make your paths straight. Prov.3:5,6

Now, with these foundational elements of our search in place, let's return to the parable of the ten virgins and put the pieces into practical terms, so that we can discern how to pay the price for the oil of wisdom and apply it in our every day lives.

"Then the Kingdom of Heaven will be like ten virgins, who took
their lamps, and went out to meet the bridegroom."Matt.25:1

Yahshua begins by telling us that this parable is giving us clues to the Kingdom of Heaven so that we will grasp its importance. Then He tells us that there are ten virgins and each have a lamp. We have established that there is only one lamp that this could be; the Menorah, and like the Holy Spirit, the Menorah is given to us as a gift. Remember too, that the lamp or Menorah is a picture of Yahshua; the Word of Yahweh in the flesh and the Light of the world.

*Your word is a lamp to my feet, and a
light for my path. Ps.119:105*

*For the commandment is a lamp, and the law a light.
Reproofs of instruction are the way of life. Prov. 6:23*

*"For You are my lamp, Yahweh;
Yahweh shall enlighten my darkness. 2Sam.22:29*

Yahshua came as the embodiment of the Lamp or Menorah, Who brought forth life and light to the Word of Yahweh!

In the beginning was the Word, and the Word was with God, and the Word was God. The same was in the beginning with God. All things were made through him. Without him was not anything made that has been made. In him was life, and the life was the light of men. The light shines in the darkness, and the darkness hasn't overcome it. John 1:1-5

The Word and the Light are one! When we accept Yahshua into our lives as King and Savior, He becomes our Lamp or Menorah, and we have His Light in our lives. As sons and daughters of the King in training for the royal priesthood, we now have an obligation to keep the light of the Menorah burning. How we are to accomplish this in the world today is found in Yahweh's Word or instructions of life, for all of Yahweh's Kingdom functions by His Covenant Torah. This is the next important key in our search for wisdom.

But seek first God's Kingdom, and his righteousness; and all these things will be given to you as well. Matt. 6:33

Yahshua tells us in this verse that when we separate ourselves from the world, and seek after His Kingdom ways, everything will come into right order and He will supply all that we need. When we become a part of Yahweh's family, we become partakers of the heavenly pattern that Yahweh revealed to His children in the Wilderness when He dwelt in their midst. The pattern of heaven, was set up in the Tabernacle in the wilderness so that Yahweh's holiness could exist with an unholy people. The Tabernacle is Yahweh's Kingdom pattern and we must seek to understand it, for we are now a part of it and He desires to dwell with us by His Spirit.

> *Don't you know that you are a temple of God, and that God's Spirit lives in you? If anyone destroys the temple of God, God will destroy him; for God's temple is holy, which you are. 1 Cor.3:16,17*

> *"See, you make all things according to the pattern shown you on the mountain." Heb. 8:5b*

We are now, individually and corporately, Yahweh's Tabernacle or Temple and bear the elements of its pattern. Yahweh's Tabernacle gives us insight and direction for how we are to serve Him and how to bear fruit. When we see ourselves as the dwelling place of Yahweh's Spirit, and His righteous servants, called to take care of the holy elements within His dwelling, it becomes clear that caring for the Menorah is our responsibility. In order to understand the *oil* for our lamp, we first need to understand the lamp or Menorah that we have been given.

We have seen that the Menorah is specially made from a single talent of gold, hammered into a seven-branched shape that resembles a tree. It is designed with a center branch and three branches that spread out on either side. The center branch is set apart as the source of life and light that the other branches abide in. Remember all that we looked at in the chapter about the Sun, and that Yahshua is the only source of light, just as the Sun is the Earth's only source of light. The center branch is called, the "yarek," in Hebrew, meaning thigh or lion, making the Menorah a remarkable picture of being grafting into Yahweh's family. We, like the branches of the Menorah, are to abide in the center branch, Yahshua.

> *I am the vine. You are the branches. He who remains in me, and I in him, the same bears much fruit, for apart from me you can do nothing. John 15:5*

But if some of the branches were broken off, and you, being a wild olive, were grafted in among them, and became partaker with them of the root and of the richness of the olive tree; don't boast over the branches. But if you boast, it is not you who support the root, but the root supports you. Rom.11:17,18

Notice that Paul is showing us how we have been grafted into an olive tree, which in turn will produce the fruit needed for the oil. The pure oil will then be used to fill almond shaped cups on the seven branches of the Menorah. The almond shapes resemble the shape of our own eyes and remind us to watch over all that matters to Yahweh's heart within His Holy Place. The seven branches remind us of what is important to Yahweh, for the number seven is repeated throughout His Masterpiece as one of His principles of design and a sign of the Artist. First in the seven days of the week, including the seventh Sabbath day, and then in His cycle or path of righteousness which includes His appointed feast days; each carrying within them patterns of seven. In the spring there are the seven days of unleavened bread at Passover, the seven Sabbaths in the counting of the omer toward Pentecost or Shavuot. Then in the fall there is the feast of Trumpets, which is appointed for the seventh New Moon that leads us to the seven days of Tabernacles or Sukkot. These and so much more reveal what the Menorah is teaching us about the glorious light of Yahweh.

He put the lampstand in the Tent of Meeting, opposite the table, on the side of the tabernacle southward. He lit the lamps before Yahweh, as Yahweh commanded Moses. Ex.40:24,25

As we come to realize, that just as the Sun is the only light for the Moon, the Menorah is the only light in the Holy Place or dwelling of Yahweh, we then can see that the light the Menorah represents is the light we are to shine and keep alive.

For the commandment is a lamp; and the law is light;
and reproofs of instruction are the way of life: Prov.6:23(NKJ)

As the *only* light in the Tabernacle and the Light of Yahweh's Word, the Menorah's light was *never* to go out! When we understand '*the Light*' from this perspective, we can also see why we cannot claim to have any light of our own. Yahweh's Light cannot be added to or taken away from; it is purely His. When we live a life that follows Yahshua and shines of Yahweh's Word, we are keeping the lamp or Menorah lit within us, and reflecting it to the world, just as the Moon reflects the light of the Sun. This was the responsibility of the priesthood then, and it is the duty of Yahshua's bride and royal priesthood now. Our life of following the Messiah as our High Priest, and keeping His commandments brings the fullness and revelation of Yahweh's Light to a dark world. Now it becomes clear why the oil is so important and why we cannot run out, especially at the end. Below is an excerpt from Brad Scott's article on the Menorah, explaining the elements of the Menorah and its relationship to watching.

According to Shemot (Exodus) 25:33-38, the single beaten work of the menorah had bowls made like unto almonds at the top of each branch to contain the oil for the light. The bowls were made like unto almonds. The word almonds shares a very interesting root with another word. The word for almonds is shaqad (שקר) which shares the exact same spelling as its verbal root. The word shaqad everywhere else is translated as watch, alert, or to be sleepless. These almond-shaped bearers of the oil for the light teach us something about the nature of being a light bearer. They, or we, are to be watchful and alert as "sons of the light". Again I quote from 1 Thessalonians:

1 Thessalonians 5:2-6

For yourselves know perfectly that the day of YHVH so cometh as a thief in the night. For when they shall say, Peace and safety, then sudden destruction cometh upon them, as travail upon a woman with child, and they shall not escape. But ye, brethren, are not in darkness, that that day should overtake you as a thief. Ye are all sons of light, and sons of the day; we are not of the night or of darkness. Therefore, let us not sleep, as do others, but let us watch and be soberminded.

Hmmm. Remember the parable of the ten virgins, five which took oil in their lamps and five which did not? Do you remember the last thing Yeshua' says in that parable? "Watch therefore;..." The "sons of light" know the word of God, obey his commandments, and keep his feasts and sabbaths. The very nature of what they are doing during the courses

of YHVH's cycles of righteousness makes them alert and watching. In the Hebrew culture the "sons of darkness", or "sons of the night", are those who do not know Torah and have not the light of YHVH.

Brad's article so beautifully weaves together all the pictures we have looked at with the importance of watching and being ready. Just as any loving bride submits to her husband and the needs of their home with joy and diligence, so Yahshua's chayil bride will take on the care of what matters to Yahshua's heart within His dwelling place. As His royal priesthood and woman of virtue, she will daily watch over and care for the flame of His Menorah so that it will *NEVER* go out!

Command the children of Israel, that they bring unto thee pure olive oil beaten for the light, to cause the lamps to burn continually. Lev. 24:2(KJV)

And you shall command the children of Israel that they bring you pure oil of pressed olives for the light, to cause the lamp to burn continually. Ex. 27:20 (KJV)

Can you see why the oil that the ten virgins needed for their lamps is so vital? The pure olive oil was to keep the light of their Beloved burning forever! So..where will we buy this oil? I used the King James version for the above two verses because the translators chose to use the words "beaten for the light," which is a more accurate translation. The Hebrew word used for beaten is Strong's #H3795, כתית kathiyth, which means; to bruise or violently strike, crush, smite. On the night before Yahshua's crucifixion, He was on the Mount of Olives with his disciples. While they slept, He went to the Garden of Gethsemane to pray. This garden was not just any garden; the name Gethsemane means Olive Press! When Yahshua went to Gethsemane, "The Olive Press," to pray, He was submitting Himself to being crushed in spirit ... to the point of shedding blood. That heart-breaking night, Yahshua revealed to us the price of the oil! After He had prayed, He was then taken into the hands of the authorities to be bruised and beaten. This, beloved of Yahweh, is the precious price of the oil and the unfathomable price of our redemption. The oil we need, is *not* free ... it carries a precious cost. If we want to keep the light of

Yahshua our Savior alive in our lives, we must pay the price for it. The light of the Menorah reflects the price that our Beloved paid for us…'His pearl of great price.'

Or don't you know that your body is a temple of the Holy Spirit which is in you, which you have from God? You are not your own, for you were bought with a price. Therefore glorify God in your body and in your spirit, which are God's. 1 Cor.6:19,20

Now great multitudes were going with him. He turned and said to them, "If anyone comes to me, and doesn't disregard his own father, mother, wife, children, brothers, and sisters, yes, and his own life also, he can't be my disciple. Whoever doesn't bear his own cross, and come after me, can't be my disciple. Luke 14:25-27

Giving up all that this world offers us and dying to ourselves to follow our Beloved Master is the cost of wisdom and the way of becoming one of the five wise. Enduring the trials and tribulations that Yahweh sets before us will produce the oil needed for our lamp. Though this is a daunting price from our perspective, it is nothing compared to the glory that awaits us if we endure.

For I consider that the sufferings of this present time are not worthy to be compared with the glory which will be revealed toward us. Rom.8:18

For our light affliction, which is for the moment, works for us more and more exceedingly an eternal weight of glory; while we don't look at the things which are seen, but at the things which are not seen. For the things which are seen are temporal, but the things which are not seen are eternal.2 Cor. 4:17,18

As we die daily, and face the persecution, trials, and heartbreak that come our way, we need to ask for wisdom from Yahweh and the guidance of the Holy Spirit to rightly apply His Word in responding to each situation, every moment of every day… with joy.

Count it all joy, my brothers, when you fall into various temptations, knowing that the testing of your faith produces endurance. Let endurance have its perfect work, that you may be perfect and complete, lacking in nothing. James 1:2-4

At times, this will feel impossible. Other times, it will crush you, and the pain will seem unbearable. Then you will need a devotion and determination like you have never had before. There will also be times when you feel alone, lost and that the odds are overwhelmingly against you. Beloved of Yahweh, you must never forget, that every one of these trials come from Yahweh's loving hand, and are designed to produce the precious oil of wisdom in our lives. For as we allow Yahweh's Spirit to have dominion in our response to these trials, the fruit of the Spirit will develop in us, and we will find that Yahweh will give us the oil we need for each situation. James continues to say,

But if any of you lacks wisdom, let him ask of God, who gives to all liberally and without reproach; and it will be given to him. But let him ask in faith, without any doubting, for he who doubts is like a wave of the sea, driven by the wind and tossed. James 1:5,6

Some may misunderstand this verse to mean that we can simply ask for wisdom and Yahweh will pour it out on us without any responsibility or effort on our part. The truth is that you do not acquire true wisdom in a life of ease. A casual attitude towards Yahweh is the mistake of the foolish. Wisdom comes to us by applying Yahweh's Word daily in each time of trial, no matter how small. We see this in the life of a child. A child that never has to endure difficult situations or disobeys the rules of the household does not learn how to truly live life or become mature. They are called spoiled. Our loving heavenly Father does not want His children to be immature or spoiled.

Therefore let us, as many as are mature, have this mind; and if in anything you think otherwise, God will reveal even this to you. Phil.3:15

For whom the Lord loves, he chastens, and scourges every son whom he receives."

It is for discipline that you endure. God deals with you as with children, for what son is there whom his father doesn't discipline? But if you are without discipline, of which all have been made partakers, then are you illegitimate, and not children. Furthermore, we had the fathers of our flesh to chasten us, and we paid them respect. Shall we not much rather be in subjection to the Father of spirits, and live? For they indeed, for a few days, punished us as seemed good to them; but he for our profit, that we may be partakers of his holiness. All chastening seems for the present to be not joyous but grievous; yet afterward it yields the peaceful fruit of righteousness to those who have been exercised thereby. Heb. 12:6-11

As many as I love, I reprove and chasten. Be zealous therefore, and repent. Behold, I stand at the door and knock. If anyone hears my voice and opens the door, then I will come in to him, and will dine with him, and he with me. He who overcomes, I will give to him to sit down with me on my throne, as I also overcame, and sat down with my Father on his throne. Rev.3:19-21

When we humbly submit to our heavenly Father's discipline, He also strengthens us to become wise in our actions and responses. The oil of wisdom gives us the tools we need to walk out difficult times in a way that shines of Yahweh's presence in our lives. These daily encounters with trial are where we acquire the oil. Often though, when we are faced with a trial, we want to react out of our fleshly and emotional nature. Consequently we miss gaining wisdom and find pride raising up. Remember, fear is the key to wisdom and it is so important to wait, allowing Yahweh to lead us in His way. His ways are higher and contrary to our nature.

In this you rejoice, though now for a little while, if necessary, you have been grieved by various trials, so that the tested genuineness of your faith—more precious than gold that perishes though it is tested by fire—may be found to result in praise and glory and honor at the revelation of Jesus Christ. Though you have not seen him, you love him. Though you do not now see him, you believe in him and rejoice with joy that is inexpressible and filled with glory, obtaining the outcome of your faith, the salvation of your souls.1Pet. 1:6-9

Our prideful flesh naturally wants to take control of things and often seeks to draw attention to hardships as though we are victims and entitled to our rights. When the truth is, each difficult time we experience is meant to take us to our knees in prayer, repentance, and forgiveness. There in the healing presence of Yahweh, we are cleansed from all unrighteousness, bitterness and hurt. As we humble ourselves before our King, He then restores us, purifies our hearts, and the oil is made pure.

*Blessed are the pure in heart,
for they shall see God. Matt.5:8*

"Blessed are you when people reproach you, persecute you, and say all kinds of evil against you falsely, for my sake. Rejoice, and be exceedingly glad, for great is your reward in heaven. For that is how they persecuted the prophets who were before you.Matt.5:11,12

The pure oil of wisdom is needed for us to have the light of our Messiah for our lamp and for us to be holy as He is holy. This oil was seen in the pure olive oil that was also used in Yahweh's dwelling for sacrifices, and more importantly to anoint those chosen to serve Him.

"You shall take the anointing oil, and anoint the tabernacle, and all that is in it, and shall make it holy, and all its furniture: and it will be holy. Ex.40:9

"You shall bring Aaron and his sons to the door of the Tent of Meeting, and shall wash them with water. You shall put on Aaron the holy garments; and you shall anoint him, and sanctify him, that he may minister to me in the priest's office.

You shall bring his sons, and put coats on them. You shall anoint them, as you anointed their father, that they may minister to me in the priest's office. Ex. 40:12-15

Anointing was also applied to kings and others who were chosen to serve Yahweh, but above all, it is true for our King, Yahshua. The Hebrew word for anointed is Strong's #4886 mashach, which is the root word for Messiah, or Mashiach in Hebrew. When we call Yahshua the Messiah, we are calling Him "The Anointed One." He is anointed as Yahweh's only Son, and the only One worthy to die and make restitution for the Covenant. As we become His bride we will also become partakers of His anointing.

You have an anointing from the Holy One, and you all have knowledge. 1John 2:20

You prepare a table before me in the presence of my enemies. You anoint my head with oil. My cup runs over. Ps. 23:5

The Hebrew word used for oil is Strong's #H8081 שמן, shemen meaning; oil or grease, as from the olive; richness, to wax fat; anointing. Shemen comes from the Hebrew word shawman, which has the same spelling and means; to shine. Shemen is also connected to the Hebrew word for eight, which is Strong's #H8083, shemonah. Remember, eight is the number for new beginning. Here again we find that all the words for oil knit beautifully together with the ways of the Moon, and Yahweh's picture of the pearl of great price. Each month the Moon travels through eight phases, beginning in darkness and then waxing fat until it shines rich and full, like its source of light, the Sun. All of these words relate back to their Hebrew root word, shem for name, which as we saw earlier, stands for character. As with most brides we are to come under our Beloved's Name or character which is Yahshua; Yah's Salvation. Below is a list of the Hebrew words, including ones that we have looked at throughout this book, that show how Yahweh's masterful design reveals Yahshua's bride within Yahweh's Love Story!

H8034 - Shem; honor, authority, character

H8085 - Shema; to hear attentively; perceive, obey

H8120 - Shemash; to serve

H8121 - Shemesh; to be brilliant; the sun

H8081 - Shemen; oil, as from an olive

H8080 - Shawman; to shine

H8104 - Shamar; to guard, to protect; to be circumspect; to watch, to wait

When we put these words together we have, 'Those who hear and obey their authority, serving Yahweh with honor, and guarding His Kingdom, are those who shine as brilliant as the Sun, watching and waiting for Yahshua's return.' Amazing! People should be drawn to our light, not because of who we are … but because of Who He is, as Isaiah proclaims:

"Arise, shine; for your light is come, and the
glory of Yahweh is risen on you.
For, behold, darkness shall cover the earth, and
gross darkness the peoples; but Yahweh will arise
on you, and his glory shall be seen on you.
Nations shall come to your light, and kings to
the brightness of your rising. Is.60:1-3

In the parable of the ten virgins, five of the virgins missed this understanding. Yahshua warns us that the five foolish had let the world and their flesh become the master of their responses. They enjoyed having the lamp (Yahweh's Word) in their lives, but could not accept the cost of humbly seeking wisdom and enduring the discipline of the Father. Like the grasshopper, they choose to be at ease rather than enduring the cost of acquiring the pure oil needed to keep the precious light of the Menorah alive. Like the ten spies who saw themselves as grasshoppers, they feared man more than Yahweh. In the end, they saw no need for an extra vessel of oil, and disregarded what the Menorah's light truly stands for, as it says in Job.

A lamp is despised in the thought of one who is at ease;
It is made ready for those whose feet slip. Job 12:5(NKJ)

Keeping the Menorah lit requires a heart that is willing to learn the ways of Yahweh. We must allow Yahweh to reveal His heart to us through trials and tribulations. Then as we dwell in secret place, He will give us the pure oil of wisdom.

> *But you have desired the truth and you have shown*
> *me the hidden things of your wisdom. Ps.51:6 (ABPE)*

> *Listen to counsel and receive instruction,*
> *that you may be wise in your latter end. Prov.19:20*

The above verse from Proverbs, could also read; 'Shema (hear and obey) advice and take hold of discipline and warning so that you will be wise during your last days.' When we see the lamp or Menorah as an instrument that displays the Word or Commandment of Yahweh, and not simply a source of light, we can then understand the heart wrenching response the five foolish virgins received from the bridegroom. Their lack of pure oil was a sign to him that they disregarded the things of his heart and so they were not welcome to come into his chamber.

> *While they went away to buy, the bridegroom came, and those*
> *who were ready went in with him to the marriage feast, and the*
> *door was shut. Afterward the other virgins also came, saying,*
> *'Lord, Lord, open to us.' But he answered, 'Most certainly I tell*
> *you, I don't know you.' Matt.25:10-12*

> *When once the master of the house has risen up, and has shut*
> *the door, and you begin to stand outside, and to knock at the*
> *door, saying, 'Lord, Lord, open to us!' then he will answer and*
> *tell you, 'I don't know you or where you come from.' Luke 13:25*

How could this happen? Again, I believe that the five foolish virgins were lulled into one of two deceptions. The first deception is in following false teachers that claim there is no need to keep the Commandments of Yahweh by His Spirit's leading and that it if you do you are in bondage. The second deception comes in trying to keep Yahweh's Commandments according to man's ways and not His. With false assurance, the five foolish virgins claim to follow Yahshua without truly having an intimate relationship with Him. Then suddenly, at the end, they are found with no oil and grieving outside the chamber of their Beloved.

> *Oh that they were wise, that they understood this,*
> *that they would consider their latter end! Deut.32:29*

Yahweh is sovereign, and His Word is the foundation that sets us free to know His ways and to love Yahweh according to His heart.

> *This is how we know that we know Him, if we keep His commandments. One who says, "I know Him," and does not keep His commandments, is a liar, and the truth is not in him. 1 John 2:3,4*

Sadly, I believe it is the five foolish virgin's disregard for the truth and their attitude toward His discipline that causes them grief and regret at the end. The same is true with the rich man in the story of Lazarus. He thought that his own judgment and ease was important. Imagine the shock the virgins had in missing something so crucial! As impossible as it may seem, I believe the underlying reason for their mistake may be very subtle, and that none of us are exempt from making the same mistake!

Often we associate foolishness with someone who is silly and lacks knowledge, yet this is not the case with the five foolish virgins, for they were not *ignorant*. Foolishness is quite different from ignorance. No one considers him or herself a fool, unless they have come to true repentance. The Modern Dictionary describes a fool as; lacking forethought or caution. Noah Webster's Dictionary 1828, on the other hand defines a fool as; one who does not exercise reason; one who follows his own inclinations, who prefers trifling and temporary pleasures to the service of God and eternal happiness. Not so surprisingly, both of these descriptions of a fool display the character qualities of the grasshopper. I am convinced that the five foolish virgins did not see their foolishness at all. In fact, I submit to you that the five foolish thought with all their heart that they were indeed pure in heart and wise. They may have even thought that they were wiser than the other five virgins. The scene that Yahshua paints for us describes both sets of five so alike, that I believe the five foolish virgins *were* filled with wisdom. Their mistake lies in *who* they acquired their wisdom from.

Their wisdom was not Yahweh's wisdom… it was man's wisdom…, which in the end is not wisdom at all, but foolishness! Why else would they be shocked and ashamed when they didn't have enough of what the other five had? James describes the wisdom, that I believe the five foolish virgins found gratifying like this.

> But if you have bitter jealousy and selfish ambition in your heart, don't boast and don't lie against the truth. This wisdom is not that which comes down from above, but is earthly, sensual, and demonic. For where jealousy and selfish ambition are, there is confusion and every evil deed. James 3:14-16

These are harsh words; 'confusion and every evil deed?!' You may have experienced this kind of wisdom in your life, for it has torn apart Yahweh's people for years. What man thinks is right or lawful is often contrary to Yahweh's Word. Man's wisdom is typically rooted in pride and finding favor with man.

> For it is written, "I will destroy the wisdom of the wise, I will bring the discernment of the discerning to nothing."

> Where is the wise? Where is the scribe? Where is the lawyer of this world? Hasn't God made foolish the wisdom of this world? For seeing that in the wisdom of God, the world through its wisdom didn't know God, it was God's good pleasure through the foolishness of the preaching to save those who believe. 1Cor.1:19-21

> Let no one deceive himself. If anyone among you seems to be wise in this age, let him become a fool that he may become wise. For the wisdom of this world is foolishness with God. For it is written, "He catches the wise in their own craftiness"; and again, "The Lord knows the thoughts of the wise, that they are futile." 1Cor. 3:18-20

Paul is trying to warn us of something very serious. The avalanche of knowledge and self-preservation that comes to us each day is intriguing;

even exhilarating at times. Often worldly knowledge makes us feel important, capable and confident. Regardless, Scripture clearly warns us that there is only one way to know Yahweh, and avoid the wisdom of the world. As we have discovered, the way is death to ourselves and seeking humility.

When pride comes, then comes shame, but
with humility comes wisdom. Prov.11:2

Seek Yahweh, all you humble of the land, who have kept his
ordinances. Seek righteousness. Seek humility. It may be that
you will be hidden in the day of Yahweh's anger. Zeph.2:3

Note that the five foolish do not question the need to buy oil and quickly run to purchase some. Again, this was foolishness, for the appointed time had already passed! The five foolish had simply neglected to pay for it in advance and now it was too late.

Why is there in the hand of a fool the
purchase price of wisdom,
Since he has no heart for it? Prov.17:16 (NKJ)

The five foolish virgins had spent their days disregarding the price of the oil, which also reveals that they did not have a healthy fear of Yahweh. They chose to take man's way of ease and acceptance, not considering the cost of taking up their cross daily to follow Yahshua and the principles of life laid out in His Word.

The way of a fool is right in his own eyes, but he who is wise
listens to counsel. Prov.12:15

There is a way which seems right to a man, but in the end it
leads to death. Prov.14:12

For which of you, desiring to build a tower, doesn't first sit
down and count the cost, to see if he has enough to complete
it? Or perhaps, when he has laid a foundation, and is not
able to finish, everyone who sees begins to mock him, saying,
'This man began to build, and wasn't able to finish.' Or what

king, as he goes to encounter another king in war, will not sit down first and consider whether he is able with ten thousand to meet him who comes against him with twenty thousand? Or else, while the other is yet a great way off, he sends an envoy, and asks for conditions of peace. So therefore whoever of you who doesn't renounce all that he has, he can't be my disciple. Luke 14:28-33

The cost of following Yahshua is something that the flesh cannot pay, and that is why He sent us help. Some may ask, 'Why then did Yahshua tell us that His yoke is easy?' The key is that He did not mean it was the way of ease. On the contrary, Yahshua is telling us that as long as we remove ourselves out of the equation, and submit fully to Yahweh, then we will be able to overcome. His yoke is easy, when we abide with Him and submit to the guidance of the His Counselor and Teacher; the Holy Spirit.

But the Counselor, the Holy Spirit, whom the Father will send in my name, he will teach you all things, and will remind you of all that I said to you. John 14:26

Now the natural man doesn't receive the things of God's Spirit, for they are foolishness to him, and he can't know them, because they are spiritually discerned. 1Cor.2:14

Many mainstream religions believe in the saving grace of the Messiah and love Him for all that He did for us on the cross, but they are not willing to receive the entirety of His Word into their hearts and walk the narrow path. They try to follow Yahshua guided by the wisdom of man, and driven by the ways of the world. When this happens we experience confusion and frustration, which is often followed by a lukewarm attitude. The parable of the seed reveals this. Though all the seeds were alike, only a few make it. As Yahshua's bride, our goal is to accept the seed of Yahweh's Word into soft soil (our humble hearts) and receive new life. Yahshua's bride will also seek to find the narrow way of the path of righteousness. As we saw in the linen garment, you cannot have two conflicting frequencies or messages together in one because they cancel each other out. Yahshua's desire for us is to be either hot or cold. He is admonishing us to be clear in where we stand and to not mix His ways with man's ways.

I know your works, that you are neither cold nor hot. I wish you were cold or hot. So, because you are lukewarm, and neither hot nor cold, I will vomit you out of my mouth. Rev.3:15,16

But let your 'Yes' be 'Yes' and your 'No' be 'No.' Whatever is more than these is of the evil one. Matt.5:37

We battle this war every day. Principalities, worldviews, and the wisdom of man bombards us on all sides. Still, we must be single-minded in our heart towards our Beloved and how we follow Him. Though Elijah stood alone and was being persecuted, he still believed in Yahweh's power and challenged four hundred and fifty prophets of Baal ... alone! He held His ground and challenged them to a duel, to prove that His God was the One true God and all powerful! When the prophets of Baal failed to prove their god was real, Elijah then gathers twelve stones for an altar as a picture of restored righteousness. When he set things in order, Yahweh came in all His power and might!

Elijah came near to all the people, and said, "How long will you waver between the two sides? If Yahweh is God, follow him; but if Baal, then follow him." The people answered him not a word. 1Kings 18:21

I hate double-minded men, but I love your law. Ps.119:113

We all grow weary of fighting the good fight, especially when we are alone. Nevertheless, these times of weakness are the times when Yahweh shines greater in our lives. It is in these times that we must hold on to Him more than ever and not give up; for in our weakness, His strength is revealed. When we, like Elijah, set things in Yahweh's righteous order in our lives we too will see Yahweh move in power!

Let us not be weary in doing good, for we will reap in due season, if we don't give up. Gal.6:9

We are pressed on every side, yet not crushed; perplexed, yet not to despair; pursued, yet not forsaken; struck down, yet not destroyed; always carrying in the body the putting to death of the Lord Jesus, that the life of Jesus may also be revealed in our body. For we who live are always delivered to death for Jesus' sake, that the life also of Jesus may be revealed in our mortal flesh. 2 Cor. 4:8-11

Be sober and self-controlled. Be watchful. Your adversary, the devil, walks around like a roaring lion, seeking whom he may devour. Withstand him steadfast in your faith, knowing that your brothers who are in the world are undergoing the same sufferings. 1 Pet. 5:8,9

Therefore, my beloved brothers, be steadfast, immovable, always abounding in the Lord's work, because you know that your labor is not in vain in the Lord. 1 Cor. 15:58

The ways of Yahweh's Kingdom and His patterns are the foundation that we can build our faith upon. Yahshua came as the Way, the Truth and the Life to establish them and make a way for us to return to them. He is our Rock and our firm foundation. Remember how Psalm 27, like Psalm 91 exhorts us to seek refuge in Yahweh's dwelling place. There we will be hidden and restored on the Rock of our salvation, especially in the times when we are weary of the world.

God is our refuge and strength,
a very present help in trouble. Ps. 46:1

During these times of refuge, our intimacy with our Beloved is nurtured. One day the old saying that goes, "It's not *what* you know, but *who* you know," will have a sobering reality. In the end, it will be those who disregard Yahshua, His Torah and the leading of His Spirit that will be told to depart because they do not know Him. Those who know Yahshua will enter into His chamber with joy.

This is eternal life, that they should know you, the only true God, and him whom you sent, Jesus Christ. I glorified you on the earth. I have accomplished the work which you have given me to do. Now, Father, glorify me with your own self with the glory which I had with you before the world existed. John 17:3-5

A fool fears man and what man thinks more than what Yahweh thinks. They are content with the wisdom and favor of men; especially men of worldly renown.

"Everyone therefore who hears these words of mine, and does them, I will liken him to a wise man, who built his house on a rock. The rain came down, the floods came, and the winds blew, and beat on that house; and it didn't fall, for it was founded on the rock. Everyone who hears these words of mine, and doesn't do them will be like a foolish man, who built his house on the sand. The rain came down, the floods came, and the winds blew, and beat on that house; and it fell—and great was its fall." Matt. 7:24-27

As enticing and self-gratifying the wisdom of the world may be, it is most often lead by pride and gain. Scripture warns us not to be deceived by shepherds or leaders who desire prideful gain. These ones seek to be accepted on a worldly scale and put themselves and those they influence in a dangerous place, especially as the world spirals deeper into deception and darkness. There needs to be evidence in leader's lives of humility, the fruit of the Spirit and a life that upholds Yahweh's Word.

When pride comes, then comes shame, but with humility comes wisdom. Prov.11:2

I don't receive glory from men. But I know you, that you don't have God's love in yourselves. I have come in my Father's name, and you don't receive me. If another comes in his own name, you will receive him. How can you believe, who receive glory from one another, and you don't seek the glory that comes from the only God? "Don't think that I will accuse you to the Father. There is one who accuses you, even Moses, on whom you have set your hope. For if you believed Moses, you would believe me; for he wrote about me. But if you don't believe his writings, how will you believe my words?" John 5:41-47

Be careful that you don't let anyone rob you through his philosophy and vain deceit, after the tradition of men, after the elements of the world, and not after Christ. Col.2:8

These are murmurers and complainers, walking after their lusts (and their mouth speaks proud things), showing respect of persons to gain advantage. Jude 1:16

Remember, the fear of Yahweh keeps us on the path that leads to wisdom. He is the Almighty King of the Universe, and there is no other! If we lack fear of Him, we will find ourselves concerned with what people think of us more than what He thinks of us. If we fear man's thoughts or judgment over Yahweh's, we immediately compromise our ability to have true wisdom. Those who are foolish have little or no fear of Yahweh. They have taken a complacent attitude toward how holy and righteous He truly is. Many even see Him as a loving God to the point of being tolerant of the world's ways, but this is not true. We are saved by grace with a purpose and brought into Yahweh's family *for* good works; the work of His kingdom. Every picture we have seen in Yahweh's Word, His Creation and His patterns confirms this. Just as the Moon witnesses to us each day; reflecting and keeping the light of Yahshua alive, comes from a life surrendered to following Him and reflecting His Light, which is Yahweh's entire Word. His Commandments reflect His heart, and when we guard them, and do them, we show the world that we love Him and the ways of His household.

So then, my beloved, even as you have always obeyed, not only in my presence, but now much more in my absence, work out your own salvation with fear and trembling. For it is God who works in you both to will and to work, for his good pleasure. Phil.2:12,13

There are many teachers in these last days; more than ever before, and each one has something different to offer us. Many teachings are good, sound and true; bringing Yahweh's wisdom to the hearer. Some though, are misleading, dangerous and twist the truth.

> But know this, that in the last days, grievous times will come. For men will be lovers of self, lovers of money, boastful, arrogant, blasphemers, disobedient to parents, unthankful, unholy, without natural affection, unforgiving, slanderers, without self-control, fierce, no lovers of good, traitors, headstrong, conceited, lovers of pleasure rather than lovers of God; holding a form of godliness, but having denied its power. Turn away from these, also. For some of these are people who creep into houses, and take captive gullible women loaded down with sins, led away by various lusts, always learning, and never able to come to the knowledge of the truth. 2Tim.3:1-7

> But evil men and impostors will grow worse and worse, deceiving and being deceived. 2Tim. 3:13

May we never forget that the world, the knowledge of man and our own selfish ways have serious consequences. Yahweh's Word warns us over and over of the dangers of loving the world and of following after men.

> ...therefore, behold, I will proceed to do a marvelous work among this people, even a marvelous work and a wonder; and the wisdom of their wise men will perish, and the understanding of their prudent men will be hidden. Is.29:14

If we do not have a sound foundation, built on the principles and patterns that Yahweh has displayed for us, we may find ourselves falsely led by man, our own efforts or false signs and wonders. False prophets will increase in the last days and can be very deceptive, especially if they bring signs and wonders to their presentation, but we must endure by faith, no matter what.

> "If a prophet or a dreamer of dreams arises among you and gives you a sign or a wonder, and the sign or wonder that he tells you comes to pass, and if he says, 'Let us go after other gods,' which

you have not known, 'and let us serve them,' you shall not listen to the words of that prophet or that dreamer of dreams. For the LORD your God is testing you, to know whether you love the LORD your God with all your heart and with all your soul. You shall walk after the LORD your God and fear him and keep his commandments and obey his voice, and you shall serve him and hold fast to him. Deut.13:1-4(ESV)

If a false teacher has ever led you astray, you know how disheartening the journey can be and that it often causes people to give up on God altogether. The enemy loves it when this happens. Scripture so adamantly tells us that wisdom is more valuable than all the riches of this world, because it builds our faith and deepens our understanding of Yahweh and His Word. Wisdom gives us the tools to discern between the lies and the truth. In Proverbs 7 we are admonished as, "sons of Yahweh," to keep Yahweh's commandments by wisdom to avoid being snared and deceived by a harlot. Let's carefully read through this warning.

My son, keep my words,
And treasure my commands within you.
Keep my commands and live,
And my law as the apple of your eye.
Bind them on your fingers;
Write them on the tablet of your heart.
Say to wisdom, "You are my sister,"
And call understanding your nearest kin,
That they may keep you from the immoral woman,
From the seductress who flatters with her words.
For at the window of my house
I looked through my lattice,
And saw among the simple,
I perceived among the youths,
A young man devoid of understanding,
Passing along the street near her corner;
And he took the path to her house
In the twilight, in the evening,
In the black and dark night.

And there a woman met him,
With the attire of a harlot, and a crafty heart.
She was loud and rebellious,
Her feet would not stay at home.
At times she was outside, at times in the open square,
Lurking at every corner.
So she caught him and kissed him;
With an impudent face she said to him:
"I have peace offerings with me;
Today I have paid my vows.
So I came out to meet you,
Diligently to seek your face,
And I have found you.
I have spread my bed with tapestry,
Colored coverings of Egyptian linen.
I have perfumed my bed
With myrrh, aloes, and cinnamon.
Come, let us take our fill of love until morning;
Let us delight ourselves with love.
For my husband is not at home;
He has gone on a long journey;
He has taken a bag of money with him,
And will come home on the appointed day." Prov.7:1-20(NKJ)

The first thing to notice in this Proverb, is that it reads like the loving words of a father sending his son out into the world. While in the world though, the son is admonished to stay on the right path, which can only be the path of righteousness. The father tells his son that *there is* a way to safeguard himself from the harlot that wants to lure him away from the path. He carefully reminds him that he must not leave the path to his destination or he will fall into danger. The son is admonished to take wisdom and understanding with him as close relatives that will keep him from being enticed by the flattery and lusts of the harlot.

The next part of this Proverb, sets the scene of the harlot waiting with her bed of tapestry and sweet perfume to lure and snare unsuspecting sons into her grip. Proverbs 7 is a specific warning to all who are called the sons/daughters of Yahweh to not be slack, or at ease in our walk with Yahweh or we risk being seduced by the harlot. Notice that the son disregards the warnings at the beginning of the Proverb, and then in the evening (when you can't see clearly) he wanders toward her house.

Listen, my son, and be wise, and keep your heart on the right path! Prov.23:19

The harlot sees the son coming and boldly, 'like a spider,' she catches the son and kisses him. She tells the son how she has waited and prepared for him. A similar situation happened to Joseph while serving in Potiphar's house. Potiphar's wife, acting like a harlot, tried to appeal to Joseph's pride and waited for an opportunity to grab him. She wanted him to seduce her, but Joseph responded with wisdom and fled away. The enemy always takes the position of a harlot, trying to lure Yahweh's sons and daughters away from their commitment to Him with the lusts and pleasures of this world. We must submit to wisdom and understanding as our closest kin, holding fast to the path of righteousness. The enemy is cunning and uses crafty, seductive words to give us a false sense of security and distract us from the truth. His ploy is to persuade us to be like the grasshopper and choose a life that is at ease and is not concerned with the return of the Messiah.

This is now, beloved, the second letter that I have written to you; and in both of them I stir up your sincere mind by reminding you; that you should remember the words which were spoken before by the holy prophets, and the commandments of us, the apostles of the Lord and Savior: knowing this first, that in the last days mockers will come, walking after their own lusts, and saying, "Where is the promise of his coming? For, from the day that the fathers fell asleep, all things continue as they were from the beginning of the creation." 2Pet.3:1-4

Then the lawless one will be revealed, whom the Lord will kill with the breath of his mouth, and destroy by the manifestation of his coming ;even he whose coming is according to the working of Satan with all power and signs and lying wonders, and with all deception of wickedness for those who are being lost, because they didn't receive the love of the truth, that they might be saved. Because of this, God sends them a working of error, that they should believe a lie; that they all might be judged who didn't believe the truth, but had pleasure in unrighteousness.2 Thess.2:8-12

Be sober and self-controlled. Be watchful. Your adversary, the devil, walks around like a roaring lion, seeking whom he may devour. Withstand him steadfast in your faith, knowing that your brothers who are in the world are undergoing the same sufferings.

But may the God of all grace, who called you to his eternal glory by Christ Jesus, after you have suffered a little while, perfect, establish, strengthen, and settle you.1 Pet. 5:8-10

Let's now compare these elements with the account of Adam and Eve. They had the privilege of dwelling in direct fellowship with Yahweh in paradise. One might say that they dwelt in the secret place of the Most High. Yahweh directly attended to their every need, and they spoke with Him face-to-face daily. There was nothing in all the world for them to want. So what went wrong? What caused them to let their guard down? What changed?

At first, Adam and Eve are content and they trust Yahweh, like a child trusts their parent, obeying Yahweh's instructions. Then comes the lie. The seductive words of the serpent play on their curiosity, emotions, and pride and undermine their trust in Yahweh. Their fatal response was to doubt Yahweh. Satan loves to snare us with this. His main purpose is to cause us to doubt Yahweh's Word and submit our own rational. If satan can't convince us that there is no God, then he will try to deceive us into thinking there is better or more enlightened truth, just as he did with Eve in the Garden. Satan convinced Eve that Yahweh was trying to keep something from her and that the fruit from the Tree of the Knowledge of Good and Evil would enlighten her and make her wise.

The woman said to the serpent, "Of the fruit of the trees of the garden we may eat, but of the fruit of the tree which is in the middle of the garden, God has said, 'You shall not eat of it, neither shall you touch it, lest you die.'" The serpent said to the woman, "You won't surely die, for God knows that in the day you eat it, your eyes will be opened, and you will be like God, knowing good and evil." When the woman saw that the tree was good for food, and that it was a delight to the eyes, and that the tree was to be desired to make one wise, she took of its fruit, and ate; and she gave some to her husband with her, and he ate.Gen.3:2-6

But know this, that in the last days, grievous times will come. For men will be lovers of self, lovers of money, boastful, arrogant, blasphemers, disobedient to parents, unthankful, unholy, without natural affection, unforgiving, slanderers, without self-control, fierce, no lovers of good, traitors, headstrong, conceited, lovers of pleasure rather than lovers of God; holding a form of godliness, but having denied its power. Turn away from these, also. For some of these are people who creep into houses, and take captive gullible women loaded down with sins, led away by various lusts, always learning, and never able to come to the knowledge of the truth. 2Tim. 3:1-7

We must heed the warnings and not run the risk of growing satisfied with the wisdom of this world or lulled into the standards of the culture we live in. There are many seducing words that sound close to the truth, but even 1% of a lie mixed into the truth is deception. We dare not succumb to the comforts of what seems right in our own eyes, or desire any fruit other than that of the Tree of Life; for the Tree of Life gives us the peaceable fruit of wisdom that will touch the lives of all those around us.

The fruit of the righteous is a tree of life. He who is wise wins souls. Prov.11:30

For, uttering great swelling words of emptiness, they entice in the lusts of the flesh, by licentiousness, those who are indeed escaping from those who live in error; promising them liberty, while they themselves are bondservants of corruption; for a man is brought into bondage by whoever overcomes him. For if, after they have escaped the defilement of the world through the knowledge of the Lord and Savior Jesus Christ, they are again entangled in it and overcome, the last state has become worse for them than the first. For it would be better for them not to have known the way of righteousness, than, after knowing it, to turn back from the holy commandment delivered to them. 2Pet.2: 18-21

Returning to Proverbs 7, we find at the end that the harlot is boasting that the husband or goodman, (as it is translated in the King James) is away on a long journey, and won't return until the appointed day, or as some translators write, 'the full moon.' This is fascinating because it is the same word used for 'full moon' in Psalm 81:3, which is Strong's #H3677 כסה keseh!

For my husband is not at home;
He has gone on a long journey;
He has taken a bag of money with him,
And will come home on the appointed day(keseh)."Prov. 7

Blow the trumpet at the New Moon,
at the full moon(keseh),on our feast day. Ps.81:3

If the translators had chosen to use 'appointed day,' as it is translated in Proverbs 7, instead of 'full moon' in Psalm 81, it could then have been written as, "Blow the trumpet at the New Moon at the appointed day, on our feast day." Could it be, that Proverbs 7 is a warning to us about Yom Teruah and the return of our Beloved Bridegroom? This knits perfectly together with the parable of the ten virgins. Proverbs 7 is exhorting us to seek the oil of wisdom and to not be lead astray by seducing words or worldly pleasures. In fact, Proverbs 7 appears to be a direct warning to the five foolish virgins!

Now let's look back to the latter verses of Psalm 81, where our search for the New Moon began, and hear the disappointment Yahweh has for His people who do not listen to His voice.

"Hear, my people, and I will testify to you,
Israel, if you would listen to me!

There shall be no strange god in you,
neither shall you worship any foreign god.
I am Yahweh, your God,
who brought you up out of the land of Egypt.
Open your mouth wide, and I will fill it.
But my people didn't listen to my voice.
Israel desired none of me.
So I let them go after the stubbornness of their hearts,
that they might walk in their own counsels.
Oh that my people would listen to me,
that Israel would walk in my ways!
I would soon subdue their enemies,
and turn my hand against their adversaries.
The haters of Yahweh would cringe before him,
and their punishment would last forever.
But he would have also fed them with the finest of the wheat.
I will satisfy you with honey out of the rock." Ps.81:8-16

These words should deeply move our hearts! Yahweh is speaking here of all the good He wanted to do for His people had they listened to His leading and His warnings which were expressed in Proverbs 7. Instead His people (or may I say five of the virgins) walk in their own counsels and are seduced into the world's ways. The New American Standard Version translates Psalm 81:15 as;

"Those who hate the LORD would pretend obedience to Him,
And their time of punishment would be forever.

We find in this translation that there is a subtle deception in the ways of those who actually hate Yahweh. They *pretend* obedience, but do not truly love Him. In the end, these ones bear the consequences of their stubborn, prideful hearts forever. How devastating! ... when instead Yahweh desired to satisfy them with honey out of the rock! How can we ever think we can pretend or be deceitful toward the King of the Universe? Paul admonished those who were followers of Yahshua in Corinth, about listening to other teachers who were puffed up in their approach to life and to Yahweh's Word; giving a distinction between the two kinds of wisdom.

My speech and my preaching were not in persuasive words of human wisdom, but in demonstration of the Spirit and of power, that your faith wouldn't stand in the wisdom of men, but in the power of God. We speak wisdom, however, among those who are full grown; yet a wisdom not of this world, nor of the rulers of this world, who are coming to nothing. But we speak God's wisdom in a mystery, the wisdom that has been hidden, which God foreordained before the worlds for our glory, which none of the rulers of this world has known. 1 Cor. 2:4-8

For who among men knows the things of a man, except the spirit of the man, which is in him? Even so, no one knows the things of God, except God's Spirit. But we received, not the spirit of the world, but the Spirit which is from God, that we might know the things that were freely given to us by God. Which things also we speak, not in words which man's wisdom teaches, but which the Holy Spirit teaches, comparing spiritual things with spiritual things. Now the natural man doesn't receive the things of God's Spirit, for they are foolishness to him, and he can't know them, because they are spiritually discerned. But he who is spiritual discerns all things, and he himself is judged by no one. 1 Cor. 2:11-15

The oil of wisdom found in Yahweh's Word and taught by Yahweh's Spirit is the single most powerful resource we have in this world, especially in these last days. Yahshua's chayil or woman of virtue, will walk out Yahweh's Word as seen in Proverbs 31, fully trusting Him and enduring the trials set before her to produce the oil of wisdom she needs to keep her lamp lit.

Buy the truth, and don't sell it.
Get wisdom, discipline, and understanding. Prov. 23:23

But whoever listens to me(wisdom) will dwell safely,
And will be secure, without fear of
evil."Prov. 1:33 (brackets mine)

These precious few, are the ones who will become Yahshua's pearl of great price as seen in the faithful witness of the Moon. For now, they are scattered among the nations, which can be likened to the seas; hidden until

Yahweh comes to gather them to Himself. Yahshua paints this picture for us in His parable of a dragnet.

> *"Again, the kingdom of heaven is like a dragnet that was cast into the sea and gathered some of every kind, which, when it was full, they drew to shore; and they sat down and gathered the good into vessels, but threw the bad away. Matt.13:47,48 (NKJ)*

Remember, like the altar stones, men also seek after pearls beneath the water. Many are chosen and gathered, but only a few treasured ones are found. Just as only a few seeds found good ground to grow and flourish in, only a few find the narrow way. The narrow way is navigated with the wisdom of Yahweh and established in fear. The few who find it will have paid the price for the oil of wisdom by walking out Yahweh's Word through the trials of life. They will lay down their selfish desires and the ways of the world to be led by Yahweh's Spirit alone. Their hearts will be filled with love for Him, which is expressed through their care for His Commandments, and their love for others.

> *You, through Your commandments, make*
> *me wiser than my enemies;*
> *For they are ever with me. Ps.119:98*

> *The wise shall inherit glory,*
> *But shame shall be the legacy of fools. Prov.3:35*

How fitting that the description of Yahshua's bride would be found in the final verses of Proverbs the Book of Wisdom. The bride of the Messiah sees wisdom as a valuable treasure and seeks for it diligently because she knows it is the only way to be equipped for His kingdom; to rightly divide His Word and fulfill the duties of her Beloved. With our vessels filled with oil, may we then be counted worthy to be clothed in the priestly wedding garments of white linen and be His pearl of great price.

> *There is desirable treasure,*
> *And oil in the dwelling of the wise,*
> *But a foolish man squanders it. Prov.21:20(NKJ)*

We have looked at many patterns and pictures found in Yahweh's Creation. There within them all, we have seen the beauty and wonder of Yahweh's awesome Love Story and Song. Yahweh's character is displayed throughout each piece of His magnificent Masterpiece; His love is unmatched and His mercy endures throughout all generations. Now, as the final verses to Yahweh's Song rise above the chaos of this world and the climax of His Love Story unfolds, His invitation to come and be in harmony with His symphonic Masterpiece rings out to all who have the ears to hear. Again... this is no ordinary invitation! It is the invitation of all time, to be one with Yahshua as His bride at the wedding supper of the Lamb. Each of us needs to determine our own response. In Yahshua's parable of the wedding feast, many who received an invitation were too busy to change their plans for the king.

When one of those who sat at the table with him heard these things, he said to him, "Blessed is he who will feast in God's Kingdom!"

But he said to him, "A certain man made a great supper, and he invited many people. He sent out his servant at supper time to tell those who were invited, 'Come, for everything is ready now.' They all as one began to make excuses.

"The first said to him, 'I have bought a field, and I must go and see it. Please have me excused.'

"Another said, 'I have bought five yoke of oxen, and I must go try them out. Please have me excused.'

"Another said, 'I have married a wife, and therefore I can't come.'

"That servant came, and told his lord these things. Then the master of the house, being angry, said to his servant, 'Go out quickly into the streets and lanes of the city, and bring in the poor, maimed, blind, and lame.' Luke 14:15-21

What will your response be? I know for many people today there is resistance, just as those in Yahshua's parable. They make excuses why they cannot commit to Yahweh and His invitation or they choose to delay their response to a later time, as though there is no need to be prompt with the King.

> *Jesus answered and spoke again in parables to them, saying, "The Kingdom of Heaven is like a certain king, who made a marriage feast for his son, and sent out his servants to call those who were invited to the marriage feast, but they would not come. Again he sent out other servants, saying, 'Tell those who are invited, "Behold, I have prepared my dinner. My cattle and my fatlings are killed, and all things are ready. Come to the marriage feast!"' But they made light of it, and went their ways, one to his own farm, another to his merchandise, and the rest grabbed his servants, and treated them shamefully, and killed them. Matt.22:1-6*

Nevertheless, the opening lines of Proverbs, begins with warnings to those who refuse to listen to the voice of wisdom. These are the ones who will be shocked in the end to find that Yahweh is a righteous Judge and that there is consequences to our choices and the way we live our lives.

> *Wisdom calls aloud in the street. She utters her voice in the public squares.*
>
> *She calls at the head of noisy places. At the entrance of the city gates, she utters her words:*
>
> *"How long, you simple ones, will you love simplicity? How long will mockers delight themselves in mockery, and fools hate knowledge?*
>
> *Turn at my reproof. Behold, I will pour out my spirit on you. I will make known my words to you. Because I have called, and you have refused; I have stretched out my hand, and no one*

has paid attention;but you have ignored all my counsel, and wanted none of my reproof;

I also will laugh at your disaster. I will mock when calamity overtakes you; when calamity overtakes you like a storm, when your disaster comes on like a whirlwind; when distress and anguish come on you.

Then will they call on me, but I will not answer. They will seek me diligently, but they will not find me;because they hated knowledge, and didn't choose the fear of Yahweh.

They wanted none of my counsel. They despised all my reproof.

Therefore they will eat of the fruit of their own way, and be filled with their own schemes.

For the backsliding of the simple will kill them. The careless ease of fools will destroy them.

But whoever listens to me will dwell securely, and will be at ease, without fear of harm." Prov. 1:20-32

At the end of Proverbs or 'the Book of Wisdom,' the writer asks the rousing question, 'Who can find a virtuous woman?' We have seen that this question could also read, 'Who can find a chayil; a woman of valor, strength, and integrity?' If we seek Yahweh with all our heart and join in harmony with His awesome Song and Masterpiece…if we humble ourselves and choose to reflect His light alone, which is fueled with the oil of Yahweh's wisdom, then Yahshua will find His woman of virtue or pearl of great price. She will be His royal priesthood; 'Fair as the Moon' and as awesome as an army with banners, prepared with enough oil to be counted as wise and waiting for Him at the trumpet's cry.

The Marriage Feast of Yahshua *will* come, as it has been ordained from the very beginning of time. Our responsibility is to shine His light to those who are lost in the darkness of the world, as the Moon faithfully does, month after month. As we follow Yahshua and dwell in the secret place, He will renew and strengthen us to continue on His path of righteousness. Each New Moon we will be hidden within His glorious presence to praise Him for all He has done to keep us and cover us throughout each month.

"Let your waist be dressed and your lamps burning. Be like men watching for their lord, when he returns from the marriage feast; that, when he comes and knocks, they may immediately open to him. Luke 12:35,36

May you find great joy and peace in seeking Yahweh in all His glory, so that you are prepared and waiting at the final hour of His return.

> *To God our Savior,*
> *Who alone is wise,*
> *Be glory and majesty,*
> *Dominion and power,*
> *Both now and forever.*
> *Amen.*

PRACTICE

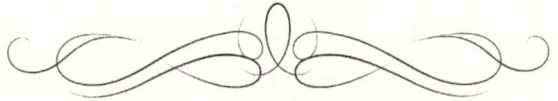

Rosh Chodesh

*It shall happen, that from one new moon to
another, and from one Sabbath to another,
shall all flesh come to worship before
me," says Yahweh. Is.66:23*

AS THE WANING CRESCENT MOON GROWS SMALLER AND SMALLER IN THE
Eastern sky, it can be seen in the early morning hours as we rise to
seek Yahweh. There in the first quiet moments of the dawn, we have an
opportunity to thank Yahweh for restoring and protecting us through the
darkness and covering of the night and then bringing our hearts concerns
before Him.

*Yahweh, in the morning you shall hear my voice. In the
morning I will lay my requests before you, and will watch
expectantly. Ps.5: 3*

Then, as we watch the Moon diminish and the old month fade away, a
new month also approaches. Soon the Moon will vanish into the awesome
light of the Sun, as it rises in the East. Halleluyah! What a breathtaking
picture of the bride drawing ever closer to her Bridegroom and His overwhelming Light! Rosh Chodesh is the rehearsal of Yahshua's soon and
eminent return! As our hearts fill with the anticipation of being in the

presence of Yahshua at last, there is no other response but to celebrate and sing for joy to our King, Savior, and only source of Light.

You who fear Yahweh, praise him!
All you descendants of Jacob, glorify him!
Stand in awe of him, all you descendants of Israel! Ps.22:23

Our great King gave up everything for us. Daily He lavishes us with His love, mercy and grace. How much of our lives shall we return to Him? Especially when the overwhelming truth is that our bodies serve as the dwelling place for His Spirit! This phenomenon can be easily be taken for granted. Yet, it is the one thing that should take our breath away each and every day, for it is the testimony of Yahweh's loving desire to be in relationship with His people.

With this in mind, consider each approaching Shabbat, New Moon or appointed feast day. We have been given the extraordinary opportunity of hosting the King of the Universe in our home individually, as well as corporately. Remember, the word chodesh used for the New Moon holds the meaning of unity. The oneness that comes through the pictures of the New Moon are so beautiful. One of the most intriguing of these pictures is seen in the Tabernacle. The Hebrew word for Tabernacle is Strong's # H4908 mishkan, which means; dwelling place, residence, habitation, etc. Just as we saw in the pictures of the Garden of Eden, Yahweh desires to dwell with His people and as with all good stories this is how Yahweh's story will end. His bride will dwell with Him forever.

> *Then I saw a new heaven and a new earth; for the first heaven and the first earth passed away, and there is no longer any sea. And I saw the holy city, new Jerusalem, coming down out of heaven from God, made ready as a bride adorned for her husband. And I heard a loud voice from the throne, saying, "Behold, the tabernacle of God is among men, and He will dwell among them, and they shall be His people, and God Himself will be among them, and He will wipe away every tear from their eyes; and there will no longer be any death; there will no longer be any mourning, or crying, or pain; the first things have passed away." Rev.21:1-4*

Dwelling in the secret place is at the very heart of the New Moon celebration, and Yahweh's desire for us all is to tabernacle together as ONE individually and corporately. The Tabernacle in the Wilderness foreshadowed this as many parts fashioned in wisdom and joined together as one central place for Yahweh's presence to dwell. Clearly, Yahshua came to Earth to bring us back to oneness with Him and His Father. Now, we are called to be the Holy Tabernacle of Yahweh; His dwelling here on Earth, until He returns.

For as the body is one, and has many members, and all the members of the body, being many, are one body; so also is Christ. For in one Spirit we were all baptized into one body, whether Jews or Greeks, whether bond or free; and were all given to drink into one Spirit.For the body is not one member, but many. 1 Cor.12:12-14

Now you are the body of Christ, and members individually. 1 Cor.12:27

For even as we have many members in one body, and all the members don't have the same function, so we, who are many, are one body in Christ, and individually members one of another. Rom. 12:4,5

As the Moon takes its place in the glorious light of the Sun at the New Moon, so too, the bride or body of the Messiah will take her place at the side of her Beloved. There under the covering of His presence, she will rejoice and worship her Savior and King. At this time there is no image of the Moon in the heavens for our eyes to seek after, and no matter where the body of the Messiah lives, we as one body, are called to be under the covering of Yahweh. This aligns with the second Commandment that Yahweh gave us, stating that we are to have no image before Him.

Yahweh is calling us to intimacy. I cannot emphasize enough what an awesome privilege this is! All that we might do for worldly guests (no matter how famous or well loved) becomes a mere shadow of how we are to prepare for Yahshua. There is none to compare with our King and

Beloved Bridegroom. He is worthy of our all, and we have an opportunity to bless Him when we prepare a place for Him.

Our lives today are filled with many things that demand our attention. Some things we simply enjoy as apart of life, and others are the many needs and responsibilities we have to take care of. Still, we need to find time to give all that we can to make a set apart time and place for our Beloved, a time that is unlike the common things of everyday. This will show Yahweh how special He is to us, and it will speak to others of our heart toward our King. If you have family, these special times will also make patterns and lasting memories for your children.

I know that there are difficult circumstances for many people that sometimes hinder the freedom to do what is in your heart, but remember Yahshua also told us that we can go into our closets and close the door to have intimate fellowship with Him. I encourage you, in whatever way you are able, to set apart time alone with Yahweh to bless His heart as well as yours. Take this time to show your gratitude to Him for His unfailing love and protection, and for all the ways that He answers your prayers and cares for you.

The key to any celebration is to find the heart behind it and then design your activities to enhance it. The main theme or heart of the New Moon or Rosh Chodesh is the rehearsal of His return, the time when we will be in the presence of the King hidden in the glory of His Light forever. The New Moon stands as our reminder to be humble, like our King, for we have no light of our own.

Have this in your mind, which was also in Christ Jesus, who, existing in the form of God, didn't consider equality with God a thing to be grasped, but emptied himself, taking the form of a servant, being made in the likeness of men. And being found in human form, he humbled himself, becoming obedient to death, yes, the death of the cross. Phil.2:5-8

Rejoice in this time of remembering and being remembered. The New Moon is our precious time of being hidden or concealed in His Holy of Holies; renewed and restored to reflect the light of our Beloved. Remember how the chuppah at a wedding is a picture of the covering and protection that the groom will give to his bride, just as Yahshua promises covering and protection for His bride. Traditionally a bride wears a veil or covering as she walks toward the chuppah where her beloved is waiting. As she approaches, the bridegroom extends his hand to welcome her under his covering, and into an intimate time of covenant promises that they will speak to each other.

Similarly, after we accept Yahshua as our Savior, we walk with a veil over us toward His extended invitation to come under His covering and protection. The chuppah is a physical picture of the covering that the word keseh is revealing. The Hebrew word chuppah is Strong's #H2646 which means: a canopy; chamber, closet, defense. When Yahshua told us to go into our closet to pray, it was with this picture in mind. As our Bridegroom, He extends His hand to us each New Moon to come into His chamber and speak the things of our heart to Him in prayer and worship. The following verses from Isaiah speak of how Yahweh will provide a chuppah or covering for His people in the future.

> *Yahweh will create over the whole habitation of Mount Zion, and over her assemblies, a cloud and smoke by day, and the shining of a flaming fire by night; for over all the glory will be a canopy. There will be a pavilion for a shade in the daytime from the heat, and for a refuge and for a shelter from storm and from rain. Is.4:5,6*

The word canopy in the above verse is the Hebrew word chuppah, and the word used for refuge is from the word keseh. Once again, we see Yahweh expressing His heart to cover us under the shadow of His presence and keep us safe. When the bride is beside her Beloved under His chuppah, Yahshua will lift the veil from our eyes to see as He sees. There in the safety of Yahweh's covering we are able to see His Covenant as never before.

> *But their minds were blinded. For until this day the same veil remains unlifted in the reading of the Old Testament, because the veil is taken away in Christ. 2Cor.3:14(NJK)*

I encourage you to embrace the wonder and the beauty of the New Moon; set apart each month for this most precious and glorious time with our Beloved.

This is how we know that we know him: if we keep his commandments. One who says, "I know him," and doesn't keep his commandments, is a liar, and the truth isn't in him. But whoever keeps his word, God's love has most certainly been perfected in him. This is how we know that we are in him: he who says he remains in him ought himself also to walk just like he walked. 1John 2:3-6

Praise Yah!
Praise Yahweh from the heavens!
Praise him in the heights!
Praise him, all his angels!
Praise him, all his army!
Praise him, sun and moon!
Praise him, all you shining stars!
Praise him, you heavens of heavens,
You waters that are above the heavens.
Let them praise Yahweh's name,
For he commanded, and they were created.
He has also established them forever and ever.
He has made a decree which will not pass away. Ps.148:1-6

An Evening with the King

AS WE COME TO THE CLOSING CHAPTERS OF THIS BOOK, I WOULD LIKE TO sum up the pictures we have seen of the New Moon and what they mean to each of us individually and corporately. We have seen that each and every piece within Yahweh's Masterpiece aligns with His pattern of life, which is revealed in the covering of darkness first and then the manifestation of life and light. As Yahshua's bride we are to seek to become His most precious treasure; His chayil or pearl of great price, delighted to follow Him and reflect His light alone. As we learn to walk the path that He has set before us, we become more in tune with His heartbeat and Song. This is how we come to know Him and be known by Him. We have seen how the trials that He sets before us are designed to refine us as we saw in the name levana for Moon, causing us to cling to the Rock of our Salvation as never before; and to become a sweet smelling aroma to Him through our prayers as we saw in the frankincense tree.

We also need to have a righteous fear of Yahweh as we saw in yarach for Moon. Just as Esther honored and feared her King by her preparation and prayer, finding favor in his presence, we too, through our prayers and preparation will find the favor of our King and be protected in His presence. Esther's name in Hebrew is Strong's #H635, estar, אסתר, which is said to be of Persian origin. Yet, if we look closer at this word we find the first Hebrew letter, the aleph א, which is the letter that represents Yahweh, followed by another Hebrew word סתר satar, which is Strong's #H5643, and means; to hide, secret, conceal, covering. The secret to Esther's name appears to hold the meaning of being hidden by Yahweh. Where was she hidden? In the king's dwelling! Each New Moon the heavens declare this same picture for us. Like Esther, we are to prepare to come before our King with the sweet fragrance of our prayers and worship, for our King is far beyond any earthly king.

Like Esther, our prayers and service in His presence will give us the wisdom and light we need to impact the lives of those who are lost. Each generation has had its place in Yahweh's story, but the last generation will usher in the return of the King. Is this the last generation? Only time will truly tell, but one thing is sure, you *were* born for such a time as this, and your life is a gift. Each choice that we make has eternal consequences, and so we must choose to do things that prepare us and those around us for our eternal life with our Beloved. All that we do has purpose and meaning, but what we do in the secret place is most important.

> *But you, when you pray, enter into your inner room, and having shut your door, pray to your Father who is in secret, and your Father who sees in secret will reward you openly. Matt.6;6*

> *What I tell you in the darkness, speak in the light; and what you hear whispered in the ear, proclaim on the housetops. Matt.10:27*

> *For there is nothing hidden, except that it should be made known; neither was anything made secret, but that it should come to light. Mark 4:2*

As we come before our Savior in the glory of His presence, let us join together as one in humility and love to bring honor and glory to His Name and to be made new in His presence. Then we will be prepared to reflect His light to a world that is being enveloped in satan's darkness and deception. From one New Moon to the next, we have an opportunity to diligently do the work of His royal priesthood and pearl of great price, so that we will acquire the oil of wisdom that will keep the light of our Beloved burning until the end.

For this reason, other than Shabbat, the New Moon is celebrated more than any other of Yahweh's appointed days, revealing the importance of Yahweh's design and helping us rehearse for the appointed day Yahshua will return for His bride. Each New Moon, the two Silver Trumpets ring out in heartfelt anticipation of our Bridegroom's return and the joy of us all being together as one. Until that most glorious day, may we find peace or shalom in knowing that His return is soon and that wherever we are scattered across the world, we are not alone. His Song resonates across the heavens and to the ends of the Earth … for those who have ears to hear.

I have listed a few ideas for celebrating, but these are simply to inspire you to do what works best in your home; knowing that your efforts are to bring honor to the Name of our King... your guest!

- Bring out a tablecloth, candlesticks, etc. appropriate for the King.

- Prepare food that you don't have everyday, something that you look forward to.

- Possibly invite guests to share in the beauty of this day.

- Read Scripture together that speaks of the essence of the day and the desires of His heart, for example, Psalm 27 and Psalm 91.

- Honor Yahweh with praise and thanksgiving for what He has done to keep you since the last New Moon. Pray for the month that lies ahead, including the needs of family, friends and the lost.

- Worship the King and give Him all the honor and glory He deserves.

- Find music that speaks of the beauty of New Moon and fill your home with songs that glorify Him.

A few songs that express the significance of the New Moon:

Sun and Moon, by Phil Wickham

You are the Sun, by Sara Groves

Song of My Father, by Urban Rescue

You are My Hiding Place, by Selah

Remember to take time to pray and pour out your gratitude to Yahweh for all He has done for you in the month that has just past, and all that He has planned for the month that lies ahead; knowing that each New Moon is a step further along His path of righteousness to His return. Most of all, delight yourself in the presence of your King and His glorious light. Let Him shine His light upon you and overcome all the darkness that the world tries to impose upon you, so that you are restored and renewed in His presence.

Below is a lovely hymn by Fanny Crosby that speaks of all we have looked at.

IN THE SECRET PLACE OF HIS PRESENCE HE WILL HIDE ME

In the secret of His presence He will hide me,
From the burden of a weary world of care;
Overshadowed by His mercy, calmly resting,
My Redeemer will protect me there.

Refrain:
He will hide me, safely hide me,
Where no sorrow nor temptation can betide me;
He will hide me, safely hide me;
In the secret of His presence He will hide me.

In the secret of His presence He will hide me,
And the brightness of His glory He will show:
While He covers me with light as with a garment,
O the rapture that my heart will know! [Refrain]

In the secret of His presence He will hide me,
In the secret of His blessed, boundless love;
There communing and abiding with my Saviour,
What a foretaste of the joys above.

May Yahweh bless you and keep you safely in His arms of love as you seek for truth and test all that you have read. Let's join together to serve Him with oneness of heart and anticipate the coming of our Bridegroom and King.

> Then those who feared Yahweh spoke one with another; and Yahweh listened, and heard, and a book of memory was written before him, for those who feared Yahweh, and who honored his name. They shall be mine," says Yahweh of Armies,"my own possession in the day that I make, and I will spare them, as a man spares his own son who serves him. Then you shall return and discern between the righteous and the wicked, between him who serves God and him who doesn't serve him. Mal.3:16-18

POSTLUDE

The Heavens Declare

THIS GENERATION IS LIVING IN AN EXTREMELY DIFFERENT WORLD THAN it was 50 years ago. If you are younger, it may be difficult to imagine a world without a cell phone of any kind, only rotary dialed land lines, attached to the wall with no call display or answering machines. There were no music downloads, only eight track tapes and cassettes, and the thrill of that time was to own your own color TV, ...with six channels. We have come so far in our technology in such a short time. In many ways, it is an exciting time to be alive, but with the ease of communication and technology at our fingertips, there also comes a responsibility. Scripture tells us that to whom much is given much will be required.

> *To whoever much is given, of him will much be required; and*
> *to whom much was entrusted, of him more will be asked.*
> *Luke 12:48b*

Now that we are able to see, do and know so much, we have no excuse, especially as we see prophecy advancing at an accelerated rate. The tension between world powers is mounting, there are increasing reports of violence, and natural disasters are becoming common. What used to be headline news on a yearly or monthly basis is now daily news. Consequently, when we see unusual signs appear in the heavens, it captures our attention, as it did with the Blood Moons of 2014 and 2015. These heavenly signs stirred peoples interest all over the world, and brought varying opinions of what they meant. Some people saw them as confirmation that something big was coming. Others saw them as confirmation of things that had past. Still others did not see any significance in them at all.

Before we continue, please let me say that I am not writing to suggest that I have the answers. On the contrary, I stand before Yahweh with fear and trembling. But I do believe that there is a common thread through all that we are seeing that aligns with Scripture. Signs from Yahweh, as with all He has designed, are meant to bring warning, confirmation, comfort, and exhortation to His people. Throughout history many eclipses have come and gone, many which have landed on Biblical feast days because it simply is the way Yahweh designed it. Yearly, we see partial solar eclipses, annular solar eclipses; partial lunar eclipses and penumbral lunar eclipses. A total eclipse is more rare and rarer still, when we see it displayed in a pattern. The interesting picture that came out of the patterns of the lunar and solar eclipses of 2014 and 2015 is that they seem to reveal the same message that we have seen in the New Moon. Remember a solar eclipse of any kind can *only* happen at the time of New Moon, which is what ties them together. We will look at this more later, but I believe the message of safety found in the New Moon, is at the center of the Blood Moon's message as well.

As we draw near to the ending of Yahweh's story, the adversary's final attempts to deceive the world are being unleashed. The evil schemes of satan are permeating everything, and the war for our souls is raging. In the midst of all this, Scripture also warns us that if we do not love Yahweh and His Word that He will send a strong delusion or 'a working of error' as it is called in the Word English translation.

> For the mystery of lawlessness already works. Only there is one who restrains now, until he is taken out of the way. Then the lawless one will be revealed, whom the Lord will kill with the breath of his mouth, and destroy by the manifestation of his coming; even he whose coming is according to the working of Satan with all power and signs and lying wonders, and

with all deception of wickedness for those who are being lost, because they didn't receive the love of the truth, that they might be saved. Because of this, God sends them a working of error, that they should believe a lie; that they all might be judged who didn't believe the truth, but had pleasure in unrighteousness. 2 Thess. 2:7-12

Over the last five hundred plus years, there have been two other sets of Blood Moon tetrads. One set of tetrads came in 1493, after Yahweh's people were expelled from Spain in 1942 when the Americas became a safe place for Yahweh's people. Then another set came in 1949 after Israel became a nation in 1948, which created another safe place for Yahweh's people. The repeated pattern appears to be that the Blood Moon tetrads followed the discovery of a safe place for Yahweh's people and appeared in the heavens during their relocation. We cannot help but wonder then, what the Blood Moon tetrads of 2014 and 2015 were following. Could it be that we have experienced another important shift for Yahweh's people that we are not fully aware of? In the previous sets of Blood Moons, Yahweh's people were expelled from one place to travel to another safer place. I wonder if, like Noah we are being called out of this world to the safety of Yahweh's presence as never before? I believe that as we have seen pictured in the New Moon, that Yahshua is calling His sheep to follow Him away from the lies of the world to the safety of His presence.

But no one knows of that day and hour, not even the angels of heaven, but my Father only. "As the days of Noah were, so will be the coming of the Son of Man. For as in those days which were before the flood they were eating and drinking, marrying and giving in marriage, until the day that Noah entered into the ship, and they didn't know until the flood came, and took them all away, so will be the coming of the Son of Man. Matt. 24:36-39

Can we hear Yahweh's call in the midst of the eating, drinking and marrying? Yahweh's heavenly signs, especially the signs of the last days appear to be similar to the message that was written on the wall at king Belshazzar's party. While everyone was eating, drinking and abusing vessels that were meant to be holy, a message suddenly appears as handwriting on the wall. This alarming account of king Belshazzar's feast appears to foreshadow the days we are in now.

> *Belshazzar the king made a great feast to a thousand of his lords, and drank wine before the thousand. Belshazzar, while he tasted the wine, commanded to bring the golden and silver vessels which Nebuchadnezzar his father had taken out of the temple which was in Jerusalem; that the king and his lords, his wives and his concubines, might drink from them. Then they brought the golden vessels that were taken out of the temple of the house of God which was at Jerusalem; and the king and his lords, his wives and his concubines, drank from them. They drank wine, and praised the gods of gold, and of silver, of brass, of iron, of wood, and of stone.*

> *In the same hour came forth the fingers of a man's hand, and wrote over against the lampstand on the plaster of the wall of the king's palace: and the king saw the part of the hand that wrote. Then the king's face was changed in him, and his thoughts troubled him; and the joints of his thighs were loosened, and his knees struck one against another. Dan.5:1-6*

The culture we are living in today, as with the culture of Noah's time, is filled with eating, drinking, and marrying, just as Yahshua told us it would be. Many people today also have a casual attitude toward Yahweh's holy things as it was at king Belshazzar's feast, treating them as common and profaning them to suit their own agenda.

> *As it happened in the days of Noah, even so will it be also in the days of the Son of Man. They ate, they drank, they married, they were given in marriage, until the day that Noah entered into the ship, and the flood came, and destroyed them all. Likewise, even as it happened in the days of Lot: they ate, they drank, they bought, they sold, they planted, they built; Luke 17:26-28*

When king Belshazzar's party was interrupted by a hand writing a message on his wall, he shook with fear, and called his trusted wise men to help him. Then a very interesting scene takes place.

Then came in all the king's wise men; but they could not read the writing, nor make known to the king the interpretation. Then was king Belshazzar greatly troubled, and his face was changed in him, and his lords were perplexed. Dan. 5:8,9

King Belshazzar's trusted men were specially chosen to serve the king because of their wisdom, but their wisdom was of no use to them in interpreting the writing. As we have discovered when looking at the difference between the wise and foolish virgins, the wisdom of the world is foolishness to Yahweh. Yahshua rebuked the five foolish virgins because they did not know Him and were not known by Him. It then stands to reason, that those who did not know the Author of the writing could not interpret the writing on the wall at king Belshazzar's party. They could not understand Yahweh's message because they did not have a relationship with Him. They could only understand and interpret the wisdom of the world.

I have heard of you, that the spirit of the gods is in you, and that light and understanding and excellent wisdom are found in you. Now the wise men, the enchanters, have been brought in before me, that they should read this writing, and make known to me its interpretation; but they could not show the interpretation of the thing. Dan.5:14,15

Daniel, on the other hand, was well acquainted with the Author of the writing. He knew Yahweh's heart and was known intimately by Him. Their relationship gave way for Daniel to be trusted with the message. This was also true with Joseph who was given the interpretation of Pharaoh's dreams. Both Daniel and Joseph, were entrusted with the wisdom needed to deliver Yahweh's message.

Daniel answered, Blessed be the name of God forever and ever; for wisdom and might are his. He changes the times and the seasons; he removes kings, and sets up kings; he gives wisdom to the wise, and knowledge to those who have understanding; he reveals the deep and secret things; he knows what is in the darkness, and the light dwells with him.

I thank you, and praise you, you God of my fathers, who have given me wisdom and might, and have now made known to me what we desired of you; for you have made known to us the king's matter. Dan.2: 19-23

Joseph answered Pharaoh, saying, "It isn't in me. God will give Pharaoh an answer of peace."Gen.41:16

Notice that both Joseph and Daniel give Yahweh full credit for the wisdom that they have. Their humility and fear of Yahweh brought a relationship of trust. Those who are considered wise by worldly standards become fools when it comes to the things of Yahweh. Throughout history this has proven true. We need to know Yahweh, and seek His wisdom more than ever, to discern what Yahweh's Spirit is saying, and what we are seeing written in the heavens. Yahweh's signs are the writings of His hand upon His heavenly storyboard, and it appears that they carry a similar message to the one written to king Belshazzar; *'we too have been weighed in the balance and found wanting.'*

This is the writing that was inscribed: MENE, MENE, TEKEL, UPHARSIN. This is the interpretation of the thing: MENE; God has numbered your kingdom, and brought it to an end; TEKEL; you are weighed in the balances, and are found wanting. Dan.5:25-27

What does it mean to be weighed in the balance and found wanting? I believe the answer for us is found in the first three chapters of Revelation. The message that Yahshua spoke to the seven assemblies gives us a detailed message of the broader statement of being weighed in the balance and found wanting. In other words, though they claimed to walk with Yahweh, there was something in their life that was not pleasing to Him. Yahshua exhorts each of the seven churches by saying, "I know your works." He sees their efforts and knows that there is good work, but each assembly has serious things in their lives that need to be addressed. All except the church of Philadelphia. The church or assembly of Philadelphia had found the way to walk with Yahweh and the message to them stands out as one of encouragement. We should not be surprised that Philadelphia means "brotherly love,"revealing again that if we want to have favor with our Master, we need to love one another fervently and consider others before ourselves.

> *Let love be without hypocrisy. Abhor that which is evil. Cling to that which is good. In love of the brothers be tenderly affectionate one to another; in honor preferring one another; not lagging in diligence; fervent in spirit; serving the Lord; rejoicing in hope; enduring in troubles; continuing steadfastly in prayer; contributing to the needs of the saints; given to hospitality. Rom.12:9-13*

> *This is my commandment, that you love one another, even as I have loved you. Greater love has no one than this that someone lay down his life for his friends. John 15:12,13*

> *Seeing you have purified your souls in your obedience to the truth through the Spirit in sincere brotherly affection, love one another from the heart fervently: 1Pet.1:22*

Yahshua also exhorts Philadelphia for their endurance.

> *Because you kept my command to endure, I also will keep you from the hour of testing, which is to come on the whole world, to test those who dwell on the earth. I am coming quickly! Hold firmly that which you have, so that no one takes your crown. Rev.3:10,11*

For those who are walking with Yahweh as the church of Philadelphia, the signs in the heavens may simply be a reminder to endure all that they are facing, but like the other churches mentioned in Revelation, many of us need to take stock of our lives and draw nearer to Yahshua, remembering that we are called to love and encourage one another.

If there is therefore any exhortation in Christ, if any consolation of love, if any fellowship of the Spirit, if any tender mercies and compassion, make my joy full, by being like-minded, having the same love, being of one accord, of one mind; doing nothing through rivalry or through conceit, but in humility, each counting others better than himself; each of you not just looking to his own things, but each of you also to the things of others. Phil.2:1-4

So, with Yahweh's patterns and pictures in mind, and with His heart's desire as the motivation for our study, let's take a deeper look at the message within the signs that have appeared in the heavens in the years 2014 and 2015.

There is an intriguing method of observing and studying literature, which looks at an author's work through chiastic structure. This method looks for the symmetry that the author placed in the sentences, phrases, and paragraphs to find the central point of his or her message. As the original Artist, Author and Composer of all, Yahweh's writing naturally holds this structure and so much more. Again, the reason an author uses chiastic structure or chiasms is to beautifully bring attention to the important central point. Below is a description and example of chiastic structure found in Matthew 6, but once you see this pattern you will find that all of Scripture contains this poetic method.

No one can serve two masters.

Either he will hate the one

and love the other,

or he will be devoted to the one

and despise the other.

You cannot serve both God and Money.

(Matt 6:24 NIV 1984)

Chiasms are usually arranged in the same top-to-bottom form as they appear in the text: Matt 6:24

A No one can serve two masters.

   B Either he will hate the one

      C and love the other,

      C′or he will be devoted to the one

   B′and despise the other.

A′You cannot serve both God and Money.

(Matt 6:24)

To many people, this verse conveys the thought that we must choose which master we will serve: God or money. While I believe that is correct, we can see a far more profound understanding when looking at it from the standpoint of a chiasm.

Note how the verses A and A′ have similar themes, as do B and B′, and C and C′. This chiasm uses three themes: serving one of two masters (God or money), hating one of the masters, and loving the other master. The theme in the middle portion of this text is called the center point – in this case, C and C′ are that center point. Most of the people that have studied the chiastic approach agree that the portion in the center generally contains the most important part of the chiasm – it is usually the emphasis of the passage.

Thomas B. Clarke

Using the chiastic structure we can easily see that, though there is more than one thing being said in Matthew 6:24, the central point is to love your Master, Yahweh. There may be more than one picture within a message, but if we don't discover the central point, we will have difficulty applying it to our lives. Chiastic structure from an artistic standpoint can be compared to a reflection in the water. For example, when a person stands by a shoreline, their reflection will fall across the water at their feet. Their feet then become the meeting point of the mirrored image. The same imagery is true with chiastic structure; the beginning of the chiasm is a reflection of the ending. Amazingly, the pattern of the heavenly signs in 2014/2015 follows Yahweh's chiastic structure. The first set of Blood Moons reflects the second set, with the Solar Eclipse of March 20, 2015, at the center. Using the chiastic structure, the total Solar Eclipse then becomes the heart of the message. If this is true, the solar eclipse of March 20, 2015, is key to understanding Yahweh's heart in the tetrads and it would be unwise to overlook it without digging deeper.

As you know a solar eclipse *always* happens at the conjunction of the New Moon, because, of course, that is when the Sun and Moon are closest in the heavens. At a total solar eclipse, the Sun and Moon's ecliptic paths cross, and the Moon moves directly in front of the Sun. During all other New Moons, the Sun and the Moon are close together in the heavens, but their paths do not cross. It's only when their ecliptic paths cross that we have an eclipse. The more common Solar eclipses are a partial Solar eclipse, when the Moon is not in direct alignment with the Earth or an annular Solar eclipse when the Moon is in alignment, but its distance from Earth makes so that the Moon does not completely cover the Sun. The perfect alignment of the Sun and Moon's ecliptic path, where the Moon fits perfectly in front of the Sun, is more rare, and why a total eclipse captures the attention of people across the world. When we account for the fact that the total solar eclipse of March 20, 2015, landed in the center of the tetrads, it becomes even more fascinating.

First let's look at the natural scientific facts surrounding the solar eclipse of March 20, 2015. As we discover what happened in the natural, we will also gain understanding of all Yahweh wants us to see in the spiritual, for the natural or physical things are designed to show us what will happen in the spiritual.

> However that which is spiritual isn't first, but that which is natural, then that which is spiritual. 1 Cor. 15:46

Scientists proclaimed the March 20, 2015, solar eclipse to be extremely rare. How rare? Well, one element of this solar eclipse was that is was, what some call, a supermoon, which is when the Moon has its closest approach to the Earth, also called perigee- syzergy in the astronomical community. A supermoon is also known as a Super Full Moon, Super New Moon or Perigee Moon. Below are a couple descriptions from online of the March *super* New Moon.

On March 20, 2015, the larger-than-average new supermoon swings right in front of the sun to totally block out the solar disk. Earthsky.org

And this eclipse was caused by a super moon, occurring roughly 13 hours after it has reached its perigee — its closest point to Earth for the month. That means the new moon was nearly as large as it could get for this particular eclipse. For the regions that could see the total eclipse, it was completely block out the sun.

Scott Sutherland; Weather Network

It should be noted that the next "supermoon" happened at the time of the lunar eclipse on the first day of Tabernacles September 27, 2015, (according to the conjunction) making two of the heavenly signs that year larger than average!

The other intriguing part about this eclipse was that it marked the first day of the Hebrew year and month Nissan, or Aviv, as it is called in Scripture. This combination of a supermoon during a total solar eclipse, on the first of Nissan was remarkable, but it didn't stop there. To add to the event, the New Moon/solar eclipse landed on the same day as the spring equinox. Individually, each of these events have a yearly reoccurring pattern and do not stand out on their own; but their alignment on the same day, grabbed the world's attention. There is still one more notable piece to this amazing picture, and that is the path that the solar eclipse took.

The stormy North Atlantic in late winter is hardly a popular tourist destination. Nevertheless, the track of the March 20, 2015, total eclipse passes right through the region and is still drawing many eclipse chasers. The eclipse path forms a backward C-shaped curve that ends at the North Pole.

Fred Espenak and Jay Anderson, Sky and telescope.com

Notice that the path of the eclipse is described as a backward C-shape. I find this especially intriguing because a backward C-shape is the shape of the Hebrew letter kaph, which we will look at more closely later. This kaph shaped path of totality completed its course at the North Pole or True North; known as an international site owned by no one nation.

There will be a total eclipse of the sun for two minutes over the North Pole on Friday, March 20, the day of the Spring Equinox which coincides with the beginning of the Hebrew month of Nissan, the first month in the Biblical calendar year, a solar occurrence that has never happened before in human history.

Tuly Weisz, Breaking News Israel, March,12th.

I have shared with you many pictures surrounding the New Moon in hopes, not of changing your mind, but of showing you the wonder and beauty of Yahweh's design. Each of us will make our own choices as to how and when we will meet with Yahweh, but the wonder of His design is too breathtaking to be overlooked. In the midst of our wrestling with the dates and times of Yahweh's appointed days, March 20, 2015, became a phenomenal day of unity. For on that glorious day, most of the world agreed that it was the New Moon, a new year and a new season, all happening over international common ground in the North, which is a barren place, or as some call it, a wilderness.

Calling the North the wilderness is fascinating, because the Hebrew word for wilderness is Strong's #4057 מדבר midbar, which means; to speak. Midbar comes from the root word, debar which is Hebrew for, word, a word spoken or to speak. Throughout Scripture, when Yahweh wants to reveal something to His people, He has taken them to a wilderness place, away from the distractions of the world to speak to them. Amazingly, it appears that Yahweh chose the same pattern for this total solar eclipse! Yahweh drew all our eyes and ears away from the things of this world, to observe His sign and hear His voice. Another remarkable piece to this event is the Hebrew word for North, which is Strong's #H6845 tsaphan, also means; to hide, protect, conceal; secret place; once again aligning with all that we have discovered about the New Moon. The New Moon (which is a picture of being hidden in the secret place) of the Biblical New Year of

Aviv 2015 came over an area that means to hide, protect, conceal! Could these phenomenal pictures set before us, on March 20, 2015, reveal that Yahweh wanted to speak to His people about unity and protection in the secret place? Yes, there will be ominous events coming, but that is why Yahweh's message of protection is so important.

Now let's take a deeper look at the significance of the North in this picture. For those of you who spend time outdoors or know the ways of a compass, you know that North is our navigational point of reference, and the North Star, Polaris or what is sometimes called the Pole star is our trusted guide. Some even call Polaris the Pathway or Gateway to Heaven. Polaris is located in the constellation Ursa Minor or what is commonly known as the little bear. Ursa Minor and Ursa Major are a part of the Constellation Cancer.

Most of the meanings attached to the Constellations have been twisted over the centuries to fit the beliefs of pagan god worship and worldviews. Yet because they are declaring glory of Yahweh it is our responsibility to look beyond the surface to see the original message and story that the Author and Creator designed. We find this is especially true for the Constellation of Cancer. Right away we are faced with its modern negative name, but when we look beyond we find something wonderful. Below is an excerpt from 'The Gospel in the Stars' by Joseph A. Seiss, which describes the true meaning behind the constellation of Cancer.

The Egyptians called this sign Klaria, the Folds, the Resting places. We call it Cancer, which in later vocabularies means the Crab, but which, in its Noetic roots, explains what we are to see in this Crab. Khan means the traveller's resting-place, and ker or cer means embraced, encircled, held as within encircling arms. And so Cancer means Rest secured the object of desire at length reached, compassed, possessed, and inalienably held. Hence also the chief star in this sign is named Acubens, the sheltering, the place of retirement, the good rest. Hence also other names in this sign (Ma'alaph and Al Himarein) mean assembled thousands, the kids or lambs; whilst Syriac by a name which signifies holding, possessing, retaining. It is the sign of the saints' everlasting

rest, in which the head of the Serpent is beneath their feet, as under the feet of this Crab.

Here Joseph A. Seiss is revealing to us that the North Star is the sign of Yahweh's elect and that the constellation of Cancer is a picture of His gathered sheepfold safely resting with the Good Shepherd. How breathtaking and awesome is the Mighty Hand of our Creator who set the solar eclipse of March 20, 2015, in the North, to draw attention to the place that declares, 'those who dwell in the secret place will find safety under His covering and will be protected in the times of trouble.' Here is another witness to all that the New Moon is revealing!

Now returning to the path of totality that the solar eclipse took; observers reported that it looked like a backward letter C, which I mentioned before. The path of totality followed the same shape as the Hebrew letter kaph כ, which in its paleo picture form, is a palm (of a hand) or a wing. Here we find yet another piece to Yahweh's Masterpiece and more confirmation to the heart behind Yahweh's message of the New Moon and this solar eclipse; to cover and protect His people. Each piece weaves together a picture of complete unity! I believe this is Yahweh's message to the world.

> *Draw near to God, and he will draw near to you. Cleanse your hands, you sinners; and purify your hearts, you double-minded. Lament, mourn, and weep. Let your laughter be turned to mourning, and your joy to gloom. Humble yourselves in the sight of the Lord, and he will exalt you. James 4:8-10*

Now is the time to draw near to Him, for the world stage is changing rapidly. The nations are heating up in anger and decisions are being made that will drastically affect our future. His call is ringing out to all who listen, "Come to Me, before it is too late!" Those who chose to dwell in the secret place, in harmony with the Master of the Masterpiece will abide under the shadow of the Most High. This is the core message of the March 20, 2015, solar eclipse, which I believe was delivered to the Northern tribes of Israel or Ephraim scattered among the nations.

In the Exodus account, after Yahweh had saved Israel, His firstborn, from slavery and death, He took them to the Wilderness. There in the

Wilderness, He tested their hearts and gave them (through Moses) His Covenant and the plans for His dwelling place. People, who were gifted with wisdom, were called to fashion and complete the Tabernacle according to the pattern given to Moses; which is the same pattern as the dwelling of Yahweh in Heaven. The intricacy and design of the Tabernacle, is a shadow picture of the body of the Messiah; and an amazing portrait of the many parts of His body being fitted together as one. In keeping with Yahweh's patterns, Bezalel was the name of the first man chosen to oversee the making of the Tabernacle's vessels. His name is Strong's #H1212 and means; under the shadow or protection of Yahweh. The one chosen to help Bezalel is Oholiab, Strong's #H171, which means; the tent, tabernacle or covering of a father. Wow! How can you not love Yahweh? His ways are consistent and beautiful! Everything has meaning, purpose and weaves together as one. It's important to notice that the ones He chose to do the work of preparing His dwelling place had wisdom.

Yahweh spoke to Moses, saying, "Behold, I have called by name Bezalel the son of Uri, the son of Hur, of the tribe of Judah: and I have filled him with the Spirit of God, in wisdom, and in understanding, and in knowledge, and in all kinds of workmanship, Ex.31:1-3

And I have put my words in thy mouth, and I have covered thee in the shadow of mine hand, that I may plant the heavens, and lay the foundations of the earth, and say unto Zion, Thou art my people. Is.51:16

Each piece of the Tabernacle was designed to declare the glory of Yahweh and to be fitted together as one dwelling. Note also that the Tabernacle was adorned with linen curtains and covered or keseh with skins. When each piece for the Tabernacle had been carefully completed, and the day arrived for each of them to be fitted together, they were raised up as one! This glorious day was the New Moon of the Hebrew New year; Nissan or Aviv! ... the same day as the total solar eclipse of March 20!

Yahweh spoke to Moses, saying, "On the first day of the first month you shall raise up the tabernacle of the Tent of Meeting. Ex.40:1

What a wonderful message of unity to us all! We are all designed with our unique purpose and place as Yahweh's dwelling and as the body of the Messiah. In Yahweh's Masterful design, He revealed this to us, on a New Moon with a total solar eclipse that happened over a place globally referred to as the Wilderness, on the same day as the Tabernacle was raised up centuries before.

So then you are no longer strangers and foreigners, but you are fellow citizens with the saints, and of the household of God, being built on the foundation of the apostles and prophets, Christ Jesus himself being the chief cornerstone; in whom the whole building, fitted together, grows into a holy temple in the Lord; in whom you also are built together for a habitation of God in the Spirit. Eph. 2:19-22

This magnificent solar eclipse appears to be Yahweh's sign of confirmation for the purpose and timing of the New Moon. March 20, 2015 shouted unity and protection to the body of Messiah! It declared the glory of His heavenly design and was meant to bring His people Israel together as one body. The verses in Exodus 40 continue to tell us that once the Tabernacle was raised up, the first and most treasured article in the Tabernacle was set in the Holy of Holies. This, of course, was the vessel that holds the treasures of Yahweh's heart, the Ark of the Covenant found in the secret place. The order of Yahweh found in His dwelling place, is the order for our lives and us. The treasures of Yahweh are His Covenant on the tablets, the rod of Aaron that displayed His choice of leadership and the container of Manna that revealed His sovereign provision and lovingkindness. These are forever safeguarded in His Ark to remind us of His heart; His love, His mercy, and His righteous authority. Remember too that the Ark of the Covenant is where our King is seated ... upon His throne (kisseh) of authority!

The next piece that was set in order after the Ark was the Table of show-bread on the *North* side of the Tabernacle.

> *He put the table in the Tent of Meeting, on the side of the tabernacle northward, outside of the veil. He set the bread in order on it before Yahweh, as Yahweh commanded Moses. Ex.40: 22,23*

There in Yahweh's Holy Place is a vessel for twelve loaves that represents His twelve tribes or the gathering of His people 'on the North side' of His dwelling. This Table of Shewbread is a picture of Yahweh's order for His people. The order of the twelve tribes will be re-established at the end when all Israel is gathered together and enters through the twelve gates of pearl to the heavenly Jerusalem. As Yahshua's bride and royal priesthood we need to be mindful of the order that Yahweh has designed. We see it in the twelve stones on the High Priest's garments, the twelve stones that Elijah gather at the altar, Yahshua's twelve disciples, etc. As we have seen, when Yahweh's righteous order is in place Yahweh's presence comes. This is what happened in the Wilderness! All that was required for the Tabernacle was completed, assembled and raised up and it was then when all were in one accord that Yahweh came in a cloud that covered (keseh) the Tabernacle. His glory filled His dwelling place and He took His place upon His throne (kisseh) in the Holy of Holies or secret place!

> *He raised up the court around the tabernacle and the altar, and set up the screen of the gate of the court. So Moses finished the work.*

> *Then the cloud covered the Tent of Meeting, and Yahweh's glory filled the tabernacle. Moses wasn't able to enter into the Tent of Meeting, because the cloud stayed on it, and Yahweh's glory filled the tabernacle. Ex.40:33-35*

Each of us has a specific part in the Tabernacle or dwelling of Yahweh according to the order and leading of His Spirit. Sadly competition and pride keep us from seeing each other's gifts, and encouraging one another to fulfill Yahweh's calling on our lives. As a result, many turn to the ways of the world for confidence and acceptance, but this is not the way of Yahweh's heart. We need to humbly accept His leading in building one another up in His righteous order.

> *If there is therefore any exhortation in Christ, if any consolation of love, if any fellowship of the Spirit, if any tender mercies and compassion, make my joy full, by being like-minded, having the same love, being of one accord, of one mind; doing nothing through rivalry or through conceit, but in humility, each counting others better than himself; each of you not just looking to his own things, but each of you also to the things of others. Phil. 2:1-4*

> *Let another man praise you, and not your own mouth; a stranger, and not your own lips. Prov.27:2*

> *Therefore exhort one another, and build each other up, even as you also do. 1 Thess.5:11*

The message of the total solar eclipse that was written upon the heavens on March 20, 2015, to Yahweh's people sums up the message of this book. In the previous tetrads Yahweh's people physically moved to safety first and then came the confirmation of the tetrads later. Now, as the world grows more evil, it appears that there has been a call for us to remove ourselves from the world and into to the safety of Yahweh's secret place and the confirmation came to us in the heavens.

Yahweh is declaring His glorious Love Story to the world! He has made a way for us to return to His Covenant ways and to be in harmony with His magnificent Masterpiece, Love Story and Song. The New Moon at conjunction is our rehearsal for being ready and watching as the darkness closes in on the world. There in the secret place of the Most High is where there is safety and protection. As the time now draws near for Yahshua to return for His virtuous bride, we must set our hearts and lives in the righteous order of His Kingdom. His desire now is the same as He declared to His people before He died for them, which was to gather them under His wings as a mother hen gathers her chicks under her wings for protection

... but they would not listen. ...Are we listening? It is time to hear the Great Shepherd's voice and allow Him to gather us together under His wings of protection.

Be merciful to me, God, be merciful to me, for my soul takes refuge in you. Yes, in the shadow of your wings, I will take refuge, until disaster has passed. Ps.57:1

Yahweh's Word tells us that a house divided will fall and though His people have learned and experienced many things, we are still quite divided and at risk of falling.

If a kingdom is divided against itself, that kingdom cannot stand. If a house is divided against itself, that house cannot stand. Mark 3:24,25

There are many groups of people that claim to know Yahweh; each having a different way of following and serving Him. How does one choose the path of truth and righteousness when Yahweh's people as a whole are suggesting that there are many paths to choose from? Is our message to the world summed up in the phrases "to each his own" or "let's agree to disagree?" How can this be? Especially when we consider the precision of Yahweh's Word and His Creation? Instead of giving up on unity, we need to seek it all the more, but not in our own strength. The vision of the Menorah shown to Zerubbabel in Zachariah, reveals again that pure olive oil was being poured out to keep the lampstand lit.

He said to me, "What do you see?" I said, "I have seen, and behold, a lampstand all of gold, with its bowl on the top of it, and its seven lamps thereon; there are seven pipes to each of the lamps, which are on the top of it; and two olive trees by it, one on the right side of the bowl, and the other on the left side of it."
I answered and spoke to the angel who talked with me, saying, "What are these, my lord?" Then the angel who talked with me answered me, "Don't you know what these are?" I said, "No, my lord." Then he answered and spoke to me, saying, "This is

the word of Yahweh to Zerubbabel, saying, 'Not by might, nor by power, but by my Spirit,' says Yahweh of Armies. Zech.4: 2-6

Just as we saw with the parable of the ten virgins, this vision confirms the picture of the oil of wisdom, which comes from Yahweh. Our own wisdom or strength will not keep our lamps lit at the end. Notice that the oil is being poured out through two olive trees or branches that represent those who have suffered trial as Yahshua did. When we allow Yahweh's Spirit to lead us into true unity we will find harmony with our King. Then as one body with many parts He will show us how to work together for His goals and outcomes; caring deeply for each other before ourselves.

Now I beg you, brothers, through the name of our Lord, Jesus Christ, that you all speak the same thing and that there be no divisions among you, but that you be perfected together in the same mind and in the same judgment. 1 Cor.1:10

Finally, be all like-minded, compassionate, loving as brothers, tenderhearted, courteous, not rendering evil for evil, or insult for insult; but instead blessing; knowing that to this were you called, that you may inherit a blessing.1 Peter 3:8,9

Do two walk together, unless they have agreed? Amos 3:3

Remember the word for agreed in the above verse is Strong's #H3259 ya'ad, which means; to fix upon by agreement or appointment; by implication to meet at a stated time; to summon to trial, to engage in marriage. There is no room for casual indifference in this word! Amos challenges us to seek unity on Yahweh's terms. Walking together can ONLY happen when we agree on His path, signs and the appointments that we are journeying towards. We must allow Yahweh's Spirit to align us with Him and His heart's desire above all, for He desires to keep us safe as we endure to the end. My prayer is that Yahweh's Spirit will lead each of us down the narrow path to truth and unity, so that those who are seeking the truth will not become confused or disheartened.

Yahweh's signs have gone out to call His people, many of which have become preoccupied and absorbed by the things of this world, to be still and know Him for who He truly is.

Be silent at the presence of the Lord Yahweh, for the day of Yahweh is at hand. For Yahweh has prepared a sacrifice. He has consecrated his guests. Zeph. 1:7

There are many prophecies in Scripture that need to yet unfold, but the signs are revealing that we are in the time that Yahshua referred to as "the beginning of sorrows." The trials that we are facing and our reactions to them are preparing us for what lies ahead.

As he sat on the Mount of Olives, the disciples came to him privately, saying, "Tell us, when will these things be? What is the sign of your coming, and of the end of the age?"

Jesus answered them, "Be careful that no one leads you astray.

For many will come in my name, saying, 'I am the Christ,' and will lead many astray. You will hear of wars and rumors of wars. See that you aren't troubled, for all this must happen, but the end is not yet. For nation will rise against nation, and kingdom against kingdom; and there will be famines, plagues, and earthquakes in various places. But all these things are the beginning of birth pains. Matt. 24:3-8

Still, Yahweh's Love Story is so utterly breathtaking and heart wrenching, that all other stories especially other love stories, fade as mere copies of His. We have the privilege of living near the time referred to 'as *the end of the age' or* we could say, the postlude of His Love Story and Song! We need to be sober and alert, so that we can discern the signs in the heavens and the things that are affecting us daily. In Yahweh's mercy, He is showing us these signs to awaken His sleepy, distracted people and warn us, for the battle for Yahshua's bride is at hand.

Do this, knowing the time, that it is already time for you to awaken out of sleep, for salvation is now nearer to us than when we first believed. The night is far gone, and the day is near. Let's therefore throw off the works of darkness, and let's put on the armor of light. Rom. 13:11,12

Wake up righteously, and don't sin, for some have no knowledge of God. I say this to your shame. 1Cor. 15:34

Therefore he says, "Awake, you who sleep, and arise from the dead, and Christ will shine on you." Eph.5:14

In closing, I would like to bring your attention another total solar eclipse that swept over the United States on August 21, 2017. This solar eclipse marked the sixth New Moon of the Biblical year. Remember, the sixth New Moon is the day that begins the month of Elul which is understood to be the acronym for, "I am beloved's and my beloved is mine." How fitting that Elul would begin with a total solar eclipse, where the Moon or bride steps in front the of Sun, the picture of her Beloved, to allow all people to view His glory. Also, like the story of the grasshopper and the ant, this solar eclipse began the time of focused preparation for the New Moon of the seventh month of Tishri, which will soon herald Yahshua's return.

Another interesting piece to the heaven's storytelling order is that the twelve constellations are known to have a beginning and an end that reflect the work of our Messiah and King. The first constellation is Virgo, the sign of the virgin. Virgo is the constellation that heralded the first coming of the Messiah, for it is believed that it was within this constel-lation that the Magi saw the sign of Yahshua's birth. The last and twelfth constellation is Leo, the sign of the Lion. Leo is the constellation that represents the Lion of the Tribe of Judah and the return of Yahshua as the conquering King. Consider this description of the sign Leo, from the Gospel in the Stars, by Joseph A. Seiss.

And here, in the sign of Leo, is this very Lion, thoroughly aroused, salient, and full of majesty, the same in all the pictorial Zodiacs of all

nations. It is the same "Lion of the tribe of Judah " to which the text refers, for in the Jewish astronomy this twelfth sign was the sign of Judah. He is the Lion of Judah in the text, and He is the Lion of Judah in the Zodiac. The record of the signs and the record of the Word are here precisely identical. The coincidence is positive and absolute, and rests on no mere inferences from mere likeness or concurring circumstances. The picture in the sky is one and the same with the picture in the Revelation as shown to John in his visions in Patmos.

In the Apocalypse the Lion-Lamb takes the roll from the hand of eternal Majesty amid thrills of exultation which shake the whole intelligent universe from centre to circumference. He tears asunder seal after seal, until the very last is reached and broken, and with each there bursts forth a divine almightiness, seizing and convulsing the whole world as it never before was affected. The white horse of conquering power, and the red horse of war and bloodshed, and the black horse of scarcity and famine, and the cadaverous horse of Death with Hades at his heels, dash forth in invincible energy upon the apostate populations of the earth. The heavens are shaken, and seem to collapse like a falling tent, the earth is filled with quaking, the mountains and islands are moved out of their places, and the mightiest and bravest, as well as the weakest, of men are filled with horror and dismay. The great tribulation, the like of which never was — and never again shall be, sets in.

Beloved of Yahweh ... this is your King, and His power is unmatched!! Leo, the great Lion faces the Crab or Cancer, which is the eleventh constellation that we looked at in the March 20, 2015, total solar eclipse and if you remember, is the constellation that represents a protective sheepfold or resting place for Yahweh's people. Yahweh's message now comes to a greater magnitude, for the total solar eclipse of the first of Elul 2017 was in the majestic constellation of Leo, the twelfth and final constellation in the heavens! Here again, we can see the pieces that we have looked at coming together as one. First the call went out to draw people to Yahweh's salvation and safety in the previous signs, and now a sign has come in the twelfth constellation which represents Yahweh's Kingdom order, to declare that He is going to reveal His Almighty power as the final chapters of His Awesome Story unfold! Furthermore, as this phenomenal eclipse moved through totality, it was noted by many that as the daytime sky became dark as night, you could see Leo's brightest star Regulus, known as the king star beside the Sun and Moon's conjunction! How awesome! The Master and Composer of all the Universe designed a breathtaking moment in the heavens; a moment that revealed the bride and her Beloved Bridegroom together in the final majestic constellation in the heavens, in the presence of the king star. Without a doubt, the heavens truly are declaring the glory of the King of the Universe and His majestic Love Story! In Yahweh's unfathomable love, mercy, and grace He is giving us signs that call us to hear and repent. These amazing signs come to us with excited anticipation and then they are gone. Still, their message remains. What will your response to His call be?

Beware, brothers, lest perhaps there be in any one of you an evil heart of unbelief, in falling away from the living God; but exhort one another day by day, so long as it is called "today;" lest any one of you be hardened by the deceitfulness of sin. For we have become partakers of Christ, if we hold fast the beginning of our confidence firm to the end: while it is said, "Today if you will hear his voice, don't harden your hearts, as in the rebellion." Heb.3:12-15

Seek the LORD while He may be found;
Call upon Him while He is near.
Let the wicked forsake his way
And the unrighteous man his thoughts;
And let him return to the LORD,
And He will have compassion on him,
And to our God,
For He will abundantly pardon. Is.55:6,7

The total solar eclipse of August 21, 2017 stands out as a warning, and an exhortation to those who live in North America, especially the United States, to prepare themselves in heart and deed for what is about to come to them, as the fulfillment of the last choruses of Yahweh's Song play out. The time has come to hear what the Spirit is saying to the people of Yahweh and join in harmony with the chorus of the heavens in anticipation for the long awaited return of our Beloved! May we be found hidden in the secret place of the Most High and prepared as His spotless bride at the call of His shofar! Halleluyah!

I would like to thank you for taking the time to read this book. May Yahweh bless you as you seek to follow Him with all your heart. I leave you now with Psalm 20 as a prayer.

May Yahweh answer you in the day of trouble.
May the name of the God of Jacob set you up on high,
send you help from the sanctuary, grant
you support from Zion,
remember all your offerings, and accept
your burnt sacrifice. Selah.

May He grant you your heart's desire,
and fulfill all your counsel.
We will triumph in your salvation.
In the name of our God, we will set up our banners.
May Yahweh grant all your requests.
Now I know that Yahweh saves his anointed.
He will answer him from his holy heaven, with
the saving strength of his right hand.
Some trust in chariots, and some in horses, but
we trust the name of Yahweh our God.
They are bowed down and fallen, but
we rise up, and stand upright.
Save, Yahweh! Let the King answer us when we call!

Reference List

The World English Bible, (WEB) Public Domain ,
Modern English translation of the Holy Bible.

The New King James Version, (NKJ)
Commissioned in 1975 by Thomas Nelson Publishers

King James Version, (KJV) 1611, 1987 printing

The English Standard Version, (ESV) 2016.
by Crossway, a publishing ministry of Good News Publishers.

Etymological Dictionary of Biblical Hebrew,
by Rabbi Matityahu Clark, Feldheim Publishers, 1999

American Dictionary of the English
Language, Noah Webster 1828,
reprint 1967 & 1995.Published by the Foundation
for American Christian Education

The New Strong's Exhaustive Concordance of the Bible.
by Thomas Nelson Publishers 1990

Hebrew Word Pictures by Dr. Frank Seekins
by Living Word Pictures Inc. 2003

CPSIA information can be obtained
at www.ICGtesting.com
Printed in the USA
LVHW02s0505240118
563484LV00001B/14/P